·MASTERING·

CHEESE

·MASTERING·
CHEESE

LESSONS FOR CONNOISSEURSHIP FROM A MAÎTRE FROMAGER

MAX McCALMAN • DAVID GIBBONS

Clarkson Potter/Publishers
NEW YORK

*To my mother, who gave me
appreciation for all living things;
and to my father, who helped me
articulate that love.*

All rights reserved.
Published in the United States by Clarkson Potter/
Publishers, an imprint of the Crown Publishing
Group, a division of Random House, Inc., New
York.
www.crownpublishing.com
www.clarksonpotter.com

CLARKSON POTTER is a trademark and
POTTER with colophon is a registered trademark
of Random House, Inc.

Cheddar Cheese Lexicon chart reprinted from the
Journal of Food Science, vol. 66, no. 9, p. 1424, by
permission of Blackwell Publishing, gratefully
acknowledged.

Library of Congress Cataloging-in-Publication
Data available upon request.

ISBN 978-0-307-40648-4

Printed in China

Design by Goodesign (www.goodesignny.com)

10 9 8 7 6 5 4 3

First Edition

Two Spanish classics: Left, Ibores and Garroxta.
OVERLEAF: *Chua Fladä: A spectacular Swiss artisan cheese.*

CONTENTS

A sheep out to pasture at Ancient Heritage Farm, Oregon.

FOREWORD

AT THE TURN OF THE TWENTY-FIRST CENTURY, WE WATCHED THE American specialty-foods market grow even more sophisticated. People didn't just want tomatoes, they wanted heirloom ones. Our parents never ate sushi, let alone talked about grape varietals and *terroir;* now, we do so all the time.

Our company, American Home Food Products, acquired artisanal Premium Cheese in August 2007. Born in the dining room of a Michelin two-star restaurant in Manhattan, the brainchild of Chef Terrance Brennan, and developed through the total commitment of a dynamic group of cheese people, headed by Max McCalman, Artisanal is America's newest luxury food brand.

When I discovered Artisanal, my eyes opened to the excitement brewing in artisan cheeses. Experiencing the amazing aromas and flavors of fine cheeses is great, but it's only half the fun. Learning their stories and comparing notes with fellow cheese lovers, adds a whole new fascinating and energizing dimension.

Max and Dave's books go hand in hand with what we're trying to accomplish at Artisanal Premium Cheese. Our efforts are all about exposing people to the best cheeses and encouraging them to taste the difference. From the kitchens of Las Vegas casinos to the corner bistros of Manhattan, Americans are learning to appreciate great artisanal cheeses.

Max is one of the most knowledgeable people in the entire artisanal cheese world. At Artisanal, Max and his colleagues are our professors of cheese. As someone who values a good education, I have a deep respect for people like them, who tackle a subject intellectually. *Mastering Cheese* is Max's ultimate course that I hope will broaden any cheese lover's experience of fine cheese.

—DANIEL W. DOWE, CEO, ARTISANAL PREMIUM CHEESE

A tasting plate shows the impressive variety among artisanal blue cheeses: From top, Beenleigh Blue, Fourme d'Ambert, Stilton, Rogue River Blue, Roquefort.

INTRODUCTION

IT IS CERTAINLY A BLESSING AND A GIFT TO DISCOVER ONE'S TRUE vocation in life. Some lucky people just roll naturally into their careers from early hobbies, interests, and passions; perhaps they're able to translate academic success to "the real world" and build compelling careers. Others may never find fulfilling work, toiling away at lucrative—and even interesting—professions but without any real sense of mission.

For me, a career path was not revealed till my early forties. I knew I loved cheese and always had. One of my earliest childhood memories is of sitting at my mother's kitchen counter one day when I had a cold. A piece of cheese beckoned. Yet Mom told me not to touch it, no doubt because she thought I might transmit my germs to it. This was pretty much what we were all taught in the United States during the cold war—that we should be afraid of *all* bacteria. Hovering near the top of the list of foods to be avoided was cheese.

Quite probably the cheese I was told not to touch represented precisely the nourishment that would have benefited me the most when I was under the weather. As is so often the case, the foods we like are ultimately the ones that are best for us. Much later, it was one of the questions I was most frequently asked: Is cheese really good for you? Early on, I asked myself the same question and the answer was yes—contrary to what I was told growing up in the 1950s and '60s and to the public consciousness of emerging "health concerns" in the '70s and '80s.

Three formidable artisan cheeses: Clockwise from above center, Idiazábal, from Spain; Nettle Meadow Kunik, from New York's Hudson Valley; and Appenzeller, from Switzerland.

Checking on some cheeses in one of the caves at the Artisanal Premium Cheese Center.

After that early incident in the kitchen, I don't remember seeing any cheese on my family's table for the rest of my formative years. You might say I was essentially drawn to cheese because I was denied it when I was young. Having been cheese starved early in life, I've been trying to get my hands on it ever since—for nutrition and also for enjoyment and pleasure.

By the early 1990s, I had worked for more than a decade at various jobs in the restaurant and service industry, including Sommelier and Maître d'. I discovered that my new employer, Chef Terrance Brennan of Picholine, wanted to start a European-style cheese program at the restaurant. Terrance asked the staff for volunteers to assume responsibility for the cheese. It fell to me. I thought, "This could be fun, a nice change of pace, and maybe I'll learn something new." Little did I know where it would lead! Fast forward nearly 15 years, thousands of cheese plates, and (I hope) many satisfied customers later. . . .

Cheese has become my life mission, a passionate pursuit, and a professional calling card far beyond any dreams or expectations. One of my biggest goals is education—spreading the word about the curd. This book has grown organically out of my urge to teach people about cheese and get them as excited about it as I am. It is set up in the manner of a course syllabus, accessible and user friendly for a general audience but also pertinent to serious connoisseurs and professionals in training.

It's all happened so quickly, sometimes I feel like I need to stop and catch my breath. Almost immediately after we launched the cheese program at Picholine, people started clamoring to buy all our wonderful cheeses at retail. Before the year 2000, this wasn't so easy. You could make a pilgrimage down to Murray's Cheese Shop in Manhattan's West Village or to Fairway on the Upper West Side. There were a few other real-cheese emporiums sprinkled across the land; Whole Foods hadn't quite exploded with its program yet, but it was brewing. Other than that, the real-cheese landscape across America was a little bleak.

When Terrance opened the Artisanal Bistro in 2001, he set it up with a retail cheese counter in the back. But our foodie customers—the specialty cheese market in industry parlance—demanded more, so the Artisanal Premium Cheese Center soon followed (in 2003). An educational component was added: A classroom was built and a website created not only for retail sales but to disseminate cheese knowledge. My job responsibilities have evolved considerably over the past 8 to 10 years. Now, as *maître fromager* and dean of curriculum at the cheese center, I'm responsible for sourcing and selecting cheeses, training fromagers, and also designing and implementing the roster of classes at the center.

Cheeses ready for shipment from the Artisanal Center.

During the time when my first two books were published I began fielding regular requests for tastings and classes beyond the walls of the restaurants and the center. These engagements began at Macy's De Gustibus. Soon, I made appearances at the Culinary Institute of America (both in New York and California); at New York University; at Peter Kump's cooking school (now known as the Institute of Culinary Education); the New School; Disney World's Epcot Food and Wine Festival; on several food-and-wine cruises with Radisson Seven Seas (now Regent Seven Seas) and the Holland America line; an appearance at my alma mater, Hendrix College, in Arkansas; at meetings such as the Mediterranean Diet Conference sponsored by Oldways Preservation and Exchange Trust and the Mediterranean Foods Alliance; the list continues . . .

My first book, *The Cheese Plate,* provides an introduction to fine cheese—a celebration, too, as "the real stuff" gained appreciation here in the United States. My second book, *Cheese: A Connoisseur's Guide to the World's Best,* is more of a reference to selected fine cheeses, with tasting notes, recommended producers, ratings, and specific wine pairing advice. Following on the success of these two publications, I felt there was an urgent need to address many of the questions I've been continually asked for the past decade and a half. These have come not only from students in classes and diners in the restaurants but also from people within the cheese industry itself, from producers to distributors, from cheese lovers to enthusiastic foodies to nutritionists and others in related fields.

This book presents a broader view aimed at demystifying all aspects of fine cheese and to address specific concerns cheese lovers may have—from production to care to nutritional values to how to get maximum appreciation and enjoyment out of it. My hope is to set artisanal cheese firmly on a throne in the realm of fine foods, to help ensure its elevation and survival, so it will continue to be available in delicious and ever-improving form henceforth.

Like any good general-education course, *Mastering Cheese* provides plenty of illustrative examples, in the form of numerous

What do you need to know to master cheese? You need to know what great cheese is; where it comes from; what makes it great; where you can find it; how it is made, bought, and sold; and how to get the most out of it.

suggested tastings and also a series of composed plates—carefully planned and coordinated progressions of cheeses—that are positioned throughout its pages. It also offers review sections—like crib sheets—at the end of each chapter-lesson. There is a lot to mastering cheese and becoming a connoisseur; nevertheless, it's meant to be fun and accessible. We've attempted to fulfill both goals here: to make it a serious, useful, complete compendium while at the same time facilitating easy reference and access to simple, practical ways of enjoying great cheeses without too much fuss.

The book has lots of cross-references, so you can dip in and out of the information stream at will or look up a particular subject of interest quickly and efficiently. We fancy that it has good narrative flow. Much of the technical knowledge we felt is necessary to mastery has been excised from the narrative and placed in sidebars where we do our best to explain it in layperson's terms. The chapter reviews are meant as refreshers. They closely resemble the bulleted lists of basics I include in presentations for classes and seminars.

What do you need to know to master cheese? You need to know what great cheese is; where it comes from; what makes it great; where you can find it; how it is made, bought, and sold; and how to get the most out of it. If this book does nothing else for you, it should outline all of this and quickly point you in the direction of some great cheeses.

Mastering Cheese features many celebrated cheesemakers and their cheeses not so much to tell you these are the ones I like so you should like them too, but simply to provide a few lessons and examples so you can build a strong foundation to launch your own cheese adventure. To paraphrase the old fish proverb: Give a person a cheese and you make them happy for a day; teach them about cheese and you make them happy for a lifetime ... (By the way, we offer some science to explain why cheese makes you happy on page 25.)

Real cheese has been around for a long time, but it almost disappeared. Now it's back and it's here to stay. We are in the midst of a tremendous explosion of artisanal cheeses in the United States. Like wine's explosion beginning in the mid-1970s and early '80s, cheese has carved out a significant niche in the fancy food sector. Gourmets are now taking it as seriously as wine. Cheese connoisseurship can be every bit as multifaceted and challenging as wine connoisseurship. In fact, there's an argument that cheese is *more* complex than wine. In any case, cheese *terroir* is a vast, wide-open frontier. Apart from providing layperson's explanations of cheese science and an insider's view of the fine-cheese business, *Mastering Cheese* aims to be stimulating and thought provoking, to turn you on to some of the more esoteric and intellectual pleasures of enjoying fine cheeses.

In researching *Mastering Cheese,* we've spoken with many of the stars of the new American artisan renaissance. Throughout the book, you'll hear not only my opinions and observations, but also those of many curdmeisters such as Peter Dixon and Cary Bryant, both master cheesemakers; Allison Hooper and Judy Schad, U.S. artisan pioneers; Catherine Donnelly and Paul Kindstedt, professors of cheese science and founders of the Vermont Institute of Artisan Cheeses at the University of Vermont; Rolf Beeler, "the Pope of Swiss Cheeses" (see sidebar, page 298); and Anne Saxelby, a leading Generation X retailer. Would that I were able to invite these fine-cheese superstars and many others of their ilk to co-teach classes and seminars. But they're too busy either making or caring for cheese.

FROM TOP: Preparing to teach a class at the center; drums of Kirkham's Lancashire at Neal's Yard Dairy, London.

This first part of *Mastering Cheese* is designed as an introductory course to include all the basic background you need to begin your journey toward connoisseurship. Part II is the equivalent of an intermediate course, starting to delve into some of the finer points. Part III features my picks of the best cheeses from among the major countries and categories of artisanal production. The emphasis is on cheeses that, as I taste and evaluate them daily, consistently jump out at me and assert themselves as worthy of the tag "great." Cheeses are produced in every state of the Union, at least on a commercial level, with the possible exception of Arkansas (since my friend Donna Doel abandoned her dairy there for points north), and on every continent except Antarctica. Of course, this doesn't mean all these regions yield the kind of fine cheeses we're seeking.

Surveying cheese from a global perspective, the notion of *terroir* rings more loudly than ever as an expression of regions, locales, and microclimates: One pasture or one family can make one very specific, excellent cheese. As we'll see, culture, history, and geography all contribute to its character. A French cheese is a

French cheese; a French-*style* cheese, made in America, is similar but different. Imitation cheeses, unwilling or unable to assert their own unique traits, don't qualify under any aspect of my definitions of *real, artisanal, genuine,* or *great,* and therefore you won't find them in these pages. (A definition of *artisanal* is proposed in the following section.)

The rapid growth of a sophisticated cheese market in the United States and the native artisans who've arisen to supply it is one of our most exciting food developments in years. People are going to farmers' markets and real-cheese shops, supporting ecologically minded, sustainable, organic/natural food production, buying local, and showing a willingness to pay a premium for authentic artisanal foods. This is the biggest story of all. Yet many questions, concerns, and missteps—from production all the way through to consumption—remain. I hope this book can become a valuable companion and make a significant contribution to all the valiant efforts of people in the artisan cheese movement who seek to address these issues, to motivate, to organize, and to educate.

WHAT IS ARTISANAL CHEESE?

The dictionary definitions of the noun *artisan* and the less-common adjective *artisanal* almost always include some reference to skilled manual craftsmanship as well as a contrast to industrial production. Before the Industrial Revolution of the nineteenth century, almost everything manufactured was made by artisans. So these terms were used almost exclusively for dry goods until quite recently; the idea of applying them to food had hardly occurred till the late twentieth century. Beginning in the 1970s, the back-to-the-land, sustainable agriculture, and nouvelle cuisine movements began to train the spotlight on food artisans and the many benefits of their wonderful products.

Real cheese is defined by the distinction between industrial and artisanal. Making real cheese—as opposed to the industrial stuff—is a multifaceted, labor-intensive process, highly dependent on the quality and integrity of its raw materials. The term *artisanal,* as applied to food in general and cheese in particular, has taken on quite a few interesting associations. It refers to traditional, old-fashioned, pre-industrial methods and small-scale manufacturing—although small does not necessarily guarantee artisanal and large does not always preclude it. *Artisanal* is largely synonymous with local, distinct—preferably unique—character, reflecting the notion of *terroir*.

When we use the term *real cheese,* by the way, it is in the sense of Patrick Rance's Campaign for Real Cheese (see page 44) and it embraces the notions of genuine, traditional, and authentic. Other terms helpful in defining artisanal cheesemaking include *specialty, farmstead* or *farmhouse (fermier* in French), *cooperative,* and *industrial.*

Recently, U.S. cheesemaking pioneer and former American Cheese Society President Allison Hooper, speaking to a master class I was teaching on restaurant service, reminded us of one of the most important differences: In artisanal cheesemaking, to maintain quality, you do not alter your raw materials; rather, you adjust your recipe. In industrial cheesemaking, the opposite is true: The raw materials are altered—with various treatments and additives—in order to conform to the recipe.

All cheesemakers strive for quality and consistency. Artisans emphasize purity of ingredients; they celebrate diversity, and they accept natural variation from season to season, from pasture to pasture, from cheese to cheese. For industrial cheesemakers, a totally predictable and completely identical result is the goal.

An important subset of *artisanal* is *farmstead.* This means the milk production and the cheesemaking occur on the same farm, and the family or company in charge is responsible for both operations. Milk quality is the first crucial element to guaranteeing the excellence of a cheese; a single, known, controlled source of milk is ideal, which is why an honest farmstead cheese is almost always your best bet.

Artisanal cheesemaking is not always farmstead; there are many fine examples where the milk producers and the cheesemakers are separate entities. As in much of artisanal cheese production, there's an analogy here to the wine business: Not all grapes for fine wines are grown on the producer's own land, i.e., not all great wines are estate bottled.

FROM TOP: Astraea Morford making cheese at Three Ring Farm, Oregon; part of the herd at Silver Falls Creamery, Oregon.

Bleu de Termignon: A rustic, naturally blueing (and not-so-blue in this photograph) artisan delight.

CHAPTER 1

CHEESE IS GOOD—AND GOOD FOR YOU

VERY OFTEN THE OPENING STATEMENT OF ANY CLASS OR SEMINAR I teach is: "Cheese is good food." It is near-perfect, primordial nourishment, the preserved form of the newborn mammal's first source of nutrition and calories—its mother's milk. Indeed, I always like to say a chunk of real cheese is arguably a better food than the incredible, edible egg.

Cheese is a delicious and tremendously efficient source of nutrition. It supplies many valuable nutrients, including proteins, sugars, vitamins, minerals, and trace elements. A 4-ounce piece of solid farmhouse cheese, for example, supplies more than half the adult nutritional requirements for protein, fat, calcium, and phosphorus as well as significant portions of vitamins A, B_2, and B_{12}. If you compare the nutritional content of a 3.5-ounce (100-gram) chunk of a hard, aged cheese such as Cheddar or Emmental to an equivalent amount of chicken eggs (two eggs are about 100 grams), the cheese contains about twice as much protein and one quarter the cholesterol.

The miracle of evolution has ensured that milk is an extremely nutritious food. After all, without it how would mothers, down through the eons, have guaranteed the survival of their precious newborns? Cheese has the same nutrients as the milk it came from except they are much more concentrated, which makes it a highly efficient delivery method. Another advantage to cheese is that its nutrients are "predigested" by bacteria and enzymes during cheesemaking and aging. This means the process of breaking down its proteins, fats, and sugars has already begun before our digestive systems goes to work.

Harbourne Blue, which has demonstrated the "cheese-of-the-moment" phenomenon (see page 107).

A Brown Swiss cow at Shelburne Farms, Vermont.

Plants in the pasture have absorbed nutrients from the soil; the dairy animals have extracted those nutrients, packaging them in the form of milk. The cheesemakers have concentrated and preserved that milk. Good news: A lot of the work has already been done for you. Your body has to devote less effort to processing cheese than it does with many other comparably nutritious foods.

It seems to me people who eat fine cheeses are rarely obese—or at least not morbidly so. Cheese is an important element in the Mediterranean Diet, a superior model for human food consumption, which also includes olive oil, wine, plenty of fruit and vegetables, less meat, more whole grains and nuts, some fish, and espouses the notion of "more is less." It's interesting to note that three of the world's highest per capita cheese-consuming countries—Greece, Italy, and France—have some of the lowest rates of cardiovascular disease and some of the longest-lived populations. A number of foods included in the Mediterranean Diet can elevate good cholesterol (HDL), cheese among them.

Nutrition experts increasingly recognize that fat tastes good and satisfies us and also that there are beneficial fats available in milk. Many of them work as antioxidants and also provide fat-soluble vitamins good for our skin and other organs. In cheese, milk fats undergo lipolysis, which breaks them down into more easily absorbed and beneficial fatty acids, some of which in turn enable us to metabolize the fats from other foods. Calorie intake should be the focus. The calories we consume must be expended; otherwise, we end up with a surplus and we gain weight.

Many people may conclude—not entirely unreasonably—that a high-fat food such as cheese is "a heart attack on a platter." It is true cheese has some "bad fats"—the saturated type from animal sources, which are associated with bad cholesterol—but it also has a lot of good ones. Cheeses, especially those made from the milk of grass-fed animals, are a good source of conjugated linoleic acid, or CLA, a highly beneficial nutrient, which is considered an antioxidant, a cancer fighter, and (miraculously) a fat-reducing fat. (Studies have shown people and animals consuming more CLA eat less.)

NUTRITIONAL CONCERNS

Because cheese contains fat, naturally, it raises concerns. I get a lot of questions about this in the Cheese 101 classes and the various other seminars I teach. Following is how I address some of the most commonly voiced concerns about fat and also about allergies and intolerances.

Among the main points to keep in mind is that real cheese delivers a lot of bang for your buck. It represents very good and very concentrated nutrition, but a little bit goes a long way. You don't guzzle Château Margaux or vintage Krug Champagne and you don't gulp large quantities of the world's finest cheeses. If you so desire, you can quite easily keep track of your fat intake from real cheeses; many of them are labeled according to their fat content, and with those that aren't, you can estimate this according to their type.

Vacherin Mont D'Or, spoonable and delicious.

One subtext to the "cheese is good food" argument is "don't be afraid of fat." Keep track of it, and consume moderate amounts. But unless you are especially overweight or have extremely high cholesterol, you need not be frightened by it. *Be aware, but don't be scared.*

Eating good cheese within the context of a balanced diet is good for you. The key is to eat moderate amounts alongside other healthy foods, especially fruits, vegetables, and other fiber-rich items—again, the Mediterranean Diet model. A 2- to 4-ounce chunk of real cheese with an apple or a pear constitutes a balanced, healthy small meal or snack.

I feel I'm personally a walking advertisement for eating fine cheese. My "bad" cholesterol is a lot lower than my genetics would predict, and many days I eat little more than cheese, fruit, and the occasional two-egg frittata (with cheese scraps if they're around). Although I've consumed a lot of it over the years, I don't overeat cheese—never too much in one sitting—and I never forget to supplement it with my fruits and fibers. In fact, I'm convinced that because I am a cheese eater, I eat better "other foods"—and I eat a lot less in general.

If you wish to track your fat intake, you should be aware that contrary to appearances, hard, grainy cheeses such as Parmesan may actually contain more fat than creamy, luxurious ones such as Explorateur. These rich triple-crème types are labeled "75 percent butterfat" while a Parmigiano-Reggiano claims around 35 percent butterfat. The trick is that cheeses are labeled by percentage of fat in their *solid* materials, not in their total weight. Cheeses do retain water, even after much of it is extracted during cheesemaking. The less water a cheese retains, the harder or more dense it will be.

Wedges of Laguiole await plating for a tasting seminar.

A dense cheese with, say, 50 percent butterfat, could actually deliver more fat per serving than a soft, runny one with 70 percent butterfat.

Generally speaking, whole-milk cheeses have about 45 to 50 percent fat content. The double crèmes have 60 to 75 percent fat and the triple crèmes 75 percent or more. To learn the fat content of a cheese, look for the terms *butterfat content, fat in dry matter* (FDM), or *fat on a dry basis* (FDB) or their equivalents in the languages of other cheese-producing nations—for example, *matière grasse* in French—on its label.

Another concern is lactose intolerance. Well-made, aged cheeses are actually one of the few dairy products that will not cause problems for people with this difficulty. The first and most important step of cheesemaking, alongside protein coagulation, is the conversion of lactose into lactic acid—the souring or fermentation action of lactic acid bacteria on milk. The small amount of lactose left over after active cheesemaking ends is further broken down by glycolysis during aging. What this means is, for people whose systems have trouble digesting lactose, it's already been done for them by the cheesemaking and aging process.

WHY CHEESE MAKES PEOPLE HAPPY

Another of my favorite mantras is "Cheese makes you happy." I'm convinced of this; I've felt cheese's uplifting effect on my own physique and psyche, and I've witnessed it so many times in so many other people. Nevertheless, I've often wondered whether it has any scientific basis. While researching this book, I met Dr. Thomas C. Morell at a cheese event in Florida. A neurologist based in Fort Myers, Dr. Morell specializes in pain management, helping patients deal with chronic afflictions such as arthritis. He is also a cheese lover and has been a happy customer at Picholine and the Artisanal Bistro.

Dr. Morell often delves into "nutritional neuroscience," which investigates how certain foods can make our brains and nervous systems function better. He offered some intriguing explanations of the mood-elevating properties of cheese—its physiological and psychological benefits.

"Why cheese makes us happy" all starts with tyrosine, an amino acid discovered in the mid-nineteenth century and found to exist in relatively high concentrations in cheese. In fact, its name is from the Greek root *tyros*, which means "cheese." (It's also the root for the word *tyrophile*, or "cheese lover.") Amino acids are complex molecular chains known as the building blocks of many proteins crucial to the proper functioning of the human body and brain. Because our bodies cannot manufacture tyrosine, many people have low levels of it, and we must obtain it from outside sources.

When we eat cheese, molecules of casein (milk's primary protein) are broken down and digested by our stomachs and intestines, and this action releases tyrosine for absorption into our bloodstreams. Casein is also broken down into a "feel-good chemical" called caso-morphin, which is an opioid (in the same family as morphine and heroin) and likely accounts for the addictive properties of cheese.

There is a section of the brain stem called the olfactory bulb, which contains relatively large concentrations of an enzyme called tyrosine hydroxylase. This enzyme reacts with the tyrosine to form certain well-known neurotransmitters, among them epineph-rine (aka adrenaline), norepinephrine, and dopamine, which in turn have many positive mental and physical effects. Epinephrine rapidly increases the flow of oxygen and glucose to the brain and muscles in order to elicit the "fight or flight" response to stressful or threatening situations. Norepinephrine helps fight depression and it also increases our attention skills and ability to focus. Dop-amine activates the brain's reward system, unleashing pleasurable feelings from survival activities such as eating, seeking shelter, or having sex and also from aesthetic pursuits such as listening to music or looking at pretty pictures. When you put all this together in the context of consuming fine cheeses, it really starts to make sense why they make us feel so good.

Tyrosine is a precursor to many hormones, including levodopa (aka L-dopa), which is made by the adrenal glands. Synthetic L-dopa is used to treat Parkinson's disease; ergo, ingesting tyrosine by eat-ing cheese may help alleviate this and other similar ailments. Tyrosine is also a precursor to melanin, the skin pigment that guards against sun damage and is also associated with the production of insulin, which regulates blood sugar levels and prevents diabetes.

Our sense of smell, largely responsible for taste, is headquar-tered in that olfactory bulb of the brain stem. Smell receptors in the nose, which detect volatile compounds in foods via the retronasal passage at the back of the throat, are connected to the olfactory bulb by the first cranial nerve.

Naturally, the olfactory system has some very important practical functions; for one, it has evolved as a method of sorting out edible substances. Your sense of smell tells you what you *can* eat, and also what you *want* to eat. If something smells good—or interesting—you are tempted to try it. If it smells putrid or harsh, you stay away from it. More often than not, what is delicious is also nutritious.

Beyond these highly practical, survival-related functions, the olfactory bulb is very much associated with a part of the brain called the limbic system, which is responsible for our memories and emotions. It is considered a key to unlocking all the feelings and perceptions of our formative experiences.

I often meditate about cheese as primordial food, our earliest sustenance, a taste we crave from the deepest recesses of our collective subconscious, a human species memory. Neuroscientists like Dr. Morell echo these thoughts: "I can't help but wonder if there isn't something in our genetics, in our limbic systems, in our memories, produced by cheese," he told us. "Maybe there's something in our brain wiring that gives us these pleasurable sensations from cheese." Cheese is the ultimate childhood comfort food, capable of triggering a Proustian moment, just like the famous Madeleine cake early in that French novelist's masterpiece *Remembrance of Things Past*, which more or less kicked off an 800-page flashback, or the ratatouille at the end of the film of the same name, which brought on the food critic's touching reverie of his mother's recipe.

Further to "why cheese makes you happy," I've always been convinced it was *the* food for helping our ancestors survive long, cold winters, and ancient periods of drought and famine. Perhaps now, the notion is obtaining some scientific backing. Dr. Morell cites studies showing that tyrosine is helpful during periods of stress, cold, fatigue, prolonged work, and sleep deprivation. It also appears to improve cognitive and physical performance, making people more alert and leading to better functioning in the workplace: "If your mood is normal and you ingest tyrosine you may not notice much change," he told us. "But if you're going through a stressful period, it's possible that increasing your tyrosine intake can improve your mood. During times of stress, you lose certain chemicals that are necessary to feelings of comfort and well-being. By taking in tyrosine, you actually build them back up."

By the way, if you've ever wondered what are those little crunchy pockets that develop in the paste of such well-made aged cheeses, such as genuine Dutch farmhouse Goudas or Parmigiano-Reggianos, they're crystals of tyrosine embedded within the long chains of amino acids comprising the casein molecules. When they make your mouth water, they are not only providing prodigious cheese-eating pleasure but they're also putting into motion a whole series of very real and tangible benefits to your body and brain.

Cheese Is Good—and Good for You

- [ ] Cheese has many highly beneficial nutrients; it is a "near-perfect" food.
- [ ] Concerns about the fat and cholesterol content of cheese are alleviated as follows.
  - Avoid eating excessive amounts (a little bit of real cheese goes a long way).
  - Eat cheese as part of a balanced and healthy (Mediterranean-style) diet.
- [ ] Milk is about 87 percent water; it also contains significant amounts of proteins, fats, and minerals.
- [ ] Cheese is concentrated milk and thus contains all of milk's essential nutrients, except in an advantageous "predigested" form.
- [ ] Aged cheeses contain very little if any residual lactose; virtually all the milk's lactose has been converted to lactic acid during cheesemaking and ripening.
- [ ] Cheese makes us feel good because it contains relatively high concentrations of tyrosine, a chemical building block of many important neurotransmitters, among them several of the brain's "feel good" substances.

CHAPTER 2

A TASTE OF
CHEESE HISTORY

THE ORIGINS OF CHEESE ARE SHROUDED IN THE MISTS OF PREHISTORY: It is believed that simple, fresh lactic-fermentation cheeses were made shortly after the domestication of sheep and goats roughly 11,000 years ago.

Archeological evidence of cheesemaking dates back approximately 7,000 years to the Sumerian and Mesopotamian civilizations in the Fertile Crescent, between the Tigris and Euphrates rivers, the location of present-day Iraq. The ancient Egyptians definitely practiced cheesemaking. There is also evidence of it in pre-Roman cultures in both northern Europe and the Italian peninsula (with the Etruscans), more than 3,000 years ago. Homer's *Odyssey,* believed to have been written in the eighth century BC, mentioned cheesemaking: Odysseus and his men had a run-in with Polyphemus, the foul-tempered Cyclops who was a shepherd and is said to have made cheese from the milk of his ewes.

The Romans left the first written accounts of cheeses and cheesemaking, such as in the works of Marcus Gavius Apicius (first century BC), and Columella, (first century AD). The Romans made Parmesan-like cheeses in the Italian peninsula; as their empire expanded, they not only exported their cheeses, but they also "discovered" local delicacies in conquered territories, ancient precursors of modern cheeses such as Cheshire and Lancashire in England; Roquefort, Cantal, and Salers in France; Mahón in Spain; and Sbrinz in Switzerland.

The hillside dug-out aging cave at Willow Hill Farm, Vermont, recalls ancient cheese farming.

With the exception of empire-driven trade, most artisanal cheeses were consumed where they were made. In fact, they were so local they didn't even have names at first. Once political power was centralized and great city-states came to rule entire countries, fine local cheeses were summoned to the royal courts. When they began to travel, it became necessary to distinguish them by their place names. What was simply "cheese" in Brie, for example, became *fromage de Brie* (cheese from Brie) in Paris, and later merely "Brie" for short.

Beginning in Renaissance times and extending through the seventeenth and eighteenth centuries, it was not only the aristocracy that spread the fame and fortune of great cheeses. The growing middle ranks of the bourgeoisie—the merchant and professional classes—began to enjoy an improved lifestyle and made farmhouse delicacies such as cheese part of it. This phenomenon continues today with the specialty foods sector, of which sophisticated luxury cheeses are an increasingly important segment.

Rich local traditions still survive in many ancient cheesemaking regions, and many local cheeses remain unknown to the outside world. If you go to the places where they make famous cheeses such as Taleggio or Pecorino Toscano, you'll also find some equally great, little-known, unadvertised local types as well as some more rustic, more authentic versions of those better-known cheeses.

Many of the modern advances of the nineteenth and twentieth centuries have actually hurt the cause of traditional cheeses more than they've helped. The Industrial Revolution led to the construction of cheese factories and the invention of mass-market cheeses beginning in the mid-nineteenth century in both Europe and the United States. This move toward modernization, along with the two world wars, almost wiped out traditional artisanal cheesemaking. A big step in the development of commercial cheeses and, in most respects, a setback for artisanal ones was the widespread implementation of pasteurization in dairy production in the 1940s in response to disease outbreaks. Another important early twentieth-century development was the introduction of commercially manufactured starter cultures. Prior to that, cheesemakers relied strictly on ambient, naturally occurring lactic acid bacteria to ferment their milk for cheese—a more old-fashioned, "genuine" or "authentic," approach guaranteeing a more natural expression of *terroir*.

Large-format Italian mountain cheeses, another ancient type.

Today, artisanal cheesemaking survives, to a great extent, in spite of modern advances. Twentieth-century dairy practices have delayed and hindered its rebirth, driven by the application of "practical, efficient" food science, fueled by increasing knowledge of microbiology and epidemiology, fanned by the popular notion that "all germs are bad" and overseen by bureaucracies such as the U.S. Food and Drug Administration. Yet a growing number of independent cheese artisans are not just surviving but thriving through grassroots initiatives, their own cooperative efforts, the support of the specialty cheese market, and by putting science to work in the service of their art. They apply up-to-the-minute sanitizing procedures and use advanced measurement and control devices. They introduce premade starter cultures and employ the latest in dairy science, including advanced breeding know-how, to maintain high milk standards and produce the best cheese possible—at great expense of time and money.

EVOLUTION OF CHEESE TYPES

Genuine cheese character is all about where a cheese comes from and how it is traditionally made. Real cheeses are a holistic, integral reflection of local history, geography, and social structure. Authentic cheese types arose out of cheesemakers' ingenuity in response to specific circumstances and challenges. Modern industrial cheeses can simulate many components of real cheeses, but they can never achieve true specificity of character because they cannot re-create the exact conditions of artisanal production.

Detail of Willow Hill Farm's cave, a return to old-style ripening.

Let's take a look at how one particular type—the large, aged Alpine cheeses of France, Italy, and especially Switzerland—evolved.

To survive the long, cold winter months when fresh food was scarce and outdoor hunting, gathering, and cultivation almost impossible, hearty mountain tribes developed big sturdy cheeses—hard yet still elastic—which could be stored and even brought to market over steep trails on the backs of pack animals. Softer, wetter, more fragile cheeses would not have survived—plus, why transport all that water weight when you could save effort by carrying more concentrated nutrition?

The hard Alpine cheeses grew out of a social structure in which groups of small farmers, who owned just a few cows each, pooled their resources to form cooperatives or associations. Their animals, organized into larger herds, followed the seasonal migratory grazing pattern called *transhumance*, wherein they move from their spring grazing grounds in the lower valleys up into the mountains to spend the summer in high-altitude pastures. Certain members of the community lived in small huts high in the Alps for the summer to tend those herds and make cheese from their milk.

This scenario presented certain logistical and technological challenges. First, the cheesemakers had limited space and a limited ability to haul large pieces of equipment up to their huts. With one small- to medium-sized vat or copper cauldron, they would make cheese twice a day, once after the morning milking and once after the evening one.

There were a number of ways cheesemakers could achieve their goal of large, solid (low-moisture) cheeses. One solution would have been to start with a slightly soured portion of milk from an earlier milking and combine it with the fresh milk from the most recent milking. This method would ensure more acid development in the curds, which would therefore expel more whey and yield a less moist cheese. With no way of storing milk overnight, however, mountain cheesemakers would have to find another less acidic path to the desired result. Salting would have been another route to low-moisture curds for big, durable cheeses, but hauling large bags of salt up to their mountain chalets was an impractical option. Instead, they used their knives to cut the fresh curds into very small pieces for better drainage, and then they cooked those curds over wood fires. There were plenty of trees to provide fuel. There were also plenty of rocks and timber beams, which were used to press more moisture out of the curds. Thus was born the family of cooked, pressed Alpine cheeses.

Such a "make procedure" (cheesemaker-speak for recipe) also resulted in several other distinctive traits long associated with Swiss-style mountain cheeses. Relatively low-acid curds yield a cheese with relatively high mineral content (for chemistry buffs, mostly calcium phosphate). This situation encourages the growth of *Propionibacterium shermanii*, which gives off carbon dioxide, creating not only the signature holes and/or fissures inside these types but also their typical deep, rich nutty flavors.

Given the proper temperature range and enough humidity during aging, the low-acid nature of these large Alpine types also makes them hospitable to surface growth of *Brevibacterium linens*. This friendly bacterium helps form a natural rind and promotes flavorful ripening in certain cheeses, particularly Gruyère and its close relatives.

CHEESEMAKING IN BRITAIN

The cheese history of England and the British Isles reflects a few important historical trends that, first, gave us some very familiar modern types, next, nearly sunk farmhouse production, and eventually, led to the modern artisanal renaissance. There is evidence of dairying and cheesemaking in pre-Roman Britain, more than 2,000 years ago. Most experts agree there was an "ancient widespread type" (Patrick Rance's words, see sidebar on page 44) prior to the Roman conquest. This British *ur*-cheese likely evolved into modern cheeses of the Cheshire or Lancashire type. Such a cheese is mentioned in *The Domesday Book,* William the Conqueror's 1086 survey of Britain, considered the first codified public record.

During the Middle Ages, peasant farmers (vassals or serfs) worked the land for the benefit of the lords of the manor and for their own survival. The peasants tended relatively small herds and made mostly small, locally consumed soft-ripened cheeses similar to those of northern France. They often paid their rents, taxes, and tributes in cheese.

As in the rest of Europe, the monasteries of medieval Britain were also agricultural centers. They often employed local peasants as sharecroppers and developed more complex, labor-intensive cheeses. At the time of the Norman conquest in the eleventh

A SAINT FOR CHEESE LOVERS

We have St. Benedict to thank for inspiring the construction of monasteries throughout medieval Europe, which in turn led to the creation of a great modern cheese type: washed-rind stinky "monk cheeses." Benedict of Nursia was a young Roman nobleman from Umbria who lived in the fifth and sixth centuries AD. He became a man of God, led a quiet life of contemplation, eschewing earthly pleasures, and wrote the precepts for the monastic life. Benedict founded the first abbey, at Monte Cassino, Italy, where he died circa 547 AD; he was canonized by the Catholic Church in 1220.

HOW TWO FAMOUS TYPES DIVERGED

Professor Paul Kindstedt
displays his first book, in which

he explains in
fascinating
detail how two
very distinct
cheese families
of northern
France, the
bloomy rinds
(Brie, Camembert, etc.) and the
washed-rinds (Maroilles,
Munster, Époisses), evolved from
similar milk because of the
different schedules and responsibilities of their makers,
farmhouse wives and monks,
respectively. The former, with
many other chores to attend,
began by mixing the two daily
milkings so their curds acidified
more quickly and thoroughly; the
latter had larger herds so they
kept the milkings separate, which
led to slower, gentler acidification. The farmhouse wives had
families to feed, so they sold or
consumed their cheeses young.
With greater resources, the
monks were able to age their
cheeses more extensively and to
develop elaborations, such as
washings. From these fundamental differences emerged all of
the contrasting traits and flavors
of two famous historical cheese
types.

century, for example, monks in north-central England were making ewe's milk blue cheeses very similar to Roquefort—a far cry
from the familiar British types of today.

By the fourteenth century, artisanal cheesemaking was a
thriving cottage industry on the manors and in the monasteries.
In a peasant farming family, the husband worked in the fields
growing produce and tending the herd while the wife worked in
the kitchen, making food and producing cheese. Quaintly enough,
this division of labor survives in many small cheese-farming
operations.

CHEESE GOES TO MARKET: THE END OF FEUDALISM AND THE RISE OF AGRICULTURAL CAPITALISM

Several key events conspired to hasten the collapse of feudalism
and usher in the era of agricultural capitalism, which had a profound effect on cheese. The first of these was the bubonic plague
epidemic, also known as the Black Death, in the mid-fourteenth
century, which killed a third to a half of the Earth's population,
decimating the peasant workforce of Britain. Manorial lords no
longer had an automatic supply of workers to sustain large farms
and they were forced to give out landholdings to their peasants,
who became sharecroppers. Some peasant entrepreneurs were
able to accumulate property; they became yeoman farmers, com-
moners with more than just a single family farm.

In the 1530s, King Henry VIII had himself appointed head of
the new Church of England and shortly thereafter began the dis-
solution of the monasteries, another blow to traditional medieval
cheesemaking practices. As feudalism collapsed and the yeoman
class arose, ancient market towns grew in size and influence. The
modern urbanization of Britain had begun. Once again, cheese
culture evolved in response to historical circumstances: The softer,
fresher, local types faded while the bigger, harder, more market-
able ones came to the fore.

Eventually, British farmers and cheesemakers began to focus
more on entrepreneurial efficiency as opposed to self-sustaining
farming. The main center of dairying and cheese production in
England beginning in the Elizabethan era (sixteenth century) and
extending through the Enlightenment (seventeenth century) was
East Anglia, the large bulbous peninsula jutting out in a north-
easterly direction from London. This fertile region became the

supplier of cheese and other dairy products for the big-city markets. It was the beginning of modern English—and, by extension, American—cheese history. It was also the beginning of the near extinction of artisanal cheese.

By the late eighteenth century, Cheshire and Somerset, to the west of London, had also converted to the new market-oriented system; what I call *big-boss cheeses* from that area, most notably one by the name of Cheddar, turned up in London. What was the common man's food of the Middle Ages became a prime source of solid nutrition for the urban proletariat, eventually helping to fuel the Industrial Revolution.

Apart from Cheddar, another delicacy destined to become world famous for centuries was also evolving in north-central England. The earliest records of Stilton, under another name, are from around 1720, although the recipe for England's greatest blue cheese may have been passed down through local families for more than 100 years prior.

Wheels of Sparkenhoe Red Leicester, a traditional British farmhouse cheese, at Neal's Yard Dairy, London.

THE CRADLE OF CHEESE: HIGHLIGHTS OF FRENCH HISTORY

At the beginning of his *grande oeuvre, The French Cheese Book,* Patrick Rance riffs on the question "How many cheeses are there in France?" He quotes General Charles de Gaulle's oft-cited quip to Winston Churchill about the impossibility of governing a country with 324 cheeses. Rance's rather vague conclusion, based on the 7 years he spent driving around the country with his wife, Janet, a journalist, looking for every French cheese, was there were over 700. After all this research, Rance was left wonderstruck and befuddled: "No definitive account of French cheese can ever be arrived at," he said. "French cheeses are in a constant state of flux. Some go by a multitude of names; other names cover a multitude of varieties. Some of the rarest and most succulent bear no name at all."

In his *Guide du Fromage* (original French edition, 1971; English edition, 1983), Pierre Androuët came up with a number closer to 500. Most experts eventually throw up their hands and admit France's cheeses are uncountable. Of course, it does depend on how you distinguish separate cheeses. If you fully subscribe to the notion of *terroir,* then you're forced to conclude that two identical cheeses from two different places, even if they're only separated

Robiola Rochetta, made by the ancient practice of mixing milks (see page 40).

by a few kilometers, are actually distinct and require different names.

In any case, local cheese culture in France is a far wider, broader, deeper canvas, with a greater multitude of cheeses and place-names, than in any other cheesemaking country. As with other traditional foods, the French have farmed milk and made cheese with a skill, commitment, and passion hard to match. This state of affairs is a matter of pride for the French and it's deserving of wonder and respect from the rest of us. I like how Patrick Rance expressed his appreciation, marveling at how all those old place distinctions, across the entire French countryside, had "survived even the Procrustean superimposition of the Revolutionary departmental system."

Some extant French cheeses were likely invented centuries before the Roman conquest of Gaul, which lasted from the second century BC to the mid-first century AD. They include Laguiole, Cantal, and Salers; the superstar sheep's milk cheeses in the Ossau-Iraty family of the Pyrénées; Roquefort, along with some of the other blue *fourme* cheeses of the Massif Central, and such Alpine large-format ones as Beaufort and Comté. During the Middle Ages, French monasteries gave birth to many a great cheese, including Maroilles in the north, Époisses, in Burgundy, and Abbaye de Tamié in the Haute-Savoie.

Another decisive event in French cheese history was the invasion of the Saracens—Arabs from northern Africa—in the early eighth century AD. They occupied the country as far north as the Loire Valley and brought their goat-herding culture to the area. Although the Saracens were driven out after their defeat in the famous Battle of Tours (October 10, 732 AD), the Loire Valley remains the world's most famous goat-cheese producing region, home of such classic place-named chèvres such as Selles-sur-Cher and Pouligny-Saint-Pierre. Farmhouse cheeses flourished in France in the late Middle Ages and throughout Renaissance times.

French cheeses did suffer some of the same setbacks as their English cousins, yet they were apparently already more firmly established and proved more resilient. Catholics were persecuted in France, but not until the Revolution, which meant the monasteries had a free pass for an additional two and a half centuries after Henry VIII's suppression in England. Later, in the eighteenth century, local specialties went to market and became

CAMEMBERT AND MORE

CHEESE MYTHS AND LEGENDS

According to legend, a farmhouse wife named Marie Harel invented and perfected the cheese that became famous as Camembert in 1791 during the French Revolution. Madame Harel is a national heroine. Her statue now stands in the village square of Camembert, Normandy, and her cheese is the biggest symbol of tradition and pride for the world's greatest cheesemaking nation.

Since there aren't a lot of verifiable historical facts about cheeses, the myths tend to take over. People's beliefs about a cheese—the stories they pass down through the generations—outshine whatever bits of muddled trivia exist. The sociologist Pierre Boisard wrote a clever book-length study called *Camembert: A National Myth,* dissecting the legend of Marie Harel, tracing this cheese from its origins as a local village staple and examining its myth from every imaginable angle.

Some unembellished accounts simply state Madame Harel was the first person to make Brie—a cheese

characterized by gentle ladling of relatively unmanipulated curds—in the molds used for Livarot. This implies Camembert is nothing more than Brie from a nearby town made in a different shape. Others attribute the recipe to a young priest on the run from revolutionaries who were determined to chop off his head. According to this version, Madame Harel hid the priest in her farmhouse and he thanked her by giving her his cheese recipe. It ascends quickly to the level of archetype: A divine secret in the form of a cheesemaking recipe for the ages is revealed to a humble farmhouse wife because of her courageous act of kindness.

The Camembert myth is just one of many noteworthy cheese legends, most of them French. Several common themes run throughout, including the magical, restorative powers of cheeses and the serendipitous nature of their discovery. In another archetype, often attached to Roquefort but also to other blues, a young shepherd leaves his lunch, a quotidian cheese sandwich, in a cave where he sought shelter. When he goes back for it a day later, he notices the cheese has grown some mold, which makes it taste much more interesting. (Blue cheeses are most often explained as "happy accident" discoveries.) In the Gorgonzola version of this tale, the

young shepherd hurries off one evening for a tryst with his girlfriend and leaves his cheesemaking vat open overnight. Much later, he returns to discover his curds have gone slightly moldy; they're still edible, though, with a pleasant little bite.

Saint-Marcellin, a soft, tasty little dollop of a cheese from the mountains of southeastern France, became famous when King Louis XI, while still prince-in-waiting and lord of the Dauphine region, became separated from his hunting party there and was rescued by local woodsmen, who gave him some of their cheese. Naturally, it became one of his favorites.

The truncated pyramid shape of the Loire Valley chèvre Valençay is mythologized as follows: Napoleon visited the statesman Talleyrand at his estate, the Château de Valençay, and tried the local goat cheese, made in the shape of a four-sided pyramid. Somebody—perhaps the emperor himself, using his ever-present sword—chopped off the top of the edifice in recognition of what a hard time his armies had fighting in Egypt. The cheese is still made in the same truncated-pyramid shape, and no doubt the genuine raw-milk AOC versions taste the same as the one Napoleon ate with Talleyrand.

famous under such place-names as Camembert, Pont l'Évêque, and so forth.

Many French cheeses did—and still very much do—suffer from industrialization. (Remember, Louis Pasteur, inventor and namesake of pasteurization, was a Frenchman.) In the late nineteenth

"A slice of good cheese is never just a thing to eat. It is usually also a slice of local history: agricultural, political, or ecclesiastical. . . . The cheeses of France are redolent of her history. Her traditional cheeses and pays *are endless, inseparable mysteries."*

PATRICK RANCE,
The French Cheese Book

and early twentieth centuries, as the railroads and large factory-style dairies began to exert their influence, these same cheeses began to develop international reputations. The Brie you could buy in your average American supermarket beginning in the mid-twentieth century was a modern, industrial, pasteurized imitation of the French original perfected in the farmhouses of Normandy and Île-de-France about 150 years earlier.

This cradle of cheese also has far more iconic cheeses than any other country. Brie and Roquefort are two of them. Roquefort is perhaps the most famous cheese in all of human history. Caesar's centurions encountered it in the first century BC during their conquest of Gaul, and it was mentioned by Pliny the Elder (Gaius Plinius Secundus) in his *Naturalis Historia* (Natural History), a multivolume encyclopedia dated AD 79.

Primitive forms of Brie—handmade, ladled, lactic fermented, young farmhouse types—were definitely around during Roman times and probably before. Brie-style cheese, in a form close to what we know today, was likely being served at least 1,200 years ago. The emperor Charlemagne enjoyed them in the eighth century BC, and they were being sold in Parisian markets as early as the thirteenth century. We would certainly recognize the *fromages de Brie* that graced the tables of the succession of French kings named Louis.

Brie de Meaux and Brie de Melun received their AOC (Appélation d'Origine Côntrollé, or Appellation of Controlled Origin) designations in 1980. Unfortunately, this coincided with a decline in artisanal standards. This was due to numerous factors, including less available milk from ancient local cow breeds; shortcuts or compromises in cheesemaking—for example, cutting the curds—and poor *affinage* (ripening). It was also due to market pressures: international demand for France's "name cheeses" and the prospects of increased profits led to industrialization and commercialization of artisanal cheeses across the board.

ANCIENT CHEESE TYPES: SUGGESTED TASTINGS

SELLES-SUR-CHER—Unadorned Loire Valley chèvres such as this one are descendants of the cheeses of the goat-herding Moors (called Saracens), who occupied western France in the Dark Ages. The youngest ones just taste like milk, not even fermented milk. I like them with enough aging so they just start to turn chalky while

remaining creamy and mild. Even an outstanding raw-milk version tastes simple, pure, and refreshing.

BRIN D'AMOUR OR FLEUR DE MAQUIS—I think of this as a primordial type: lactic fermented, unpressed, unaged, without extraneous bacteria, with just a coating of herbs to protect it. These types are still soft and fresh, their flavors still mild, but their mouth feel is more buttery. They have none of the chalkiness exhibited by the chèvres; however, they do possess more heft, being in the sheep's milk medium.

AMARELO DA BEIRA BAIXA OR ROBIOLA ROCCHETTA—Another ancient farmhouse type: simple, young, and made from mixed milk, a technique typical to small single-family farms. The Amarelo is an animal-rennet sheep-goat mix, rendering it significantly gamier and meatier, with stronger aromas than the previous cheese(s). Its consistency is thick and buttery and its more com-

A taste of ancient types: Clockwise, from top left, Fleur de Maquis; Selles-sur-Cher; Amarelo da Beira Baixa; Laguiole; Idiazábal; Sbrinz; Brie de Nangis; Munster; Fourme d'Ambert.

An Ayrshire cow at Jasper Hill Farm, Vermont.

plex profile, featuring fairly assertive flavors, tells you it's a raw-milk cheese. An alternative would be the Robiola Rocchetta, made from cow's, goat's, and sheep's milk, which invites an interesting species comparison (see chapter 6) and not as meaty or rustic as the Amarelo.

BRIE DE NANGIS—Cheeses of this type are the modern versions, perfected in the eighteenth century, of ancient lactic-fermented and/or mold-ripened (bloomy-rind) farmhouse cheeses. Mushroomy is the first flavor note, which comes from one of the *Penicillium* species—either *candidum* (for Bries) or *camemberti* (for Camemberts). The Brie is smooth, buttery, and mild, with barely a hint of cowy flavor. Its rind is perfectly edible but it may have a bit of metallic flavor, which can cause a clash with wines. An alternative would be a genuine AOC Camembert or Brie de Meaux.

IDIAZÁBAL—Any complete historical tasting must include one pressed, aged, hard, *tomme*-style mountain sheep's milk cheese. Idiazábal is from the northeastern Navarra region of Spain, not far from Rioja. It is traditionally a smoked cheese, which reflects a preservation method that was a significant historical advance in cheesemaking. Nutty in flavor, and slightly granular in texture; like many of its type, its profile includes rich olive oil notes. Two fitting alternatives, RONCAL, also from Navarra, and OSSAU-IRATY from another ancient sheep-dairying region, the Pyrénées.

MUNSTER—A fine representative of the stinky washed-rind monastery types, descended from medieval monk's cheeses. Munster is semisoft and buttery. Its aroma, an important part of its overall profile developed via the washings, is a little fetid and barnyardy: call it "cowy." On the attack, its flavor is a little salty; as it develops you get a lot of really pleasant *umami* and meaty character.

CANTAL—Pressed drums, these types were contemporaries of the Parmesan-style cheeses from the Italian peninsula, all of them ancient commodity cheeses from long before the development of Cheddar, a more modern member of this class. Cantal's profile is bigger and deeper than even the Idiazábal, with a longer finish; its flavors are familiar from many fine harder cow's milk cheeses, bold yet balanced. The British alternative is CHESHIRE, for which I have a lot of respect. The Cheshire has most of the same traits as the Cantal but with more of a maritime tang.

SBRINZ—This represents the harder, longer-aged ancient cow's milk (cooked and pressed) types, which, we can imagine, have not changed all that much in 2,000 years. I think of Sbrinz as the great-grandfather of modern Parmigiano-Reggianos. It's got plenty of strong flavors that announce themselves loud and clear all over your mouth, Sbrinz has good underlying fruitiness. It has a longer finish than any of the preceeding cheeses; only well-aged Gouda or a full-fledged blue cheese will linger more on your palate. A genuine DOP (Denominazione d'Origine Protetta) PARMIGIANO-REGGIANO would be a good alternative to the Sbrinz as a genuine ancient type.

FOURME D'AMBERT—The name alone (*fourme* is an archaic word for "cheese") evokes the ancient cheese traditions of the Massif Central region of south-central France. The Fourme has a little salt and good cow's milk flavors. It's smooth and creamy, with a nice *P. roqueforti* accent. Among the blues it has a medium intensity: Roquefort is stronger; BEENLEIGH BLUE is a little sweeter. BLEU D'AUVERGNE is a good alternative to the Fourme, with an equally ancient feel to it.

CHEESEMAKING IN AMERICA

English-style cheesemaking of the seventeenth and early eighteenth centuries migrated to the New World with the Puritans who settled in New England. True, there were Franciscan friars manning the California missions and bringing Spanish cheese savvy up from Mexico, beginning in 1769. And as Europeans moved west into the nineteenth century, there was some diversification among pioneering dairy farmers: Groups of Germans and Scandinavians, for example, brought their cheese-making and beer-brewing skills to Wisconsin and other parts of the midwestern farm belt. But for their first 300 years, American cheeses remained largely Cheddar and Cheddar style.

In the early eighteenth century, Puritan groups had begun to break off from the original Massachusetts Bay Colony—some of them, ironically, to escape religious intolerance among their own. They established dairy farms in Connecticut, Rhode Island, and New Hampshire and began exporting their British farmstead-style cheeses both to America's southern colonies and to the West Indies in exchange for molasses and to England for other neces-

The Neal's Yard Dairy store in Borough Market, London.

sary goods. Settlers of primarily English descent brought their dairy-farming and cheesemaking skills up the Connecticut River Valley to Vermont and also west to New York's Hudson Valley. They began to ship their ageable cheeses to urban markets in growing cities such as Montreal, New York, Philadelphia, and Boston.

New England farmers had already moved into New York State by the time of the Revolutionary War, but the big push westward toward Ohio began with the opening of the Erie Canal in 1825. The canal made it possible to ship hard cheeses down to New York City and other mercantile hubs. By the middle of the nineteenth century, New York was the number-one cheese-producing state in the union, followed by Ohio and Vermont. But cheese production was gradually shifting to rural areas of the Midwest, thanks to the canal and the huge demand created by the fast-growing cities of the Northeast.

Westward migration continued to be important, but the Industrial Revolution had an even bigger impact. First, clothing could now be manufactured in factories, freeing America's farmwives from many hours spent spinning wool, which allowed more time for cheesemaking. Also, farms now had more modern tools available, which could increase efficiency in all pursuits, including cheesemaking.

By midcentury, the railroad had come to the Midwest, and Wisconsin would become America's perennial number-one dairying and cheesemaking region. (It was finally surpassed by California in the late twentieth century.) Then came a devastating blow to American farmstead cheesemaking. In 1851, a dairy entrepreneur named Jesse Williams built America's first industrial cheese factory in Rome, New York.

Williams's upstate New York factory not only cleared a path toward production of mass-market processed cheeses, but it pretty much wiped out American artisanal production. Cheese factories proved to be at least five times more efficient at churning out cheese than any large farm to date. Within 15 years of the opening of Williams's first factory, there were about 500 of them in New York State alone. By the end of the 1800s, America was exporting huge amounts of cheese to Britain, whose cheesemakers could not keep up with domestic demand. To milk the British export market (pun intended), American cheese manufacturers skimmed off their cream and sold it for extra income as butter. By cutting corners and shipping out inferior cheeses, they were able to turn a better profit.

Throughout the first part of the twentieth century, real cheese in America maintained isolated outposts; there were a few respectable Vermont Cheddars and also some from Wisconsin; there was the Vella Cheese Co., in Sonoma, California, with its Monterey Jack types. The overwhelming majority of American cheeses, however, were made in large factories, by mechanized production. Artisanal cheesemaking was moribund and it remained so until the 1960s, when a back-to-the-land movement arose out of the hippie era. Vermont and California were centers for this type of activism and so naturally those states were where artisanal production began to percolate.

Dr. Frank Kosikowski, dairy scientist and ACS founder.

The next big development in American artisanal cheese was the founding of the American Cheese Society (ACS) in 1983 by one of our great modern cheese heroes, the dairy scientist, Professor Frank Kosikowski. This part of the story continues, under "The Great American Cheese Renaissance" (page 45), but first a brief digression to Britain.

NINETEENTH- AND TWENTIETH-CENTURY BRITAIN

Back in England, traditional real cheese encountered similar woes, attributable to a culture of industrialization and modernization. First came the railroads, which made it easier to transport fresh milk from outlying farms to urban markets so it was no longer as necessary to preserve it in the form of cheese. Then, as in America, came the construction of cheese factories, in the 1860s and '70s. World War I was a major setback for British artisanal cheesemaking. In the 1920s, commodity milk and cheese prices fluctuated, putting financial pressure on dairy businesses; in 1933, the British government set up a centralized system of distribution and price controls called the Milk Marketing Boards. While this mandatory cooperation stabilized the dairy market and made life easier for small producers, it also further undermined traditional artisanal methods and values.

World War II was another setback—nearly fatal—to whatever British farmhouse tradition was left. Many farmworkers, cheese

CHEESE HERO

PATRICK RANCE:
INTERNATIONAL CHEESE HERO

In 1971, four serious fans of traditional brews sought to offset industrialization and homogenization by launching the British Campaign for Real Ale. Cheese merchant Patrick Rance, inspired by their example, started his Campaign for Real Cheese in 1973. Rance soon won a commission from the National Tourist Board to write a book about British cheeses. Aside from providing an invaluable reference, based on nearly a decade of research, *The Great British Cheese Book,* which was published in 1982, also launched a strong defense of traditional artisanal raw-milk production. It laments the decline of several of England's big-boss cheeses: authentic Cheshire was made on 405 farms in 1939 and, by 1948, only 44; in the same period, farmhouse producers of Lancashire dropped from 202 to 29 and Wensleydale from 176 to 9. By 1970, authentic, traditional Lancashire was made on fewer than seven farms and today (as of this writing) it is made on just one, the Kirkham family operation in Gosnargh.

The original cover of *The Great British Cheese Book* sports a photo of Major Rance—he had served in the British Army—wearing his signature monocle and a sign-of-the-times paisley shirt, presiding over a large stack of real cheeses, an endearing image that reminds us of Rance's huge influence in reviving artisanal cheeses. Rance went on to author *The French Cheese Book* (1989), which turned out to be at least as important as his first book. He passed away in 1999 after a life devoted to championing real cheese and remains an inspiration to us all.

Patrick Rance, champion of real cheeses.

producers among them, were either sent off to war or to work in the war effort. The government was forced to ration foods and mass-produce cheese in factories. All those wonderful old historical types were being transformed into "block" or "supermarket" cheeses and this trend would continue to run rampant during the rebuilding and recovery after the war.

Into the second half of the twentieth century, just a few resilient British cheese heroes (and heroines) remained committed to and were able to keep the old ways alive, the Kirkhams of Lancashire fame and the Applebys of Cheshire among them. (Lucy Appleby, age 88, passed away in April 2008, but her family's cheese continues.) With his Campaign for Real Cheese, Patrick Rance launched the British artisanal cheese revival and Nicolas Saunders, who founded Neal's Yard Dairy, gave it an early boost. Neal's Yard Dairy opened in July 1979, on a small street of the same name (Neal's Yard) in London's Covent Garden district, as a creamery. Saunders's right-hand man, Randolph Hodgson, made Greek-style yogurts and fresh cheeses, which were sold from the shop. When

Saunders moved on to focus on other businesses, Hodgson took over and gradually built it into Britain's preeminent cheese *affineur*, wholesaler and retailer, one of the most influential such operations in the world.

THE GREAT AMERICAN CHEESE RENAISSANCE

Spurred by 1960s counterculture, farmhouse cheesemaking in America began returning to its roots, mostly in New England and California. Late twentieth- and early twenty-first century artisans, like the Kehler brothers in Vermont's Northeast Kingdom, very clearly echo the hippie farmers of their parents' generation. They also consciously evoke their cheesemaking forebears, all the way back to pre–Revolutionary War times. (The Kehlers have named some of their cheeses after heroes of that era.)

The culinary revolution jump-started by Alice Waters with the founding of Chez Panisse in 1971 and marked by the Judgment of Paris wine tasting in 1976 (where California wines bested some French greats) aroused the great sleeping "foodie" within the American public. Several pioneers of our real-cheese renaissance started their dairy farming and cheesemaking operations in the late 1970s and early 1980s, coinciding with the arrival of nouvelle cuisine. They include Laura Chenel, whose "California chèvres" began to appear on the menus at Chez Panisse in 1979; Judy Schad, Capriole (1978); Jennifer Bice, Redwood Hill Farm, (1978); Marjorie Susman and Marian Pollock, Orb Weaver Farm (1982); Mary Keehn, Cypress Grove Chevre (1983); and Allison Hooper, who founded the Vermont Butter & Cheese Company, with partner Bob Reese, in 1984. These top cheese farmers have become the visible faces of modern American cheese artistry.

Allison Hooper recalls how things were back in the days when she first started marketing her chèvres-style cheeses: "Nobody in America ate goat-milk cheeses. The French chefs we approached in New York City would all say, 'American goat cheeses? *Mais non!*'" Over a quarter century later, Allison's company is still going strong and she has become an influential voice in the artisanal food business.

A cornerstone for today's real-cheese revival was laid in 1977 with the founding of a gourmet food shop in Manhattan's trendy SoHo district by a team of entrepreneurs, Joel Dean, a business manager in book publishing, and Giorgio DeLuca, a former school-

FROM TOP: Allison Hooper and Bob Reese of Vermont Butter & Cheese Co.; Jennifer Bice of Redwood Hill Farm; Randolph Hodgson of Neal's Yard Dairy.

Ricki Carroll of New England Cheesemaking Supply Co.

"I had heard about farmstead cheese-makers, whom I glibly concluded were leftover hippies from the 1960s who had taken a shine to raising goats. I viewed farmstead cheesemaking as an anachronism. . . . I asked myself why I should waste my precious time orchestrating a conference for these idiosyncratic nonconformists? Kosi knew better."

PAUL KINDSTEDT, PH.D., FROM
AMERICAN FARMSTEAD CHEESE

teacher. Dean & DeLuca's first employee was a somewhat manic character from among the large ranks of New York's proverbial struggling actors, Steve Jenkins. (See sidebar, page 47.)

As Jenkins was developing the template for specialty cheese retailing, first at Dean & DeLuca and later at Fairway, Rob Kaufelt was learning the grocery trade from his father and grandfather in New Jersey. In 1991, Kaufelt took over an old-time Little Italy cheese shop (Murray's), eventually building it into a fine-cheese destination. Rob, Steve, and people like Cathy Strange of Whole Foods Market are the trendsetters of U.S. cheese marketing, helping stimulate and drive worldwide demand for artisanal cheeses.

A catalytic moment for the American cheese renaissance occurred in 1983 when Frank Kosikowski, a professor of dairy science at Cornell University, announced at a meeting of his grad students his intention to found the American Cheese Society (ACS). Paul Kindstedt, who was among this group of cheese Ph.D. candidates, recalls being dismayed: All the organizational work would sap him of valuable research time. At the time, Kindstedt was busy deconstructing the cheesemaking process in order to make it more efficient and factory-like. Luckily the good professor prevailed and was able to recruit him to become the ACS's first vice president. From a gathering of 150 core experts and enthusiasts in its first year, the organization has grown into a driving force for real cheese in America with well over 1,000 members and counting.

Other key developments in the U.S. cheese renaissance include the mainstreaming of health foods and development of real-cheese programs by natural food retailers such as Whole Foods; the rise of the Slow Food movement; and the founding of cheesemaking guilds in the United States. (For a list of these and other organizations, see appendix 3.) Also worth mentioning are the efforts of importers such as Henry Kaplan of Amazon de Choix, who was among the first to bring French soft cheeses to the U.S. market; Sara Stern, Debra Dickerson, and Jason Hinds of Neal's Yard Dairy, who brought the great British cheeses to the United States; Lou DiPalo and Dick Rogers for their Italian-cheese importing efforts; and Caroline Hostettler for bringing in the real Swiss cheeses. Ricki Carroll also deserves a niche in U.S. cheese history for starting her New England Cheesemaking Supply Company (in 1978) to provide not only equipment, rennet, and cultures but also valuable cheesemaking education.

STEVE JENKINS: AMERICA'S FIRST CHEESEMONGER

Steve Jenkins is a pioneer of American real-cheese retailing and importing. He may even have coined the term *cheesemonger*—and he certainly did popularize the trade. In the late 1970s, Steve was the first hire at Dean & DeLuca, a new upscale deli catering to the hippest, trendiest crowd in Lower Manhattan's latest art colony (SoHo). Steve developed their cheese program for two years, traveling to France and Italy to source delicacies such as Loire Valley chèvres and genuine Italian mozzarella di bufala and Parmigiano-Reggiano, introducing indigenous European artisanal cheeses to American palates—in many cases, the authentic versions never before tasted on these shores.

In 1980, Steve was hired by Fairway, where he launched its cheese program, eventually building a remarkable smorgasbord of as many as 400 selections. Before long, Steve became the first American to be inducted into France's exclusive cheesemongers' guild, the *Guilde des Fromagers, Confrérie de Saint-Uguzon*. In 1982, he was made an official *taste-from-age,* an honorary French designation for cheesemongers. He was at Fairway for eight years then spent another eight as a consultant, helping other businesses set up their cheese operations and also writing his book, *The Cheese Primer* (1996), which became a standard reference in the business. Steve received a Lifetime Achievement Award from the American Cheese Society at its 2008 convention in Chicago.

Steve oozes infectious humor and relentless enthusiasm. On the one hand, he admits to never having entertained an original thought and having stolen all his good ideas—mostly from the French. On the other, he claims to have invented specialty cheese retailing as we know it. Can he have it both ways? Why not? In any case, Steve is an American cheese hero.

By the early 1990s, real cheese had become as a significant segment of the U.S. specialty foods sector. It steadily built momentum, and in the first decade of the twenty-first century, it exploded, (see Chapter 14).

TASTING PLATE

American Pioneers

HOJA SANTA
(The Mozzarella Company, Dallas, TX)

HUMBOLDT FOG
(Cypress Grove Farm, Arcata, CA)

PANIOLO
(Willow Hill Farm, Milton, VT)

PIEDMONT
(Everona Dairy, Rapidan, VA)

MONT ST. FRANCIS
(Capriole, Greenville, IN)

VELLA DRY JACK
(Vella Cheese Co., Sonoma, CA)

GRAYSON
(Meadow Creek Dairy, Galax, VA)

CABOT CLOTHBOUND CHEDDAR
(Cabot Creamery, Cabot, VT)

GREAT HILL BLUE
(Great Hill Dairy, Marion, MA)

One of the goats at Tumalo Farms, Oregon.

OPPOSITE: "American pioneer" cheeses: From above left, Hoja Santa; Humboldt Fog; Paniolo; Piedmont; Mont St. Francis; Vella Dry Jack; Grayson; Cabot Clothbound Cheddar; Great Hill Blue.

All of these American originals have been produced artisanally since before the turn of the twenty-first century—true, some of them only since the mid- to late-1990s, but they are products of the twentieth century. They represent a pretty good sweep of our country's geography and its varied pockets of cheese *terroir,* leaving out only the Northwest, which is well represented in chapter 14.

We start with the mild, fresh, pasteurized goat's milk Hoja Santa, made by Paula Lambert's dairy in Dallas. Paula is a U.S. trailblazer, creating superb artisanal cheeses in an urban factory setting since 1982. The Hoja's main expression of *terroir* comes from being wrapped in leaves of the plant from which it gets its name, the *hoja santa,* also known as *yerba santa,* or root beer plant, which lend a hint of sassafras flavor.

The progression moves to another pasteurized goat's milk cheese, Humboldt Fog, which announces its *terroir* not only with its name but also its appearance, the gray-tinged rind from ripening *P. candidum* molds recalling the fog rolling into California's Humboldt County off the mighty Pacific. Mary Keehn established her farmstead cheesemaking operation in 1983, and this cheese is a fine representative of the "California chèvre" style. More mature and crumblier than the fresh Hoja Santa, it exhibits some earthy notes yet remains light and creamy. We move on to a raw washed-rind cow's milk cheese, Willow Smart's Paniolo, still on the young and fresh side but a logical next step past the two goat's milk openers. Paniolo is a twenty-first-century cheese, though owner Willa Smart has been producing cheese since the 1990s. It's not unlike Ireland's Durrus, mild and milky but with some nice spunk and illustrates how a relatively recent (2008) American farmstead original can equal the European greats while expressing its classic Vermont *terroir.*

What follows is an artisanal sheep's milk cheese from the mountains of western Virginia first made in the late 1990s, in the style of a great European antecedent. The Piedmont is a Pyrénées type (firm, pressed, aged) and, with its nutty, sweet, grassy notes, definitely a bigger, bolder cheese than the Paniolo.

We progress back to a goat cheese, also made from raw milk, this time in the washed-rind monastery style. Mont St. Francis has some stink to it and a big flavor profile, reflecting its roots in "Kentuckiana," a region of southern Indiana topographically much more akin to the nearby hills of Kentucky than the flatter farm

U.S. artisan terroir: Cato Corner Farm, Connecticut (see also Chapter 8).

country in most of the rest of the state to its north.

In the category of twentieth-century True American Originals, the next cheese has to be considered the granddaddy of them all. Vella Dry Jack was created by Tom Vella in the 1930s as a gratable variation on the Monterey Jack style, intended for his fellow Italian immigrants in California. For this plate, I'd recommend the Special Select version, aged 12 to 24 months, although the regular, which is aged 7 to 9 months, can also be very nice. The Dry Jack's texture and consistency are somewhere between a Piave and a Keen's Cheddar; its flavor profile is mellower than a classic British farmhouse Cheddar, though, and not as fruity as the Piave.

Another Virginia mountain farmstead cheese, Grayson, follows. It is washed-rind, pungent in aroma, and meaty in flavor, reminiscent of both Taleggio and Livarot. The Feete family has been making it since the late 1990s, but it really hit its stride more recently, in 2006 and 2007. It was a standout in the blind tasting for the Raw Milk Cheese Presidium at the Artisanal Premium Cheese Center in the summer of 2008. Actually, depending on how ripe it is, the Grayson might switch places with the next item, Cabot's Clothbound Cheddar. Cabot was established in 1919 and its label is very familiar to supermarket shoppers. As compared with their British farmhouse cousins, Vermont Cheddars are more acidic, they offer that signature tang, and they present a more focused, not as mellow and round, flavor profile.

Our American Pioneer finale comes in the form of another cheese born in the late 1990s. Great Hill Blue provides a little bit of everything Americans are looking for in their blue cheese: some salt, some acid, a taste of the *P. roqueforti* mold, and a hint of underlying sweetness. Great Hill is located on the southern Massachusetts coast, in Plymouth County, less than 25 miles south of where the Pilgrims landed the Mayflower in 1620, bringing things full circle. The dairy buys its milk from local farms whose herds graze pastures bathed in the fog rolling off Buzzard's Bay.

An Outline of Cheese History

☐ Cheesemaking is believed to have been first practiced in prehistoric times, about 9,000 to 11,000 years ago, in the area around the Fertile Crescent of Mesopotamia.

☐ The oldest archeological evidence of cheesemaking in Europe dates back about 3,000 years.

☐ Modern cheese types evolved from specific sets of cultural circumstances and logistical requirements; real cheeses reflect their geographical and historical origins.

☐ St. Benedict and the proliferation of monasteries in Europe profoundly impacted cheese development.

☐ Local cheeses became known by their place-names with the modernization of European nations and the dawn of agricultural capitalism in the seventeenth and eighteenth centuries.

☐ American cheesemaking and cheese types came largely from East Anglia via the Puritans and other English settlers.

☐ The Industrial Revolution and the advent of cheese factories in the United States and Britain nearly wiped away artisanal farmhouse cheesemaking.

☐ America's first cheese factory opened in 1851 in New York State.

☐ World War I and World War II both caused the near extinction of artisanal cheeses in England.

☐ Patrick Rance founded his Campaign for Real Cheese in 1973 in England.

☐ France has more cheeses and more cheese history than any other nation.

☐ The renaissance of American artisanal cheesemaking began in the late 1970s and early 1980s; it gathered momentum throughout the 1990s and it exploded between 2000 and 2005.

CHAPTER 3

ALL ABOUT CHEESEMAKING: THE EIGHT BASIC STEPS & BEYOND

I'M A FIRM BELIEVER THAT THE MORE YOU KNOW ABOUT HOW SOMETHING is made and what goes into it, the better you can appreciate it. Understanding cheesemaking fundamentals is part of mastering cheese: It clarifies the differences among types and also helps explain how individual cheeses express their distinctions and character.

Professor Frank Kosikowski, the same American cheese hero who founded the American Cheese Society (ACS), outlined the eight basic steps, which have become the cheese equivalent of Newton's Laws of Motion. You'll see these listed in some form in just about every professional volume and featured in most serious classes on cheesemaking. (Professor K taught them in his courses and also explained them in Volume 1 of his textbook *Cheese and Fermented Milk Foods,* the third edition of which was coauthored by his former student Vikram Mistry and came out in 1997, two years after the professor's death.)

First, following up on our history chapter, we'll look at how various procedures evolved, then we'll consider exactly what goes into cheese (always know your raw materials) before launching into a layperson's overview of Kosikowski's Eight Basic Steps.

Parmigiano-Reggianos ripening at the Cravero facility in Bra, Italy.

Newly formed cheeses draining at Three Ring Farm, Oregon.

CHEESEMAKING DEVELOPMENTS: STEP BY STEP

From a historical viewpoint, each of the basic steps represents one in a series of technological advances. In the centuries-long evolution of this artisan craft, these advances led to innovations in the cheese recipe; they added complexity, created distinctions, and thereby defined the various modern cheese types.

The first step, acidification of milk, remains the basis for all cheeses. (In fact, some still don't require much more than that.) Prehistoric fresh types, which were not all that far removed from today's sour cream, clotted cream, or quark, eventually evolved into something resembling a basic farmer's cheese, also known as white cheese or, in Spanish, *queso blanco* or *queso fresco*.

After simple souring to make fresh cheeses, the next big step is the coagulation of milk to form curds, which is generally done via the proteolytic enzymes contained in rennet from the stomachs of young ruminant animals, the very substances that helped those sucklings break down the proteins and digest their mothers' milk. You could say this was the beginning of modern cheesemaking because it opened the door to the curing and aging steps. It is assumed this advance was a "stumble discovery." Some clever shepherd used an animal stomach to transport milk, noticed the milk spoiled in a different way, and developed a useful procedure for preserving it in tasty, transportable form. Modern cheese was born.

Further developments, beginning in Roman times and extending and into the Industrial Revolution of the eighteenth and nineteenth centuries, included more extensive draining as well as cooking, pressing, molding, milling, and salting. These procedures result in harder cheeses that can be aged, stored, and/or transported, rendering them a major food staple and commodity for trade. They also pose logistical challenges requiring the manufacture of mechanical devices such as vats; baskets or colanders; pots; kettles; and knives; and other efficient cutting, cooking, and draining tools.

Here are some of cheesemaking's "developmental steps":

LARGE-FORMAT "COMMODITY" CHEESES—By Roman times, cheesemakers had established recipes for big, hard cheeses; they utilized rennet coagulation as well as cooking, pressing, and salting. To make rennet, they would either dry the young ruminant stomachs, cut them in strips, and add them to the milk in that form or create a rennet solution with brine, then mix it in.

BLUE CHEESES—Encouraging blue molds to ripen cheeses such as Roquefort dates back to pre-Roman times. The Roquefort recipe, which includes propagating the molds in large loaves of bread, specifically baked for that purpose, was codified over 300 years ago, and in 1925 it became the first cheese to receive legal designation and protection, launching the French AOC system.

SMOKING—Ancient artisans making cheeses in mountain huts would keep themselves warm, shoo away flies, and dry their cheeses by building little fires inside. (Necessity as the mother of invention.) As an added benefit, their cheeses would acquire pleasant smoky flavors. Two Spanish cheeses, Gamonedo and Idiazábal, carry on this tradition as do two modern American originals, Rogue Creamery's Smokey Oregon Blue and Three Ring Farm's Up In Smoke.

David Gremmels of Rogue Creamery picks syrah grapevine leaves at Carpenter Hill Vineyard, Oregon, for wrapping Rogue River Blues.

MIXED MILK—Small family farms would make young cheeses for their own consumption from the milk they didn't drink. They had perhaps one or two cows, a sheep, and a goat—not enough of one species to fill the cheesemaking vat. So they blended the milks and discovered delicious results.

LEAF WRAPPING—Soft and semisoft primordial types, represented today by such cheeses as Banon and Brin d'Amour, were often used as currency and sometimes brought to market. For this, they needed protection, so they were wrapped in leaves. Early cheesemakers found this technique also offered some nice flavor benefits. Today, cheeses such as Rogue River Blue, which is wrapped in pear-brandy-soaked Syrah grapevine leaves, recall this ancient method.

COMMODITY CHEESES—Among the cheesemaking steps defining what I call British boss cheeses beginning in the sixteenth and early seventeenth centuries was partial skimming. The cheesemaking milk would undergo higher and more rapid acidification, its cream removed to make butter. More acidification resulted from using milk from two or three consecutive milkings. This was a first step toward bigger, harder, lower-moisture cheeses. Further steps included scalding, pressing, cheddaring (a form of "passive pressing" achieved by repeatedly cutting and stacking

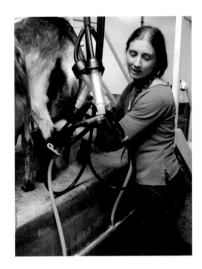

FROM TOP: *Andhi Reyna milks her goats at Fern's Edge Goat Dairy, Oregon; a spotless stainless steel collection can for fresh cheesemaking milk, Pholia Farm, Oregon.*

Among the handful of professional mantras I chant every day is "Cheese is a moving target." This starts with the changing nature of the raw material itself.

blocks of curds), and salting of the curds themselves (as opposed to external salting of the formed cheeses).

EARLY "VEGETARIAN" CHEESES—Sephardic Jews in Iberia (western Spain and eastern Portugal) invented—or at least advanced—the practice of thistle-renneting (plant coagulation) of curds to make cheeses according to their kosher diet, beginning about 1,500 years ago. Animal renneting could be interpreted as violating the prohibition against seething the calf in its mother's milk. These were the precursors of the modern *torta*-style cheeses.

"MONK" (OR MONASTERY) CHEESES—Washed-rind cheeses began to evolve about fifteen centuries ago, with the gradual spread of Christianity and construction of monasteries across Europe. Their modern descendants are the medium-sized semisoft luxury cheeses such as Munster and Époisses, which survive pretty close to their original form. The monks were prodigious farmers and dairymen, who also developed fermented, brewed drinks such as abbey ales, which they often used to wash their cheeses.

BLOOMY-RIND CHEESES—Cheeses of the Brie and Camembert types—made with rich milk acidified overnight, gently ladled into draining and shaping forms, and ripened by external molds—had likely been produced, in rustic versions, in the kitchens of small dairy farms, since at least late medieval times. They originated in the Île-de-France region, not far from Paris, and in nearby Normandy. This type was descended from simple, ancient lactic fermentation cheeses (with no renneting) and improved with the discovery of mold ripening.

WHAT'S IN CHEESE?

Since cheese is essentially concentrated, preserved milk (with salt added), in order to answer this question, we need to take a step back and answer a more fundamental one: What's in milk?

The solid content of milk runs from approximately 12.5 percent in cows to about 19 percent in sheep. Its principle solids are the protein casein, the sugar lactose, and butterfat, all of which are dispersed in the medium of water. The fact that all of milk's solids are not completely dissolved but rather float in somewhat self-contained units within an emulsion is what makes cheesemaking possible (i.e., that the curds can be separated from the whey so they can be preserved and aged).

Milk components are as follows:

WATER: At about 80 to 87 percent, water is by far the major component of milk. It is present largely in the form of hydrogen ions, which are electrically charged molecules of water. Not to delve too deeply into organic chemistry, but the fact they have a slight electrical charge means they are readily able to bond with other substances, in this case all the solid components of milk.

FAT: Milk fat exists in the form of globules, emulsified in whey, which is a thin solution of mostly water with small amounts of fat and protein. As the whey is drained away and dried up during cheesemaking, the fat globules become integrated into the body of the cheese and are subject to breakdown into free fatty acids by the action of enzymes from various microflora.

PROTEIN (CASEIN): Milk protein (casein) exists in the form of micelles, the protein equivalent of a fat globule, suspended in solution. Through the process of proteolysis, the casein in milk is broken down into amino acids such as tyrosine, tryptophan, lycine, valine, and taurine.

SUGAR (LACTOSE): Milk sugar is very similar to table sugar in chemical makeup. It is very water soluble and provides "food" for bacteria in the milk, including those introduced as starter cultures to convert the lactose to lactic acid. The vast percentage of lactose in milk is fermented into lactic acid during cheesemaking; a small amount is drained away with the whey and another very small amount remains in the cheese to provide energy to bacteria during the aging process.

VITAMINS: Milk contains the vitamins A, B_1, B_2, B_3, B_6, B_{12}, D, E, and K. Although these and the minerals (below) account for less than 1 percent of milk's total volume, they are significant nutrients.

MINERALS: Minerals contribute flavor and texture or substance to the body of a cheese; they are also potential nutrients. The principle minerals in milk are calcium and phosphorus (in the form of calcium phosphate); it also contains sodium, potassium, and magnesium as well as trace elements, including zinc, iron, manganese, and copper.

ANCIENT RECIPE

ROMAN CHEESE RECIPE

Cheesemaking can be quite complicated, but there are certain aspects common to all recipes. Here is a cheese recipe from the first century AD—from the Roman food writer Columella, as quoted (in translation) by Frank Kosikowski in *Cheese and Fermented Milk Foods* via French professor Germaine Mocquot, a microbiologist and historian:

- Heat cheese milk to a warm temperature.
- Add animal or plant rennet to the milk.
- Remove free whey and press with weights.
- Place fresh cheese in a cool area and salt surfaces.
- Periodically brush and work cheese surface.
- Allow cheese to ripen.

Andhi Reyna checks feeder pipes in her cheesemaking room at Fern's Edge Goat Dairy.

"... the amount of casein in milk will directly influence coagulation time and curd firmness. Milk with high casein contact, such as sheep's milk, like that from a Holstein cow, coagulates more slowly to form a weaker curd. As the casein content of milk changes across seasons, so, too, will the coagulation properties."

PAUL KINDSTEDT, PH.D., FROM
*American Farmstead
Cheesemaking*

VARIABILITY OF MILK COMPOSITION

Among the handful of professional mantras I chant every day is "Cheese is a moving target." This starts with the changing nature of the raw material itself. The overall solid content of milk—as well as the ratio of its fat and protein content—changes daily, monthly, and seasonally.

Milk composition varies as the animals go through their yearly lactation cycles (and also from morning to evening; see opposite). At the very beginning of a cycle, during the first week after the birth of the calf, kid, or lamb, the milk is thick, yellowish, and contains high levels of the antibody immunoglobulin to supplement the newborn's fragile immune system. This milk is called colostrum, or beestings, and is not appropriate for cheese-making. (Colostrum does not coagulate properly and can't make a viable cheese: its protein-to-fat ratio is way off.) Throughout the early part of the cycle, the milk is relatively concentrated and high in fat and proteins, again to nurture the small growing offspring. As the lactating mother approaches midcycle, the volume of milk increases, but it becomes more diluted. Toward the end of the cycle, the volume decreases and the milk becomes more concentrated again.

Seasonal variation in the solid content of milk—its combined casein (or protein) and fat—can be as much as 40 percent, from a high in the late fall or winter to a low in the summer. The percentages of those two key solids increase and decrease together; the P/F ratio between them, an important parameter in cheese-making, also fluctuates, although within a smaller range. The higher the concentration of these two key solids is, the higher the cheese yield.

Generally, it takes between 6 and 12 units of milk to make 1 unit of cheese. (Dairy farmers, by the way, tally their animals' milk using solid units—pounds or kilos.) A large Alpine-style cheese—Emmentaler, which ranges in weight from about 90 to 110 kilos (198 to 242 pounds), is one impressive example—requires about 320 gallons of milk to make a 220-pound wheel. This really underlines the notion of cheese as a concentrated, preserved form of the precious nutrients in milk. Sheep's milk yields relatively more cheese since it is more concentrated; its milk-for-cheese ratio is about 6 to 1 (although an individual ewe yields a lot less milk than a cow). Softer cheeses require more milk since they have higher liquid content—and milk is, after all, mostly water.

Different species have different breeding and lactation cycles—determined by their different gestation periods and expected ranges for weaning. This is the main reason most traditional cheeses are not made year round. Breeding can be staggered to extend a herd's milk-production cycle. A farm can manipulate the breeding cycle, using artificial insemination to extend its milk production year-round, although one must question whether this type of "modern farming technique" is at all advisable. Does it fall into the category of "fooling with Mother Nature" and can such an approach ever bode well for artisanal cheeses?

Dairy animals are usually milked twice a day, and the evening milk generally has a lower fat content than the morning milk. How the milk from the two daily milkings is stored and combined—or not—is an important factor in cheesemaking.

Another crucial factor determining milk composition is *terroir*—all the components of environment and geography, water, and feed. Water will affect milk and cheese character on two counts: first, via the ground and/or melt water, which irrigates the animals' plant foods; and second, via the drinking water given to the animals. (Water has a third potential influence: Young cheeses are sometimes given baths to enhance ripening.) A self-contained farmstead using pure drinking water from a local underground spring and relying on pristine rains from the sky and untainted stream water from the melting snows for irrigation would be ideal, but is not always possible. Whatever special local traits the water possesses—certain mineral flavors, for example—are likely to show up in a cheese.

What the animals eat will also help determine the taste of the milk and the cheese. The fundamental contrast is between a diet of dry feed in the winter and pasture plants in the summer. Winter feed can consist of so-called TMR (total mixed ration), the dairy-farming term for a prepared, solid "formula food," and/or hay, which is composed of dried grasses with the occasional flowers or legumes mixed in. Silage, which is hay and other plant fodder in a silo, can also be fed to dairy animals, but it is potentially problematic since "off flavors" from the fermentation can work their way into the milk and eventually the cheese.

LEARN FROM MISTAKES

ONE PERCENT CAN MAKE A BIG DIFFERENCE

If a cheesemaker finds a batch is not up to standards, he or she will need to go back and examine, minutely, microscopically, each and every detail of cheesemaking to analyze and try to determine where things got off track. This can be tricky. It may be just one or two variables were off by a hair. Perhaps the moisture content of your Cheddar was 38 percent instead of 37 percent, or the fat content of your milk was off by a small percentage. Maybe you used a fraction of a teaspoon too much or too little starter culture, or your curds acidified a few minutes too fast. In any case, you wound up with a cheese that didn't reflect your intentions and probably had to be thrown out so as not to risk damaging your reputation.

FROM TOP: Cary Bryant and Marc Druart pouring fresh milk for a cheesemaking demonstration at the 2008 Oregon Cheese Festival; forming cheeses at Caseificio Pinzani in Tuscany.

TMR generally results in slightly higher solid content—both protein and fat—in milk and, at the same time, a slightly higher P/F ratio. In other words, dry formula feed yields slightly more dense milk that is slightly higher in protein.

The P/F ratio, even with relatively small variations, is a prime factor in the decision of what type of cheese to make. Assuming the goal is to achieve consistent results, fluctuations will dictate adjustments in the cheese recipe. Like the other factors in milk composition, the P/F varies not only seasonally but also by animal type. (More on all this can be found in "Changes in Milk Composition," page 65, and also in chapters 4 and 6.)

KOSIKOWSKI'S EIGHT BASIC STEPS OF CHEESEMAKING

Now that we know what's in milk and cheese, we can discuss how cheese is made, following the good professor's outline of the fundamental recipe steps.

Step 1: Setting the Milk (Acidification and Coagulation)

This first step involves two important, somewhat related and overlapping occurrences: acidification and coagulation. Fine cheese starts with clean, fresh milk from the most recent milking, perhaps mixed with milk from a previous milking (or milkings). The milk is soured, its lactose (milk sugar) converted to lactic acid by bacteria. Ideally, fresh milk is made into cheese immediately—or, in any case, the sooner the better. Any delays or extra handling steps may introduce unnecessary variables and, in the worst-case scenario, even risk of contamination. If fresh milk is stored in a refrigerated tank, it must be reheated to begin cheesemaking.

ACIDIFICATION AND STARTER CULTURES Acidification will occur naturally if milk is left to sour on its own: Inherent and/or ambient bacteria will ferment its lactose into lactic acid. Cheesemakers normally add bacterial starter cultures to jump-start the process. Traditional cheese recipes involve creating a starter by using a small amount of the naturally soured milk from the day before, the same way as yogurt is handmade at home. Bulk cultures can be created by adding a small amount of starter culture to a portion of the cheesemaking milk, maintaining it day to day and using just enough of it to start each batch of cheese. It's possible to make cheese by these strictly old-fashioned methods, but it can be difficult and time consuming. Nowadays, cheesemakers often add bacteria via commercially prepared starter cultures in the form of freeze-dried powders or frozen liquid concentrates.

Commercial starters offer the advantages of greater predictability, consistency, and control. Dairy supply companies have isolated many species of starters and defined how they affect acidification and coagulation and also what flavors and textures each one is expected to contribute. A possible disadvantage of commercial starters is a loss of natural character since the influence of the milk's inherent microflora can be overshadowed.

After completing acidification, starter bacteria die and release their enzymes, which contribute to the breakdown of proteins and fats—key steps in successful cheese ripening and flavor formation. These enzymes also affect cheese texture, assist in expelling moisture from the curds, and inhibit spoilage.

As the bacteria convert lactose into lactic acid, temperature and time measurements are critical. Bacteria multiply very rapidly, especially under conditions highly favorable to their species. And although this window of proper conditions may be fairly narrow, if it is left open, lactic acid bacteria may continue their fermentation for a long time during cheesemaking (i.e., both during and after coagulation), when the milk has turned into a mass of curds. The rate of acidification is the most important measure of a starter culture because it determines the curds' (and cheeses') eventual pH (acidity) as well as their moisture and mineral contents. The acidity level has many repercussions throughout the course of cheesemaking.

SECONDARY CULTURES So-called secondary cultures are often added to the acidifying, coagulating milk and curds. They can be applied to or encouraged to grow on a forming cheese. Each culture has unique flavor and texture effects, which help distinguish one cheese type from another. Among them are a number of yeasts, molds, and bacteria that have many strains and sub-strains and may be added in various combinations. The main species of secondary cultures are:

• PROPIONIBACTERIUM (SEVERAL SPECIES), which give Swiss-style cheeses certain characteristic flavors as well as holes due to carbon dioxide release in the cheese's interior

"MAKING CHEESE IS LIKE FARMING BACTERIA."

—ANONYMOUS

Some wise cheesemaker—I wish I could remember who it was to properly attribute the quote—once told me, "Making cheese is like farming bacteria." Part of mastering cheese is learning to love and understand the "bennies"—all those friendly little microbes that help us make cheese. We shouldn't be scared of them. What we *should* be scared of is the widespread use of herbicides, pesticides, and genetically modified organisms. Making real cheese has nothing to do with those practices.

CHEESE CHEMISTRY

TYPES OF CULTURES

Of the many different types of starter cultures, there are two main categories: mesophilic and thermophilic. Mesophilic cultures function best at temperatures close to the body temperature of the dairy animal, around 86 to 98 degrees F, though their growth range can be as low as 50 degrees F and as high as 102 degrees F. Thermophilic cultures function best at higher temperatures—91 to 111 degrees F—with a growth range from 68 degrees F to as high as 131 degrees F. The latter heat-loving cultures are used to make cooked-curd types such as Gruyère and also *pasta filata* cheeses such as Mozzarella and Provolone; mesophilic cultures are appropriate for most recipes where the temperature in the cheesemaking vat milk is not as high.

- GEOTRICHUM CANDIDUM, a white mold (with yeast-like traits) that contributes to surface-ripening of bloomy-rind cheeses as well as some washed-rind ones
- PENICILLIUM GLAUCUM contributes dark blue–green colors and piquant flavors to Gorgonzola and other blues
- PENICILLIUM ROQUEFORTI, which has a similar effect on Roquefort and related blue cheeses
- PENICILLIUM CAMEMBERTI, which is crucial to Camembert-style cheeses (it turns a young cheese's rind white at first then changes to gray after a few days)
- PENICILLIUM CANDIDUM, the equivalent for Brie types (it stays white and accounts for flavor variations)
- BREVIBACTERIUM LINENS, a moist, reddish smear of bacteria that helps ripen many washed-rind and *tomme*-style cheeses

Within each species of microorganism, there are different local substrains, which can account for subtle variations in cheeses. This is how the effects of *terroir* are played out at the microscopic level. Mother Noella Marcellino, a microbiologist known as "The Cheese Nun," has described this phenomenon, studying indigenous molds in various ripening caves of France, recording and describing them for the advancement of cheese science and the preservation of tradition.

COAGULATION This has to be considered first among the microbiological miracles without which cheese as we know it would not exist. A natural chemical reaction, it transforms fresh liquid milk into one of the world's most delicious solids. Coagulation is a result of two different chemical reactions occurring during Step 1 of cheesemaking: the fermenting action of lactic acid bacteria and the clotting action of the enzymes in rennet.

As previously mentioned, traditional animal rennets are extracted from the stomachs of young ruminants. (For those organic chemistry buffs out there, the two principle enzymes in rennet are chymosin and pepsin). There are two other types of milk coagulants: microbial, which are synthesized by implanting genetic material into molds, and "vegetable," aka vegetarian, which come from various plants, most notably the cardoon thistle (*Cynara cardunculus*).

CHEESE CHEMISTRY

HOW COAGULATION WORKS

Molecules of milk protein (casein) consist of long chains of amino acids, which fold and form into round submicelles, and which in turn are bonded together by calcium phosphate into larger, spherical micelles. These micelles are suspended in the solution that is milk, which is mostly water. Because of their ion composition, the casein molecules in milk can bond with water and can also transmit calcium phosphate, an important nutrient, to the suckling animal or, more relevant to this discussion, the cheese.

In coagulation, rennet enzymes go to work on the casein micelles and cause them to reconfigure into an interconnected matrix or lattice-work, which is the structural foundation of curds. As they begin to coagulate, the casein micelles lose their water solubility; that is, they begin to separate from the whey, which is the remaining liquid portion of the milk. The new casein matrix begins to trap fat globules, which are much larger and also suspended in the milk solution, and form into a more solid, uniform, smooth curd mass. The whey can then be drained or pressed away, leaving the curds to be transformed, by a few further steps, into cheese.

The whey is quite nutritious: It contains some lactose and a portion of uncoagulated, dissolved casein called whey proteins. Once drained off, it can be used as fertilizer, animal feed, or to make ricotta-type cheeses. (*Ricotta,* by the way, means "recooked" in Italian and refers to the fact that the whey is heated another time to make cheese.)

Cheesemakers must monitor and control acidification and coagulation very carefully because these two aspects of Step 1 have such profound effects on cheese formation. Cheesemaking is a process of concentrating not only casein and fat but other solid milk components, including calcium and phosphorus.

Lactic acid buildup in the milk helps break down its casein micelles, causing them to release calcium phosphate into the whey, where it dissolves and drains away. When and how much acidification occurs determines how much of these minerals are retained. Higher acidity in the cheesemaking milk and ensuing curds will result in greater breakdown of casein and greater release of minerals. Longer, slower, gentler acidification allows the curds to retain more of their minerals (or, in cheesemaker-speak, "ash"). Although the actual amount of calcium phosphate in curds is quite small, it is one of several important ingredients that helps dictate aging parameters and determine not only a cheese's nutritional content but also its flavor profile.

Rennet-induced, or enzymatic, coagulation takes about a half hour to an hour; this amount of time varies according to the cheese-making recipe, the temperature and characteristics of the milk, and the type of coagulant used. Acidification continues until the lactic acid bacteria have ceased to function because the temperature is no longer conducive, the acid level in the curds is too high for them, or simply because they've run out of lactose to ferment.

Acidification also has a coagulating effect of its own. Curds formed by acid coagulation are generally less firm and elastic than those formed by rennet coagulation; they are more fragile and lead to a softer cheese, that is, one with higher moisture content. All milk bound for cheese is acidified; some cheeses are made via lac-

Here is a list of some vegetarian rennets, which are mostly associated with fresh cheeses and farmstead or homemade production.

FICIN—from the fig tree

PAPAIN—from the papaya

BROMELIN—from pinapple

URTICA DIOICA—from stinging nettle

GALIUM RERUM—from Lady Bedstraw

CALOSTROPIS PROCERA—a juice extract from this tropical plant

CYNARA CARDUNCULUS—from thistle flower

tic fermentation (acidification) alone, with no rennet coagulation. The majority of cheeses, however, rely on a combination of both types of coagulation.

The acid level inside a newly formed cheese is a key to how it will age and ripen. It determines what types of microflora can survive and thrive and how the different chemical breakdown reactions proceed toward developing texture, aroma, and flavor. Cheesemakers measure the amount of acid by testing for pH; as acidity increases, pH values decrease (see sidebar, page 66). As fresh milk is transformed into a Cheddar-style cheese, for example, its pH typically decreases from about 7.0 to about 5.0.

OTHER IMPORTANT CONSIDERATIONS Here are a few other key concerns for the early stages of cheesemaking.

PASTEURIZATION AND OTHER HEAT TREATMENTS—Cheesemaking milk may be pasteurized according to various goals, rules, and regulations. Other heat treatments, which involve lower temperatures than pasteurization, can also be applied; the principal one of these is called thermization. Pasteurization kills virtually all microbes in milk, affecting the entire process of producing cheese. It necessitates recipe adjustments to reintroduce acidifying and coagulating agents and to replace the natural aroma- and flavor-inducing enzymes in the milk. Heat treatments also affect coagulation, resulting in more fragile curds and higher moisture content. (For more on this topic, see chapter 7.)

MICROFILTRATION—This process involves forcing the milk through a porous membrane to separate out bacteria, mold spores, and/or other particles. Membranes with smaller pores perform more selective filtering known as ultrafiltration or nanofiltration. These filtration procedures are typically used to augment pasteurization, kill bacteria, and thus increase the shelf life of commercial milk and milk products. They can also be used to alter casein-to-fat ratios (elevating protein content) and are not considered compatible with artisanal cheesemaking.

TEMPERATURE—The higher the temperature, the faster the chemical reactions. Cheesemakers regulate milk temperature in Step 1 usually between 86 and 96 degrees F, sometimes up to 110 degrees F. If the milk is too cool, Step 1 won't proceed properly; if it's too warm, the curds may become rubbery and/or Step 1 may stall. The temperature in the cheesemaking room is also crucial: For exam-

ple, if it's cooler in winter, the milk will need to start out slightly warmer to compensate. Small fluctuations in this and other key parameters can wreak havoc with a cheese recipe.

CHANGES IN MILK COMPOSITION—Smart, skilled cheesemakers start out by choosing their recipe based on the makeup of their raw material; second, they adapt and adjust their recipe as the milk changes. Milk with relatively higher protein (casein) content coagulates more quickly and yields firmer curds; sheep's milk is a good example of this. Milk with lower protein content—from Holstein-Friesian cows, for example, or for that matter any cow grazing in lush summer pastures—will undergo slower coagulation and produce thinner, more fragile curds. Variations in acidity and mineral content affect the speed and character of coagulation as well. Abnormally high levels of bacteria in the milk can also affect coagulation owing to unwanted, early proteolysis.

SCHEDULE OF ACIDIFICATION—Milk goes sour pretty quickly on its own. At warmer temperatures, without hindrance, lactic acid bacteria will make an unpalatable mess of it in little time. Cheesemaking is controlled spoilage, and many of the early steps in a recipe involve putting the brakes on acidification, so it can continue at a measured pace until the elevated acid level within the curds or cheese body and/or the presence of other agents—salt, heat, drying, other bacteria, or molds—cause it to cease.

"EASY DOES IT"—Successful artisan cheesemaking requires a gentle hand, literally and figuratively. Milk fat molecules form into globules surrounded by a protective membrane. Excessive agitation, causes the globules to break up and the fat molecules to separate, in which case you wind up making butter instead of cheese. Gentle stirring during cheesemaking allows the fat globules to remain emulsified (suspended in the milk solution) as curds form and as the whey is drained off. If kept intact, the fat globules become fully integrated into the forming cheese and are allowed to make their delectable contribution to flavor and texture.

Step 2: Cutting the Curds

Once the curds have coagulated into a smooth, regular mass, they will naturally begin to contract and expel their whey, which mostly consists of water. The technical term for this process is syneresis.

HOW COAGULATION DISTINGUISHES TWO FAMOUS CHEESES

The two AOC variants of Brie—Brie de Melun and Brie de Meaux—have an interesting distinction with respect to coagulation. Brie de Melun relies almost entirely on gradual lactic coagulation and the process is stretched out over as many as 18 hours. Brie de Meaux, on the other hand, involves traditional rennet coagulation, which takes as little as half an hour. These are two very fine, very similar, traditional cheeses with a few interesting differences: in a comparison tasting, the first difference I notice is the Brie de Melun, which has a fuller, meatier flavor than the Brie de Meaux, which has a flatter, milkier profile.

THE IMPORTANCE OF pH

The pH scale measures the concentration of hydrogen ions (charged molecules of hydrogen), which is how acidity is defined.

The higher the concentration of these ions in a solution, the more it will react with other molecules, more readily creating bonds within and thereby breaking down or corroding those other molecules.

The center point of the pH scale is assigned a value of 7.0, which is neutral—neither acid nor alkaline (aka basic)—and is represented by water. Anything from 7.0 down to zero is acidic and from 7.0 up to 14.0 is basic. It is a so-called logarithmic scale wherein, as with the Richter scale to measure earthquakes, each unit represents a tenfold increase. So a pH of 6.0 indicates a concentration of ten times more hydrogen ions than one of 7.0, and one of 5.0 is a hundred times more than 7.0 and so forth.

Cheesemaker Jason Garcia stirring curds at Rogue Creamery.

The more surface area the curds have, the more syneresis will occur. This means the more the curds are cut—that is, the smaller the pieces—the less moisture they will retain. To produce a softer cheese with higher moisture content, the curds will be left larger, whereas for a harder cheese with less moisture, they'll be cut smaller.

The cheesemaker keeps watch on the firmness of the curds in order to determine when they are ready to be cut. This pivotal decision involves a critical judgment, exercised by inserting a small knife, spatula, or finger into the curd and pulling out a sample section to see how it separates, which is called "the break." The cheesemaker looks for a clean break so the curds don't get torn, frayed, crushed, or splayed, which will lead to mushy or ragged curds. The curds must maintain clean edges so the whey can leach out properly. If they're cut when too soft or too firm, the leaching-out process may go awry, in which case a cheese's target moisture content is off and its texture and consistency suffer.

The cut curd particles should be uniform in size and shape to ensure consistent moisture and texture throughout the body of the final cheese. Traditional cheese recipes instruct that they be cut to the size of such familiar items as grains of rice, peas, or walnuts.

Various types of knives are used for cutting. One design consists of a series of wires evenly spaced inside a metal frame that is called a harp, because it resembles that musical instrument. The cheesemaker passes this device through the mass of coagulated curd—first in one direction and then at the perpendicular—to cut it into small cubes. (Some cheeses are barely cut, if at all; their curds are gently ladled into vessels to yield a very soft, smooth consistency. In this sense, Step 2 can be considered optional.)

Step 3: Cooking and Holding

This third basic step involves some amount of heating or cooking of the curds as well as a holding period during which they are left to sit in the vat while the effects of acidification, cutting (if applicable), and heating proceed. Throughout the cheesemaking process, the curds require gentle treatment so that they won't break up and will be able to dry out at a measured pace. Timing is crucial: The time and temperature of cooking is adjusted according to the composition of the milk and the nature of the curds. The smaller the particles, for example, the hotter they will get.

Generally, cheesemaking vats are made of stainless steel with "jacket" walls, meaning they are hollow inside so hot water can circulate and heat the curds. This allows for gradual heating and control. If curds are heated too quickly, they can become overcooked and develop a hard outer skin, which hinders whey expulsion.

During heating, curds may be stirred to prevent them from clumping or matting together. When stirred, they bump into each other and this has an effect akin to pressing, which further promotes moisture loss. The more heat and the more stirring, the greater the moisture loss in the curds and the harder and denser the resulting cheese. Curds intended to become softer, higher-moisture bloomy-rind cheeses, such as Camembert, will undergo relatively mild heating, a gradual cooling, and a resting period, with little or no stirring. Semisoft types may receive slightly more heating and some gentle stirring. Curds for harder cheeses are "cooked"—that is, they're heated to higher temperatures—and also stirred more.

Like the decision of when to cut the curds, the decision of when to stop cooking and/or stirring is critical to the success of the operation. Cheesemakers apply their savvy and intuition to exercise judgment about curd development based on a manual test. They scoop out a sample of the curds and squeeze it, rubbing it between their hands to get a sense of texture and consistency. Next, they may allow a portion of curds to settle on a finger, then turn that finger over to see to how much it sticks. This is called the grip. Both the previously mentioned break and the grip reflect the lev-

FROM TOP: Cheesemaker Cary Bryant cuts curds at Rogue Creamery; cut curds showing uniform shape and consistency.

els of acidity within the curds, which can also be tested with instruments.

An optional step at this stage is to drain some of the whey from the vat as it seeps out of the curds and replace it with water—a procedure known as washing the curds. This can help lower the acidity as well as raise both the moisture and lactose content of the curds, depending on when it's done in relation to the heating or cooking. The cheesemaker's job at this point is to coordinate the firmness of the draining curds with their acid development and figure out exactly when they are ready to be removed from the vat and undergo the next steps toward becoming cheese.

Step 4: Dipping and Draining

Dipping is the term for transferring the curds, by way of a scoop or ladle, to some sort of draining receptacle or mold. Draining vessels are usually some form of basket or colander, but occasionally a large cheesecloth bag is used. At this point, the cheesemaking milk has separated into curds and whey, whitish or cream-colored solids and greenish or yellowish liquids, respectively.

Dipping is itself a form of draining, since the solid curds stay in the basket or bag during transfer and the liquid leaks away. Another form of draining is simply to open a valve at a bottom edge of the cheese vat and let the whey run out.

Soft, moist curds will settle and meld into a mass of cheese, taking on the shape of the hoop or mold into which they've been dipped. Some finished cheeses even retain the imprint of the basket or colander on their exteriors, a badge of handmade authenticity.

Step 5: Knitting (Curd Fusion)

During this stage, the curd particles fuse together into a uniform body and begin to attain a distinct consistency. Depending on the recipe and the eventual cheese-type goal, knitting can occur in the vat, in a draining vessel (hoop, mold, basket), or in a press, where weight is applied. Not all of the steps of cheesemaking occur sequentially. Some of them overlap and proceed simultaneously, which is a principle reason why cheesemakers must be adept at juggling their various effects and interactions.

Cheddar and other similar cheeses undergo a unique type of knitting called cheddaring wherein the masses of curds are swept or brushed to the sides of the vat, allowed to fuse and then

CHEESE RECIPE

A REAL CHEESE RECIPE

Following is a recipe for a *tomme*-style cheese courtesy of master cheesemaker Peter Dixon from his website www.dairyfoodsconsulting.com, where you can peruse more than twenty other basic "make procedures."

- Heat milk to 90° F.

- Add a bulk, mixed mesophilic/thermophilic culture: Use ½% for pasteurized milk and ¼% for raw milk.

- After 30 minutes add 9-ml single-strength rennet per 100 lb. milk.

- Check for curdling time and multiply this by 3 to get the time from adding rennet to cutting.

- Rest curd 5 minutes.

- Begin heating: 1° F every 2 minutes to 95° F, then 1° F every minute to 100° F. Total heating time is 15 minutes.

- Cook higher (up to 102° F) when milk solids are low and lower (down to 98° F) when milk solids are high.

- Cook at 100° F for 10-30 minutes to firm curds until they are springy in the grip of your hand.

- Let curds settle for 5 min., then drain off whey to the level of curds. Scoop curds into cheese hoops (round forms) lined with cloths. Knead curds into hoops, place follower* on top and press with 2 lb. weight per 1 lb. curd.

- After 30 min. remove weights, take cheese wheels from cloths, turn, replace cloths and press for one hour more. Repeat this procedure two more times.

- After 3½ hours of pressing turn cheese out of cloths and hoops. Cheese should have pH 5.7- 5.8. Move cheese wheels to cellar at 55-58° F.

- After 3 hours, put cheese in saturated (23% salt) brine. Brine cheese 4 hours per lb.

- Finished wheels are 8-9 inch in diameter and 3 inches thick and weigh 5 lb.

- Aging: After the cheese wheels are removed from the brine, place on shelves and turn every other day. Eventually a moldy coat will grow, in about one month. After this, brush the rind every few days to keep it from being too thick.

*The follower is a circular piece that fits into the hoop and covers the curds; weights are placed on top of it to press and form them into a cheese.

---

cut into slabs, stacked, and restacked in order to force out more whey. Cheddar curds are also milled: After cheddaring and prior to molding, salting, and pressing, they are passed through a cutting device, which once more alters their texture. These steps further solidify the cheeses and ensure a more dense consistency, allowing for development of the moist yet crumbly quality of a fine Cheddar.

Step 6: Pressing

This step takes anywhere from a few hours to a few days and is designed to exert varying degrees of pressure to achieve the desired moisture content, density, and texture of a cheese. Soft and semisoft cheeses, bloomy or washed rind, are drained gradually and subjected to very little, if any, pressure. Often, these types of

OPPOSITE FROM TOP: Peter Dixon hand-stirring curds; Dixon placing curds in basket molds to form cheeses; young, forming goat cheeses draining at Fraga Farm, Oregon.

QUESO BLANCO

A SIMPLE CHEESE YOU CAN MAKE AT HOME

This recipe for *queso blanco* is adapted from the New England Cheesemaking Supply Co., courtesy of its founder and owner, Ricki Carroll. The company's website (www.cheesemaking.com) features many home recipes as well as ingredients and supplies. This one yields approximately 1½ pounds of cheese. Like Indian *panir,* which is essentially identical, it can be cut into ½-inch cubes for use in various recipes and will not melt—even if you fry it. (Always remember: the better the milk, the better the cheese. So try this recipe with a good, local, organic whole milk and enjoy the cheese's mild, sweet taste.)

> 1 gallon whole milk
> ¼ cup vinegar (cider, grain, or
> herbal type)

Place the milk in a large, nonreactive pot over medium heat, stirring often to prevent scorching. When the milk reaches 195°F, stir in the vinegar then turn off the burner and allow the hot milk to set for 5 minutes. It will quickly coagulate into curds (solid, white) and whey (clear, green liquid).

Line a colander with fine cheesecloth and pour the contents of the pot into the colander to drain off the whey. Gather the ends of the cloth and tie them with a string to form a bag. Hang the bag of curds over your sink to drain for 1 hour or until they reach the desired consistency. Remove the cheese from the cloth, cover loosely in plastic wrap and refrigerate until ready to use.

cheeses are said to be pressed "under their own weight," which is enough to ensure the appropriate amount of drainage. Harder types may have weights placed on top of them or pressure applied by various devices. How much pressure is applied and for how long helps determine moisture content, density, and texture.

Bacterial cultures are still active; acidification proceeds and must continue to be monitored and controlled, along with temperatures in the vat and in the cheesemaking room. Modern technology in the form of electronic and/or computerized monitoring devices can be a big boon to artisan cheesemakers—as opposed to the past when navigation was done strictly by dead reckoning. This is not to say instinct and experience are any less crucial; only that it's nice to have confirmation via instruments.

Step 7: Salting

Salt is a main ingredient in cheese not only for taste but for moisture reduction and control of bacteria and molds. It can be applied in two ways: dry or wet. Dry-salting can occur either before or after pressing. In the former case, the salt is sprinkled directly in and on the curd mass where it begins to exert its effects on the development of a cheese more immediately. In the latter case, the salt is

SOME PEOPLE JUST HAVE THE KNACK

We've all heard of the proverbial green thumb—people who just seem to have that magic touch in the garden. Well, I've come to believe there's a cheesemaking equivalent: the yellow thumb. There are some cheesemakers—and also *affineurs*—who demonstrate a consistent ability to produce great cheeses.

No doubt, the yellow thumb starts with an extraordinarily discerning palate; you have to be able to taste and recognize a great cheese. Beyond that, these people possess an uncommon talent for understanding their raw materials and knowing how to transform them into unique and highly expressive edible artifacts. They know how to source the finest milk, often husbanding their own herd of animals to produce it, how to choose the recipe best suited to the character of that milk, and how to adapt and adjust the recipe to changing conditions. When it comes to ushering milk through the curd stage and into cheese, they seem to possess heightened perceptions and to exercise superior judgment.

Different cheesemakers show different affinities. Cary Bryant of Rogue Creamery has a special knack for making blue cheeses. Although he's quite new at the game, Cary has been able to turn out an outstanding roster of as

many as seven blues at a time. (He's a bluesman with a yellow thumb.) Likewise, Mateo Kehler of Jasper Hill Farm—with a huge assist from his brother Andy—has shown a talent for both the bloomy-rind and the washed-rind types. The Kehlers produce a couple of very fine blues, but their bloomy-rind Constant Bliss and their washed-rind Winnimere are outstanding. And again, they've only been doing it since the year 2000.

Who are some of the other yellow thumbs? Peter Kindel, a roving cheesemaker and former colleague at Picholine, seems to have "it" with regard to goat's milk. I remember tasting a fresh goat cheese Peter made when he was at Consider Bardwell Farm in western Vermont. David Lockwood of Neal's Yard Dairy and I were on an ACS panel tasked with making recommendations for improving specific cheeses. We quickly concluded that Bardwell cheese "couldn't have been any better. " (Ergo, it might very well have been perfect.)

More yellow thumbs: Jamie Montgomery for English farmhouse Cheddar; Anne Wigmore for aged sheep's milk cheese as in her Spenwood; Josef Barmettler for the younger washed-rind types (sheep and cow), including Stanser Röteli (formerly known as Innerschweizer Weicher) and Innerschweizer Schäfchas. Among *affineurs*, of course, William Oglethorpe of Neal's Yard (along with his boss Randolph Hodgson) seem to have the touch for all manner of traditional British farmhouse types; Rolf Beeler, "the Pope of Swiss Cheeses" is another yellow thumb.

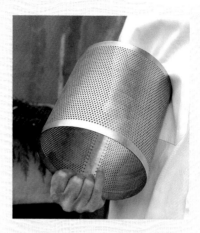

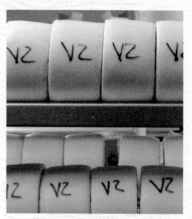

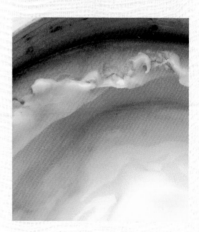

FROM TOP: A stainless steel draining mold; Young Crater Lake Blues at Rogue Creamery; it takes a deft touch to make washed-rind types like this Vacherin Mont D'Or.

Newly formed cheeses being pressed under their own weight.

sprinkled or rubbed onto the surface as it's about to enter its aging period: This treatment is slower to take effect and its main goal is a gradual drawing out of moisture.

Wet-salting is properly referred to as brining. For this technique, cheeses are immersed in a saltwater solution for anywhere from several hours to several days. Brine recipes, and brining procedures, vary and have subtle yet significant effects on the final results. Washed-rind cheeses have brine—among other solutions—rubbed onto them during aging (see "Step 8: Special Treatments," below).

Alongside the draining step, salting is the most important determinant of a cheese's moisture content; relatively small differences can seriously affect results. Every cheese has a target range for moisture content. When salt removes moisture from a young cheese, it puts a brake on lactic-acid bacteria, slowing down their ongoing fermentation of lactose. This, in turn, affects the pH level—and all that follows—inside the developing cheese.

Salt is also a major contributor to rind formation: It causes moisture to evaporate from the entire cheese, but more so from its outer edges. The other main factor in rind formation is the growth of various bacteria and/or molds, determined both by the recipe (especially Step 8) and also by the surface environment. The amounts of salt and moisture on the outside of a cheese, in turn, are important factors in determining which microorganisms can thrive. In other words, salt works on a cheese's surface in two ways: It dries it out and also helps dictate what will or won't grow there.

Step 8: Special Treatments (Curing)

This step—a series of treatments, many of them optional—marks the end of the active phase, the formation process, and the beginning of ripening. The curds are now cheese, but they have a long way to go before they become *great* cheese. Their traits have been etched but their true character has yet to emerge.

"Curing" is a term to describe treatments introduced for desired effects during aging. These might include rubbings, brushings, sprayings, wrapping in cloth or leaves or bark, and regular turnings. For example, ash, which is alkaline, may be rubbed or brushed onto a cheese to help balance its acidity. Washes increase a cheese's surface moisture, creating a more hospitable environment for bacterial growth. If the wash is a fermented drink, it may directly introduce yeasts, which can also contribute to flavor development.

Ripening agents (see "Secondary Cultures," page 61) grow on cheeses and release their enzymes. These enzymes work their way into the cheeses, breaking down the proteins, fats, and residual sugars and thereby releasing aroma- and flavor-giving compounds—thus the terms *surface ripened* or *mold ripened*. Some of these agents may have been introduced directly into the curds. They may have been applied and/or encouraged to grow by curing treatments, or they were simply allowed to exist in the cheese-forming environment, alight on the cheeses, and do their magic of their own accord. The fuzzy white, grayish "flowering" of certain molds, among these agents, also contributes to rind formation.

Traditional Cheddars and Cheddar-style cheeses receive interesting variants of "special treatments;" namely they are often rubbed with butter or lard and/or wrapped in cloth (sometimes called a bandage). Some Italian types (including Parmigiano-Reggiano and Pecorino Toscano) are rubbed with olive oil and/or tomato paste mixed with oil; certain Italian and Iberian types receive rubs made with paprika or *pimentón* (Spanish paprika). Washed-rind cheeses with a tendency to ooze amorphously may be fitted with a band of spruce bark (as with some of the Swiss mountain styles).

Some of the harder, longer-lasting types, such as the aged farmhouse Goudas of Holland or the genuine Parmesans of Emilia-Romagna, are aged 3 to 4 years. Some Dutch Roomanos are aged for 6 years, an extreme. Ideal aging conditions for cheeses include moderate temperatures, relatively high humidity, good ventilation, and a "clean" environment in the sense that no outside (nonindigenous or uninvited) pests or pathogenic microorganisms should sneak in. These aging parameters are monitored and controlled by cheesemakers and *affineurs*. In traditional operations, when the weather changed and the humidity went up or down, cheesemakers had to find ways to adjust conditions back to a consistent, optimum ripening range.

From the connoisseur's viewpoint, the most important result of the curing and ripening stage, beyond completion of the breakdown reactions that yield aromatic substances, is the melding and

SALT: A STARRING ROLE

Salt is crucial to cheesemaking for:

- Dehydration of surface and interior
- Rind formation
- Influence on cheesemaking microflora (inhibition of lactic fermentation)
- Inhibition of undesirable microorganisms (preservative or protective effect)

Young cheeses receive a brine bath.

The treatments applied in Step 8 continue to emphasize broader distinctions among cheese types; they also signal subtler differences within those types.

- Spray application of surface molds such as *P. camemberti* for bloomy-rind cheeses

- Inoculation of curds with spores of such molds as *P. roqueforti,* for blue cheeses

- Rubbing or "washing" with brine or *morge* (a concoction of wine, whey, and perhaps some cheese scraps) to promote *B. linens* surface-ripening bacteria (this may occur repeatedly and regularly, at varying intervals, as a cheese ages over a period of weeks and/or months)

- Coating goat cheeses with a layer of ash

- Lancing or piercing blue cheeses to admit air and promote interior mold growth

balancing of a cheese's aromas, flavors, and textures. (For more on this, see "Assessing and Judging Cheese," page 104, and "What Makes a Cheese Great?," page 109.)

AFFINAGE: THE FINISHING TOUCHES

By the time they're shipped from their makers, some cheeses are fully aged and ripened while others may need days, weeks, or even months to reach their peak. Traditional cheesemakers often relied on specialists called *affineurs* (ripeners) to bring their cheeses to their final ready state. Such arrangements were part of a tiered system where dairy farms supplied their product to larger dairies or cooperatives, which still exist in many traditional cheesemaking societies. In this type of system, smaller producers benefit from economies of scale, increased marketing clout, and faster cash flow.

This tiered system is still in effect for many of the larger Alpine cheeses as well as for Roquefort and other famous Old World types. Likewise, many of the top northern Italian cheeses are selected, ripened, and exported by Guffanti (see page 76 and also chapter 17).

Most relationships between cheesemakers and *affineurs* are historical, and many are regulated so you can be assured your cheeses are authentic. Roquefort's appellation rules, for example, specify not only the breed of sheep from which the milk must come and the permissible production zone but also its ripening, which must occur in the caves of Combalou beneath Roquefort-sur-Soulzon. Many of the cheeses are made outside the town itself, but all of them are ripened by producers who own sections of those caves. Roquefort ripening is a well-defined procedure, lasting at least 3 months but often as many as 8 months.

Affinage is about nurturing cheeses and letting them ripen in their own time in order to bring out their best qualities. To be successful, an *affineur* must have full knowledge of the entire equation, beginning with land stewardship, animal husbandry, and milk production, and extending right through each step of cheesemaking. The *affineur*'s skills include selection, tasting, and the application of ripening treatments.

Although active cheesemaking officially ends with Step 8, some of the *affinage* treatments are extensions of earlier procedures and may appreciably improve a cheese. *Affinage* depends on managing a set of variables with minute attention to detail. Among these variables are the setup of the cave; the temperature and humidity conditions (adjusted to proper levels); the duration of aging; and the type, degree, and frequency of treatments.

Depending on what type of cheese is being ripened, high, arched ceilings, providing just the right amount of natural air flow, can make all the difference in an aging cave. The number of cheeses in a cave can also be tremendously important, particularly for encouraging beneficial bacteria to ripen washed-rind types. An empty cave will be too dry and breezy; a cave with too few cheeses won't attract a big enough colony of bacteria. A well-filled one, its damp shelves brimming with plump, slimy cheeses, provides a much more welcoming environment and thus much better aging potential for its cheese inhabitants.

The Importance of *Affinage*

Different experts attach varying degrees of importance to *affinage*. Randolph Hodgson of Neal's Yard Dairy, perhaps too modestly, says it's only a matter of "not screwing it up." Jamie Montgomery, of Cheddar fame (see chapter 20), many of whose cheeses Hodgson handles, echoes this sentiment. Montgomery's majestic clothbound Cheddars are more stable and slow developing so they may require less babysitting than some other types. The moist Stiltons, made for Hodgson by Joe Schneider, are more delicate and perhaps want less tinkering.

Giovanni Guffanti Fiori, of the famed family firm Luigi Guffanti 1876, also downplays the *affineur*'s role, saying you can't salvage a poorly made or defective cheese through *affinage,* but you could theoretically ruin a good one. Fiori's cheeses, aged in his caves not far from Milan, come from scores of small producers all over Italy. He and others stress that sourcing and selecting the best cheeses, vetting producers, and working with them to improve materials and processes is the biggest part of their job.

Rolf Beeler echoes this sentiment but also expresses his belief that an *affineur* can make or break a cheese. Some of the larger format hard *alpage* cheeses he works with, including massive wheels of Gruyère (weighing 80 pounds or more), are aged for 12 to 18 months and require frequent turnings and washings. Regulat-

FROM TOP: A mechanical piercing device for blue cheeses; just-pierced cheeses, before blueing has kicked in; syrah grapevine leaves, macerated in pear brandy, for Rogue River Blue wrappers; David Gremmels checks leaf wrappers at Rogue Creamery.

CHEESE CHEMISTRY

THE MIRACLE OF CONTROLLED SPOILAGE

What causes successful cheese aging? Beginning with Step 1 and continuing throughout cheesemaking, there are three basic chemical reactions occurring: glycolysis, the conversion of sugars into acids; proteolysis, the breakdown of proteins by enzymes; and lipolysis, the breakdown of fats by other enzymes.

Proteolysis begins when the enzymes in rennet begin to turn the milk to curds. Proteins are made up of chains of amino acids that bond together and twist to form large, complex molecules. As the enzymes within the body of a ripening cheese break down, those proteins release fragmentary chains, like peptides, which contribute to flavor.

In lipolysis, the enzymes from bacteria, molds, and yeasts break down butterfats and release chains of free fatty acids, many of which are also flavor-giving compounds. Without proper moderation and control—without the steady guiding hand of the cheesemaker—these free fatty acids can produce defects such as rancidity, as in spoiled butter or oil. For many fine cheeses, there's a thin line between rancidity and all kinds of lip-smacking flavors.

ing the final salt content of these cheeses, largely through adjusting the strength of the brine used to wash them, is crucial to Rolf. So, naturally, he would assign a greater impact to *affinage.*

In connection with *affinage,* I always conjure another French term, *élévage,* which means "rearing," as in the raising of human children and also domesticated animals. Like rearing, cheese *affinage* is done with selection and care. Cheesemakers baby their curds when young; *affineurs* judiciously steer their cheeses as they age into adolescence and approach maturity. The other part of the term *élévage* I feel applies to cheese is the tantalizing possibility of raising up the cheeses, of making them even better than they already are.

TASTING PLATE
Tasting the Eight Basic Steps

1. **SETTING THE MILK (ACIDIFICATION AND COAGULATION):**
   Langres

2. **CUTTING THE CURDS:**
   Lancashire

3. **COOKING AND HOLDING:**
   Beaufort

4. **DRAINING AND DIPPING:**
   Vermont Shepherd

5. **KNITTING (CURD FUSION):**
  Tomme de Savoie

6. **PRESSING:**
  Piave

7. **SALTING:**
  Mahón

8. **SPECIAL TREATMENTS (CURING):**
  Rogue River Blue

Here's a plate wherein you can discern each of the fundamental steps by tasting their specific effects on flavors and textures. There are certain cheeses whose most prominent traits seem to highlight one of the eight steps. Apart from salting, the basic steps seem to show themselves more through consistency and mouth feel than they do by way of flavor. This makes sense when you consider that a cheese's form and structure are determined very early on by how a recipe transforms the milk; its flavor, however, emerges later as a result of more gradual developments.

LANGRES—This is a light, mild cheese with a simple, straightforward profile featuring the flavors of rich, creamy, gently soured milk. From a cheesemaking standpoint, it comes from an old-style ladled-curd recipe, relying on lactic fermentation.

LANCASHIRE—A traditional British farmhouse cheese with fabulous texture—light and crumbly yet moist—Lancashire harks right back to that moment when its fresh, firm curds were cut, well before they began to fuse. The delightful mouth feel of this cheese gives the impression of small, precisely cut, discreet curd particles. You can feel this first by picking up a little piece and grinding it lightly between your fingers.

BEAUFORT—Large-format mountain cheeses represent an important historical type, largely defined by the procedure of cooking their curds in big old cauldrons. This dries and concentrates them, helping to focus their broad, complex flavor profiles. A cheese like Beaufort is dense and hard but, when properly aged, dissolves quite easily on your palate. Step 3 also lends "cooked milk" flavors reminiscent of the steamy froth on top of your morning cappuccino.

VERMONT SHEPHERD—This and other similar Ossau-Iraty-style cheeses accentuate the draining step, which brings the tasty pro-

The Keys to Successful Affinage

"Affinage is an exercise in consciousness, being able to deconstruct or diagnose the cheese-making process by looking at the cheese. It's all about understanding the cheeses, monitoring rind and flavor development, moving them from one place to another. You really need to pay attention and be able to manage in detail their needs—batches within cheese types and individual cheeses within batches."

MATEO KEHLER, CHEESEMAKER AND AFFINEUR, JASPER HILL FARM

teins and delectable butterfats of sheep's milk to the fore. The weight and texture of a cheese like Vermont Shepherd makes me think of a child's bucket of wet sand at the beach. It's thick, dense, and has gravitas. Yet it remains moist and quite pliant on the inside.

TOMME DE SAVOIE—Consistency and texture are, again, among the outstanding features of the Tomme de Savoie. The curds have ceded their boundaries and merged into a uniform, fairly dense mass akin to smooth, hardened farmhouse butter. It's quite the opposite of Lancashire's moist/crumbly feel, which borders on open textured.

PIAVE—In all my cheese-tasting years, this one represents the most successful pressing job of all. If a cheese like Tomme de Savoie is firm yet moist and, one would suspect, eminently friable, the Piave is hard and resistant to melting. Piave's curds, cut quite fine and drained extensively, are pressed into a substantial, dense mass similar to Parmigiano-Reggiano but more uniform and less crumbly or granular.

MAHÓN—I don't think I've ever tasted a Mahón in which the salt was not highly prominent. Salt is probably the number-one flavor in all cheese; this one highlights briny flavors from both its seaside *terroir* and the seventh basic step of cheesemaking. Yet it's almost never oversalted; the rich, buttery character of its cow's milk renders it admirably balanced, approachable, and delicious.

ROGUE RIVER BLUE—The blues represent Step 8 because they undergo some of the most specific and interesting special treatments. Mold spores are sprinkled into the curds of forming cheeses; formed cheeses are pierced for aeration to encourage further mold growth. One can taste these steps in Stilton and in Roquefort, which also reflects a fascinating "external procedure"—baking large loaves of bread to grow the molds in the first place—as well as very specific aging parameters. But Rogue River shows a few further steps, including handpicking of Syrah grape leaves and steeping them in pear brandy to create wrappers for the cheeses. I remember the first time I tasted a Rogue River Blue. There was a big "wow" followed by "There is a lot going on in this cheese."

OPPOSITE: Tasting the Eight Basic Steps: From top, left to right, Rogue River Blue; Piave; Mahon; Vermont Shepherd; Tomme De Savoie; Lancashire; Beaufort; Langres.

WINTER CHEESE, SUMMER CHEESE

At Jasper Hill Farm, the Kehler brothers make a washed-rind cheese called Winnimere from winter milk. Their herd of Ayrshire cows stays in the barn and eats strictly dry feed—farm-grown hay and small amounts of grain—which means they produce less milk but it's thicker and fattier. This higher-fat winter milk is better suited for a gooey, high-moisture cheese. "Grass is 90 percent water and hay is 90 percent dry matter," explains Mateo. "So, in the winter, they have to chew their cud a lot more to produce more enzymes in their saliva. They break those carbohydrates into fats and proteins more effectively than with grass, which kind of shoots right through them." In summer, the casein-to-fat ratio goes up—there is more protein in fresh plant fodder than in dry winter feed—as does the overall solid content. So once the Jasper Hill cows go out to pasture in late May, the Winnimere is replaced in the farm's cheese-making schedule by a Stilton-like cheese called Bartlett Blue. Blue cheeses and some of the semihard aged types tend to do better when made with less fatty milks, since rancidity—from gradual oxidation of fats during aging—is a threat.

CHAPTER REVIEW

All About Cheesemaking

- ☐ Technological advances led to step-by-step developments in cheesemaking, which are reflected in modern cheese types.
  - Simple lactic fermentation for fresh and/or unpressed types
  - Renneting (animal, vegetable, and microbial)
  - Cooking and pressing for large-format, aged "commodity" cheeses
  - Internal mold for blue cheeses
  - Washed rinds for "monastery" cheeses
  - External mold ripening for bloomy-rind types
  - Other special treatments including smoking, leaf wrapping, and mixing of milks
- ☐ Acidification, or the souring of milk, is achieved by various species of lactic-acid bacteria, which convert lactose (milk sugar) into lactic acid.
- ☐ Milk can be soured "naturally" (by inherent or ambient lactic acid bacteria) or by adding starter cultures.
- ☐ Coagulation of casein (milk protein) is encouraged by the introduction of enzymes contained in rennet from an animal, plant, or microbial (synthesized) source.

- [ ] Curd formation via coagulation is a chemical reaction wherein casein molecules, which exist in loose spheroid agglomerations called micelles, are reorganized into a more rigid matrix or lattice-type structure.
- [ ] Attention to detail and a steady, guiding hand with a light touch are crucial to successful cheesemaking. Special attention is paid to monitoring acidification and temperature, and to adjusting recipes based on milk composition and the effects of pasteurization or other heat treatments.
- [ ] Milk curds naturally contract and expel whey. The more cutting, heating, stirring, or pressure applied, the more whey is extracted.
- [ ] Salt is a ubiquitous ingredient in cheesemaking. It adds flavor, dehydrates the interior and exterior of forming cheeses, and inhibits pathogenic contamination.
- [ ] Curing marks the end of active cheesemaking and leads into the ripening and *affinage* stages.
- [ ] Enzymes secreted by ripening agents (bacteria, molds, and yeasts) are responsible for the three basic chemical reactions occurring during cheese ripening: lipolysis (breakdown of fats), proteolysis (breakdown of proteins), and glycolysis (breakdown of sugars).

Discussing the finer points of cheesemaking with Pierre Kolisch, right, at Juniper Grove Farm.

- [ ] *Affinage* is the practice of ripening cheeses beyond Step 8 until they are ready to be sold; although it is more passive than cheesemaking, it requires a good deal of skill and intuition.
- [ ] Different types of cheeses require different—and highly specified—aging and ripening conditions.
- [ ] Some cheese producers perform ripening and *affinage* on their own cheeses; some leave it up to other professionals.
- [ ] *Affinage* can make a good cheese better, but it probably cannot salvage a bad cheese.

CHAPTER 4

CHEESE FLAVOR: WHAT IT IS AND WHERE IT COMES FROM

IN CHAPTER 3, WE LEARNED ABOUT HOW COMPLEX ORGANIC COMPOUNDS in milk are transformed during the cheesemaking and aging processes. Many of these are broken down into other water- or fat-soluble compounds. Some of them are volatile, which means they can be detected as flavors or aromas by our taste buds and the smell receptors in our noses, respectively. In this chapter, we'll explore where these flavors and aromas come from, and in the next we'll delve into how we perceive, describe, and compare them.

Whether professional or amateur, the way all cheese people approach the subject of flavor is framed by Professor Frank Kosikowski's theory of component balance. According to Kosikowski's model, very specific compounds in very specific amounts and combinations are responsible for the often mind-boggling array of flavors detected in cheeses, yogurts, and other dairy products. When we talk about a cheese's flavor profile, we're referring to its overall taste as comprised by multiple individual components.

Any fine artisanal cheese has many distinct aroma and flavor components, which, when well put together, form a whole greater than the sum of its parts. While each fine cheese is unique—with individual pedigree and identifiable *terroir*—it is also similar to others of its type; in fact, it distinguishes itself precisely because of the way its many volatile compounds combine, interact, and

Spenwood: A great repository of beautifully balanced sheepy, grassy, and underlying sweet flavors.

Bourboule: A cheese redolent of its terroir; rough on the outside, subtle and sophisticated within.

balance each other to present a signature flavor profile. The more components a cheese has in its flavor profile, the more complexity it is said to possess. If one or more of those components dominates and drowns out the others, we can say the cheese lacks balance. If it only has a few of them, we can say it lacks complexity.

WHERE DO THE FLAVORS COME FROM?

The three principle nutritive substances found in cheese—casein (milk protein), butterfat, and lactose (milk sugar), which is converted to lactic acid—are the building blocks of its flavor. Those volatile compounds we perceive as cheese aroma and flavor, often referred to as "aromatics," come from two principal sources: first, the plants the animals eat and the breakdown of chemical compounds in those plants during the animals' digestion process; and second, the action of key enzymes, secreted by microorganisms, in breaking down those three "building blocks" during the cheese-making and ripening processes.

Dairy and flavor scientists who've studied cheese generally estimate 20 to 30 percent of aromatics come from the feed the animals eat (and the water they drink). The remaining 70 to 80 percent is determined by cheesemaking and ripening parameters. As we learned in chapter 3, making cheese is mostly a process of dehydration, that is, of increasing the percentage of a milk's solids; in terms of taste, the flavors of these aromatics become more focused and concentrated.

You might think water would have less influence than soil as a factor of *terroir*. Yet it is still significant. I've seen plenty of examples of cheeses produced very close to each other from virtually identical recipes, using the same animal breed raised on the same local vegetation, that taste quite different because of varying watersheds. This can be seen as just another manifestation of the wine-growing concept of microclimate. All other factors being equal, vines from adjoining vineyards, with nothing more than a few degrees difference in slope or aspect (the direction they face the sun) can end up projecting significantly different personalities.

If you want to taste the simplest, most fundamental cheese flavors, try a *queso fresco* or a *queso blanco*, the fresh farmers'-style cheese popular in Central American cultures. They are gently acidified, coagulated milk protein and concentrated fats with some salt added. Once you take the next step, adding a starter culture, it

CHEESE CHEMISTRY

SOURCES OF FLAVOR COMPLEXITY

As we learned in chapter 3 (see sidebar, page 76), flavors and aromas arise from an assortment of complex organic compounds released by chemical reactions at the microbiological level. Casein is broken down into peptides, amino acids, acetic acid, ammonia, aldehydes, alcohols, and sulfur compounds, among others. Milk fat is broken down into free fatty acids (including acetic, butyric, and hexanoic acids), methyl ketones, and lactones. Lactose and citrate are broken down into lactate, diacetyl, acetaldehyde, ethanol, acetic acid, carbon dioxide, and other compounds. Short-chain fatty acids, abundant in the milk of pasture-grazing animals, have a lot of aroma and flavor potential, which is realized when they're broken down into free fatty acids during ripening. This, by the way, is where we discover the fine line between desirable sharp, peppery, spicy flavors and undesirable (borderline rancid) ones.

Scientists have been able to isolate an impressive number of these chemical compounds and to associate them with specific flavors.

Among all these compounds with rather complicated, esoteric names, there are a few familiar cognates: Vanillin, for example, has been detected in Gruyères and Emmentalers, which is why we can often taste a hint of vanilla flavor in the finer versions of these cheeses. Esters such as ethyl butanoate and ethyl hexanoate are responsible for fruity flavors, a bubble gum–like one in the former case and a ripe berry-like one in the latter. Phenylacetaldehyde causes a "rosy, styrene" aroma and methional a "potato" one. The free fatty acids acetic, isobutyric, propinoic and hexanoic, found in many cheeses, are responsible for vinegary, sour, sour (again) and sweaty aromas, respectively.

immediately kicks off a series of biochemical reactions, eventually yielding the complex flavors found in aged cheeses.

Starter cultures release their enzymes, which continue working after the bacteria cease to function, and rennets contribute their animal or plant enzymes. These agents start the breakdown and flavor-making processes. Molds, yeasts, and bacteria introduced during cheesemaking and/or ripening secrete their own enzymes, which in turn act on the fats and proteins to create volatile compounds. Each different substance contributes its specific flavors. Brie-style cheeses, for example, obtain their delicious mushroomy flavors from the white *candidum* species of *Penicillium* mold growing on their rinds. Thistle rennets used in certain traditional Portuguese and Spanish cheeses lend a typical hint of bittersweet flavor.

TRACING *TERROIR:* FROM PASTURE TO PLATE

Common sense tells us what the animals eat will affect their milk and thus have a tremendous impact on the cheese. We can reason-

ably assume the greater the amount of natural, local food the animals consume, the more of the land's character (*terroir*) will eventually end up in the cheese. But because organic chemistry is so complex and because so many variables enter into the cheese equation, uncovering specific evidence and proof of these logical assumptions requires Ph.D.-level science.

Scientists such as Dr. Giuseppe Licitra, Dr. Stefania Carpino, and their colleagues at CoRFiLaC, a dairy research center in Ragusa, Sicily (the acronym is for Consorzio di Ricerca Filiera Lattiero-Casearia or the Cheese and Dairy Industry Research Consortium), and Dr. David Barbano at Cornell, have begun to trace back through the entire cheesemaking process to determine how certain compounds in the animals' feed are transformed into volatile flavor-giving ones in the cheese.

One CoRFiLaC study, focusing on the ancient local cheese Ragusano and published in 2002, revealed a preliminary finding—not related to aromatics but still significant because it showed there was a path—regarding the role of carotene. Carotene is the compound that makes carrots (and also sweet potatoes, mangoes, and pumpkins) orange. Its beta form also transmits vitamin A. The study demonstrated conclusively that carotene from summer pasture feed was responsible for the darker, yellower colors of summer-made cheeses as opposed to the lighter, whiter-shaded cheeses made from winter milk of animals consuming only dry feed.

Another study, coauthored by Drs. Carpino, Licitra, and Barbano and published in 2004 in the *Journal of Dairy Science*, examined the differences between Ragusano cheeses made from the milk of pasture-fed cows versus ones made from the milk of TMR-fed ones. (TMR is total mixed ration, or dry formula feed.) Researchers actually followed the cows around as they grazed, noted which plants they were eating, and then sampled and analyzed those plants, recording which compounds were present. Those results were compared with lists of compounds from analyses of Ragusano samples.

The study provides conclusive scientific evidence for two key concepts of cheese flavor origin: first, pasture feed yields more flavors and aromas; second, native plants and grasses offer unique aromas and flavors, that is, *terroir* makes a big difference. The study showed that a significant portion of the aromatics came from specific plants known to have been eaten by specific animals. As the cows chewed up grasses and flowers, crushing them and oxidizing the chemicals within, aromatics were released into the animals' digestive tracts. Those aromatics eventually made their way into the milk to emerge as aroma- and flavor-giving substances in cheeses. Some aromatics may have been merely inhaled—the quickest method of absorption into the bloodstream—bypassing the cows' digestive tracts entirely.

Species and breed of animal are important factors contributing to flavor, as are all the steps of cheesemaking. But it is these aromatics from the animals' feed that determine individual cheese character and distinguish great cheeses.

One of the most appealing traits of great cheeses is their ability to project subtle hints of *terroir*. I swear I can smell the sea salts, like a fresh breeze off the ocean, in an Appleby's Cheshire, one of England's most outstanding farmhouse cheeses. Likewise, an unpasteurized Majorero from the Canary Island of Fuerteventura offers a tantalizing whiff of the mineral-rich soil of its wild, volcanic pastures. With any great cheese, it's easy to envision all those beautiful, aromatic plants and flowers. I can see the cows, doe, and ewes grazing, and I can taste their delicious fresh milk. I can sense the goodness of these raw ingredients, transformed by the artistic techniques of honest, expressive cheesemaking. And it's thrilling to discover there is firm, scientific basis for these sensations.

HAPPY ANIMALS = TASTY CHEESES

In addition to their influence on the animals' feed, the elements of *terroir* also affect the animals' physiology and health. (*Everything* has ripple effects, *everywhere*, my friends.) Good temperature conditions, enough feed, plentiful, clean water, and not too much heat or cold means the animals are happy. The conditions enjoyed (or endured) by the animals affect the chemical composition of their milk and thus the building blocks of cheese flavor. Happy animals make better milk. This, too, is cheese science.

SENSORY ANALYSIS OF REAL CHEESE: "FLAVOR RULES!"

To separate and detect individual flavor components, dairy scientists such as Dr. Licitra and colleagues at CoRFiLaC and Dr. Mary Anne Drake at North Carolina State University use a technique called gas chromatography olfactometry (GCO), or GC sniffing. In GC sniffing, laboratory scientists dissolve samples of the subject cheese into liquid or gas form then they separate each volatile compound using a gas chromatograph. The compounds emerge one by one, so they can be recorded by detection instruments and/or sniffed by professional tasters, who can then record their findings. GCO has been applied in food science and the flavor and aroma industries since the 1960s but only more recently to cheese.

Greeting some contented cows at Shelburne Farms, Vermont.

"In 4-month-old cheese made from milk of pasture-fed cows, 27 odor-active compounds were identified, whereas only 13 were detected in cheese made from milk of total mixed ration-fed cows ... A total of 8 unique aroma-active compounds (i.e., not reported in other cheeses evaluated by gas chromatography olfactometry) were detected in Ragusano cheese made from milk from cows consuming native Sicilian pasture plants."

S. CARPINO ET. AL., "COMPOSITION AND AROMA COMPOUNDS OF RAGUSANO CHEESE: NATIVE PASTURES AND TOTAL MIXED RATIONS"

Inspired by their motto ("Flavor Rules!"), Dr. Drake and her colleagues have conducted extensive research on various cheeses. Her lab has identified between 200 and 300 volatile compounds in samples of aged Cheddar types, about 70 of which have been conclusively identified as "aroma active." A result of all this sensory analysis is a verifiable lexicon of Cheddar flavor components.

Once the aromatics have been separated from the little chunks of cheese, it's up to Dr. Drake and other "educated noses" to smell and describe them. Rigorous scientific methodology is applied not only to identifying the compounds but also to assemble and conduct the panel of experts to come up with descriptions of all these smells and tastes. Although preparing cheese samples and performing separations via chromatograph is exacting and time-consuming work, it's not necessarily complicated. "Where the real science and art come in," explains Dr. Drake, "is in figuring out which of those hundreds of volatile compounds are the ones responsible for flavor. The process of identifying the compounds in general and then selecting which ones cause flavor—that's where we're starting to get into high-level flavor chemistry."

Aromatic compounds are described by way of references to other substances with the same flavor or aroma. Many flavors and aromas are very specific; others are a bit more vague or complex. Some have clear, single references and are identified with one particular compound. Often, it's a direct reference to the active chemical itself. An example: to most people—even serious foodies—the chemical name diacetyl means absolutely nothing; the reference "movie popcorn butter," however, has immediate resonance. Its aroma is unique and has no other clear reference; in fact, the chemical was used for many years to create artificially flavored buttered popcorn.

The Cheddar Lexicon chart (page 90) developed by Dr. Drake and her colleagues has several columns of information. The first one, reading from left to right, lists the flavor or aroma. The next one provides a definition by analogy to other flavors or aromas, and the third one a brief formula for creating a reference, i.e., another food or chemical solution to provide the same taste. "Cooked," a component of milky aromas, is defined as "aromatics associated with cooked milk" while its reference is "skim milk heated to 85 degrees C for 30 minutes." In other words, if you want to taste the aroma cooked, apart from detecting them in a piece of

ISOLATING FLAVOR

CHEESE SCIENCE: HOW GLC WORKS

Gas chromatography is sometimes called GLC, or gas-liquid chromatography, since samples are often injected as liquid and then turned into gas by high temperatures in the injector port. Cheeses are sampled using several preparation techniques from basic undergraduate chemistry: by heating them gently and extracting the volatile compounds (aromatic gases) they emit; by dissolving them with inert organic solvents; or by sparging them with nitrogen (i.e., pumping this inert, neutral gas through the sample so it carries with it the aromatics to be identified).

The functional part of the chromatograph is a small tube, referred to as the column, containing inert gases in its cavity or inert chemicals in its walls that react with the chemical compounds in the samples. When the samples are injected into the column, their component compounds emerge one by one, separated, because the chemical reactions occurring as they pass through take different amounts of time. (The substances inside the column are inert in the sense that they react with the samples but do not significantly alter them.) As the chemicals emerge from the chromatograph, they are recorded and analyzed by several types of detectors, one of which is the human nose—through a "sniffing port." The portion of the column effluent that does not exit via the sniffing port can be directed into other devices, which give quantifiable measurements.

A mass spectrometer attached to the chromatograph is "the gold standard" (Dr. Drake's words) for analyzing flavor samples. As compounds emerge from the chromatograph, the mass spectrometer bombards them with electrons, causing them to fragment and give off electrical charges, which can be measured and recorded. It also creates unique patterns; the printouts are akin to chemical fingerprints of each compound. Other detectors—flame ionization and flame photometric are two of the types used—may be more sensitive than a mass spectrometer, but they don't provide this extremely useful fingerprint-type ID.

The Electronic Nose Knows

Beyond the application of GLC sniffing to label and trace specific components attributable to *terroir*, animal feed, and cheese manufacturing steps, gas chromatography on its own—with no sniffing—can also be useful for simple identifications and comparisons. Employing another type of device, the "electronic nose," a so-called black box filled with different types of detectors, scientists can create fingerprints of different foods' flavor profiles. Electronic noses can detect minuscule amounts of specific volatile compounds that even a well-trained human one might not be able to sense. They are used in the meat and fish industries, for example, to determine whether certain samples are starting to go bad and can identify spoilage before a food actually starts to smell rotten. They can also be used for testing real cheese. A known genuine sample can be compared to a pretender in order to determine authenticity. A trained nose and palate can perhaps offer strong opinions in such cases; but detection via instruments provides positive IDs, confirmed by numbers, charts, and graphs. (Cheese counterfeiters beware!)

Cheddar, you can take a whiff of heated milk. This helps create a mnemonic reference, a taste memory.

When she holds workshops for cheese people, Dr. Drake adds a cheese reference for each component's entry in the lexicon. This can reinforce her students' recognition of a particular flavor or aroma via examples from their experience. Take, for example, a Cheddar-type cheese with a distinct fruity note in its profile: Its

CHEDDAR LEXICON

Term	Definition	Reference
COOKED	Geometrics associated with cooked milk	Skim milk heated to 85°C for 30 minutes
WHEY	Aromatics associated with Cheddar cheese whey	Fresh Cheddar whey
DIACETYL	Aromatic associated with diacetyl	Diacetyl, 20 parts per million (ppm)
MILK FAT/LACTONE	Aromatics associated with milk fat	Fresh coconut meat; heavy cream; ∂ dodecalactone, 40 ppm
FRUITY	Aromatics associated with different fruits	Fresh pineapple; ethyl hexanoate, 20 ppm
SULFUR	Aromatics associated with sulfurous compounds	Boiled, mashed egg; hydrogen sulfide bubbled through water; struck match
FREE FATTY ACID	Aromatics associated with short chain fatty acids	Butyric acid, 20 ppm
BROTHY	Aromatics associated with boiled meat or vegetable soup stock	Canned potatoes; Wyler's low-sodium beef broth cubes; methional, 20 ppm
NUTTY	Nutlike aromatic associated with different nuts	Lightly toasted unsalted nuts; wheat germ; unsalted wheat thins; roasted peanut oil extract
CATTY	Aroma associated with tomcat urine	2 mercapto-2 methyl-pentan-4-one, 20 ppm
COWY/PHENOLIC	Aromas associated with barns and stock trailers, indicative of animal sweat and waste	Band-Aids; p-cresol, 160 ppm
AGE*	Flavors indicating age in Cheddar cheese	Aged Cheddar cheese (1 year or longer)
YEASTY**	Aromatics associated with fermenting yeast	Raw yeast dough; yeast in 3% warm sucrose water
MOLDY/MUSTY**	Aromas associated with molds and/or freshly turned soil	2-ethyl-1-hexanol potting soil
METHYL KETONE/BLEU**	Aroma with associated blue-veined cheeses	2-octanone, 40 ppm
OXIDIZED**	Aroma associated with oxidized fat	2,4 decadienal, 20 ppm
WAXY/CRAYON**	Aromatics associated with medium chain fatty acids	Capric acid, lauric acid, or decanoic acid, 100 mg/mL
FECAL**	Aroma associated with complex protein decomposition	Indole, skatole, 20 ppm
BELL PEPPER**	Aroma associated with freshly cut green vegetables	Methoxy pyrazines, 5 parts per billion; freshly cut bell pepper
OSY/FLORAL**	Aroma associated with flowers	2-phenethylamine, 20 ppm
SCORCHED**	Aroma associated with extreme heat treatment of milk proteins	Milk heated to 121°C for 25 minutes
BITTER	Fundamental taste sensation elicited by caffeine, quinine	Caffeine (0.08% in water)
SALTY	Fundamental taste sensation elicited by salts	Sodium chloride (0.5% in water)
SWEET	Fundamental taste sensation elicited by sugars	Sucrose (5% in water)
SOUR	Fundamental taste sensation elicited by acids	Citric acid (0.08 in water)
UMAMI	Chemical feeling factor elicited by certain peptides and nucleotides	MSG (1% in water)
PRICKLE/BITE**	Chemical feeling factor of which the sensation of carbonation on the tongue is typical	Soda water

*Data analysis indicated term is redundant and is a combination of several terms. Chemical references prepared in 95% ethanol.
**Indicates term was not frequently encountered in Cheddar cheese.

food reference would be a piece of pineapple; its chemical reference would be to smell ethyl hexanoate, an aromatic common to pineapple and also certain cheeses; and its cheese reference would be a piece of Parmesan, which has relatively high concentrations of this particular compound. If you smell "fruity" as a prominent component in three places you'll much more readily form a lasting impression and be able to recognize it the next time you come across it.

CHAPTER REVIEW

Cheese Flavor: What Is It and Where Does It Come From?

- [ ] A fine cheese has many aroma, texture, and flavor components, which together make up its flavor profile.
- [ ] Casein, lactose, and butterfat are the principal building blocks of cheese aromas and flavors.
- [ ] Enzymes from starter cultures, rennet, molds, yeasts, and bacteria break down these building blocks to produce volatile compounds, many of which are aromatics (i.e., we can detect them as aromas and flavors).
- [ ] Cheese flavor can be traced to:
  - The food (plants, feed, etc.) and water the animals consume
  - The breakdown of the three building blocks of milk
- [ ] *Terroir* has numerous effects on aroma and flavor.
- [ ] Cheese made from the milk of pasture-fed animals has a more complex and varied profile than cheese made from the milk of dry-fed ones.
- [ ] Animals consuming native plants, grasses, and flowers yield milk and cheeses with unique flavor profiles.
- [ ] The majority of a fine cheese's flavor components come from microflora introduced during cheesemaking; nevertheless, the sublety to plants and flowers eaten by the animal.

CHAPTER 5

RECOGNIZING GREAT CHEESE: HOW TO TASTE, DESCRIBE, ASSESS, AND JUDGE IT

ALL STUDYING ASIDE, TO KNOW CHEESE YOU'VE GOT TO TASTE IT—AND lots of it. By far the most crucial skill of connoisseurship is the ability to taste, first recognizing what's in a cheese and, second, articulating what it is you like and don't like about it.

Always remember that tasting a cheese in a vacuum is difficult: There is nothing to compare it to. Once you have two or more cheeses, you can develop references, see the range of possibilities, and eventually accumulate a vocabulary based on your personal library of cheese experiences.

Another illuminating way of tasting cheeses is alongside wine or other beverages, which provide further contrasts and/or complements. Sometimes a pairing will elevate both partners and in almost every case it will reveal something interesting about each of them. If you can't wait for that, please skip ahead to chapter 12. Meanwhile, let's consider . . .

HOW WE TASTE CHEESE

What we humans perceive as cheese flavor is made up of a few of fundamental components: first, the five flavors detected by the taste buds on our tongues—sweet, sour, bitter, salty, and *umami* (savory); and second, the thousands of odors we can pick up with our noses. The pleasures of cheese tasting are made possible by the incredible sensitivity of the human olfactory

Scaling the heights of flavor, a tasting of great mountain cheeses: From top, left to right, Persillé de Tignes; Serra da Estrella; Ossau-Iraty; Abbaye de Tamié; Fontina d'Aosta; Alp Dräckloch; Bleu de Termignon.

Dr. Giuseppe Licitra of the dairy research center CoRFiLaC takes a whiff of a funky artisanal cheese. (See also page 86.)

system—we can pick up something on the order of 10,000 aromas—and also its physiology, namely, the retronasal passage connecting the nose to the mouth at the top of the back of the throat. These oral and nasal perceptions, added together, comprise an overall taste impression, or "flavor by mouth." When you include the additional factor of texture, you have another compound sensation called mouth feel.

About 90 percent of what you taste in a cheese's "flavor by mouth" is aroma. Our sense of smell comes into play twice: first, when we put a cheese under our noses and, second, when we put it in our mouths. One reason for the differences between the smells and tastes of cheeses is due to our ability to smell only surface volatiles, in what flavor scientists call the "head space" of a cheese (the immediate vicinity of its surface). When we put cheeses in our mouths and begin to chew, however, all the different aromatics inside them become available.

Many of the compounds on a cheese's surface, including perhaps ammonia and quite a number of potentially stinky, barnyardy (even somewhat noxious) odiferous substances, have actually had a mellowing effect on its interior. They are among the ripening agents responsible for balanced flavor development and are one reason why a really smelly cheese can taste quite mellow and mild.

Once we put a cheese in our mouth, another breakdown process has begun: our body's own digestive enzymes, starting with those contained in saliva, go to work at releasing flavor compounds. Multiple component taste factors immediately come into play, starting with those five primary flavors of the tongue and including the tingle, rasp, or caress of the cheese's textures stimulating all those nerve endings on our palates and creating an overall impression of flavor by mouth, plus mouth feel.

We've discussed aromatics in some detail in the previous chapter. Now, let's digress briefly. If these aromatics are the difference makers in distinguishing cheese character and delineating greatness, then the five primary flavors of the tongue are the foundations of taste.

CHEESE AND THE FIVE PRIMARY FLAVORS

Of those five flavors of the tongue, fine cheeses do exhibit quite a bit of underlying sweetness and also sourness. After all, milk sugar (lactose) is one of the three building blocks of flavor, and fermentation, producing lactic acid, is the first step of cheesemaking. (Long before any ripening effects kick in, a cheese's sweet-sour components and the balance thereof has largely been determined by ongoing acidification.)

What about bitterness? Our favorite cheeses do offer occasional bitter flavors but these are mostly underlying and mostly, one hopes, balanced out by the other five. A little bit of basic bitterness goes a long way.

Next comes "salty," which is the most common flavor in all cheeses. Like any other flavor component, the salt should be in balance and it should complement the other flavors. Of all cheese defects, oversalting is the most frequent. Salt should emphasize or bring out a cheese's other flavor components—not call attention to itself.

Two contrasting items from Oregon Gourmet Cheeses.

And how about the proverbial fifth flavor? Like salt, *umami,* is perhaps more than a pure taste because it also has a separate chemical effect, with the potential to enhance or suppress other specific flavors.

Interestingly, the sharp flavor of *Penicillium* molds in blue cheeses is similar to *umami* in its role as an enhancer. Like salt, the bite of mold is capable of overwhelming a cheese's other tongue flavors and/or aromatics; it should turn up the volume rather than drown out the others. The analogy in cooking, other than salt, is the spicy-hot flavor from the compound capsaicin found in many types of chile peppers. Spicy hot is meant to bring out the charms of a dish, not eclipse them. Very hot peppers have flavor, but until you build up a tolerance all you taste is the heat. The same can be said for salty foods and blue cheeses.

Flavor scientists such as Dr. Drake classify *umami,* along with "bite," under the heading of "chemical feeling factors." "Bite," also referred to as "prickle," is a mouth feel you get from heavily carbonated beverages (with lots of tiny bubbles) as well as from sharp, focused blue cheese molds. The notion of chemical feel suggests that *umami,* spicy hot, and salty represent a kind of hybrid between an actual taste (sweet, sour, bitter) and a neutral-tasting agent capable of simply "turning up the volume." They seem to have two separate effects: one a definite (if somewhat elusive) taste, the other a chemically induced enhancement. Glutamic acid and its synthetic equivalent, MSG (monosodium glutamate), do taste a little salty (see sidebar, page 95), but they also embody other aspects of *umami.*

THE FIFTH FLAVOR

How the five primary flavors interact and strike a balance (or not) quickly ascends to the level of algebra. There are so many ways they can combine and/or play off each other. Both salt and the fifth flavor, *umami,* for example, tend to counteract both bitter and sour flavors. A sour and/or bitter cheese will taste less so if salt is added.

The tactile sensation of a cheese—how its texture is perceived in our mouths—is an important part of its overall profile. Whether it's satiny smooth and near liquid or crunchy and more crystalline or anywhere in between, a fine cheese's texture and consistency will settle over the tongue in a particular way to deliver a distinct impression. As with flavors and aromas, personal preference comes into play: Some people prefer softer types, others harder ones. In any case, contrasting tactile sensations can enrich a cheese experience, adding to the variety of a tasting sequence (see chapter 11). They also can be an important factor in matching cheeses with wines (see chapter 12).

HOW TO TASTE CHEESE

This is one of the shorter yet most important lessons of any Cheese 101 course. If you don't take the time to notice and enjoy everything a real cheese has to offer, you will be missing out on the most crucial aspect of true connoisseurship.

The main steps in tasting a cheese are look, touch, smell, taste, wait, think about it and reflect, and don't miss the finish. Clear your palate; do it all over again with the same cheese. Again, take your time and move on to the next one only when you're good and ready.

LOOK: Examine the rind and, if it's a cut piece, the interior or paste. Make a note of all the textures and colors there and also if there are any interesting, different, curious, or potentially meaningful markings. Think aesthetics: What is it about this cheese that looks good or bad and/or bodes well for how it might taste? Bear in mind that some very scary-looking cheeses can be very delicious indeed.

TOUCH: Poke it, tap it, run your finger over the surface, roll or press a small portion between a thumb and forefinger. (By the way, cheesemakers and *affineurs* use different types of "touch tests" frequently.) How hard is it? Does it have any resistance, any kind of springy, bouncy consistency or texture? How does it break or crumble? A tactile assessment does not make or break a cheese's reputation, but it's an interesting piece of the bigger picture. By the way, if a cheese feels too cold, give it more time to warm up to room temperature before going any further.

SMELL: Take a good sniff. One of the most common FAQs I get is, "Why do some cheeses smell a lot stronger than they taste?" This leads quickly to the realization that the character and intensity of a cheese's aromas do not necessarily coincide with its flavors. A strong cheese may have a deceptively mild aroma; a real stinker may taste mellow and mild. Also, make sure your hands are clean and free from any kind of perfume or other potentially conflicting odors.

TASTE: Take your time throughout a tasting but particularly with the all-important moments after you put it in your mouth. Keep a clean, clear neutral palate and an open mind. This is where a little bit of good white bread (classic baguette or its equivalent) and a sip of water or some other fairly neutral beverage can help clear the palate of any potentially clashing or conflicting flavors. Just a tiny piece of bread works like a swab to take the acids and fats off the tongue so you can taste a cheese more clearly.

Tasting and comparing many different types is the path to connoisseurship.

Take a small bite at first and make sure it comes into contact with every part of your tongue and as much of the inside of your mouth as possible. This is important because your taste buds are spread around the tongue and other parts of the back of the mouth and also because different receptors may focus on different flavors. Chew gently and slowly. Note all the flavors on the tongue and try to determine whether they're in balance.

Be sure to note the attack and also to what extent there's an evolution of flavors: Some fine cheeses make a strong immediate impression, especially to an uninitiated or inexperienced palate; others build from a quiet start to an impressive crescendo. As the cheese settles over your tongue and then migrates to the back of your mouth, you begin to taste its full flavor profile. Note its texture and soon its mouthfeel. Wait for the finish and see how long it lingers; great cheeses don't disappear quietly or slink away meekly, but they frequently offer distinct final impressions.

DESCRIBING CHEESE

Whether you're a dairy flavor scientist such as Mary Anne Drake or Giuseppe Licitra, a cheese professional like myself, or an enthu-

★ TAKE A ★
GOOD SNIFF

SMELLING THE RIND

The rind is a mark of authenticity and is a distinguishing feature of many artisanal cheeses (not all of them have rinds, of course). Examining it, taking a sniff, and perhaps eating at least a bit can be part of developing connoisseurship. All you can tell about a wine by smelling its cork is how the cork smells; smelling the rind of a cheese, however, may give you an extra measure of understanding or appreciation. Rinds can be funky with molds and bacteria—a few are inedible and this is easy to recognize—so eat them only if they promise interesting tastes.

siastic amateur connoisseur, you labor under a universal linguistic constraint, which is that *any* description must be done by analogy. (To say that a cheese tastes or smells cheesy or milky doesn't mean a lot; it's pretty much a tautology.) You have to describe it by comparing it to something else: "This cheese smells like fresh herbs" or "It has a taste like burnt caramel."

Terms such as *fruity, nutty,* and *grassy* are common in cheese descriptions because we're literally smelling and tasting the same flavors, from the same chemicals, as we do in those "reference" substances. Owing to the thousands of aromas and flavors we're able to sense, and because great cheeses potentially offer so many of them, cheese description can go pretty far afield. You'll find some interesting—at times quirky, quizzical, comical, and even anthropomorphic—references. Some of them are a tad alarming; some are even cute. (See sidebar on "squidgy" and "bilious," page 100.)

Descriptions can be quantitative or objective as well as qualitative or subjective. Outlining a cheese's appearance is more objective than trying to capture all its aromas and flavors. Observers can generally agree whether its rind is reddish orange or orangish red. Once taste and preference enter the equation, however, all bets are off. A cheese that tastes sour to you may seem only slightly tangy to me. One I feel is lush and luxurious may strike you as a boring tub of butterfat, but hopefully we can objectively identify and acknowledge the traits upon which we base these opinions. It can be a valuable exercise to compare tasting notes with other cheese lovers, even if you disagree on fundamental judgments.

A beginning connoisseur may find it difficult to move past such seemingly mundane adjectives as *salty* or *buttery* or *creamy.* That's fine. For starters, people attach all kinds of different tags to an item in order to keep track of it in their memory banks. A novice taster may blurt out enthusiastically, "Wow, I love this cheese. It's so buttery!" And that may be a great way to remember it. After years of tasting, there are still many cheeses I file under a simple term like *buttery* or *crumbly,* but with experience, there are many others for which I've committed full, multifaceted impressions of complexity to memory. The more fine cheeses you taste and compare, the more sophisticated your descriptions and references will become.

It's best to stay away from vague or overused terms such as *sharp.* To this day, I'm not sure whether it means "strong," "salty,"

KEEP ON TASTING: THE SAME CHEESE MAY BE DIFFERENT NEXT TIME

One of the wonderful qualities of artisanal cheeses is that not every wheel or drum or button is the same. Every single real cheese, as a living, breathing artifact, will evolve, its flavor profile developing and changing. This is why you don't want to miss the first, second, third, or any other impression. Not only will wheels differ from one to the next but the same wheel can taste better—sometimes *much* better—from one day to the next. I've noticed this phenomenon on several occasions but none more pronounced than with the Harbourne Blue. This is a fine English veined cheese made from pasteurized goat's milk. Around the year 2002, I began to notice the Harbournes were good on first tasting. We would store them and they'd taste even better on the second and third days. This was curious: Cheeses, almost without exception, taste better when fresh cut. At first I wasn't sure—perhaps this perception was coming from my appetite or some other subjective factor. After observing the phenomenon several times, I gave the Harbourne a pet nickname, "the Blue of the Moment." I began mentioning it in restaurant service, which in turn kicked off some interesting cheese conversations.

"pungent," "possessing bite," "having pronounced sour or tangy flavors," or all of the above. And, in fact, *sharp* should raise a red flag with any self-respecting cheese snob since it has become a catchall marketing tag for mass-produced Cheddar types.

Lactic is another catchall term that can benefit from a little dissection to yield some more precise flavor descriptors. If a cheese tastes lactic, exactly what flavors of milk is it exhibiting?

There are also subsets of terms as *nutty* and *fruity*. Under "nutty," expert cheese tasters have detected the aromas of hazelnut, peanut, pecan, and quite a few others. "Fruity" encompasses pineapple—the main one—but also apple, orange, melon, and if a cheese had grape must applied to its rind, grape (naturally).

Vacherin Mont d'Or

In a seminar, a tasting, or any other social gathering revolving around cheese, I encourage people to develop their own facility not only in perceiving but also in describing what great cheeses have to offer. For this reason, I ask my students to utilize a list of descriptors as a tool to start accumulating their own cheese vocabulary. This list is updated from our first two books:

COLOR: Aquamarine, blue, brown, golden, gray, green, greenish, ocher (aka ochre, which is darkish yellow or reddish brown), ivory, orange, orangish, pink, pinkish, purple, purplish, red, reddish, rusty or rust colored, white (chalky, off-white, pure), yellow, yellowish.

CHEESE TALK

DO YOU LIKE "SQUIDGY"? HOW ABOUT "BILIOUS"?

Talk to smart people who know their cheese and you are bound to encounter some interesting new terms to describe the plethora of flavors, textures, and aromas. In reviewing some of the cheeses he makes and also ripens at Jasper Hill Farm, Mateo Kehler brought up the term *squidgy* to describe a consistency somewhere in the rather vague range of "semisoft" to "semihard." Mateo explains "squidgy" as squeezable, with a lot of give, but springy, like a balloon.

We put Mateo on the spot to come up with some other notable cheese adjectives; after a brief pause, he blurted out "bilious," as in bile. It describes the borderline bitter, rancid flavor you find in traditional Italian Provolone-style cheeses, a by-product of the breakdown of the fats known as triglycerides.

Another interesting adjective you'll hear professionals use with some frequency is *friable,* which you might assume has to do with frying. Actually, it does refer to a cheese's suitability for cooking in the sense that the lower its melting point is, the more "friable" it's considered.

A cheese whose curds are cooked and pressed—Sbrinz is a good example—is less friable than one whose curds are uncooked—say, Cheshire. Cheeses with rougher textures and harder consistencies are less friable than smoother, softer ones. Cheeses made from pasteurized milk are also less friable than raw-milk ones; in essence they've already been cooked. A cogent comparison would be between two fine Spanish goat's milk cheeses: Garrotxa (pasteurized) and Ibores (raw). It's not that you couldn't melt down the former, particularly if you cut it into pieces, but rather that the latter possesses a much more pleasantly friable texture and consistency.

COLOR MODIFIERS: Bright, bleached, deep, dirty, dull, uneven, uniform, pale, shiny, smudged.

FIRMNESS OR DENSITY: Compact, dense, firm, hard, liquid, runny, semihard, semisoft, soft, tight.

TEXTURE: Airy, cracking or cracked, crumbling or crumbly, chalky, drying or dry, elastic, fissured, flaky, grainy or granular, greasy, leathery, pasty, resinous, ropey, smooth (satiny), spongy, spreadable, springy, squidgy, rough, waterless, with holes.

MOUTH FEEL: Astringent, bubbly, hard, light, prickly, rough, smooth, caressing, *umami* (MSG).

FLAVOR AND AROMA: Acidic, alcoholic, ammoniacal, barnyardy, beefy, bitter, bland, brothy (canned potato), burnt, buttery, cabbage, chalky, cooked, cloves, cowy (phenolic), cow-shed, movie popcorn butter (diacetyl), eggy (sulfurous), farmy, fecal, floral, fruity (fresh pineapple and other fruits), funky, garlic, goaty, grassy, green, herbal, lactic (milkfat/lactone), meaty, metallic, moldy, mushroomy, musty, nutty, oily, onion, rancid, rosy, salty, savory, scorched, sour (sour milk), spicy, sulfurous (burnt matches, boiled

eggs), sweaty, sweet, tangy, *umami* (MSG), vegetal (pyrazine/fresh bell pepper), weedy, woodsy, yeasty.

An assortment of Cravero selections at the Slow Food Convivium in Bra, Italy. (See page 319, Max's Picks.)

FLAVOR MODIFIERS: Harsh, mild, persistent, pronounced, rich, strong, weak.

SUBJECTIVE, QUALITATIVE, OR INTERPRETIVE: Bite (or biting), complex, concentrated, elaborate, gentle, insipid, luxurious, loud, obstreperous, opulent, powerful, rich, robust, sharp, simple, sonorous, stout, timid, unctuous, zesty.

SORTING 'EM ALL OUT: CLASSIFYING CHEESES BY TYPES AND CATEGORIES

Categorizing cheeses can be a useful extension of describing them. It helps you find substitutes or alternatives when the one you want isn't available, and it can help you create an interesting, varied selection when putting together a cheese plate.

Any categorization system that accurately describes cheese traits can be useful not only in sorting them out but also in understanding and appreciating their various qualities and attributes.

Sorting out and comparing categories is a fine aid to developing connoisseurship.

Basic Categories

FRESH—Unaged, lactic-fermented cheeses, including what are called tub cheeses (unmolded, unpressed).

CHÈVRE—Goat's milk soft-ripened Loire Valley–style cheeses. Examples: Selles-sur-Cher, Sainte-Maure de Touraine, Bonne Bouche, Wabash Cannonball. Note: Many chèvre-like cheeses can also be placed under the next category, bloomy rind.

BLOOMY RIND (SOFT RIPENED)—These unpressed cheeses result from curds that have been gently poured or ladled into molds. Examples: Brie, Camembert, Constant Bliss, Tomme Vaudoise, and the triple-crème family of cheeses.

WASHED RIND—These can be slimy (outside), melting (inside), mild tasting, and stinky (Époisses); they can also be semihard with strong, pronounced but elegant flavors (Appenzeller). Examples: Langres, Maroilles, Pont l'Évêque, Taleggio.

NATURAL RIND—Blue cheeses actually fall under this category, which can also include any cheese for which the rind is allowed to form on its own—that is, without special treatments. Examples: Orb Weaver, Piedmont, various blue cheeses.

UNCOOKED, PRESSED—These are semihard and hard cheeses that feature pressing. Examples: Bra, Caerphilly, Cantal, Laguiole, Saint-Nectaire, Tomme de Savoie.

COOKED, PRESSED—These are hard, aged Alpine, "Swiss-style" cheeses. Examples: Appenzeller, Beaufort, Comté, Gruyère, Pleasant Ridge Reserve, Tarentaise.

BLUE—This is a wide-ranging class whose cheeses are all categorized by blue-green molds, the vast majority of which occur as interior veins (in the paste) but a few of which appear only on a cheese's exterior. Examples: Fourme d'Ambert, Gorgonzola, Monte Enebro Roquefort, Stilton, Bleu de Gex.

Other Types

STRETCHED CURD (*pasta filata*)—This is an indigenous Italian style, made by hand-stretching the curds after acidification. Examples: Provolone, Caciocavallo, and Scamorza.

WHEY CHEESES—Whey from primary cheesemaking is made into cheese in a secondary process—hence the name Ricotta, from the Latin *recoctus* meaning "recooked." Example: Ricotta.

An Italian Viewpoint

In *Italian Cheese: A Guide to Its Discovery and Appreciation* by Slow Food Editore, cheeses are classified as follows.

BY FAT CONTENT—(defined by fat in dry matter or FDM)—Fat or whole-milk (42 percent FDM or more); semifat or partially skimmed (20 to 42 percent FDM); low fat or skimmed (less than 20 percent FDM).

BY WATER CONTENT—Hard (less than 40 percent water); semihard: (40 to 45 percent water); soft (45 to 60 percent water).

BY AGING PERIOD—Fresh (for consumption within a few days); young (brief maturation; up to 1 month); aged (medium maturation; 1 to 6 months); extra aged (long maturation; more than 6 months).

An American Melting Pot

The American Cheese Society awards have a huge number of categories. Maybe they're diluting things a little for the purpose of making their competitions inclusive, but I like the spirit.

Cheeses can dry out and look sketchy but still taste great: Cornish Yarg at Neal's Yard Dairy, London.

FRESH UNRIPENED—Cow, goat, sheep or mixed, Mascarpone, Ricotta.

SOFT RIPENED—Cow, Brie, Camembert, goat, sheep and/or mixed, flavor added, triple crème.

AMERICAN ORIGINALS—Cow, goat, sheep and/or mixed, Monterey Jack, Monterey Jack with flavors, Colby.

AMERICAN-MADE/INTERNATIONAL STYLE—Dutch style (all milks), cow, goat, sheep and/or mixed.

CHEDDARS—Aged (all milks; 12 to 24 months), flavor added, cow (less than 12 months), goat, mature (aged 25 to 35 months), mature (over 49 months).

BLUE MOLD—Blue-veined cow, blue-veined goat, blue-veined sheep and/or mixed; external mold (all milks).

HISPANIC AND PORTUGUESE STYLE—Ripened; fresh, unripened (*queso blanco/queso fresco*); flavor added.

ITALIAN TYPE—*Pasta filata,* grating types, Mozzarella types, fresh Mozzarella types.

FETA—Cow, goat, sheep, flavor added.

LOW FAT, LOW SALT—Goat, sheep, water buffalo; light/lite; flavor added.

FLAVORED—All peppers, herbs, fruits, vegetables, flowers, syrups; crushed or whole peppercorns or savory spices; goat, sheep.

SMOKED—Cow, goat, sheep, Italian styles, Cheddars.

FARMSTEAD—All milks, aged over 90 days, cow, goat, sheep, flavor added.

FRESH GOAT—Flavor added.

FRESH SHEEP—Flavor added.

MARINATED—Cow, goat, sheep.

AGED SHEEP

AGED GOAT

WASHED RIND—Cow, goat, sheep.

ASSESSING AND JUDGING CHEESE

Use common sense. If a cheese looks really dry, cracked, bulging, or otherwise damaged, smells especially putrid or "off," don't jump to conclusions, but do consider that it might not be right. However,

SEEKING PERFECT BALANCE

A cheese's peak, that stage where everything has come together in perfect harmony and you say with conviction, "It can't get any better than this," can seem elusive. You might taste a great cheese not quite at peak and it will reveal its potential, but one or more of its components may be out of whack. Not too long ago, Dave and I were sampling cheeses from the cave at Picholine. We came across a Rolf Beeler–aged Sbrinz—consistently a world-class cheese and one of my personal favorites. This particular wedge had so much of that pronounced super-fruity flavor note it was almost cartoonish. It tasted like pineapple-flavored bubble gum. Clearly this was a remarkable cheese, but just as obviously it needed more time to achieve balance. Would I serve it to my diners? Perhaps, but it might have been more appropriate for a master class. A cheese where one flavor jumps out and dominates so blatantly is an interesting curiosity. It illustrates valid points about ripening and component balance. It does not, however, represent its type fairly and may give the wrong impression to paying customers. At the restaurant, I should probably send it back to the cave for a while, although once cut open it is much less likely to achieve ideal balance unless it's a blue-of-the-moment type like the Harbourne (see page 99).

even if it looks funky or smells questionable, if it appears a bit beat up or stinks a little, it might be at peak. Or, as I sometimes say, "It's screamin' to be eaten." A whiff of ammonia can be okay—it's a natural by-product of ripening—but a lot of it that doesn't dissipate could be a problem. The same with excessive putrefaction: The cheese should smell alive. A soupçon of baby diapers or ripe, teeming barnyard is one thing, but corpses and rot another.

Ripeness

Of course, any retailer or restaurateur will claim to take great care to sell or serve all cheeses at peak ripeness. Making your own critical judgments, however, is part of becoming a connoisseur.

One cannot stress enough the point that fine cheeses evolve, going through various stages of development. In this cheesemongering business of ours, we have a concept—naturally French—of a cheese being *à point,* or at peak ripeness, which is a nice idea but perhaps a bit abstract. I had given this quite a bit of thought, based on repeatedly tasting hundreds of types of cheeses and thousands of individual examples, when I came up with the "seven degrees of ripeness" model for our first book (see sidebar, page 106). Part of the point is that while most cheeses are best at their peak, many are good at several stages.

THE SEVEN DEGREES OF RIPENESS

1. Too young. Fully formed but not ready to eat.

2. Still tender, but somewhat one-dimensional. Edible but not showing full potential.

3. Flavors emerge, character development and potential is evident. Very edible, but not exhibiting deeper, richer flavors or full complexity.

4. Peak. Get it while you can! Flavors are complex, profound, and balanced; overall profile creates a memorable impression; texture and mouthfeel are optimal.

5. Still eminently edible and tasty but just past peak. Intimations of faded glory.

6. Remains edible, but definitely fading. Faults may emerge; flavor profile may lose harmony and balance. Texture is declining: It's either too dry or too liquid.

7. Over the hill. Barely edible—if at all.

Softer, younger, more moist and fragile cheeses naturally have shorter peak periods. Classic Loire Valley chèvres and similar fresh goat types are a good example of this. These and some of the other soft and semisoft mold-ripened cheeses—the ones that mature relatively quickly from the outside in—have anywhere from three or four days to about a week when they're at their best.

Washed-rind, stinky types can have a short peak period, where they go from eye opening (and nostril flaring) to just plain over the hill. The harder, drier, bigger sturdier cheeses have much longer periods of optimum ripeness. But the same principles hold: Regardless of whether it's hard or soft, of relatively obstreperous or gentle character, a perfectly ripe cheese should have lip-smacking and mouthwatering flavors and textures, a balanced profile and uniform consistency. Furthermore, it should not exhibit any obvious defects (see "A Checklist of Defects and Faults," page 108). Although optimum ripeness is hard to define objectively, one thing is for sure: A great cheese has a host of attractive traits, all of which should be clearly displayed when it's *à point*.

As they ripen, most cheeses eventually dry out, become harder and more dense, and their flavors become more concentrated. Surface-ripened cheeses, however, will go through a stage where they are softening and becoming creamier, their texture and flavor profiles smoother and more melded. Most connoisseurs of these types—the bloomy rind and even some of the washed-rind varieties—would prefer their cheese still have a "heart" not entirely liquefied; they should be creamy, with the consistency of soft (although not melting) butter. Using a sharp knife, you should be able to cut all the way through with almost no resistance, indicating ripening has penetrated the entire cheese. Eventually they'll go into decline, melting into nothingness à la Wicked Witch of the West or drying out and evaporating.

Certain goat cheeses provide good examples of how very different stages of ripeness can be equally pleasing. A traditional Loire Valley chèvre will start out light and fresh, creamy and moist, with mild flavors and not very assertive character. It will become chalkier, drier, and more dense, and its flavors will become more focused as it matures. The same cheese may continue to evolve and eventually reach a stage where it melts into a satiny smooth, gooey puddle at room temperature, especially if it's made from pasteurized milk and/or has received insufficient *séchage* (drying) in its youth. At that point, the chèvre can still taste very good indeed, but it has definitely turned the corner: It's now behaving much more like an Époisses. I once taught a seminar where I presented a Garrotxa, the excellent Catalonian bloomy-rind goat cheese, at two stages of ripeness distinct enough that most people mistook them for two completely different cheeses.

The notion of peak ripeness is subject to personal preference and habit. As we said in our first book, I may take my Époisses a day or two closer to the compost heap than you do. I might enjoy a very mature chèvre, one that melts like an Époisses or has become drier and chalkier instead, but it would be hard to argue with a purist who claimed this cheese was overripe and no longer in character.

Fine cheeses are often marketed and consumed at several distinct stages of ripeness. This, too, is a reflection of habit and preference, as well as tradition. Many traditional cheeses have long been preferred locally—within their ancient production zones—at younger, less mature stages. The longer-aged, stronger versions rarely saw the light of day until the late twentieth century, when they became hot items in the fancy food sector. This is particularly true of some of the large-format Alpine cheeses such as Comté and Gruyère. It is also true of the Dutch farmhouse (Boeren Kaas) aged Goudas as well as quite a few of the traditional Italian ones, including Taleggio and Pecorino.

A young Taleggio is pure, moist, smooth, and milky, but relatively unsophisticated in terms of its tremendous potential when meltingly ripe and irresistibly meaty; I might even classify it as a "sandwich cheese" rather than the "fine table" one it can become. Fine traditional Tuscan Pecorinos are also sold in quite a few distinct ripeness categories, some of which are closer to that "sandwich" class. Mahón, an aged cow's milk delicacy from the Spanish island of Menorca available in raw-milk farmhouse versions, provides another good example of a cheese sold at several stages: *tierno* (young), 15 to 30 days old; *semicurado*, up to 2 months of aging; *curado*, 3 to 6 months; and *viejo* or *añejo*, 9 to 12 months.

Overripeness

The first telltale sign of an overripe cheese is loss of balance. It gets out of whack and one particular trait—not necessarily a defect but often not a clear asset—takes over. Overripe cheeses can

THE CHEESE OF THE MOMENT

Among my favorite sayings is "The cheese shows up on its own time." What this means to me is a given cheese will have times of the season, the month, the year when it's at its very best. This may have to do with production factors (e.g., the milk it comes from is best for making it at a given time of year) or aging ones (i.e., it's pretty good after 6 months of ripening but best after 7 months). We commercialized the cheese-of-the-moment phenomenon on the Artisanal Premium Cheese website with a feature called "Max's Picks." About once a week, I post the three cheeses I think are showing best at that time, constantly tasting and keeping track of their fluctuating fortunes so we can highlight individual items at peak.

become too sharp or rancid, "goaty" or "sheepy"; too hard, too soft, too salty or too runny; or soapy tasting ("saponified"). Washed-rind types should not be cracked, bulging, collapsing, or completely stuck to their wrapping or packaging.

Other signs of overripeness include excess dryness or graininess—except in the Parmesan or Grana types, which are designed to be this way; lack of uniform flavor or texture; excessively bitter flavors; persistent ammonia; black external molds; and blue, gray, or green internal molds in a cheese other than blue.

A Checklist of Defects and Faults

Imperfections can be caused by poor manufacturing, subpar raw materials, overripeness, and abuse suffered during transportation or storage. Certain typical (desirable) flavors and aromas can become faults if excessive. ("Cowy" or phenolic, "eggy" or sulfurous are two examples of the latter.) The stronger and/or more rustic a cheese, the closer it may be to crossing the line from "interesting" to "off." Here's a checklist of defects, updated from our first book.

TASTING AZEITÃO

ODE TO A GREAT CHEESE

Permit me to share a tribute to one cheese I consider great: Azeitão. This little Portuguese sheep's milk drum makes me really happy. First, there's the anticipation, laced with curiosity: Every Azeitão is a bit different; not one has ever disappointed. When I get my hands on one, I can't wait to cut into it. A ripe Azeitão is a cheese I can enjoy on its own—no bread, no wine, not even any company required. And there's always the temptation to eat

one whole, right down to the rind—it's just that good.

Ideally, an Azeitão will be a little plump and quite soft. Its aroma, exuding from the rind alone, will be green and grassy with a note of olive. To be in a room thick with the scent of several of these tender young things transports me to the south of Portugal in a heartbeat. If it's soft and melting and nobody's looking, I'm tempted to cut out the top of my Azeitão, scoop out a delicious dollop with one finger and quickly pop it into my mouth.

The Azeitão's first taste impression is buttery, with a scarce bit of salt thrown in. The flavors widen quickly, however, offering vegetal notes; a trace of avocado appears,

with a few drops of lemon juice for accent. Then, a meatiness descends further back on the tongue—filet mignon . . . no, tenderloin of lamb, yet with a light fullness balanced by a lingering hint of bitterness. Essence of ripe mango comes into play, its juices visiting the outer edges of the tongue. This is getting really interesting: I don't want it to end! The thick, creamy Azeitão falls away gracefully with a touch of peach and ground almond lending a tantalizing and refreshing sweetness to the finish. I might try some of the rind to make sure I didn't miss anything. Then I'll dive back into the paste to savor another leisurely mouthful of its delights.

□ **PHYSICAL:** Bulging, bloating, heaving; flat or collapsed shape; unwanted interior holes or fissures; cracked and/or slimy or drying, pockmarked, rough, leathery rinds; unwanted molds, particularly black ones; discoloration or uneven coloration of rind or paste (spotty, smeary, mottled); cracking or bulging of paste; reddening of paste; mites, which appear as a brownish, curry powder–like dust that actually moves if you watch it closely.

□ **TEXTURE:** Uneven interior; excessively open or airy in hard cheeses or hard in soft ones; inappropriate interior consistency, including brittle, chalky, pasty, greasy or soapy, gummy, lumpy, mealy, rubbery (tough or corky), spongy, or sticky.

□ **AROMA:** Ammoniated; excessively strong, acrid, pungent, sour, putrid, or "barnyardy"; medicinal.

□ **FLAVOR:** Too strong (harsh) or too weak (flat); excessively sour (acidic) or bitter or salty; strongly ammoniated; "off" flavors not normally associated with milk or cheese, for example pronounced onion, garlic, metallic, musty, stale, yeasty, weedy, burnt, sulfurous (rotten eggs); oxidation ("cardboardy"); rancidity (oxidation of fats or oils); overly fermented or overly fruity.

WHAT TO LOOK FOR

CRITERIA FOR CHEESE GREATNESS

- Purity of ingredients (raw milk; nothing artificial; all natural, as organic as possible)
- Distinct character; unique personality
- Expression of *terroir*
- Memorable aromas, textures, and flavors (not necessarily high volume or strong but unmistakeable and leaving a lasting impression)
- Evolution of flavor: stimulating on the attack, in the development and at the finish
- Complexity and depth: a complete flavor profile
- Balance: no one trait dominates or drowns out the others; no extremes in the profile
- Consistent quality (though not sameness or uniformity)
- Offers good pairing potential with wines and other beverages (optional)

What Makes a Cheese Great?

Having outlined a cheese's trajectory and discussed signs of failure, let's turn to some standards for greatness. If a cheese has all of them or enough of them in abundance, it can be elevated from the level of "merely good" to "outstanding" or "great."

Some of the traits I look for in assessing greatness are complexity of aromas and flavors, stimulating texture(s), balance, distinct or unique character, and impact—in the sense of making a memorable impression. You might taste a cheese once, perhaps not even remembering its name, but you can't get it out of your mind. It doesn't necessarily have *strong* aromas or flavors—after all, great cheeses can be very subtle—but it begs you to try it again.

If a cheese is unique, it may qualify as great. But, to be exceptional, it doesn't absolutely have to be one of a kind. Cheeses that are variations or even imitations of great types should not be automatically ruled out. They may be very similar in character but at the same time could possess enough individual personality to stand out.

Another key question: Does it truly express its *terroir*? Great cheeses, like great wines, have an uncanny ability to transport you. Merely good cheeses taste like a type; great ones taste like the place they're from. An outstanding Chianti beams you right to a sun-drenched hillside vineyard beside a dusty road in Tuscany. Likewise, a taste of a perfectly ripened Appenzeller takes you to a flowered mountain meadow with a backdrop of majestic glaciered Alps.

Great cheeses live and breathe; they evolve and grow—not just from cheesemaking through ripening but on your palate when you taste them. Cheeses with profound, complex flavor profiles inhabit your mouth and offer a broad evolution. They start with an attack, subtle or not so subtle, hitting the taste buds of the tongue with

CULTURAL AFFAIRS

LOVE FOR A GREAT CHEESE RESTORED

Spenwood—a pressed, aged, raw sheep's milk cheese made by Anne Wigmore in Berkshire, England— was great for a long time. Then it wasn't so great for a while. What happened?

By 2005, I had been receiving Spenwoods in consistently excellent form for over a decade. In our second book, I gave it a near-perfect rating. The edited manuscript went off to press, and then the Spenwoods started to drop off. They lost some of their profile: That focused, refreshing brilliance had somehow gone away. The texture was still good, but the flavors had gone a bit flat.

After a few more batches, it was clear that Spenwood had been overtaken by Berkswell, the Chevy to Spenwood's Cadillac. As an everyday working cheese connoisseur, it's the sort of reversal that makes you question your own palate. Was I losing it or had something gone awry with this cheese?

How was I going to deal with the depression caused by the decline of yet another of my favorite cheeses? In the old days, my blood pressure would go up every time a shipment of Spenwoods arrived. I couldn't wait to taste them. They made my day. Now the love affair was over— or was it?

At Picholine, we bought our Spenwoods through Randolph Hodgson at Neal's Yard Dairy. I mentioned my misgivings to Randolph, and he responded confidently, saying the problem had already been taken care of. Within a few months, Spenwood was back in form and taking its habitual place of honor on our cheese boards. It turned out Mrs. Wigmore had changed her starter cultures. When the cheese took a wrong turn, she was quickly convinced, via feedback from Randolph (and myself and others), to restore the status quo.

There are several morals to this story. First, "If it ain't broke don't fix it." Second, for a cheese to be great, every little detail has to be right. If you mess with just one, you risk throwing off the entire delicate balance. This Spenwood incident drove that point home once more.

fundamental flavor highlights. Those flavors develop and expand, melding and competing with myriad aromas, working their way back through the retronasal passage and up into the intellectual and memory centers of your brain. You're excited, stimulated, challenged. Tasting a great cheese makes you say, "Wow." Strong or mild, hard or soft, you're bowled over by its brilliance.

CHAPTER REVIEW

Recognizing Great Cheese

TASTING

- [ ] Flavor by mouth consists of aroma plus the five fundamental flavors of the tongue: sweet, sour, bitter, salty, and *umami*.
- [ ] A cheese's aroma and its flavor do not necessarily coincide; a stinky cheese can taste mellow and mild.
- [ ] Apart from its aroma (how it smells), most of a cheese's flavor (how it tastes) is made up of retronasal aromas.
- [ ] Mouth feel consists of flavor by mouth plus texture.
- [ ] Imbalance and oversalting are common defects in less-than-ideal cheeses.
- [ ] Excessive acid development is a frequent flaw.
- [ ] Before putting a cheese in your mouth, look at it, touch it (optional), and smell it.
- [ ] When tasting a cheese, take your time, keep a clear palate and an open mind; note its attack, development, and finish.
- [ ] Taste a cheese multiple times in one session and also in multiple sessions; cheeses can and do change.

DESCRIBING, ASSESSING, AND JUDGING

- [ ] Cheeses, like other fine foods, are described by their components, mostly using analogies.
- [ ] Cheese descriptions have both quantitative (objective) aspects and qualitative (subjective) ones.
- [ ] Fine cheeses should be given the benefit of the doubt; some of the funkiest, scariest-looking ones may taste great.
- [ ] The concept of *à point,* or peak ripeness, is fairly abstract.
- [ ] Younger, fresher, more moist cheeses have shorter "windows of opportunity" than older, harder, drier aged ones.
- [ ] Great cheeses exhibit complexity, balance, and distinct character; they make a memorable impression and reflect their *terroir*.

CHAPTER 6

AROUND THE BARNYARD: SPECIES AND BREEDS

THE MORE I STUDY CHEESE, THE MORE I PONDER ALL THE INS AND OUTS of artisanal production, the more certain truths are hammered home. Among the principal ones is the preeminence of raw materials. As we've learned, without great milk, you cannot make great cheese. Quality is crucial; the next consideration, very shortly thereafter, is character. Two of the most important factors in determining milk composition and cheese character are animal species and breed.

In our first book, I quoted the old adage that goat's milk is best for drinking, cow's milk best for making butter, and sheep's milk best for cheese. Goats yield pure white, mild-tasting, pleasantly drinkable milk. Cows yield much more milk, which is thinner but nonetheless very tasty and nutritious. Sheep's milk is the most concentrated (i.e., already closer to cheese), and ewes produce relatively less of it. By the way, cheese can be made from the milk of many different animals. (I've tried some tasty yak's milk cheeses from the steppes of central Asia and some interesting camel's milk ones from from the deserts of northern Africa, but, alas, no reindeer yet. So many cheeses, so little time . . .) But the remarkable fine artisanal cheeses relevant to this discussion are all made from the milk of these three species. First, let's take a look at the differences among them and how the composition of their respective milks affects the cheeses we know and love.

An East Friesian ewe at Willow Hill Farm: Sheep's milk is particularly suited for cheesemaking. (See also page 118.)

An Ayrshire cow at Jasper Hill Farm.

SPECIES TRAITS

Cows

Cows have a lactation period of about 300 days, so with a little help from staggered breeding, a herd can produce milk for cheese-making year round. Being much larger animals, cows produce more milk than sheep or goats, but it is not *proportionally* more. A 1,500-pound cow will produce up to 120 pounds of milk per day, which is less than 10 percent of her body weight. (Dairy professionals refer to milk in units of dry weight; a pint is about a pound.)

Although they are magnificent beasts, dairy cows are less manageable and require more attention than goats or sheep. All dairy animals require TLC because if they aren't happy and healthy they will not produce good milk. Not only do healthy animals make better cheese, but they are also less of a burden on the farm, the environment, our planet, and everybody's karma.

Sheep

Sheep are quite hearty, relatively easy to manage, and versatile, although they do need to be sheared, which is hard work. Sheep farming is much less common in the United States, perhaps because cow dairying is so ingrained in our culture. Sheep thrive in much more sparse conditions than cows. This is why they—and their cheeses—are more prevalent where pasturelands are higher, rockier, and more barren. In Spain, for example, sheep dairying occurs on the central mesa whereas cows inhabit the greener, lusher north. In Italy, too, the wetter north, including the foothills of the Alps, is mostly for cows while the drier, more exposed mountains of the central and southern regions are sheep country.

The gestation period for sheep is 5 months; the lambs are weaned when they are 1 month old and ewes continue to produce milk for up to 8 months, making their lactation period about 150 to

MILK COMPOSITION SPECIES COMPARISON: AVERAGE PERCENTAGES OF SOLIDS				
	fats	protein (casein)	sugar (lactose)	total solids
COW	3.7	2.6	4.8	12.7
GOAT	3.6	2.6	4.5	12.5
SHEEP	7.4	3.9	4.8	19.5

240 days. A-150 pound ewe will produce up to 4.5 pounds of milk per day, which is about 3 percent of her body weight.

Sheep's milk is just as sweet as cow's milk but has as much as double the fat, with 50 percent more protein and 50 percent more total solids—significantly higher numbers, which have important ramifications for cheesemaking.

A doe at Tumalo Farms.

Goats

Goats are hardy omnivores and are able to free-range in relatively sparse areas. There is a bit of a popular misconception of them as ornery scavengers who can survive almost anywhere under almost any conditions. The animals that produce the milk for the world's fine chèvres and other goat's milk cheeses, however, are relatively pampered farm animals. In fact, in terms of temperament and behavior, they are probably more like pets than the other dairy animals. And they're very often encouraged to browse in pastures, bushlands, and forests that are quite lush and green.

Female goats are called does and the males called bucks. (The equivalent terms for sheep are ewes and rams; for cattle, cows and bulls.) The lactation period for does is 10 months, beginning after they give birth, which is generally sometime between the beginning of winter and early spring. Most goat breeds produce about 6 to 8 pounds of milk per day, or 5 to 10 percent of their body weight, with the exception of the Saanen (Swiss), which can yield more than 20 pounds per day, over 10 percent of body weight.

Neither does nor their milk smells "goaty"; that odor is an aphrodisiac produced by the bucks' scent glands. If the bucks are allowed too close to the milking parlor, the odor *can* end up in the milk and cheese—a rare occurrence and a blatant defect.

Goat's milk has about the same amounts of solids as cow's. There is, however, a key difference in its proteins: Compared with cow's or sheep's milk, goat's milk has more of the beta variant of casein and less of the alpha one. This affects the way the proteins coagulate, and the result, in cheesemaking terms, is that goat's milk curds are more fragile and yield less cheese.

MILK COMPOSITION AND CHEESE RESULTS

As discussed in chapter 4, the fats in milk, particularly the short-chain fatty acids, have a great deal of aroma- and flavor-giving potential, which is realized when they're broken into free fatty

Vacherin Mont d'Or

acids (FFAs) during cheese ripening. The good news is these FFAs can offer pronounced, sharp, peppery, spicy flavors; the bad news is they often teeter on the edge of rancidity. Both sheep's milk and goat's milk have a higher percentage of short-chain fatty acids than cow's milk, which is why they typically exhibit more of these flavor traits and why they are also prone to the aforementioned defect. (Rancidity can also be caused by feeding hay to the animals or by natural changes in the milk late in the lactation cycle.)

Another key difference in milk composition is the size of the fat globules. Both goat's and sheep's milk have smaller globules than cow's, making them easier to digest (if consumed raw) and also more consistent and predictable for creating and aging cheeses.

In tasting cheeses of all three species daily, I'm constantly reminded how these differences in milk composition are played out in the flavors, textures, and aromas of my favorite cheeses. They're most clearly delineated when I conduct a seminar with a horizontal tasting of three otherwise identical cheeses, which is fairly rare and always highly edifying. I recall a recent event aboard ship on a Mediterranean cruise:

During one port call, I visited the tiny village of Soulac-sur-Mer, near the mouth of the Gironde estuary on the Atlantic Ocean, about 40 miles north of Bordeaux. At the market in Soulac, I found the stall of Hélène Athaquet, offering *fromages fermiers, spécialités des Pyrénées* (farmhouse cheeses of the Pyrénées). In Madame Athaquet's mouthwatering display, there were three virtually identical firm, pressed, raw-milk cheeses from the western Pyrénées, all whole milk and animal renneted, one from cow's milk, one from goat's, one from sheep's. This was precisely the ticket for the seminar I planned to give that afternoon!

The three cheeses, with their sandy gold-colored rinds, looked almost identical from the outside, although the goat cheese was just a little smaller. The goat cheese's paste was creamy white, the sheep's more golden, and the cow's more yellow—typical colors. Remember: How a cheese looks is significant, especially if it can tell us something about its other qualities.

Referring back to my tasting notes from that day, all the other distinctive traits among this trio are also emblematic. The goat cheese's aroma was gentle, creamy, and milky. The sheep cheese smelled grassier, nuttier, and sweeter, while the cow was more buttery and tangy smelling. The flavors followed those first aromatic impressions: The goat cheese was slightly tart, but very creamy flavored, with just a little clay texture to its mouth feel and a pleasant bit of salt in its finish. The sheep's milk version offered grassier flavors with a nuttiness typical in these types and a sweeter note in its longer finish. The cow's milk version was meatier, beefier, more buttery in flavor, and left a bigger impression on the palate.

BREED DIFFERENCES

To become a well-rounded connoisseur, you'll probably want to learn about more than just the basic differences among the three primary species of milk-giving animals. You'll want to look into particular breeds and how the distinctions in their milk are expressed in cheeses.

A common and helpful analogy is to compare animal breeds to wine grape varietals—Cabernet Sauvignon, Sangiovese, Zinfandel, etc. In wine, each varietal has certain recognizable traits, which are expressed in different ways depending on *terroir*. Likewise, each varietal has certain conditions and climates where it thrives best. In cheesemaking, the animal contributes certain traits to the raw material and is also a vehicle for expressing *terroir*. What the animals eat and drink is partly determined by *terroir* and partly a choice made by cheese farmers. It might seem a trifle simplistic, but you could say, in the case of milk, that species and breed determine character while *terroir* and feed determine composition.

MAKING THINGS INTERESTING

Mixing the milks of different species was likely first practiced by cheesemakers out of necessity when their primary dairy animals' lactation cycles were coming to an end or if they simply didn't have a large enough herd of one species to make cheese production worthwhile. No doubt, it quickly became apparent they could make some very interesting cheeses this way.

Mixed-milk cheeses offer a "best of both worlds" scenario whereby the different milks can contribute their most attractive attributes. They provide buffering and balance, so that any harshness or tilt too far in one direction can be offset by another element in another milk. For example, the Robiola family from northern Italy, has *due latti* and *tre latti* (two-milk and three-milk) versions, both beautifully balanced little farmhouse delights. Amarelo da Beira Baixa, a very traditional Portuguese cheese made from sheep's and goat's milk, is also exemplary of this attractive mixed-milk balance, as is the Spanish (Queso de la) Peral, made from cow's milk with sheep's milk cream added. The bottom line: Mixed-milk cheeses possess full-flavor profiles (see chapter 4), even when made from pasteurized milk.

"SHEEP'S MILK MAKES THE BEST CHEESE"

In making professional judgments and expert recommendations, it's important first to disclose one's personal biases and preferences. I like strong-tasting, aged cheeses—many of them washed-rind stinkers; others big, hard, old-fashioned mouthwatering, lip-smacking mountain types. I like cheeses with barnyardy aromas and gamey flavors. In case you hadn't already guessed, this means I really like sheep's milk cheeses. Probably the first cheese mantra I ever chanted

was "Sheep's milk makes the best cheese." Here are some of the reasons why.

- I like its primordial character, its evocation of subconscious, collective memory; sheep's milk cheeses strike me as being more ancient and elemental than other types.
- Sheep's milk is more concentrated—it has a higher percentage of solids and is therefore particularly suited for cheesemaking.
- It is very versatile and yields many excellent, beautifully balanced cheeses.
- It has more beneficial fatty acids than other milks; this includes conjugated linoleic acid.
- Even though sheep's milk has more fats than the other milks, its fat globules are small,

making it (and resulting cheeses) easier to digest.

- Sheep's milk cheeses pair with a larger number and broader range of wines and other beverages than cow's or goat's milk cheeses.
- Sheep's milk tolerates heat treatment—pasteurization or thermization—relatively well; the texture of its cheeses doesn't suffer as much as goat's.
- It also tolerates freezing better.
- Firm sheep's milk cheeses don't mind being encased in plastic wrap as much as other types.
- Washed-rind sheep's milk cheeses won't become as gamey or as fetid as quickly as goat cheeses.
- Pasteurized-milk sheep cheeses are longer-lived than their goat and cow counterparts.

MILK COMPOSITION, FROM BREED TO BREED

While the extent to which breed distinctions affect cheese results is an open question, we do know there are both quantitative and qualitative differences in milk composition, which definitely affect cheesemaking strategies.

Quantitative Differences

Just as between species, milk solids can vary from breed to breed. Jersey cow's milk, for example, has a higher solid content than Holstein milk; likewise, Nubian goats produce milk with more solids than their cousins, the Swiss, which are the biggest producers by volume. The levels of protein and fat also vary by breed as does their ratio, which is very important to some basic cheesemaking decisions.

Qualitative Differences

Once again—as among species—there are qualitative differences in milk from one breed to the next, starting with the size of the fat globules. Larger fat globules don't break down as quickly, which can lead to problems with oxidation, potentially contributing "off" flavors to a cheese. Younger cheeses don't suffer as much from this; some of the aged ones, particularly the blues, often do.

At Jasper Hill Farm, the Kehler Brothers, Mateo and Andy, make all of their cheeses, which include blues and washed-rind types, from the milk of their Ayrshire cows. Ayrshire milk has relatively small fat globules. Jersey milk, by comparison, has larger globules and creamier character, which is why it runs a greater risk of turning rancid or bitter. (Think fresh butter, with no preservatives.) For this reason, Jersey milk is a better fit for the more luscious, softer cheeses and/or the younger washed-rind ones.

ANCIENT AND TRADITIONAL BREEDS

On your trek through the world of fine cheeses, which would normally begin in the European hinterlands, you'd come across many ancient breeds with local place-names—Saanen goats, Simmental, Ayrshire, and Jersey cows among them.

In ancient cheesemaking regions, each village or appellation had a typical breed. A cow in one village was known to have a certain look—brownish red, say, with short horns. Meanwhile, in another village, just 10 or 15 kilometers away in the next valley, the cows didn't look the same and had at least a few of their own different traits. A cow is a cow is a cow, you might say. Yet without such a rich tapestry of local breeds and variations, the wide variety of indigenous cheeses, with the potential for distinction and greatness, would not be impossible.

In Europe, breed was never all that much of an issue because there was so little exchange between localities and because crossbreeding was not common practice. We asked Caroline Hostettler how breed differences impacted the great Swiss cheeses she's introduced to the United States (see chapter 14). At first she drew a blank. Perhaps it was like asking Escoffier what kind of butter he used in his cooking. No doubt he would have replied, *"But, of course, I use the best fresh butter from the farm down the road!"* Said Caroline, "I don't know whether it's specific to Switzerland or

"We're milking Ayrshires because they have small fat globules. A lot of American artisanal cheese producers are using Jersey milk, which has large fat globules. They are a butter and cream cow, basically bred over hundreds and hundreds of generations to produce fat. Small fat globules break down in a simple and predictable fashion. The biochemical process of breaking down a large fat globule is more complex. It takes longer and it's not necessarily as certain what direction a cheese may take."

MATEO KEHLER, JASPER HILL FARM

HOW MUCH DIFFERENCE DO THEY MAKE?

An interesting subject for discussion among cheese people is how much of cheese character is attributable to each of the fundamental factors—species, breed, *terroir,* feed, and so forth (not to mention the cheesemaking recipe . . .). Many experts maintain breed is of primary importance; others argue it's much more important what you feed the animals. Dairy scientists and cheese experts are perhaps just beginning to scratch the surface as to the relative significance of each of these factors.

Mike Gingrich is proprietor of Uplands Cheese Company in Wisconsin, producers of the award-winning Pleasant Ridge Reserve. He started crossbreeding his cows in the early 1990s and now has a very mixed herd with strains of Holstein, Jersey, Brown Swiss, Ayrshire, Normande, Tarenvtaise, Abondance, New Zealand Friesian, and New Zealand Jersey; there are no purebreds. We asked Mike to weigh in on the feed versus breed debate, and he came down about 80 percent to 20 percent in favor of feed: "When the pastures are in good condition, we get great milk for cheesemaking. I don't think the breed has much impact . . . I have tasted great cheese from Holsteins and bad cheese from Jerseys as well as vice versa. I would put my money on the pasture quality much more than breed differences."

We might quibble with Mike's downplaying of breed. If the feed is responsible for 70 or 80 percent of cheese character, then the remaining 20 or 30 percent, attributable to other factors, including animal type, may be the very part responsible for some of the most interesting distinctions.

Attempting to determine the significance of each of the many variables of cheesemaking is "immeasurably complex" (my colleague Peter Kindel's phrase). All else being equal, do different species or breeds produce different aromatics in their milk, which in turn vary the aroma and flavor profiles in their cheeses? Do different breeds, when "free-grazing," make different food choices and if so how are they reflected in the cheeses? I think these are interesting questions, worthy of investigtation and debate among connoisseurs.

Mike and Carol Gingrich survey their pastures and herd.

to Europe or to old cheese-producing cultures in general, but we don't really talk about breeds as much as is done here in the U.S." She went on to explain there are three main traditional breeds of cow in Switzerland, which are referred to by various different names in the various local dialects (see sidebar, page 124).

This ingrained concept of local breeds does not necessarily exist in America, where dairy culture was introduced much later in history and where all the means of production (the people and the animals) were imported. Perhaps U.S. cheese producers are in the middle of discovering which breeds work best in which locations, just as our winemakers did with traditional European grape varietals in the 1960s and '70s. No doubt we can look forward to many more great original American cheeses as our artisans hit a stride

HOW BREED AFFECTS CHEESEMAKING DECISIONS

One way cheesemakers know a breed's milk is well suited for making a certain type of cheese is by looking at values for what is called the protein-to-fat (P/F) ratio in different milks. They establish targets for percentage of fat in dry matter (FDM) in different cheese types and calibrate the P/F ratios in the milk with those targets.

The more fat there is in the milk, the less its curds can expel whey and take up salt. In other words, a lower P/F ratio (relatively less protein and more fat) will result in a cheese with more moisture and less salt. Milk with lower P/F ratios should be used for the softer, bloomy rind types whereas the higher P/F milk is generally used to produce harder, more aged types. As the milk composition differs from breed to breed (or season to season), the cheesemaker has a choice either to adjust his or her recipe or make a different type of cheese.

Average P/F ratios in the milks of three different common breeds of dairy cow are as follows: Jersey, 0.74; Ayrshire, 0.87; Friesian, 0.96 to 0.81. Marc Druart, cheesemaker at the Vermont Institute for Artisan Cheese (VIAC), gave us the following corresponding values for cheese types: Brie, 0.86; Gouda, 1.07; Cheddar, 0.91. So, according to these numbers, Ayrshire cow milk would be a good material for making Brie-type cheeses whereas Friesian would be better for Cheddar types.

Marc also cited these target values: Soft, bloomy-rind cheeses such as Brie and Camembert require 50 percent or greater FDM, which results from a P/F ratio in the milk of 0.85 or less; Cheddar-type cheeses require 50.8 percent or more FDM, which results from milk with a P/F ratio of 0.91; Gouda-style cheeses require FDM of 46 percent or more, resulting from a P/F ratio of 1.1. (Note: When we say "require" here we are referring to the U.S. Federal Code of Regulations standards of identity for cheeses; European DOP rules defining and regulating cheese types are even more specific.)

in expressing *terroir* through appropriate choices, not only of cheesemaking recipe but also animal and breed.

One way of preserving breed distinctions is to build them into appellation legislation. When local culture ruled, there was no need to codify or enforce these distinctions. With the political centralization of eighteenth-century Europe, followed by the Industrial Revolution, distinctions among traditional local products were threatened. Throughout the twentieth century, to salvage them, many had to be protected by enacting codified regulations.

The paradigmatic French AOC guidelines are very specific regarding the breeds employed in producing most of its protected foods. Some of the other cheese-producing EU countries have followed suit. You can peruse examples of this by visiting the websites of the AOC's governing body, the Institut National des Appélations d'Origine (www.inao.gouv.fr). I find this sort of specificity fascinating. Learning the breeds of animal used to produce certain fine cheeses—and knowing the traits they impart—is an interesting branch of connoisseurship. Wine geeks love to talk about varietals, so why shouldn't cheese nerds discuss the finer points of animal breeds?

BREED AND CHEESE CHARACTER

Mozzarella di bufala is an example of a very famous and widely commercialized cheese where the authentic version is very much defined by a specific breed of animal: the beautiful, horned *bufala*, which is believed to be related to the water buffaloes of India. This breed is raised in two well-defined zones of southern Italy. Their creamy, rich milk makes for a fuller, nuttier-tasting version of this fresh pulled-curd (*pasta filata*) delicacy. If you taste the real thing alongside an industrial version, the difference is obvious.

Most modern cheeses don't have such an overtly identified connection to the animal breed as buffalo mozzarella. This clear and extant (surviving) cause-and-effect, though, raises the question of what other cheeses may have lost some of their unique character-

HAPPY LITTLE GOATS, GREAT CHEESE

One of my favorite farmstead cheesemaking outfits in Oregon is Gianaclis Caldwell's Pholia Farm. Her Nigerian Dwarf goats produce milk relatively high in both protein and butterfat, although in fairly low quantities. Since it's more sheep-like than other goat's milk, it yields cheeses better suited for aging and less for fresh varieties. This would account for the nuttiness in Pholia's cheeses, a signature flavor usually associated with sheep cheeses. Gianaclis's Elk Mountain Tomme won Best in Show in the amateur division of the 2005 American Dairy Goat Association awards, for which I was the aesthetic judge. The technical judge, Dr. Scott Rankin, from the University of Wisconsin, and I agreed this was a masterfully crafted cheese and that Gianaclis was a cheesemaker to watch.

Was something inherent in the Nigerian Dwarf breed and its milk responsible for this spectacular cheese? One has to credit Gianaclis's skills as a cheesemaker and also as a goat farmer. Her dairy is surrounded by forests, where she encourages her does to browse and make their own plant food choices. I have no doubt their free ranging makes a considerable difference in the character of the milk. But I'm equally convinced the Nigerian Dwarf breed itself contributes to the milk and cheese quality—and I strongly doubt she'd be able to produce the same delicious cheese from Alpines, LaManchas, or Saanens alone.

Gianaclis Caldwell and a Nigerian Dwarf goat.

istics and distinctions once the permissible production zone for the milk of their traditional breed was expanded way past its old boundaries. This happened to Roquefort; for a time, milk of the Lacaune breed from as far away as Corsica was allowed. Then its AOC regulations were tightened. How much of its authenticity was lost and regained? We may never know, but in general it is reassuring to see traditions being renewed and breed distinctions being understood, acknowledged, and put into practice.

Here are some other cheeses famously associated with traditional breeds.

LAGUIOLE—The great French cheese was traditionally only made with milk from the Aubrac cow. This is an ancient breed—a large, muscular, rustic-looking animal (with the appearance of an ox or working steer), light brown or tan, hearty and sure footed, with long horns. It's raised in the mountains of the Massif Central of southern France and has a relatively low milk yield. Now, production of Laguiole has shifted almost exclusively to the milk of higher-yielding breeds such as Holstein-Friesian and Pie-Rouge-de-l'Est. It's my understanding the Aubrac milk was sweeter and more concentrated so likely the cheese's flavor profile has become less rich and well rounded.

SALERS—Like the Abondance, this one is both an ancient breed and a cheese name; it is closely associated the Cantal region of the Auvergne around the town of Salers, where 7,000-year-old cave drawings of these animals were discovered. They are big, sturdy, horned, long haired, and well adapted to the cold winters and hot, dry summers of their original homeland. Because of its build and its dark red or mahogany color, the breed is believed to be related to the Egyptian red cattle, pictured in ancient hierglyphs.

ROVES DES GARRIGUES—A very traditional fresh goat's milk cheese, it is made from the milk of the Roves breed of goats that roams the sparse Garrigue region of southern France. The breed features picturesque curved horns and produces only about 2 liters of milk per day, making it more concentrated and extra creamy. In the cheese, you taste a whiff of the wild herbs—thyme, rosemary, lavender, citronelle, and others—upon which those hearty little goats feasted. To me, it's among the best modern traditional cheeses to illustrate the importance of a specific animal breed.

"In Switzerland, the mountainous geography plays a very important role in how cheeses are designed. You couldn't just go over the hill and buy red apples when all the apples in your valley were green. It was too much of an effort. That's why we've always produced these big aged cheeses, sturdy, very easy to handle and keep. You have to deal with what you have. We still have that mentality."

CAROLINE HOSTETTLER,
SWISS CHEESE IMPORTER

SWISS COWS

TRADITIONAL BREEDS

FRIBOURGEOIS—Black and white, native to western Switzerland, and historically providing the milk for Gruyère and Vacherin Fribourgeois, among other prominent Swiss delicacies. Cattle-breeding experts consider this variation extinct since there are no longer any purebred descendants of local strains. The breed has essentially been merged into the Holstein-Friesian gene pool, becoming simply the Swiss version of the common black-and-white milk cow.

SIMMENTAL—The most common breed in Switzerland, light reddish brown and white in color, found all over the central part of the country.

BROWN COW—Known as the Brown Swiss in other countries, this sturdy, horned breed is brownish gray in color and similar to the Italian so-called Red Cow (*vacca rossa*) breed, also known as Reggiana or Formentina, which is associated with Parmigiano-Reggiano. The Brown Swiss is found all over Switzerland but primarily in the central and eastern zones and is associated with production of very ancient and traditional cheeses such as Sbrinz.

FACTORS FOR CHOOSING A BREED

- Milk production (quantity)
- Milk quality (character)
- Heartiness (is the breed appropriate for or can it adapt to the local environment?)
- Reproductive cycle
- Lactation period
- Requirements for care (what do the animals want/need?)

IBORES—This is another very traditional "national treasure" of a goat cheese, but it's from Spain, not France. There are three ancient breeds of goats in the Extremadura providing milk for the production of Ibores: the Serrana, the Verata, and the Retinta, the latter two of which are on the wane—if not actually on the "endangered" list.

CHOICE OF BREEDS

Farmhouse cheese producers are close to their animals, literally and figuratively, and they consciously and carefully choose the breed (or mix of breeds) for their herds. The two main factors to consider: what type of animal is appropriate for their particular farm environment and what the animals are like to work with. If you talk to dairy farmers, you'll very often hear them praise the breeds they've chosen, parsing their choices in terms of business or aesthetic considerations or even personal preferences.

As we learned in chapter 2, the Great American Cheese Renaissance was jump-started by a group of dynamic young goat cheese producers in the late 1970s and early 1980s. (Judy Schad, Allison Hooper, Mary Keehn, and Pierre Kolisch, all still very active in the business, were among them.) Many of these cheese pioneers had become prize-winning breeders long before they ever contemplated curdling a vat of fresh milk. At first, many of them raised goats as a hobby or a way to supply family and friends with the best, cleanest, healthiest milk. A few of them realized they'd found

COMMON FRENCH BREEDS

In most great cheesemaking regions, modern dairy animals are descended from distinct ancient breeds. Nowadays, there are many crossbreeds and fewer, if any, purebreds. Some dairy farmers and breeders strive to keep the old breeds and distinctions alive. Here is the lay of the land in France.

Sheep

BASCO-BÉARNAISE—This is the traditional Basque breed from the Pyrénées.

MANECH—Identifiable by their black or red heads, both this and the Basco-Béarnaise are native to the western Pyrénées; the milk of these two breeds is the basis for the Ossau-Iraty family of cheeses.

LACAUNE—The most common breed in France and one that has undergone the most genetic improvement through selective breeding for milk production and quality. Lacaune sheep are now found all over France, on Corsica, and also in Portugal. Among the most prominent cheeses made from their milk: Roquefort in the Massif Central; Brin d'Amour and Fleur de Maquis in Corsica; and Azeitão in Portugal. Compared with the ubiquitous East Friesian sheep breed, Lacaune milk has higher solid content, but the ewes produce less of it.

Goats

POITEVINE—From the region of western France known as Poitu-Charente, this is the original and ancient breed for production of many Loire Valley chèvres.

ALPINE—Also known as Chamoisée or Saanen, they are the most common breed in the Alps and other eastern mountain regions. Alpines are associated with such fine cheeses as Persillé de Tignes and Chevrotin des Aravis.

ROVE—A roaming, mountain breed originally from Provence in the southeast and responsible for one of France's most distinguished local cheese, Roves des Garrigues (see page 123).

PYRÉNÉEAN—The ancient (and now very rare) breed from the Pyrénées; provides the milk for the goat's milk version of Le Moulis and also for a popular, common regional cheese, Tomme de Chèvre.

Cows

NORMANDE—This is the traditional butter and cheese dairying breed from Normandy, identifiable by the large brown spots and freckles on its coat and most commonly associated with Camembert.

MONTBÉLIARDE—Known for its white head and large brownish red spots or splotches on its body, this breed is originally from the mountainous Franche-Comté region of eastern France and provides the milk for two classic cheeses, Comté and Vacherin Mont d'Or.

FRIESIAN—This is the most common dairy cow in France—and just about anywhere else, for that matter—with its black-and-white coat; originally from northern Holland, near Holstein, Germany, which is why it's also known as the Holstein or Holstein-Friesian breed. It is considered the world's highest yielding and has pretty much become *the* generic milk cow for our entire planet. As such, you can expect almost any cheese to be made from its milk.

OTHER BREEDS: Tarentaise (or Tarine); Abondance; Rouge Flamande; Salers; Vosgienne. Most of these less-common breeds are ancient ones associated with particular regions and/or cheeses. The Vosgienne, for example, is from Alsace and was the source for traditional Munster-Geromé cheeses. The brown to light brown colored Tarentaise and the brown Abondance are hearty mountain breeds of the western Alps, known for providing the milk for such famous alpage cheeses as Beaufort and, naturally, Abondance.

a vocation. The foundations of their success as cheesemakers were laid via selection and breeding.

There are as many interesting individual sagas and adventures as there are successful, independent cheese artisans today. Through

THE SHEEP AND THEIR CHEESES

I think of the sheep breeds of Spain and Portugal as more locally oriented, their populations concentrated in their native regions, and also quite closely associated with specific traditional cheeses. Here is a sampling.

AWASSI: Cabuérniga (from Cantabria)

MANCHEGA: Manchego

LAXTA AND CARRANZANA: Idiazábal

CHURRA OR CASTELLANA: Castellano, Pata de Mulo, Zamorano

MERINA, ENTREFINA, AND OTHERS: Torta del Casar

TALAVERANA: Oropesa (from Castilla–LaMancha)

CHURRA DE TERRA QUENTE (TERRINCHA): Queijo Terrincha

BORDALEIRA DA SERRA DA ESTRELA: Queijo Serra da Estrela

each of them runs the theme of a special affinity for their animals and a knack for care and husbandry. Cheese farmers all share a deep respect and also a great deal of affection for their milk-producing mammalian partners. Dairy cows are big, frequently dirty, needy animals, but they are also gentle, noble, compliant, and highly productive—as long as you treat them well. Always remember the cheese mantra: "Happy cows make good milk" (and don't forget, the same is true for goats and sheep).

BREEDING FOR QUALITY

Dairy farmers through the ages have practiced selective breeding for traits including heartiness, milk quality (higher concentrations of fats and proteins), milk yield (quantity), and personality or temperament. The second priority, after the herd's health and happiness, is milk quality. Quantity considerations aren't initial priorities, though economic pressures may force them into play and this can lead to compromises.

Artisanal cheese farmers have shown they can selectively breed their animals to produce more and better levels of fundamental components in their milk (fat, protein, lactose) without compromising their ideals, but it can be a tricky tightrope to walk. Selective breeding can be achieved with or without artificial insemination; the technique does afford more control and assurance of improvement. At Cato Corner Farm, Elizabeth MacAlister and Mark Gillman diversified their Jersey herd's gene pool by importing specific strains from regions of Denmark and Australia where creamy, rich milk from pasture-grazing cows was prevalent and introduced them to their herd via artificial insemination, a good example of a rustic family outfit using modern dairy science to improve its cheesemaking potential.

For any sustainable farming operation, keeping the herd healthy and productive is top priority. Loss of milk output owing to sick animals is a major drain in dairying. On a family farm, one animal prone to mastitis whose milk has to be discarded for fear of tainting an entire vat is problematic. Large industrial farms often overwork their cows, overloading their systems with formula feed, preemptive medications, and BST, usurping their metabolisms and shortening their life spans.

Among the key questions about any animal husbandry operation, beyond whether it is treating its herd responsibly and compassionately, is whether it is breeding for quality or efficiency. These two goals may not automatically come into conflict, but they certainly can. Do the ideals of maintaining distinct character and guaranteeing the survival of traditional breeds contradict modern farm economics? Is it necessary to create modern crossbreeds that are hardier and/or yield more milk per animal per day, at the risk of sacrificing traditional distinctions and values, in order to survive as a dairy business? I think it's a good thing for cheese connoisseurs to research, think about, and discuss these issues.

Applying the wine analogy again, do higher-yielding breeds, as with higher-yielding grapevines, produce less concentrated, less flavorful milk with less potential for crafting superior cheeses? Can a cheesemaker "make up for" any such compromises via clever manipulations of the recipe? Most dairy-farming experts and cheese producers will agree that crossbreeding is mainly practiced for economic reasons. The high cost of quality milk is the biggest expense in making artisanal cheese. Is it possible for the traditional farmstead to increase milk production and cheese output in order to make more money without sacrificing quality? In the short term, perhaps. But each operation has its limits.

CROSSBREEDING

One of the ways ancient cheese cultures are eroded is by crossbreeding. Newer, more efficient dairy animals from mixed genetic strains are substituted for the original breed used to make a cheese. Once upon a time, a cow was a cow, a sheep was a sheep, and so forth. The option of altering a breed, other than by basic selective breeding from within a herd, simply did not exist. Things have changed. Artificial insemination and genetic science are commonly used, but they can easily compromise the resulting milk, blurring distinctions and wiping out character.

If dairy farms must sell more milk to survive and if genetic manipulation offers increased production, who can fault them for using it? The unfortunate side effect is that it may threaten the very existence of fine artisanal cheeses, dragging them, inch by inch, pint by pint, toward uniformity.

In France, suppliers of cheesemaking milk are replacing traditional local breeds such as the Vosgienne, Salers, and Normande with higher-yielding breeds such as the ubiquitous Holstein-Friesian. When you have a cheese that's been great for 1,000 years

U.S. DAIRY BREEDS

Here are the main dairy breeds in the United States. (Of course, there are many crossbreeds as well as a few less-common ones in use, for example, the Nigerian Dwarf goats; see page 122.)

COWS: Ayrshire, Brown Swiss, Guernsey, Jersey, Holstein (aka Friesian or Holstein-Friesian), Milking Shorthorn

SHEEP: East Friesian, Lacaune

GOATS: Alpine, LaMancha, Nubian, Oberhasli, Saanen, Toggenburg

Janine Putnam with the herd of Jersey cows at Thistle Hill Farm.

PREFERRED ★ BREEDS ★

JUDY'S GOATS

We asked Judy Schad, one of my favorite cheese people and among America's farmstead goat pioneers, about her choice of breeds. Here's what she said.

"We have Alpines, Saanens, and some crosses. We started with Alpines because they were beautiful and we loved their outgoing personalities. They have also proven to be the strongest breed we've worked with: They have longevity, good mothering instincts, strong characters, and long lactations. All this adds up to a very interesting animal to say 'good morning' to each day. Saanens are also beautiful, strong animals, not the fighters that Alpines are and so not as long lived, but wonderful personalities. Beyond just the breeds however, we have cultivated particular bloodlines and have selected for a flavor profile in our milk.

"I think our milk is clean and sweet. We drink and cook with it. It is not exceptionally high in butterfat, which is perfect for the flavor profile we want.

"There are a few traits that make the other breeds bad choices for us. We've had Nubians who have proven not to be the best mothers, do not have long lactations, and are prone to get fat. Fat is a real problem in dairy animals and the Nubians have almost culled themselves out of the herd because of this tendency to convert food to body fat rather than milk. If they go into their dry period and pregnancy with a lot of extra body fat, they are prone to ketosis and other metabolic diseases of pregnancy. This in combination with their tendency to produce multiple kids is sort of the 'kiss o' death.' Plus they have the loudest mouths of any of the breeds.

and you switch breeds, it would seem to me you are inviting disaster. The French Montbéliard cow breed, used to make mountain cheeses such Comté, yields an average of 7,500 kilograms of milk per year. At a recent dairy show in Québec, an Ayrshire breed was trumpeted as a shining example of milk production for yielding double that. The latter might represent a boon if you're looking to supply the commodity milk market, but not necessarily for artisan cheesemaking. Another example: The old Reggiana breed of Red Cow has been almost entirely replaced by higher-yielding Holstein-Friesians in production of DOP Parmigiano-Reggiano. Many experts—some of them people involved in the Parmesan consortium's marketing efforts—claim it doesn't make a difference. But beyond traditional local character, what else are we sacrificing in resorting to alternative breeds?

BEYOND ECONOMICS

So many variables come into play in determining cheese quality and character, and I find it impossible to entirely dismiss any one of them. As we've learned, how much of a contribution breed makes to the overall quality and character of a cheese is open to speculation. Even the most exacting of connoisseurs might have a tough time picking out much of a difference between a Parmigiano-Reggiano made from Red Cow milk and one made from Friesian. Is the premium you pay for the Red Cow Parm worth it? Perhaps not. But the answer may be different for other cheeses and/or in other circumstances.

Beyond economics and aesthetics, there are ethical, moral, and philosophical issues. Preserving a particular breed may mean rescuing that breed from extinction. Do we commit to preserving a breed "merely" for the sake of tradition or to maintain biodiversity, an ideal of the Slow Food and real-cheese movements? There are economic, political, and historical pressures both for and against the preservation of breeds and cheeses. Regardless, we must ask whether the market cares enough to sustain a more esoteric cheese, made from the milk of a local, traditional, and possibly threatened breed, especially if it costs more. I certainly hope so, although, unfortunately, this does not always appear to be the case.

Janice and Larry Neilson's "Albion" goats: They are a cross between Alpines and Nubians created by specialized breeding at Fraga Farm.

TASTING PLATES

Let's put this species and breed knowledge into practice with some tastings. When I'm sampling a cheese of noble pedigree, I'll often ponder which of its special traits come from species and breed. Short of scientific evidence of these connections, tasting is a connoisseur's way of amassing "empirical proof." Here are some suggested comparisons—the best way to highlight differences—illustrating some of the animal-derived distinctions among cheeses.

Species Characteristics and Differences

LE MOULIS, a firm, pressed farmhouse cheese from the French Pyrénées, provides an excellent comparison tasting, as it comes in cow's, sheep's, and goat's milk versions. (There are some Dutch Gouda styles made with cow's and goat's milk, as well as the occasional goat Cheddar, which offer clear contrasts; Le Moulis is a rare type in offering variations from all three species.)

Another interesting species comparison would be between CASHEL BLUE and CROZIER BLUE. The Grubb family, from Beechmount Farm, in County Tipperary, Ireland, had been making

GOAT BREEDING FOR QUALITY AT REDWOOD HILL FARM

Jennifer Bice has been a committed goat breeder since she started working at her family's Redwood Hill Farm, Sonoma County, California, in 1968. She took over in 1978 and is among our best-known cheese artisans and a spokesperson for the movement. Redwood Hill is billed as the first certified humane goat dairy in the United States through an organization called Humane Farm Animal Care, which started its program in 2003. The farm has a herd of about 350 goats, which includes purebred Nubians, Alpines, Saanens, and LaManchas (registered with the American Dairy Goat Association). Redwood Hill's animals are encouraged to graze local rocky pastures and forests, but they are also kept sheltered from the wind and rain as needed. (Dairy goats like to roam, but unlike most sheep and many cow breeds, they do not tolerate staying out in stormy weather.)

Jennifer Bice, for one, doesn't buy into the financially expedient practice of crossbreeding. She keeps all four breeds she employs separate, paying close attention to their genetic strains and selectively breeding to improve their respective milk qualities. The Saanens in her herd are high-volume, low-solid producers. Nubians are considered the "Jersey of goats" for their milk's high protein and butterfat content. It contributes outstanding flavors and, like that of Jersey cows, a creamy mouth feel to the mix. The LaManchas' milk values are similar to the Nubians', while the Alpines' are in the midrange. All four milks are combined for cheesemaking, creating balance and a best-of-all-worlds scenario.

Jennifer Bice with one of her prize-winning Alpine goats.

Cashel Blue from the milk of their Holstein Friesian cows since 1984. In the early 1990s, two of their nephews started a small flock of Friesian sheep nearby; by the end of the decade, they had developed an award-winning sheep's milk blue, the Crozier.

Among the great Swiss cheeses, you can find a few interesting species comparisons. Try STANSER RÖTELI (AKA INNERSCHWEIZER WEICHER), a washed-rind, raw cow's milk Reblochon-style cheese from Josef Barmettler, alongside an INNERSCHWEIZER SCHAFKÄSE (AKA STANSER SCHAF REBLOCHON), which is a similar cheese from the same producer made with raw sheep's milk. Another fun Swiss comparison is between the cow's milk BERGFICHTE (formerly Krümmenswiler Försterkäse) and the goat's milk HOLZIGE GEISS, both from the same producer, Willy Schmid.

Typical "Species Types"

Each of these cheeses represent a distinct type that highlights particular species traits. (You can pick four to six of them to create a tasting plate; more on how to compose sequences in chapter 11.)

- Loire Valley chèvre
- Thistle-renneted Iberian sheep's milk: Torta del Casar, Queso de la Serena
- Farmhouse-style raw cow's milk bloomy-rind such as Constant Bliss or some other either Brie- or Camembert-style cheese
- Pressed sheep's milk: Ossau-Iraty, Berkswell, Spenwood
- Washed-rind *B. linens* ripened cow's milk, e.g., Durrus
- Traditional British aged cow's milk farmhouse such as Cheddar or Lancashire
- Hard aged Alpine cow's milk such as Comté or Gruyère
- Mold-ripened goat's milk such as Monte Enebro
- Superior raw-milk blue such as Rogue River (cow) or Roquefort (sheep), possibly both, for comparison

A Brown Swiss cow at Shelburne Farms, Vermont.

Breed Characteristics and Differences

Two lovely traditional Portuguese sheep's milk cheeses provide a good introduction to tasting for breed comparisons: SERRA DA ESTRELA, which comes exclusively from Bordeleira ewes, and SERPA, which is almost always from the Merina breed. While both are rustic Iberians, the Serra is quite buttery, smooth, and approachable, as compared to the Serpa, which is "rougher" and gamey, with a bigger finish. I attribute the contrasts partly to breed and partly to *terroir*, the Serpa being from a more rugged, isolated area of southeastern Portugal.

Three quite similar Spanish hard, pressed sheep's milk classics provide another interesting comparison: RONCAL, from the Laxta and Aragonesa breeds; ZAMORANO, from the Churra or Castellana; and MANCHEGO, from the Manchega.

Thistle Hill Farm's TARENTAISE, made from 100 percent Jersey cow's milk, makes for an interesting comparison to another modern American classic in the same genre, Uplands Cheese Co.'s PLEASANT RIDGE RESERVE, which comes from the milk of a mixed herd. Jersey cow milk has always intrigued me from a tasting perspective. I've consistently detected a pleasant acidic flavor note in its cheeses, which I call the Jersey tang. See if you can detect it in the Tarentaise and also in Blythedale Farms' JERSEY BLUE, comparing it to GREAT HILL BLUE, which is made from a blend of Holstein and Jersey milk.

Three Vermont artisanal Cheddars also offer a good cow-breed comparison: SHELBURNE FARMS' CHEDDAR, from its herd of Brown Swiss; CABOT CLOTHBOUND RESERVE CHEDDAR, from a mixed herd of Jerseys, Holsteins, and Guernseys; and GRAFTON CLOTHBOUND CHEDDAR, from an all-Jersey herd.

For an interesting goat-breed comparison, try the ELK MOUNTAIN TOMME from Gianaclis Caldwell's Nigerian Dwarf ewes at Pholia Farm, alongside ST. OLGA, a similar firm, *tomme*-style, lightly washed cheese, made from the milk of Pat Morford's herd of Alpines at Three Ring Farm, both in Oregon. You could make it a crowd by adding Judy Schad's OLD KENTUCKY TOMME from the mixed herd at Capriole in southern Indiana.

CHAPTER REVIEW

Around the Barnyard: Species and Breeds

- ☐ Cow's and goat's milk average about 12 percent solids; sheep's milk has about 50 percent more fats and proteins, increasing its total solids to about 19 percent.
- ☐ The P/F ratios in milk, largely determined by species and breed, are significant in choosing cheesemaking recipes and strategies.
- ☐ Milk character, partially determined by species and breed, combines with *terroir* and feed to determine milk composition.
- ☐ Cheesemaking experts differ on the question of the relative significance of breed versus feed.
- ☐ Differences in milk composition attributable to species and breed include percentage of short-chain fatty acids and size of fat globules.
- ☐ Traditional breeds and cheeses often share place-names from ancient cheesemaking regions; Manchego, Salers, and Abondance are good examples.
- ☐ Breed requirements are often part of cheese appellation-designation laws.
- ☐ Artisanal cheese farmers practice selective breeding for quality—not quantity—of milk, and most of them are also careful to maintain breed distinctions.
- ☐ Crossbreeding is done mostly for economic reasons and can potentially damage the cause of real cheeses.

OPPOSITE: *From the bottom: Chabichou de Poitu; Evora; Constant Bliss; Berkswell; Dorset; Pleasant Ridge Reserve; Roquefort (Carles).*

CHAPTER 7

RAW MILK
AND REAL CHEESE

I GET REALLY RILED UP—I MEAN BORDERLINE FURIOUS—ABOUT ALL THE assaults on the integrity of real cheese and the repeated injustices done to raw-milk production. There have certainly been too many of these in recent times. I consider them threats not only to my livelihood and beliefs but, more important, to the many artisans who work so hard making fine cheeses the right way. It doesn't take much to envision the demise of our good little cottage industry.

Raw-milk production is one of the foremost "hot-button issues" pertaining to cheese. While I can't say there aren't reasonable concerns with raw milk itself, I will state with utmost certainty that any efforts to ban, curtail, or discredit legitimate raw-milk cheeses can ultimately be traced back to fear, bad science, and a shortage of clear, rational discourse. The U.S. government bans all raw-milk cheeses, imported or domestic, if they're aged less than 60 days—a dubious regulation. Furthermore, we've seen misapplications of this and other rules as well as overzealous enforcement: Cheeses have been held up at U.S. ports of entry and border crossings; foreign cheese types, brands, and producers have been blacklisted. Thousands of pounds of fine cheeses have been damaged or destroyed. It's almost criminal.

Azeitão is a great raw-milk artisanal cheese—complex, expressive of terroir, and full of aroma, texture, and flavor. (See also page 108.)

A CLEAR DEFINITION

While we're at it, why not define raw-milk cheese? I like the wording proposed by the Raw Milk Cheesemakers Association (RMCA; our U.S. equivalent to Britain's Specialist Cheese Makers Association): "cheese produced from milk that, prior to setting the curd, has not been heated above the temperature of the milk at the time of milking." Of course, you could simplify matters by calling raw-milk cheese "any cheese made from nonpasteurized milk." The lengthier RMCA definition, however, does not allow for *any* type of heat treatment, which is why I prefer it.

Any cheesemaking environment requires careful sanitary precautions.

When the U.S. Customs and Border Control puts a halt to honest, legal international cheese commerce for spurious reasons, it's frustrating, embarrassing, and makes us look ignorant. I shouldn't have to buy a ticket to Paris if I want to enjoy a bite of a genuine raw-milk Camembert or any number of other young, "uncompromised" cheeses. Missing out on the genuine Loire Valley chèvres is particularly deplorable. Our own dairies should be able to make such cheeses, too. Forced to choose between a cheese made with raw or pasteurized milk, I'll take mine "living" over "barely breathing."

Thanks to the raw-milk cheese lobby, spearheaded by the Cheese of Choice Coalition, we now have a counterbalance to forces that would just as soon ban raw-milk cheese (or raw-milk anything), destroying a valuable part of our dairy culture, wiping out a tradition of ecologically sensible, sustainable agriculture.

Consumers ought to be allowed to make rational, informed choices using a scientifically based understanding of the risks. Fear is a powerful emotion and it can lead to misguided policies, especially in combination with misinformation and faulty intelligence. In this chapter, we aim to give you some accurate information about raw-milk cheese, starting with what can go wrong—with any type of cheese—if it isn't properly manufactured, delving into issues such as the effects of pasteurization and finishing with tastings to demonstrate the superiority of raw-milk cheeses.

BACKGROUND AND SCIENCE
Safety Concerns

Any farm or cheesemaking room is potentially a fertile and welcoming environment for many kinds of bacteria, most of them beneficial, a few of them not. Of the pathogenic microorganisms (aka bad bacteria) that can contaminate milk or cheese, The Big Four are *Escherichia coli, Salmonella, Staphylococcus aureas,* and *Listeria monocytogenes.*

Ideally, high-quality raw milk is made into cheese almost immediately after the animals are milked. Anytime milk is cooled and/or held in refrigerated storage tanks, there is a risk of contamination by pathogens, including psychrotropics (the scientific term for cold-loving microorganisms). In this sense, refrigeration can provide an illusory safety net, whereas the real goal is clean, quick handling of cheesemaking milk.

Pathogens (bad bacteria) are opportunistic. They will multiply wherever and whenever they find favorable conditions. Of course, the flip side of this equation is unfavorable conditions provide a defense against them. Cheese resists and/or succumbs to contamination by pathogens as a result of internal and external (aka intrinsic and extrinsic) parameters. Internal factors include moisture and acidity levels, nutrient content, and the presence of antimicrobial substances and/or competitive microflora. External safety factors include how the milk is handled and stored; how the various cheesemaking steps are managed; and how cheese is aged, packaged, and shipped for sale. Throughout the production and fulfillment chain, the two key questions are, what it is about the makeup of the developing cheese that may or may not provide a welcome home for pathogens, and what environmental factors may or may not expose it to pathogens?

Different species of bacteria and molds have very specific ranges of conditions within which they can survive and perhaps thrive. All other factors being equal, a given type of bacteria or mold may survive better with relatively low acidity, or perhaps relatively high moisture. Most prefer at least some moisture and low salinity. Salt dehydrates and creates an environment hostile to most bacteria. Milk also contains naturally occurring antimicrobial compounds—built-in defenses, if you will—which can be damaged or destroyed by pasteurization or heat treatment.

As luck (or fate or perhaps evolution) would have it, lactic acid bacteria provide another line of defense against pathogens. Most other bacteria—including various pathogens such as staphylococcus, listeria, and clostridium—have a tough time surviving in the relatively high-acid environment created by the former. By the same token, abnormally or unusually slow acidification can increase the risk of pathogen growth.

Careful handling of fresh goat's milk by Amelia Caldwell at Pholia Farm.

WHAT IS PASTEURIZATION?

The great nineteenth-century French microbiology pioneer Louis Pasteur invented pasteurization as a way to alleviate sicknesses caused by wine and milk. For traditional artisanal raw-milk cheese production, pasteurization is controversial to say the least. In any case, here are a few key definitions:

PASTEURIZATION—In its Federal Code of Regulations, the U.S. government defines pasteurization of milk as heating to a mini-

CHEESE SCIENCE

WHAT IS *LISTERIA*?

Of the Big Four pathogens, *Listeria monocytogenes* is the scariest and most dangerous: It is acknowledged as the leading cause of death from food poisoning in the United States. One of six species in the common *Listeria* genus, *L. monocytogenes* is the cause of listeriosis, an opportunistic infection that attacks mostly immunosuppressed people (e.g., the young, the old, AIDS patients, and unborn children). People with healthy immune systems usually have no problem fighting it off. Listeriosis causes flulike symptoms and can lead to meningitis. In severe cases, it has a high mortality rate compared to other food-borne illnesses.

Listeria are hearty bacteria with a relatively large survival window (the bad news). The good news is they are easily wiped out by basic sanitary measures such as washing all surfaces in the cheese production and handling environment with a solution of ammonia and/or sterilizing them with alcohol.

Of the documented cases of listeriosis between 1998 and 2008, most were traced to consumption of ready-to-eat meats and poultry products such as hot dogs and turkey deli meats. A minuscule percentage was attributed to cheeses and of these few almost all were from *queso fresco*–type cheeses produced in illegal factories (see sidebar, page 142).

FROM TOP: *Pasteurization equipment; fresh, pure raw goat's milk, a beautiful sight.*

mum of 143 degrees F for at least 30 minutes or a minimum of 161 degrees F for at least 15 seconds. The former is usually referred to as "batch" or "vat" pasteurization while the latter method is called HTST, for high temperature short-time pasteurization. Another form of pasteurization is UHT, ultra high temperature, or simply ultra-pasteurization, which involves flash heating the milk to as high as 350 degrees F for a fraction of a second. Any milk heat-treated for less than the time and temperature minimums listed above is considered raw by the U.S. Food and Drug Administration (FDA).

THERMIZATION—The European Community regulations define this as the heating of milk to a temperature between 57 and 62 degrees C (135 and 154 degrees F) for at least 15 seconds. Many American cheesemakers heat-treat their milk to 131 degrees F for between 2 and 16 seconds, but these treatments do not qualify as pasteurization under U.S. regulations. Thermization is a compromise, short of pasteurization, and it is applied in the case of many aged raw-milk cheeses in the United States.

IS RAW MILK SAFE FOR CHEESEMAKING?

This is perhaps first among many key questions deserving even-handed consideration. No doubt about it: Bacteria are scary. Naturally, people harbor a certain amount of fear of food poisoning. Even the slightest outbreak of a serious food-borne illness is enough to inflame near hysteria, especially when it receives the usual fanning by the mass media. My customers and students frequently seek reassurance about the safety of unpasteurized cheeses. There's no question that drinking raw milk can be risky, but it's probably a lot less risky than eating a raw oyster. I understand many people are scared of raw-milk products. I've even seen colleagues at work—people who know a lot about cheese and deal with it every day—allow irrational fears to creep into their decision making and fog their acceptance of real cheeses. So let's take a realistic look at the facts.

The fundamental fact is that eating raw-milk cheese is not equivalent to drinking raw milk. (If you forget everything else in this chapter, please remember this!) Viewed from a food-safety perspective, the cheesemaking process is nothing more than a series of steps aimed at preserving fermented milk in beneficial (and hopefully delicious) form. In addition to their flavor-giving properties, all those substances developed and/or introduced during cheesemaking—acids, salts, bacteria, molds—have preservative effects: they banish the pathogens and promote the "bennies."

IS RAW MILK *SAFER* FOR CHEESEMAKING?

In my view, the answer to this question is yes, on two major counts. First, raw milk retains its inherent, natural defenses. If you kill all the bacteria, including the good ones, there's more room for the bad ones to march in. A pasteurized-milk cheese, shorn of its natural defenses, is a friendlier environment for bad bacteria. Most scientists will not go so far as to make this assertion. They tend to focus much more on the problem of environmental contamination. You'll find them stressing that listeria and other pathogens can survive in the cheesemaking environment absent of proper cleaning procedures.

The second reason raw milk is likely safer for cheesemaking is it eliminates the supposed safety net of pasteurization and returns the focus to milk quality and safe handling at the outset. High-quality milk not only lowers the risk of contamination with pathogens, but it also yields better cheese. Safe handling—quick, efficient, and sanitary—ensures the raw material at least has a chance of becoming great cheese. Always remember: You can't make good cheese with lousy milk (although it's possible to make bad cheese with good milk).

DR. DONNELLY

Dairy scientists such as Dr. Cathy Donnelly, microbiologist and cheese expert at the University of Vermont, provide the voices of reason in the debate about raw-milk cheeses. We consulted Dr. Donnelly, among others, to help us explain the evidence in favor of raw-milk cheeses and to promote understanding by answering a few basic questions about safety, the effects of pasteurization, and related topics. Among her statements, during an extensive conversation about the subject of raw-milk cheeses:

"You wonder why we have to pasteurize commodity fluid milk [for the consumer mass market]: It's because of all the abuse and how we really try to push its shelf life. If you're milking that cow and not letting that milk sit, but making cheese right away, you're really reducing the risk substantially."

The official line on raw milk for cheesemaking, often repeated by government bureaucrats, is that the acknowledged risks of consuming raw milk are transferred to raw-milk cheese. We asked Professor Mary Anne Drake of North Carolina State University, microbiologist and cheese expert, whether this was true. Her reply: "No, the qualifier there is *potentially*. Potentially or theoretically, they carry the same microbial risks." She added that all the major steps of cheesemaking—acidification, drying, cooking, salting—are what help minimize the risk. But it's easy to see how taking that first assumption at face value—that raw-milk cheese is as risky as raw milk itself—might cause people to adopt an irrational stance toward real cheeses.

WHAT DOES PASTEURIZATION DO TO CHEESEMAKING MILK?

With pasteurization, there's good news and bad news. The good news is pasteurization kills the four main pathogens that can invade milk and cheese. The bad news is it kills just about everything else, including a lot of the friendly bugs without which you can't make fine cheese. As a result, beneficial microflora have to be introduced (and at times *reintroduced*) into the milk: Check out a recipe for pasteurized-milk cheese: you'll note it calls for much more starter culture—often double—than a raw-milk recipe does.

Pasteurization affects aromatic and flavor-giving compounds. In killing the milk's indigenous microflora, it damages or destroys local character, essentially canceling the expression of *terroir*. "There might be some elements that shine through if they were dramatic beforehand," says cheesemaker Cary Bryant, "but they're going to be just the residual flavors."

Many cheesemaking experts will tell you pasteurization imparts "cooked" consistency and flavors to the milk. I do know from thousands of tastings that it tends to render a cheese's texture more pasty or rubbery and also to flatten out its flavor profile.

On the strategic level, the main knock against pasteurization is it can create a false sense of security and perhaps even encourage producers to relax their vigilance vis-à-vis milk and cheese safety. The impression that zapping the milk once with high heat is some sort of guarantee is wrong.

One of my favorite passages regarding the specific ill effects of pasteurization is from Patrick Rance's *The Great British Cheese*

Book, where he quotes a four-volume study by British food scientist John Gilbert Davis: "Dr. Davis mentions, among others, the following disadvantages of pasteurization in his work *Cheese:* increased cost; encouragement to use low-quality milk; no natural ripening in the event of starter failure; poor renneting (prolonged cheesemaking); weak curd; slow drainage; inferior body and texture of cheese; insipid taste." Davis also enumerated many other potential problems with ripening and flavor development owing to the destruction of the milk's natural enzymes. When we asked Dr. Cathy Donnelly to comment on all this, she said, "I generally agree with these perspectives, especially the notion that pasteurization is used as a substitute for good-quality raw-milk production."

ASSURING CHEESE SAFETY: WHAT RESPONSIBLE CHEESEMAKERS DO

The U.S. government, strict in applying its blanket 60-day minimum aging requirement for raw-milk cheeses, ironically does not have much in the way of established enforced safety and quality standards for cheese milk. Instead, it's largely left up to the cheesemakers to take the necessary steps. What better guarantees of quality and safety could we ask for than a dedicated cheese farmer whose professional reputation and livelihood depend on keeping things clean? Cheese artisans voluntarily establish their own testing and monitoring systems for the entire milk- and cheese-producing chain, based on what are called GMPs (good manufacturing practices) and the HACCP approach.

HACCP is the acronym for Hazard Analysis Critical Control Point, a food safety system developed by Pillsbury for NASA's manned space flights in the 1960s. (Who ever said the space program was a complete waste of money?) HACCP identifies all critical points in a food's entire production and delivery process where contamination might occur; it then institutes measures to monitor, correct, and control those vulnerabilities. Cheesemakers combine the HACCP approach with microbiological screening of raw milk, environmental testing and the establishment of GMPs to ensure high-quality, safe cheese.

The top artisan cheesemakers actually set the bar higher for themselves than the government demands. Beginning with Slow Food USA's Raw Milk Presidium, which led to the formation of the Raw Milk Cheesemakers' Association, U.S. raw-milk

CHEESE SCIENCE

THE EFFECTS OF PASTEURIZATION

- Pasteurization kills potential pathogens in milk but it also kills just about everything else. (It is no guarantee of what happens next.)

- Cheesemakers employing pasteurization need to replace lost microflora in their milk by introducing more outside cultures.

- Pasteurization gives "cooked" textures and flavors to cheesemaking milk.

- Pasteurization is likely to drastically reduce, if not eliminate, local character (*terroir*) from cheese-making milk.

- Pasteurization also may present a false safety net.

DIRTY BUSINESS

THE JALISCO FIASCO

The year 1985 witnessed one of the darkest interludes in American cheese history: a serious outbreak of listeriosis. The victims were largely pregnant Hispanic women, their fetuses, babies, and young children. In the end, about 180 people got sick, and it is estimated 60 died.

This was the first *documented* incident of its kind in American history and the first time a widespread investigation involving bacteriologists, epidemiologists, and food-processing analysts was launched. The Centers for Disease Control and Prevention in Atlanta began by locating the victims, all of which were in an area of Southern California. When their consumption was examined, the common denominator turned out to be cheeses from a company called Jalisco Mexican Products, which made *queso blanco, queso fresco,*

and other Mexican-style cheeses for the regional market and also for distribution to Mexican restaurants across the country.

The company claimed to have pasteurized all of its milk, but further investigation revealed that about a third of it was left raw—and the cheesemaking environment was unsanitary. The plant was filthy, plagued with an ant infestation, among other problems. Jalisco executives were charged with a series of crimes; the CEO fled to Mexico, and one vice president served jail time.

In the end, the cause of this disaster turned out not to be raw milk but rather dirty milk—milk that was not properly selected, handled, or tested and was used to make illegal, underaged cheeses with fatal results.

Why dwell on—or even mention—this tawdry tragedy in a book purporting to celebrate fine table cheeses? Mainly as a cautionary tale but also to put things in perspective. It's exactly this type of extreme situation that not only inflames people's irrational fears about real cheeses but also has a ripple effect—more like a tsuna-

mi—on businesses throughout the industry. The minute the words *cheese* and *bacteria* become connected in the public consciousness with "fatal disease outbreak," especially in the presence of scary and not well-understood terms such as *listeria* and *listeriosis,* the damage is done.

The Jalisco fiasco documented what can go wrong if food safety guidelines are not followed. It also lent weight to the argument that in order for people to get sick or even die from cheese, there has to be a great deal of conscious wrongdoing.

In spite of all the efforts of raw-milk cheese advocates to keep things clean, problems of this nature do not seem to go away so easily. The smuggling in of illegal, improperly manufactured cheeses of the types produced at Jalisco continues. If there's a market for them, there's only so much the authorities can do to stop the flow. And unfortunately, it remains a threat to give real cheese a bad name and encourage crackdowns that extend to legitimate raw-milk products.

cheesemakers got together to define their standards for milk quality, quite consciously and intentionally establishing them higher than the EEC (European Economic Community) equivalents. Now, *that's* what I call a safety net.

The British Specialist Cheesemakers Association's website (www.specialistcheesemakers.co.uk) is a good place to familiarize yourself further with raw-milk producers' safety procedures. The Raw Milk Cheesemakers' Association (www.rawmilkcheese.org)

has taken up the same mantle in the United States. Another excellent summary of safety measures can be found in the American Raw Milk Cheese Presidium's mission statement and protocol (www.slowfoodusa.org/raft/raw_cheese.pdf).

WHAT THE U.S. GOVERNMENT DOES (AND DOESN'T) DO

Our federal government regulates interstate cheese commerce primarily in the guise of the FDA and the U.S. Department of Agriculture (USDA).

In general, there are a lot of well-meaning, well-informed scientists and bureaucrats involved in government regulation of cheese. But naturally, they tend to become heavy handed, overprotective, and patronizing. (It's their *job*, folks!). Real-cheese people are understandably wary of dealing with the government; just about everybody has at least one anecdote about how their favorite raw-milk cheese was assaulted or insulted.

The basic U.S. government rule for raw-milk cheeses is pretty straightforward. (Its simplistic nature, in fact, is a big part of the problem.) In the United States, it is legal to produce (and to import) raw-milk cheeses as long as they're aged at least 60 days at a temperature of no less than 35 degrees F. State and local authorities, who oversee agricultural products across our great nation, are given leeway to enforce stricter standards.

Sometimes, as Americans, we have to look abroad, or at least next door, for more enlightened policies. The government of Québec, for example, recently launched an initiative to lower its raw-milk cheese aging minimum to 30 days from 60 and to concentrate more on the issue of milk quality. Says my good colleague Dénis Cottin, Canadian *affineur* and expert on all French-style cheeses, "What we want is for our producers to be clean and to use clean milk. Anything that can go wrong happens within 30 days. With Époisses-type cheeses, the *B. linens* bacteria occupy the territory for 60 days. Then they die and the listeria can move in. So the problems happen *after* 60 days—not before."

MORE "SAFETY NETS": SPOT TESTING AND THE AMERICAN APPROACH

The way the U.S. government regulates and tests cheesemaking milk does not adequately address the issues of concern to raw-

"[Pasteurization] seems almost arrogant. Of course, milk should be safe. If you've got bad milk, you should kill everything. If you're starting with nice, clean, beautiful milk, it's silly to kill everything."

CARY BRYANT, ROGUE CREAMERY CHEESEMAKER

WHY THE 60-DAY RULE DOESN'T WORK FOR RAW-MILK CHEESES

This famous rule itself is an example of how U.S. cheese policy does not make sense when it comes to traditional raw-milk cheese-making. The fact is a soft surface mold-ripened cheese actually becomes *riskier* with age.

First of all, a contaminated cheese, regardless of whether it's made from raw or pasteurized milk, becomes more dangerous as it ages because the pathogens have more time to multiply. The pivotal event occurs during cheesemaking when that one little germ alights in your cheese milk or your ripening curds and starts multiplying. If a listeria bug snuck in on Day 1, it will have grown to half a million bugs after 10 to 20 days and to well over a million after 30 days, easily attaining levels able to make a person sick. (Remember: Good, clean cheesemaking from conscientious artisans is your best bet.)

Mold-ripened cheeses start out with a good amount of acidity—their pH values are around 5.5—which acts as a buffer against pathogens. As they age through their first and into their second month, the surface molds, which are naturally more basic (less acidic), begin to lower their acidity toward a neutral value of 7.0 on the pH scale. This melds and mellows the flavors, and by about 50 to 55 days, the cheeses are ripe and ready to eat. Their diminishing acidity, however, also starts to render them (theoretically, at least) more vulnerable to bacterial contamination. As Dr. Cathy Donnelly makes clear, 60 days is actually too long for certain cheeses: "The FDA gives cheesemakers a choice: either you make a Camembert from pasteurized milk or you age it for 60 days. But if you age a Camembert 60 days, you create *more* risk. According to its French AOC rules, it cannot be aged for more than 57 days. Again, we have taken this simplistic American approach that cheese is cheese is cheese and all rules apply equally."

milk producers. It's clearly a system based on industrial mass production as well as on certain assumptions, including that pasteurization is some sort of magic bullet.

In the United States, there is no overall legal requirement to test cheese for specific microbial pathogens, largely because it is considered a safe food. Milk, however, is tested for microbiological factors: standard plate count and coliform counts. Standard plate count is an enumeration of *all* bacteria in a food. A sample of that food is placed in a petri dish and its bacteria are allowed to grow into individual colonies and then measured. A high plate count in milk does not necessarily equate with a higher risk of getting sick. All it really means is there are more bacteria present; and in the case of milk bound for cheese, they could be the good ones.

Coliform counts measure the amount of fecal bacteria present and are a good indication of whether or not a food is clean (i.e., if there has been contamination from external sources). This method is better at predicting whether salmonella or listeria could be present than taking a standard plate count, but it is still far from ideal.

Beyond these standard plate and coliform counts, the United States has no specific legal limits for pathogens. What the law does state is that cheeses found to be adulterated (i.e., not conforming to specific U.S. government definitions and parameters) must be banned or recalled. Technically, contamination by pathogens falls into this "adulterated" category. The focus of this approach appears to be off.

In 1998, the FDA instituted its Domestic and Imported Cheese and Cheese Products Food Compliance Program, which requires random inspections of cheesemaking sites and spot testing of cheese samples. These tests, conducted by the FDA, the U.S. Customs and Border Control, and state and local officials, do specifically target listeria, salmonella, *E. coli,* and staphyloccocus. Positive results mandate bans or recalls of specific products, identified as tainted, and the companies trafficking in them. Despite the noble intentions of these officials to protect the American public from food-borne illness, misdirected efforts in these areas have resulted in much harm being done to real cheeses.

Starting in the late 1970s, plenty of authentic raw-milk cheeses were coming in under the U.S. government radar, courtesy of cheesemongering pioneers the likes of Steve Jenkins. This state of affairs eventually came to the attention of the authorities, beginning with an article by Bryan Miller, which appeared in the *New York Times* on April 13, 1983. (Some say this was part of "a goose that laid the golden egg scenario," in that the impetus to publicize and market this delicious contraband was the beginning of its demise here.) A coterie of clever, sophisticated, Francophile foodies had flaunted their enjoyment of these illicit items for long enough! It was time for a crackdown, which indeed came in the form of the FDA's compliance program and a more than decade-long serious consideration of an all-out ban on raw-milk cheeses. By the early twenty-first century, government forces had backed off the threat of an all-out ban. But the compliance program and its effects on the real-cheese business continue.

Testing samples—and imposing bans and recalls—is a classic illustration of an apt cliché: closing the barn door after the cows got away. The most effective way to encourage prevention is environmental testing. If listeria is detected anyplace in a cheesemaking plant where it might make its way into the milk or the cheese, cleaning up that area and shoring up the plant's defenses

SOMATIC CELL COUNTS

Taking a somatic cell count (SCC) is one way cheese producers monitor the quality of their milk. Somatic cells are white blood cells (leukocytes) that are the mammalian body's main defense against potentially infectious bacteria: When invading bacteria are detected, leukocytes are dispatched to the site of the breach. There, they go to work swallowing and digesting the invaders. If a cow has high SCC in her milk, it indicates bacteria such as staphylococcus have attacked her udder—possibly causing mastitis. In dairying, the SCC is measured in terms of number of cells per milliliter of milk. A healthy cow (or herd, if the milk is being measured in a bulk tank) will have a count of no more than 100,000. Counts exceeding 200,000 indicate the presence of mastitis among at least some animals in a herd. European milk standards outlaw any commercial use of milk with a SCC of over 400,000; in the United States, the legal threshold is higher (750,000), meaning the standard is lower. Responsible raw-milk producers often voluntarily set tougher limits.

are the best guarantees of a safe product.

It's somewhat hard to believe, but very few if any of our government policymakers and regulators have visited farmstead cheesemaking operations. Catherine Donnelly encourages them to do it so they can see the type of care taken. What they'll find is hardworking cheese farmers doing everything in their power to ensure high-quality milk and optimum manufacturing, aging, and storage conditions. The reality is they devote at least half their labor to cleaning up. Sanitation is a huge priority, cleanliness a dominant theme on these farms. This would surely impress our conscientious federal inspectors.

THE 60-DAY RULE AND CHEESE IMPORTS

The FDA periodically issues directives to U.S. Customs and Border Control called import alerts. Customs agents place cheeses under quarantine, sometimes until they die, based on concerns and suspicions arising from tests for pasteurization and adulteration. Cheese types as well as producers, *affineurs,* exporters, and importers can be placed on banned lists. Many of these alerts or bans are based on false alarms, including false-positive tests for pathogens.

Once a cheese or a company is blacklisted, it is a long and difficult process to have it reinstated. Meanwhile, it's an open secret in the business that the U.S. authorities have no test to determine the age of a cheese. If a cheesemaker or importer declares a cheese to be of raw milk but claims it is aged 60 days or more, there is no way to tell.

French cheeses have been subject to extra scrutiny and many people in our industry believe there was a political motive. As of this writing, all young French raw goat's milk cheeses are being prevented from entering the United States. This means none of the genuine Loire Valley chèvres can reach U.S. consumers. All I can say is *quel dommage!* What a crying shame . . .

U.S. barriers are so tough that the French have pretty much given up on even trying to send any real raw-milk cheeses to these shores. They want to preserve what business they can and anyway they realize you can't fight city hall. So, ironically, while the American artisanal cheeses they largely inspired are on the upswing, real French raw-milk cheeses are on the decline and are seldom available in the United States. According to Rolf Beeler, who alongside his artisanal Swiss selections has been an importer and *affineur* of

Piper's Pyramid from Capriole.

DEALING WITH THE ANTI-RAW MILK BUREAUCRACY

Dénis Cottin, a veteran of the Canadian and French cheese wars, recalls how one little slip of the tongue—or rather pen—from a government bureaucrat put a big crimp in his business.

Dénis had applied to the Canadian authorities for a license to export his raw-milk cheeses to the United States; they, in turn, sent a request to the USDA. Their letter was directed to Jack Mowbray, an official with the USDA's Food Safety and Inspection Service. Mowbray sent an official response stating unequivocally that *no* Canadian raw-milk cheeses were allowed into the United States. Dénis, eager to tap into the U.S. market, traveled to Washington, D.C., with a copy of Mr. Mowbray's response. At a public hearing, Dénis, brandishing the letter, was able to get the USDA official to admit he had overstated the rules. Typically, though, Dénis was faced with a long rehabilitation effort on behalf of his cheeses.

Caroline and Daniel Hostettler's Swiss cheese business (see chapter 15) also suffered a major hiccup owing to a similar misunderstanding—actually a misreading of one key word. In 2005, the FDA requested a sample of one of the Hostettlers' cheeses, a Prattigauer, for random testing. Daniel sent the cheese, labeled accurately as an unpasteurized-milk cheese aged over 60 days. Soon he received notice the Prattigauer had been banned from importation. After 6 weeks of back and forth, the problem came to light. The FDA inspector had misread the label as "pasteurized-milk cheese," tested the sample as such and therefore labeled it as an "improperly pasteurized cheese." Cheeses were destroyed and business was lost.

French delicacies since the mid-1980s, 91 percent of all French cheeses are now pasteurized. When Beeler discovered that raw-milk Époisses was rare if not extinct, he began to source identical and/or equivalent Swiss cheeses. Imagine a "Swiss Époisses" replacing the French one—the "imitation" out-authenticating the original.

THE EUROPEAN "RISK-BASED" APPROACH

The European Union has a different approach to regulating raw milk. It incorporates maximum tolerable limits for microbe content as well as stringent requirements for sanitation, collection, storage, and transportation. Milk is regularly tested and production sites are regularly inspected.

In the European Union, authorities regularly target specific pathogens, including listeria, monitoring whether they are within legally defined limits of acceptable risk. The more dangerous a pathogen is, the less it can be tolerated and the lower its legal limit. (An acceptable risk might be on the order of 100 individual listeria bacteria per gram of food—a very low number, given their microscopic size, and well below a level that could make you sick.) The

Kirkham's Lancashire, a traditional raw-milk British farmhouse cheese.

European approach is a scientifically sound risk-based one, quite different from the "zero tolerance" or "kill everything" one we have in the United States. It's so much easier to hide under a security blanket of simple absolutes. Many U.S. dairy scientists and raw-milk advocates are pushing our authorities to emulate the European strategies and particularly to enforce the same high standards. As you can probably guess, I'm in full agreement.

THE RAW-MILK CHEESE LOBBY IN THE UNITED STATES

Part of the FDA's mission is to conduct periodic reviews of existing regulations to make sure they are up-to-date (i.e., based on current scientific data and the latest assessments of the risks). Sometimes this has a deleterious effect on raw-milk cheeses. For example, in the 1990s, several studies that involved inoculating pasteurized cheeses with pathogens such as salmonella, *E. coli,* and listeria demonstrated these microbes could survive beyond 60 days. The FDA reacted by launching a review of the 60-day aging rule, which had been in effect since the late 1940s; there was consideration of either increasing the requirement or banning raw-milk cheeses altogether. Of course, the key words here are *inoculating* and *pasteurized.* If a cheese is kept clean, what's to survive before or after 60 days? Furthermore, if you plant pathogens in a cheese, some of them may survive *regardless* of whether it's made from pasteurized milk.

Fortunately, there are two organizations that have assumed the official mantle as lobbyists for raw-milk cheeses with our government: the Cheese of Choice Coalition (founded by the Cheese Importers Association, Oldways Preservation and Trust, and the American Cheese Society), and the Raw Milk Cheesemakers' Association (RMCA).

The main goal of the Cheese of Choice Coalition (CCC) is to encourage the U.S. government to maintain the status quo for raw-milk cheese. It keeps an eye on the priority status of the raw-milk issue within the government, monitoring statements, and alerts. It endeavors to keep good information flowing in both directions, educating both the public and government officials about the realities of raw-milk cheese production, about its benefits to biodiversity and healthy nutrition. Often, the government appears to operate without enough transparency. There have been instances in which the bureaucracy was secretive about who was part of a study group to which the CCC would have liked to submit some peer-reviewed scientific papers supporting the cause of raw-milk cheeses. (This is not about weapons of mass destruction, folks; it's about cheeses people want to eat!) The CCC also tries to initiate monthly conversations with government officials who may lend a sympathetic ear such as the FDA's John Sheehan, director of the Division of Plant and Dairy Food Safety, Office of Food Safety, Center for Food Safety and Applied Nutrition. (Sheehan helped Rogue Creamery expedite the approval process for exporting its raw-milk Rogue River Blue cheese; see chapter 14.)

In the year 2000, the lobby won a battle when the FDA decided not to tighten its rules. It seems, however, there will always be periodic alerts and temporary bans—at least for imports. Among raw-milk cheese advocates, there's a lingering fear the federal bureaucracy will once again start lurching toward an all-out, irreversible ban on raw-milk cheeses. For the CCC and RMCA, maintaining the status quo is acceptable; backsliding is not.

RAW VERSUS PASTEURIZED: CHEESE QUALITY AND CHARACTER

From my viewpoint as a professional cheese connoisseur, pasteurized milk cheeses are lacking in several respects—starting with their flavor and aroma profiles and extending to other important criteria. We've already discussed how pasteurization is an indiscriminate killer of microflora. Raw milk has more fruity, grassy, and also more cowy or phenolic (barnyardy) flavors from all those "bennies," which are removed by pasteurization. Young unpasteurized cheeses, like the raw material itself, already possess more of those natural flavors, and they continue to develop faster and more fully as they age.

Pasteurized-milk cheeses also tend to develop less desirable textures than raw-milk ones. What you usually get is a more rubbery or "plasticized" consistency; the paste shows less of a clean break. (Try prying a small chunk of cheese in half with your fingers.) Goat's milk seems to tolerate heat treatment and pasteurization even less than sheep's or cow's milk, and the effects are particularly apparent in the texture of the finished cheeses. One of the more appealing traits of fine goat's milk cheeses is their pleasant somewhat claylike consistency; the best ones also have a softness, lightness, and airiness—with no sticky or rubbery qualities—and offer a

> *"We exist today in a culture where people do not want to assume any personal responsibility or risk for the food they purchase and consume. It's a very litigious society. If one farmstead cheesemaker or one raw-milk co-op is responsible for a big outbreak, it's like a domino effect. It impacts the entire dairy industry, all the way up to the big guys, because it frightens consumers."*
>
> MARY ANNE DRAKE, Ph.D., NORTH CAROLINA STATE UNIVERSITY

highly stimulating mouth feel. Pasteurization tends to accentuate the former (negative) traits and diminish the latter (positive) ones.

The more I babysit cheeses, observing them stride toward maturity and then slither into decline, the more I become convinced the pasteurized-milk types are more vulnerable to an early demise than the raw-milk ones. I often refer to pasteurized-milk cheeses as compromised. In fact those two terms—*pasteurized* and *compromised*—have become virtually synonymous in my cheese vocabulary. It's clear to me that pasteurized-milk cheeses head south sooner: They start to smell putrid and cross the border into that inedible zone more quickly and easily than comparable raw-milk ones.

RAW MILK MAKES BETTER CHEESE: TASTING IS BELIEVING

Some experts claim the flavor differences between raw-milk and pasteurized-milk cheeses are quite subtle and would not necessarily be noticed by your "average Joe," that you would have to be an experienced connoisseur to appreciate the nuances. I disagree and I believe tasting comparisons will consistently bear out my strong conviction that there really is a big difference.

TASTING COMPARISONS:
Raw- Vs. Pasteurized-Milk Cheeses

Following are some suggested comparison tastings of otherwise identical or very similar cheeses in raw-milk versus pasteurized incarnations.

DURRUS (RAW) VS. ARDRAHAN (PASTEURIZED)—These two otherwise quite similar Irish farmhouse cheeses present an interesting comparison, particularly from the perspective of texture and consistency. The Ardrahan tends to be more rubbery. You can detect this even before you put it in your mouth by either pressing a small piece between thumb and forefinger or gently pulling apart a sample. The raw-milk Durrus demonstrates a better break, with less sponginess, and delivers a more pleasing mouthfeel. This comparison also says something about durability (although this won't be apparent in a onetime tasting). Over time, the Durrus certainly fades. Meanwhile, the pasteurized-milk Ardrahan, though delicious when at peak, can bottom out quickly and become disagreeably stinky. You could even try an experiment at home and hold a piece of each until they really start to decay. It would be kind of like an engineer doing a materials study: Stress two pieces of different alloys till they break; then figure out what this tells you about their basic properties.

IBORES (RAW) VS. GARROTXA (PASTEURIZED)—Although these two classic Spanish goat cheeses are quite different in some respects, I think they also demonstrate the textural aspect of the raw versus pasteurized comparison. While the Garrotxa can be outstanding, it doesn't necessarily have that delightful, slightly chalky, crumbly texture I look for in a superior goat cheese. Compared with the Ibores, the Garrotxa develops more of a pasty consistency, another drawback of pasteurized milk. When well made and well cared for, the Ibores has a better break and more toothsome texture, with a more stimulating mouth feel and a more diversified flavor profile.

CONSTANT BLISS (RAW) VS. CHAOURCE (PASTEURIZED)—Jasper Hill's blissful bloomy-rind cheese is constantly compared to Chaource, and indeed it's made by a similar recipe. The raw-milk Bliss offers more aroma, more flavor, and a longer shelf life. It is also more challenging—in a good way. Constant Bliss has a finish quite different from its start and a moderately funky but pleasantly edible rind. The pasteurized Chaource has a nice finish, too, but there's no hint of the farm there. A shorter shelf life is ensured simply because there's not as much life in it to begin with.

GRAYSON (RAW) VS. LIVAROT (PASTEURIZED)—Grayson is another American raw-milk gem often compared to a French classic, Livarot, which we now get in pasteurized-milk versions. The Grayson tastes like some pretty happy cows were involved here: It has full raw-milk aromas and a deep and lingering flavor profile, which is pungent and rounded out with a good helping of *umami*. The pasteurized Livarot looks good and its texture is similar to a Grayson, but it has less heft. When you cut into the Livarot, there's virtually no resistance, a clear indication of pasteurization. (By the way, I would avoid its rind, making sure not to mix any with its paste.) When fairly young, the flavor of the Livarot isn't bad; there just isn't a lot of it and there isn't much aroma to back it up either.

STICHELTON (RAW) VS. COLSTON-BASSETT STILTON (PASTEURIZED)—Ask me for an example of a great pasteurized cheese, and Colston-Bassett Stilton quickly pops to mind. (Not coincidentally, it's also one of those cheeses about which you are compelled to say. It's a tribute to its makers.) It's a masterpiece of a blue, a venerable old stalwart I can trust. I've loved it for years and it will continue to be my first choice among Stiltons. The milk flavor comes through and it displays good balance, start to finish: It's milky and buttery with just the right amount of zing. I have seen C.-B. Stiltons go south, though; they can fade and start to taste a little rusty. If there's a Stilchelton around, it will give the Colston-Bassett a run for its money. On first inspection, they look almost identical, but you can tell the difference right away from the aromas: The Stichelton's is fuller, fruity, and sweet; the Stilton's is faint and slightly musty. In the mouth, the Stichelton shoots sparks all around. Probably the most noticeable difference texture-wise is the Stichelton is not as dry. It has more give and is a tad closer to full-cream butter. This quality makes it more accessible, allowing it to spread its flavors out more extensively on your palate and linger longer. It's also more crumbly and less waxy than the Stilton.

ADDITIONAL COMPARISONS—Rogue Creamery makes pasteurized- and raw-milk versions of their Cheddar in medium, sharp, and extra-sharp gradations. Beecher's makes its Flagship in both pasteurized- and raw-milk versions as does Tumalo Farms, with its Classico. I'd recommend any of these as possibly the best way to illuminate fundamental raw versus pasteurized comparisons.

CAN PASTEURIZED MILK YIELD A GREAT CHEESE?

Although I will not back down from my assertion that raw milk makes better cheese, this does not rule out the possibility of very good cheeses being made from pasteurized milk. Can it yield great ones, though? Let's hear from several of our experts:

MATEO KEHLER, JASPER HILL FARM: "I think it's definitely possible. The truth is there are some fantastic pasteurized milk cheeses out there. Milk quality is still a determining factor as it relates to cheese quality—even of pasteurized cheeses. What you do, I think, is eliminate the peaks and valleys."

CARY BRYANT, ROGUE CREAMERY: "It is possible with added, properly defined cultures to create some very complex and delicious pasteurized-milk cheeses. But if you're starting with just pasteurized milk, you're going to get something very bland. You have to inoculate it with something. When it's pasteurized, you're much more likely to lose the *terroir*."

CATHERINE DONNELLY, Ph.D.: "It is so dependent upon microbial flora, which contribute to the fermentation and aging. We can make great cheeses from raw milk, and U.S. cheesemakers have shown that we can also make great and distinctive cheeses from pasteurized milk. Cabot Clothbound Cheddar is such an example."

MARY ANNE DRAKE, Ph.D.: "I have had some spectacular pasteurized milk Cheddar cheeses and I have had some spectacular raw-milk Cheddar cheeses."

If you'd like to taste and judge for yourself, I can suggest the following examples of potentially great cheeses made from pasteurized milk: Monte Enebro, Colston-Basett Stilton, Beenleigh Blue, Garrotxa, and Manchego El Toboso. When they're at their best, the first two on the list have to be considered among the world's finest; I gave them 95 points out of 100 in our second book, and my opinion of them hasn't wavered.

CONCLUSIONS

Regardless which experts you consult and how they must couch their statements for decorum, the main point about raw-milk cheeses is if they're made right they present extremely minimal dangers—far less than many other foods. Furthermore, the authentic ones I'm recommending taste better and more faithfully express their *terroir*.

When it comes to raw-milk cheeses, quality and choice are both fundamental. If we are afforded the option of eating uncooked fish and shellfish in the form of sushi and oysters on the half shell, then why are we denied the pleasures of eating raw-milk cheeses aged under 60 days? These cheeses may be slightly risky; however, they're most likely safer than pasteurized-milk ones in the same category. We should be treated like adults and allowed to make our own choices and take responsibility for them.

It's important to make distinctions among cheeses and not automatically lump all raw-milk ones into a "high-risk" category: Raw milk itself is not the same as "underaged" (by FDA standards) raw-milk cheese, which in turn is not *aged* raw-milk cheese. The

"Pasteurization has its place in the world. It is a way to make a safe cheese out of unsafe ingredients. If you're trying to feed a billion people, economically and efficiently, there is a place for pasteurized cheese. But there's a place for raw-milk cheese as well."

CARY BRYANT, ROGUE CREAMERY

CHEESE SCIENCE

EVIDENCE IN FAVOR OF RAW-MILK CHEESE

For anyone who would like further reassurance, there are quite a few good sources of public health science regarding the safety of raw-milk cheeses.

- The Center for Science in the Public Interest website (www. cspinet.org) has a page on food safety, with a section titled "Outbreak Alert," showing a conspicuous absence of problems stemming from cheeses in general and especially raw-milk ones.
- A Food Standards Australia New Zealand–commissioned report on Roquefort, in connection with the Aussie government's proposed lifting of its long-time ban on this raw-milk cheese, delivered by FSANZ senior food scientist Narelle Marro at the Twelfth Australian Food Microbiology Conference in Sydney, February 2006, provides a fine outline and summary of how the safety of a raw-milk cheese is assessed and confirmed.
- "Factors Associated with the Microbiological Safety of Cheeses Prepared from Raw Milk" is a review prepared by Dr. Catherine Donnelly for the Cheese of Choice Coalition that analyzes reports of sicknesses from raw-milk cheeses and concluding all the causes were "confounding parameters" other than the raw milk itself.
- Codex Alimentarius (www.codex alimentarius.net) is a joint task force of the World Health Organization and the Food and Agriculture Office of the United Nations; part of the Codex's mission is to establish and maintain world food standards and practices.
- The Institute of Food Science and Technology (www.ifst.org) is an independent standards and certifying organization in the United Kingdom.
- The U.S. Food and Drug Administration's website (www. fda.gov) includes a page titled "Recalls, Market Withdrawals and Safety Alerts Archive," which confirms that raw-milk cheeses are not the problem.
- The U.S. Department of Agriculture's website (www.usda.gov) includes sections on food safety and on research and science.
- The Code of Federal Regulations, part 133, "Cheese and Related Cheese Products," provides information on current regulations and updated standards and definitions. Go to the website www.usasearch.gov, open up to the Code of Federal Regulations main page, and search "cheese."

decision to choose raw-milk cheese must come from the top down but also from the bottom up. Supporters of artisanal cheesemaking need to follow the lead of the Cheese of Choice Coalition, the RMCA and other real-cheese champions. We need to keep a dialogue going with the governing powers and continue to educate any alarmists within the medical, government, and legislative communities who have the power to take away our choice to enjoy raw-milk cheeses.

Raw Milk and Real Cheese

- [ ] Cheese is a very safe food; the number of documented outbreaks of illness from it is relatively tiny.

- [ ] The few outbreaks that have occurred are most attributable to pasteurized cheeses and to postproduction contamination.

- [ ] There are no documented cases of death by food poisoning from legal, properly manufactured raw-milk cheeses.

- [ ] Pasteurization destroys microorganisms in raw milk that are built-in defenses against pathogens. It also destroys microorganisms responsible for aromas, flavors, and textures.

- [ ] High-quality milk and clean processing and aging facilities are the most important factors for safe (and successful) cheesemaking.

- [ ] Pasteurization is not a guarantee of cheese safety, though it helps minimize certain risks.

- [ ] Reliance on pasteurization may represent a "false safety net," resulting in lowered standards throughout production.

- [ ] The additional costs of pasteurization (in equipment, time, and energy) place a burden on small-production cheesemakers.

- [ ] Aged hard cheeses made from raw milk pose no greater health risk than cheeses made from pasteurized milk; both are considered safe foods.

- [ ] Raw milk makes more interesting-tasting cheese. High-quality raw milk makes the best cheese.

- [ ] U.S. government policies ought to be more in line with a risk assessment-based approach.

- [ ] The U.S. government does not regularly test for specific pathogens in cheeses; any such testing is conducted on a random basis.

- [ ] It is left up to U.S. cheesemakers to establish and maintain, largely on a voluntary basis, their own safety standards and procedures.

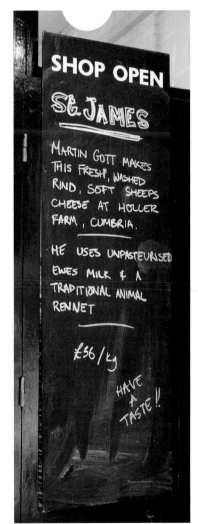

TOP: Stanser Röteli, a washed-rind raw-milk delight from Switzerland.

From top: Fourme d'Ambert and Hudson Valley Camembert.

CHAPTER 8

A CHEESE FARM VISIT: CONNECTICUT'S CATO CORNER ON THE RISE

IN LESS THAN A DECADE, A MOTHER-AND-SON TEAM IN SUBURBAN Connecticut has pulled off the surprising feat of putting their modest family farm on the world's cheese map. At first glance, Cato Corner Farm might seem an unlikely source of great artisanal cheeses or, indeed, a model for sustainable farming, but it has earned both of those accolades among cheese connoisseurs, professional and amateur alike.

Cato Corner is a pleasant enough 75-acre spread in a semirural area just 20 minutes southeast of Hartford. (Housing developments and McMansions dot the neighborhood; Manhattan is less than 2½ hours away by car.) Neither of its principals, Elizabeth MacAlister nor her son Mark Gillman, have much family history or formal training in cheese farming. Although Cato Corner has a dairy pedigree dating back at least to the mid-nineteenth century, Elizabeth herself never raised cows or made cheese from their milk until the mid-1990s. (She was an English major at Bryn Mawr and held various jobs, including caseworker for disabled people, school bus driver, and "hippie living in San Francisco.") Mark jumped on the bandwagon in 2002. That same year, when I first tasted their flagship cheese in one of the American Cheese Society convention contests, I was underwhelmed. It had an intriguing name— Hooligan—but its texture was a bit dense and rubbery and its flavors tended to be out of balance. This lovely Jersey cows' milk clearly had potential, but it wasn't being fulfilled in the cheese.

Cato Corner Farm's signature cheese, Hooligan, finds some nice pairings with beers.

FROM TOP: *Top: A storage shed at Connecticut's Cato Corner Farm; cheeses are for sale from the farm on Saturdays.*

Sometime over the next four years, a transformation occurred. Hooligan not only became one of my favorite American cheeses, but it also garnered widespread critical acclaim and won prizes. Cato Corner itself earned the 2006 Gallo Family Vineyards grand prize Never Stop Growing Award for the best traditional family farm.

To find out what elevated Cato Corner's cheeses to the threshold of greatness, we spent some time there, poking around with the kind indulgence of its owners. It would be great if anyone seeking to master cheese could pay such a visit. Unfortunately, it's not possible: Cheese farmers are too busy to conduct guided tours for the public. Consider this your virtual tour of a working cheese farm, a chance to witness the lessons of our first seven chapters firsthand.

In 1979, Elizabeth MacAlister and family (husband and two young sons) made the proverbial back-to-the-land move, buying the property at 178 Cato Corner Road in Colchester, Connecticut. (Cato was a freedman who farmed in the area in the late eighteenth century.) After her divorce in 1997, Elizabeth set out to make a business of cheesemaking. She had grown up in Rhode Island, surrounded by dairy farms, and she had a cheese-loving father. She kept some goats at Cato Corner, making "bootleg" cheese by hand. Meanwhile, Mark grew up a "farm nerd," with classmates poking fun at the fresh goat-cheese sandwiches in his school lunch box. Later, when he was teaching seventh-grade English in inner-city Baltimore, he decided to return to his farm chores. Elizabeth now manages the herd and Mark is the head cheesemaker, a reversal of traditional male and female roles.

Both mother and son are mostly self-taught in the fine arts of dairy farming and cheesemaking. Elizabeth took a course in cheesemaking at Cal Poly San Luis Obispo in 1997, and Mark took a short dairy chemistry course from Dr. Paul Kindstedt at the University of Vermont. They've both taken seminars from the likes of Peter Dixon, the well-known Vermont consulting cheesemaker.

Cheese farming starts with the animals. Cato Corner has a beautiful herd of mostly Jersey cows with a few Brown Swiss mixed in. Jersey milk is known to be rich, tasty, and sweet. If you've ever tried a swig of it fresh, it's divine: It goes down easy, like a spoonful of the best homemade ice cream. As cows go, Jerseys are relatively small, well-mannered, and easy to work with. They are also very productive, giving the same amount of milk as the Brown Swiss, but eating only half as much. Is it anything short of a miracle that an animal can eat 40 pounds of hay or grass in a day, plus drink some water, which is free (but for the well digging and pumping), and give back *the same amount* of milk?

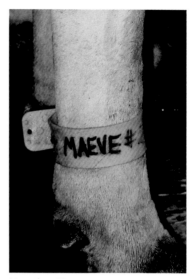

Maeve's anklet name tag.

Abby, Agnieska, Beatrice, Beryl, Doozie, Isis, Jane, Juanita, Jellybean, Koko, Maeve, Marigold, Morgan, Naomi, Phoebe, Sinead, Siobhan, Sugar, Tulip. The roster of cows at Cato Corner reveals a range of names from quaint and archaic to traditional Irish, from cute pet monikers to just plain old Jane. Naming them is one measure of the immense loving care and respect "the girls" command. (One wonders how many cows a farm would have to own before it reverted to numbering them.) Each cow has a plastic name band around her ankle where it's easy to read when she's up on the platform in the milking parlor. Practically speaking, names help a farmer identify each individual and track her progress and output, especially when she gets sick and needs special treatment. But the names also signal a deeper message: These noble domestics—friendly, curious, ponderous, needy, yet amazingly productive—are true partners in this honest endeavor of cheese farming.

Elizabeth and her farmhands keep notes on dry-erase boards posted in the barn and milking parlor and also in a logbook, which is updated at each milking (5:30 a.m. and 4 p.m. daily). Strung together, these observations form a compelling—and sometimes poignant—narrative of life on the farm. A few excerpts:

Wednesday, 6/14, a.m.
Isis temp. was 101°. She ate her grain. Please check Isis left rear ankle. Jim noticed her favoring it.

8/30/06
Jim let Althea & Kira loose. Kira stayed out for a while but got pushed around & cried to go back so we let her back.

Thursday, 9/7/06, 4:30 a.m.
Is the moon full today? It is bright as day in the barnyard—shadows.

9/8
Moon bright again. Cows all wide awake. Coyotes howling!

Tuesday, 9/12
Agnieska has 2 new calves from side pens. They have started to nurse but need encouragement & help. You can tie her with the

Mark Gillman and Elizabeth MacAlister, a mother-son cheese-farming team.

halter & show them the teat if they aren't nursing. The larger one was doing better than the small one. They can have some milk replacement if they get hungry.

Wednesday, 9/13, a.m.
Sanitizer stuck this morning. Had to move it along by hand.

Cato Corner Farm has between 30 and 40 acres of natural pastures that are divided by a series of fences into five fields with between three and seven paddocks per field. In the warmer months, the cows are led out to graze in these areas on a diet of indigenous grasses, weeds, and flowers. They are rotated from one paddock to the next, with each paddock left empty for 7 to 10 days—more or less, depending on seasonal and weather conditions. Cows are very thorough grazers—they really mow that lawn—so this rotational system gives each section of pasture time to recover. During the colder season, when they're indoors most of the time, they eat a combination of locally produced hay and natural dry feed.

Cato Corner's cows go out to pasture at the beginning of May and return to the barns for the winter in November. Seasonal changes in the milk require adjustments in the cheesemaking; for example, with less-concentrated milk (fewer solids), less starter culture is required. May is the most difficult month for cheesemaking because the milk is changing so rapidly.

Conventional wisdom might maintain that summer milk from free-grazing cows is automatically preferable since they're outdoors consuming Mother Nature's lush bounty. But it really depends on what type of cheese you're making. Blue cheeses and abbey-style cheeses—richer, uncooked, soft-ripened—are best made from winter milk, which is more concentrated. In summer, the milk is more diluted and better suited to making harder cheeses such as Cheddar and the Alpine types, where the curds are subjected to more heating and drainage, which cause further dehydration. (Cato Corner's winter milk has about 5 percent butterfat and 3½ to 4 percent protein, high numbers for milk solids but to be expected from Jerseys. In summer, the fat tends to drop to around 3 percent and the protein will rarely exceed 3½ percent.)

At Cato Corner, they considered using a cream separator to enhance the summer milk and make it more suitable for some of their signature cheeses, such as the abbey-style Hooligan, so they could be made year-round. Another option was to make the hard

cheeses in the summer and the soft ones in the winter. Given aging periods of anywhere from 3 to 7 months, this strategy posed a dilemma: many of their most popular cheeses would not be available all year. The market for luxury items such as elite cheeses can be fickle and demanding, with a short attention span. Once a cheese is in the mind of sophisticated, discerning consumers, you want to keep it there.

"We'd love to be able to make really seasonal cheeses, but we have to look at our cash flow," says Elizabeth. "If Murray's Cheese Shop wants only one or two cheeses and that can pay all our bills, then fine. But I seriously doubt that will happen. Also, we aren't going to produce a cheese that's consistent year-round. That's not what we're about."

A traditional cheese farm can only hope to sustain itself with proper animal husbandry as its foundation. The milkers are the focus, but there are plenty of other ladies-in-waiting—nonlactating cows, maturing calves, and heifers (who don't earn the title "cow" until they've given birth to their second calf). Cows generally lactate for about 10 months and go dry for the remaining 60 days of the year and/or until they're bred. The U.S. industry standard is about three lactations per cow and a life span of roughly 6 years. At Cato Corner and other smaller, humane operations, a cow's life expectancy is much higher—in the range of 12 to 13 years. "In New Zealand and other traditional dairy cultures, they always talk about longevity and their cows leading a productive life," says Elizabeth. "In the U.S., we're just starting to."

"We'd love to be able to make really seasonal cheeses, but we have to look at our cash flow. If Murray's Cheese Shop wants only one or two cheeses and that can pay all our bills, then fine. But I seriously doubt that will happen. Also, we aren't going to produce a cheese that's consistent year-round. That's not what we're about."

ELIZABETH MacALISTER,
CATO CORNER FARM

Happy cows at Cato Corner Farm consume a variety of lush pasture forage.

Lactating cows are milked regardless of their state of health, but the sick ones are said to be "out of the tank," meaning their milk must be thrown out instead of being pumped into the holding tank for cheesemaking. Cato Corner's cheese yield is 12 percent, or 12 pounds of cheese per 100 pounds of milk. A healthy Jersey cow produces, on average, about 50 pounds of milk a day—the equivalent of nearly 6 gallons. Four sick cows spell a loss of 200 pounds of milk, which translates to 24 pounds of cheese or at least $300 in revenue—*per day*. That's a lot of milk. Imagine how quickly this could eat up a farm's profits.

In dairy farming, particularly with cows, there's no avoiding the mess. They are lovely, sweet animals but not exactly dainty about where they tread. Cheese producers must spend a great deal of energy on keeping things clean. The front lines in the cheese farmer's battle against germs are first drawn in the milking parlor and then in the cheesemaking room. Sanitation is one of the first and most obvious manifestations of the virtually manic attention to detail required to become a superior cheese artisan. Without it, cheeses may not only turn out dull tasting, but they will literally go rotten.

Sanitary measures follow a strict routine. Spend a day at a cheese farm and you quickly realize that cleanup is the single most time-consuming activity. It starts with mucking out the barns and maintaining the pens. Once the milk is ready to be extracted from the cows, the routine becomes intense and detailed, starting with a Betadine swab for each teat and the use of spotlessly clean rags that, once used, are thrown directly into a washing machine located next to the milking parlor. (Betadine is a well-known brand of microbicide, essentially a povidone-iodine solution.) Conservatively speaking, a cheesemaker spends at least as much time cleaning up as making cheese.

At Cato Corner and other raw-milk producers, where there is no "safety net" of pasteurization, sanitation receives extra emphasis. Thursdays are their cleanup days: Cheesemaking takes about 4 hours but doesn't start until midday, after a rigorous (and nearly 5-hour) general wash-down of the cheese room. To save time, cheesemakers scrub and swab as they go, almost constantly cleaning during intervals. If the curds take 45 minutes to acidify after the introduction of starter culture, at least 30 of those are spent washing up. There might be a few minutes to return some phone calls and grab a quick bite to eat, but then it's on to the next step. Cheesemakers appear to change clothes more times than a runway model at a Giorgio Armani show: not a speck of outside dirt or mud or germs shall be tracked into the cheesemaking area. Vigilance is crucial and the effort is impressive.

Every step at Cato Corner is done by hand in the traditional manner: Typical of skilled cheese artisans the world over, Mark judges his curds by hand, without a pH meter or any device other than a big carving knife, noting the quality of the break as the telltale sign of proper acidification. He slides his knife into the curd mass and gently pulls it out; a triangle of glistening coagulated milk neatly splits open along well-defined edges. The curds are ready to be cut, as gently as possible, with a large harp passed smoothly in one direction, then the other, across the cheesemaking vat, a large stainless-steel tub whose hollow walls contain warm water for gradual heating. The cut aims to achieve uniform ½- to ¼-inch cubes. (You could do all this by remote-controlled machines, but it would yield "industrial" cheeses, their flavors pleasant but bland and their textures consistent but rubbery.)

To acidify his curds, Mark uses about twelve different starter cultures in different combinations depending on the recipe and seasonal variations in the milk. He has shown himself capable of producing seven cheeses (each with variations) on a regular basis, as well as at least six others in limited editions. The recipes are from various sources. Their first abbey-style cheese came from Belgian cheese guru Freddie Michels. Determined to avoid a dour male name, Elizabeth called it Bridgid's Abbey after Saint Bridgid, who lived in sixth-century Ireland. (Bridgid ran a coed monastery; her prayer is a wonderful ode in which she imagines sitting down to a feast with Jesus and his disciples at a groaning table alongside a lake of beer.) Hooligan got its name because it was a rougher version of Bridgid's. "Some of my friends in Ireland don't like the name because it reminds them of people who behave badly at football matches," says Elizabeth. The recipe for a cheese they call Bloomsday came from one of those famous fortuitous accidents. The milk for one batch acidified too long but they went ahead and added the rennet for coagulation anyway. Then they cut the curds very carefully and early but skipped the washing and cooking steps, giving the Bloomsday a distinctive Cheddar-esque heft and meaty quality, which is lacking in most washed-curd cheeses.

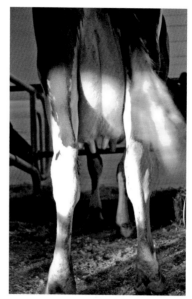

The rear end of an Ayrshire cow at Jasper Hill Farm.

FROM TOP: Curds in their draining baskets form into young cheeses; a young cheese ready for aging.

Cato Corner's cheeses are sold directly from the farm (wholesale and retail) and also at farmers' markets. Connecticut is no longer a particularly farm-oriented state—in fact, there was talk of eliminating its Department of Agriculture altogether—but it does present some strong geographical and marketing advantages such as its proximity to the major metropolitan areas of New York and Boston and the relative affluence of its population.

Although Connecticut provides no direct support to artisan cheesemakers, as Vermont and Wisconsin do, it is one of the few states where it's legal to sell bottled raw milk. Consequently, makers of real cheese can expect less meddling and more collegial collaboration from the regulatory authorities than most other places in North America. At Cato, the aging cave is an underground poured concrete structure built with grant money from Connecticut's Farm Enhancement Program, reflecting one way in which government programs can help food artisans make a go of it.

Cato Corner produced about 45,000 pounds of cheese in 2006, and they project that this amount will increase to 50,000 pounds in 2009. With a self-replenishing herd, good cheeses in high demand, and a staff with the equivalent of six full-time positions, is this quintessential family farm a truly viable operation? "We are close to making a living at it," says Mark. "We are close to the numbers we'd like. Maybe we could sell a little more cheese at a bit higher prices but we're close."

Asked to explain the evolution of their cheeses and highlight the turning point, Elizabeth starts with a fond childhood memory of a delicious Munster-like Trappist cheese from Québec. "I had a taste memory of the Fromage d'Oka, which I grew up with. We got the recipe for an abbey-style cheese from Freddie Michels. Then I fooled around with the curds and figured out the recipe for Hooligan. I didn't press them, and I drained them in baskets." Once Mark came on board, they had more time to devote to aging. They built an underground cave with its own cooling system, applied constant vigilance and made all the necessary adjustments. That's when the differences started to show. "We realized if we put in the work, we could make this cheese really good," Elizabeth says. "The recipe hasn't changed, but the handwork has."

Cato Corner produces an impressive variety, though perhaps not all of them are fully developed. When they hit all the right notes, their cheeses are sublime. The inherent risk—or perhaps we should say "charm"—of artisan cheesemaking is inconsistency. Faults can and do crop up; the good news is they may just as easily fade away or be fixed with judicious tweaks in the recipe for the next batch.

"We make cheeses we like," says Elizabeth. "We can't make bloomy cheeses; we're not set up for that. We like feisty sorts of cheeses with a couple of exceptions. Our milk is fairly assertive and that's how our tastes run. This is not to say we don't like other people's beautiful, delicate cheeses. Someday we'd like to be able to make a really good Cheddar. I grew up tasting some really good old American Cheddars."

If you asked me to pinpoint what makes Cato Corner cheeses great, I'd have to highlight the dedication, focus and passion this mother-and-son team brings. It starts with Elizabeth's commitment to the farm life and love for her animals and extends right through Mark's step-by-step precision and deft touch with the cheesemaking, all of which enables this family farm to produce excellent cheeses and remain sustainable. Elizabeth and Mark are doing great work on their little oasis amid the sprawling expanse of suburbia in America's northeast corridor. They are demonstrating the viability of preserving a productive 200-year-old lifestyle, making use of available natural resources and pleasing their public with some very tasty cheeses.

I could quibble with them on a few counts. I'd probably recommend they concentrate on making more of their most successful cheeses—in particular, the Hooligan. I can understand the temptation to flex one's cheesemaking muscles and produce a broad range of types; I can also imagine how boredom might set in. I've observed, however, that those producers who really concentrate on one special cheese are often able to bring it close to perfection over time. (A few come to mind: Berkswell, Tarentaise, Pleasant Ridge Reserve, and Flixer.) Mark Gillman is making six or eight cheeses he himself feels are best melted in a sandwich and eaten alongside a bowl of cabbage soup. I salute his unpretentious, workmanlike attitude; I urge him to keep shooting for the stars because he's coming pretty darn close to cheese nirvana.

"We make cheeses we like," says Elizabeth. "We can't make bloomy cheeses; we're not set up for that. We like feisty sorts of cheeses with a couple of exceptions. Our milk is fairly assertive and that's how our tastes run. This is not to say we don't like other people's beautiful, delicate cheeses. Someday we'd like to be able to make a really good Cheddar. I grew up tasting some really good old American Cheddars."

ELIZABETH MacALISTER,
CATO CORNER FARM

CHAPTER 9

CHEESE FOR SALE: EVERYTHING YOU NEED TO KNOW ABOUT BUYING AND TAKING IT HOME

IF YOU WANT GOOD, FRESH FOOD—OR, MORE TO THE POINT, TASTY, ripe cheese—you have to know your sources and it helps to "buy local." Ideally, you'd be able to buy all your cheeses directly from the artisans who made them—no middle person necessary. For cheese lovers, a face-to-face encounter with whomever actually manufactured the stuff is a special experience. It promises firsthand information, an assurance of quality and careful handling, a chance to make immediate judgments about the cheeses and perhaps to establish a bond with their makers. The exchange can also work both ways, because it can offer invaluable feedback to producers.

If your cheese artisans are close by and sell from little shops or counters at their creameries or from booths at farmers' markets, you've got it made. Unfortunately, we don't always have the opportunity to buy directly from the farm or dairy, so we're forced to depend on retail shops. This chapter is all about making that moment of purchase the best it can be; it aims to describe, define, and encourage the highest standard of cheesemongering. We'll cover two main areas: (1) What to expect from a cheesemonger or, put another way, how to assess a cheese shop; and (2) How to shop for cheeses, including recommendations for getting the most out of your cheese-shopping expeditions.

Robiola La Rossa with Guidalberto, a Super Tuscan wine.

"I don't tell [my cheesemakers] how to make their cheeses. The chemistry aspect is somewhat of a mystery to me. But I'll definitely let them know if there was a batch that seemed special or different or likewise if it wasn't so good. They want to hear it. Communication is definitely very important."

ANNE SAXELBY, SAXELBY
CHEESEMONGERS

CHEESEMONGERING CHECKLIST: WHAT TO LOOK FOR IN A SHOP

For me, the proper connoisseur's attitude involves keeping an open mind, training a critical eye but also looking to learn something and have fun at the same time. Discernment is key, not only when appraising the cheeses themselves but when judging also the shops where they're sold. Here is a checklist of what to look for.

ATMOSPHERE AND AMBIENCE—Take a stroll to your local cheese shop, peruse the front window display, and then step in and take a sweeping look around. Get a general feel for the place, see what type of vibe it projects, what is its overall style and ambience.

LIGHTING—Cheeses should never be exposed to direct sunlight or other heat-producing sources. There should be as much natural light as possible, to display the cheeses authentically and honestly.

TEMPERATURE—It should be comfortable, not too hot and not too cold, perhaps a little lower than the proverbial room temperature of 72 degrees F. Cheeses should be displayed and tasted at this temperature, though unfortunately state and local regulations in the United States may require refrigeration.

SOUND—Although this is not to advocate a mausoleum-like whisper and hush, I do prefer a little quiet so I can relax and focus on the cheeses. At the Artisanal Bistro, a cheese-themed restaurant with a retail counter in the back, they play background music, which I would generally deem inappropriate. On the other hand, perhaps a bit of muffled Edith Piaf to set the tone isn't such a bad thing.

SIZE—Many cheese shops cram a lot of wares into surprisingly spare square footage. Part of cheese retailing is merchandising and part of that is the theatrical element. A giant smorgasbord can be impressive. On the other hand, "going small" may represent a concerted effort to create an intense, intimate environment. This paradigm of the bustling little shop, with everybody falling all over each other, can work as long as the cheesemonger hires people who are adept at not stepping on each other's toes and can stay cheerful in cramped quarters.

OWNERSHIP/HISTORY—Is the shop family-owned and/or operated? What is its history, its traditions and roots? How does it fit in to its community? Who owns it and what is their background? Every cheese and cheesemaker has a story; the same is true of shops and their owners.

INFORMATION AND EDUCATION—Accurate information and intelligent advice should be offered and/or immediately available upon request, not only regarding all the basic facts and figures but also practical matters such as whether a cheese is ready to eat, how long it can be kept, and how. Cheesemongers should, above all else, avoid disseminating misinformation. They should also clearly separate fact from opinion. (An example: Fact: "Well-made raw-milk cheeses are safe to eat." Opinion: "We think they taste better and are better for you.") They should be able to give you interesting and relevant specifics about their cheeses, such as whether they are officially—or only de facto—organic (i.e., whether they are certified by a third party or the government, or produced naturally and organically but not certified).

FEEDBACK—All good retailers should provide a forum for information flowing in both directions—from customers to retailers to cheesemakers and back again. Regardless of the size of the operation, customer feedback should make its way along the entire supply chain. Furthermore, the interplay between cheesemakers and cheese sellers is one of the more significant behind-the-scenes aspects of fine-cheese retailing. If they aren't communicating well and implementing each other's suggestions, then they may not be serving you, the customer, as well as they could. This extends from the tastes, smells, and textures of a cheese right down to its packaging and handling.

SELECTION

This is by far the top priority, and if a retailer doesn't nail everything else, he or she has to get this right. Great shops—big or small—offer complete lineups of the best cheeses available in a variety of categories, with a coherent and inclusive scope.

Two main questions arise: (1) How wide is the selection (i.e., what is its range, breadth, and depth, geographically and in terms of cheese types?) and (2) What are the retailer's criteria for choosing a given cheese? Now, I love a big, lavish emporium that offers hundreds of cheeses as much as the next guy, but there is something to be said for a small, focused inventory with a strong emphasis on quality.

In judging a shop's selection, you might take one cheese type, such as the blues, and see how well the buyer's choices represent the varieties within that particular category. If a roster includes

DIPALO FINE FOODS FOR ATMOSPHERE

DiPalo's is an honest-to-goodness, old-fashioned, close-knit family business in the heart of Manhattan's old Little Italy neighborhood. Its window display, featuring no less than 20 full wheels of specially selected DOP Parmigiano-Reggiano, gives a strong first impression. Inside it's crowded, and if you don't mind waiting a few minutes, you'll likely have a chance to chat with fourth-generation proprietor Lou DiPalo. If your timing is right you might get to sample a fresh-cut helping of Giorgio Cravero-selected Parm—a little fruity, savory, dense, crumbly-yet-moist chunk of heaven. In DiPalo's, you get an immediate and intimate sense of what old-time cheese-shopping is about. I like what they have to offer: a strong theme, the best cheeses in their categories, tradition, hustle, and bustle.

Shopping at DiPalo's: A heartwarming experience.

STOCKING CHEESE

CRITERIA FOR SELECTION

FLAVOR—How does a cheese measure up to others already in stock? If it tastes really good, it's a candidate. If not, it won't even make the first cut.

POSITIONING/NICHE—How does it fit in with current selections? If it's a washed-rind cheese, does the shop need another one and/or is it good enough to replace one already on the roster? If the shop is short on sheep cheeses and this one is a cow, there may not be a place for it.

PRICE/PURCHASING AND MARKETING/ COMPETITION—Given the wholesale price and required markup, if the cheese would have to sell for $20 and there's an equally good one already in stock selling for $10, then it's out.

PROMOTIONS (SEASONAL, REGIONAL)— Cheeses of certain regions may be pushed for a short period of time, just to create awareness or "spice up the variety." Likewise, certain types of cheeses might be promoted seasonally. If they're quirky and/or have funny-sounding names, they might be pushed, in the short term, based on the novelty or curiosity factor.

EXCLUSIVITY—If a shop can offer the first and/or only cheese (or version of a cheese) in a particular type or category, this can be a strong selling point.

TRUSTED AFFINEURS

MAX'S *AFFINEUR* BRAND PICKS

A handful of *affineurs* have built brands that have become as close as you can get to a guarantee of fine cheese quality. Here are the ones I can recommend: Neal's Yard Dairy in Britain; Roland Barthélemy, Hervé Mons, Fromagerie P. Jacquin et Fils, Pascal Beillevaire, and Chantal Plasse in France; Guffanti and Cora in Italy; and Rolf Beeler in Switzerland.

Cambozola and Danish Blue but is missing a top Gorgonzola or Roquefort, you might reasonably question this store's standards.

Another good benchmark is the quality of a shop's lesser cheeses. Check out and compare some of its lower-tier items to top-of-the-line brands. If they carry a Montgomery's or a Keen's Cheddar, do they also have some "commodity cheeses" in the same category— respectable, well-made non-brand-name types?

Certain cheeses within a category may indicate a buyer's over-all philosophy: Are they willing to include commercial or indus-trial items, or are they exclusively supporting traditional, artisanal, raw-milk production? Are they emphasizing local and/or regional products? Are they skewed toward one country or another? What other standards do they uphold?

Next to quality, the other major factor at retail, of course, is price. The price-quality equation is not automatically in sync: The more expensive cheese is not always better—usually, but not all of the time. Also take a look to see whether there are price options within a category: Top retailers should carry the best cheese in each important class, which can be expensive. (A small-production genuine DOP Parmigiano-Reggiano is a good example of "top in class.") The next question is whether they also offer some less expensive alternatives and, if so, how those compare for taste.

"BUYING LOCAL"

Among the most significant principles espoused by the Slow Food movement, this one is of particular relevance to artisanal cheese. Except for the larger, sturdier types, most cheeses don't travel all that well, and the farther they have to be shipped, the better chance they'll arrive damaged or diminished. There are other concerns, too, not the least of which is the cost of fuel.

"Buying local" has different meanings in different places. For his *affinage* wholesale and retail business, Rolf Beeler (see chapter 15) is able to select and age the best cheeses from every corner of his native land, Switzerland, which is the size of Connecticut and Massachusetts put together. (Rolf does put a lot of mileage on his vehicles . . .) In the United States, "buying local" presents many more logistical challenges. For a cheesemaker in central or northern Vermont, it's at least a 6-hour drive to sell his or her cheeses at a regional farmer's market in New York City.

Supporting local artisans and trying to do our part to reduce the carbon footprints of our foodstuffs is a wise and admirable goal. On the other hand, another plank in the Slow Food platform is to sustain unique, inimitable products from traditional, defined production zones. Peña Blanca is a wonderfully atypical, quirky washed-rind Spanish artisanal cheese, made in sheep's and goat's milk versions (see page 309). I worry about it and would hate to see it die. What if genuine cheeses like it are unable to survive on their regional markets alone? What if, to avoid extinction, they need to find support from far-flung fancy food outlets, thousands of miles across the globe? How much gas and diesel can we condone burning to save such precious real cheeses?

SUBSTITUTIONS/ALTERNATIVES

If the cheese you're looking for is not available, at least one good alternative should be offered. There are very few cheese categories that don't include possible alternatives or substitutions. "Totally unique" cheeses without comparison are rare and mostly in a realm of curiosities (some might say monstrosities): Afuega'l Pitu, with its striking orange-shaded coloring and spunky, peppery flavors, and Blaue Geiss—wonderfully multicolored and alarmingly slimy—come to mind. If you ask for, say, a Hoch Ybrig and it's not in stock, then your cheesemonger should suggest some other delicious Swiss or Swiss-style hard, aged *alpage* cheese.

MAX'S SHOP PICKS

WHOLE FOODS FOR CONVENIENCE

In the absence of a good neighborhood mom-and-pop shop or a brand-name retailer (Zingerman's in Ann Arbor; Cowgirl Creamery in Point Reyes Station, San Francisco or Washington, D.C.; Beecher's in Seattle), your local Whole Foods Market can be a good place to start your cheese mastery. If a freestanding, medium-sized shop like Murray's carries between 150 and 300 cheeses, which is no mean feat, your average Whole Foods easily matches that while also providing some measure of informed service. Larger locations may carry as many as 800 cheeses, many of which will be local. Now that's what I call using your corporate clout to promote the good cause of artisanal cheese.

MURRAY'S FOR SELECTION

Mainly because it was near my home downtown and also because proprietor Rob Kaufelt really knew what he was doing, Murray's was a big part of my early cheese education. I'd pass by there on the way uptown to work at Picholine, tasting cheeses and often buying some to serve at the restaurant.

At Murray's, they manage to cram a lot into a limited space. On a recent visit, Murray's had 117 cheeses on display in its refrigerated cases, another 20 or more stacked in piles around the store, and at least another 20 prewrapped in plastic for self-service and a quick checkout. Murray's is always well stocked in every major category. On one visit, it offered one each of the "world's greatest blues quartet"—Roquefort, Stilton, Gorgonzola, and Cabrales—great for comparison tastings. Of the 16 blues on display, five were American and six French—an interesting comment on the U.S. artisanal boom: Before the year 2000, you would have been surprised to see more than two.

Another great way for a server to help a customer is by suggesting a more adventurous, less mundane, pedestrian cheese than the one requested. If a customer mentions a Manchego or a Morbier, there's almost always a more interesting, artisanal and/or sophisticated option. (Nothing against well-made versions of the former, but there are much more exciting alternatives in their respective categories...) These days, even with a much-loved, phenomenally tasty, genuine cheese such as Stilton, there are probably ten or fifteen equally exciting choices. The trick is for the cheese seller to engage in some discreet steering and for the customer to be open to exploration.

DISPLAY AND ORGANIZATION

How are the cheeses laid out and how are they organized? Does the layout make it easy to (1) find a specific cheese or cheeses you may be looking for, (2) shop for a variety of cheeses by category, and (3) make choices within a category?

At the Artisanal Premium Cheese Center, we divide our cheeses into the following basic categories, mostly by rind types, stacking and storing them accordingly:

- Younger, fresher chèvre styles, made at least in part, if not wholly, of goat's milk, often ash-dusted
- *Tomme* style, aged, semihard to hard, natural rinds
- Bloomy rinds: Bries, Camembert, and *triple crèmes*
- Washed rinds (both younger and aged), from Époisses to Appenzeller
- Blues (always natural-rinded)

(For more about categorizing cheeses, please refer back to chapter 5, page 101–4.)

As for the method of display, refrigerated cases may be required by local ordinances, but they cause a couple of problems: The cheese gets too cold for proper tasting and the large, enclosed cases throw up too much of a barrier between buyer and cheese. Knee- or waist-high open cases are a bit better. Ideally, cheeses are laid out on open counter tops at room temperature. Big open-air stacks, what I call the "wall of cheese" approach, can be impressive. Steve Jenkins popularized these at Fairway, adding a New York theatrical element to the more pious, restrained approach he had observed on scouting trips to France.

SAXELBY CHEESEMONGERS FOR FOCUS AND COMMITMENT

Anne Saxelby is a young Generation Xer who chose cheese over a host of other cool career options. Anne is one of my favorites among the new wave of cheese professionals. Her pocket-sized shop (just 120 square feet) in the Essex Street Market on Manhattan's Lower East Side features a precise selection of approximately thirty northeastern artisans and serves a following of loyal customers.

When she was an art student at nearby New York University, Saxelby took a trip to Italy that opened her eyes to the world of real cheese. Back in Manhattan, working at a bakery in Tribeca, she became a regular at the farmers' market stand operated by Elizabeth MacAlister and Mark Gillman's Cato Corner Farm. Anne did a cheese-making internship at Cato Corner the summer after college. Then she went to work at Murray's and became the in-house expert on American artisanal cheeses. Through Hervé Mons, the great French *affineur, négociant,* and retailer, she arranged stints at three chèvre-making farms in the Loire Valley. She also worked at Mons' shop in Roanne.

It's nice to see the big guys such as Whole Foods get into the act and exhibit a desire to do things right. At the same time, it's important for the littler ones to thrive and coexist. Saxelby Cheesemongers is just about seven city blocks from one of Whole Foods' biggest cheese showcases at the corner of the Bowery and Houston Street, a worthy temple to cheese, which should never outshine the magnificent little shrine Anne Saxelby has created. We root for the "little guys" like Anne because they're good for the artisanal movement (which is not to say the big ones like Whole Foods aren't).

Saxelby's, Murray's, DiPalo's, and Whole Foods—all more or less in my extended neighborhood, which is Lower Manhattan—fill different niches in the market and express different philosophies of retailing and cheesemongering, each with their own strengths. No doubt you'll find equivalent shops in your area. (The artisanal movement is about buying local food but also buying food locally, about supporting local producers *and* local retailers.) Anne Saxelby impresses me with her energy and commitment, but there's no lack of it in those other emporiums or in whichever fine-cheese shops stocking artisanal cheeses dot your neighborhood.

DESCRIPTIONS

What kind of descriptions and/or labels are attached to cheeses in the shop? At Dean & DeLuca's original SoHo store and later at Fairway, Steve Jenkins pioneered the genre of clever, pithy, funny (and often punny) blurbs attached to little cards on metal poles sticking into each chunk of cheese. At Murray's and other smart shops, these blurbettes are printed out as part of the price label that is used to seal each cheese package so you can take them home to serve inspirational and also mnemonic purposes.

The only downside to a retailer's catchy descriptions is they might overly influence buying decisions. Part of me feels people should be able to trust their eyes and rely on their gut instincts to pick out cheeses. If a cheese looks good, they can ask for a try. If it tastes good, they can buy some. Basic information is good, as long as it's accurate and fine cheeses are allowed to speak for

Anne Saxelby caters to her customers.

JEAN D'ALOS FOR DISPLAY

Not only does real cheese get around, but I get around because of real cheese. For me, this includes working the occasional cruise ship in the Mediterranean or the Pacific. Whenever I'm in southern France, I try to make it to the Jean d'Alos cheese shop on Rue Montesquieu in Bordeaux to stock up for shipboard events. D'Alos is not a very large store, but there's clearly a lot of love and reverence for fine cheese. It features excellent, mostly natural lighting. The cheeses are displayed in a stunning manner. They're laid out on marble counters, closely grouped but not cramped, in the open air with no sneeze guards or anything else standing between cheese lovers and their objects of affection. There is ample room for customers to walk around and examine the cheeses up close. The service is highly attentive and professional: An apron-clad female server accompanies each customer around, lavishing personal attention to assist with their cheese devotions.

themselves, especially those of lesser-known reputations or subtler character that might be drowned out by all manner of extraneous din and hype.

CARE AND HANDLING

Dealing in fine cheeses, caring for them, displaying and merchandising them properly takes quite a bit of time and physical effort, most of it behind the scenes. How serious is your retailer about ensuring its cheeses are kept in the best possible shape? What type of storage arrangements have been made? Cheese shops that have their own caves or dedicated temperature- and humidity-controlled storage areas score big points. They've taken their cheesemongering mission over the border into *affinage,* which can be a good capacity to have.

Although Anne Saxelby's retail space is relatively tiny, during her start-up she sought out a refrigeration specialist and had him build a custom 7-foot-square unit akin to those found in flower shops. It features an extra large coil to promote condensation and keep the moisture level up, addressing one of the biggest cheese-storage challenges. At Whole Foods' big Bowery location in Lower Manhattan, the cheese department (largely based on Patricia Michelson's La Fromagerie in London) features a walk-in cheese cave with an adjoining room for special care and handling that includes a row of smaller storage units with precise digital temperature controls. Murray's has a cellar underneath its flagship store with custom-built aging and storage units.

Though it's best not to refrigerate cheeses (and in any case not to get them too cold), you can't blame retailers if their local department of health mandates they hold all their cheese at 38 degrees F or lower. I recall some colleagues at a Chicago restaurant who were told by the health department their cheese cart had to refrigerated. The cheese *cart?* Please.

Our cheese cave at Picholine worked just fine, thank you very much, for well over a decade, operating at around 50 degrees F and 85 percent relative humidity. Cheese was around for a long time before the invention of 38 degree F refrigeration. Part of what I want this book to accomplish is to get the word out that if you treat cheeses carefully, in traditional fashion, nobody gets hurt and in fact everyone—producers, buyers, sellers, connoisseurs, and everyday fans—is happier.

We never had a lot of cave space or elaborate storage arrangements at Picholine. What we did have was a cozy environment, with just enough refrigeration and enough attention from me and my associates so the cheeses could settle in and stay quite happy together. Cheeses are best stored relatively snug. They tend to do better resting in their original shipping boxes, opened but carefully repacked and closed, though not taped or tightly sealed. I've often used the expression "keeping the cheeses in their own little microcosm." I firmly believe storing similar types together—in separate environments, if possible—encourages the appropriate colonies of microflora to stabilize and persist at beneficial levels, in a continuum from aging and ripening. None of this is necessarily cheese science, but I can tell you from experience it works. A good cheesemonger develops a feel for what's best for his or her cheeses, and this shows in how they present when on display in the shop.

TEMPERATURE ABUSE

Though many fine cheeses can put up with a lot, they cannot, ultimately, be ignored. They are, after all, "a living, breathing" perishable food. One of the more serious indignities a cheese may suffer is temperature abuse. As long as the relative humidity is kept high enough, cooler temperatures allow a cheese to settle into a more static state. If it's exposed to elevated temperatures for extended periods, it can literally start to cook. When kept too warm, a cheese's butterfats may begin to drain out and its enzymes may become overactive, causing excess degradations, mostly of those fats, from which it may never recover. Once a cheese starts sweating it is impossible to reinstate lost moisture. Giving a cheese a bath may help preserve its rind, but it cannot put escaped moisture back inside its body.

WHOLE CHEESES AND SHRINK-WRAPPING

Generally speaking, there is way too much shrink-wrapping of fine cheeses. Call it a necessary evil: My problem is it tends to be rampant and is usually unnecessary. There are few exceptions.

Sometimes people are looking for a quick fix: That one piece of cheese they can walk out with right away—a whole Époisses, say, or a Camembert or perhaps a hefty chunk of genuine cave-aged Gruyère. They don't want to wait for it to be cut to order and they're

STORING THE BLUES

AN EXCEPTION

Blue cheeses are the one exception to the prohibition against cold storage. At refrigeration temperatures, as long as there's enough moisture so it doesn't shrivel and dry up, a blue cheese will go into a static condition, akin to hibernation. A properly manufactured and aged blue should be at or near its optimal stage of bluing when it arrives at the shop. You don't want it to go any further and be over the hill before it's sold. If a nicely blued blue goes any further, there's no turning back. Cold storage can be a good solution in this case.

Old-style refrigerated wall display cases at DiPalo's.

CUTTING ORDER

PROGRESSION OF CHEESE TYPES

1. **HARD** (cow's and sheep's milk). Examples: Berkswell, Parmesan, Sbrinz, Zamorano.

2. **SEMIHARD.** Examples: traditional British farmhouse styles such as Cheddar, Cheshire, Lancashire.

3. **FIRM YET MOIST.** Examples: Fontina Val d'Aosta and Tomme de Savoie.

4. **SOFT RIPENED.** Examples: Pierre-Robert, Camembert and Brie styles, Pavé d'Auge.

5. **FRESH CHÈVRE STYLE.** Examples: Valençay, Selles-sur-Cher, and others.

6. **WASHED RIND, "STINKY."** Examples: Époisses, Munster, Maroilles.

7. **BLUES.** Examples: Stilton, Gorgonzola, Roquefort.

willing to buy based on a cheese's name, reputation, consistency, and reliability—that is, without tasting it. In this instance, it makes sense for the store to stock and display a certain number of whole (small- to medium-sized) cheeses and also to shrink-wrap ready-to-fly chunks of larger cheeses. But the best way to buy cheese is straight from the counter with no plastic wrap involved.

TURNOVER AND INVENTORY: THE SEASONAL EBB AND FLOW OF CHEESE

"Real cheese moves at its own pace" is one of my main professional mantras. Many a genuine article is either not available or isn't in top form year round. If a cheese is made for 8 months of the year and it requires 4 months of aging, you can do a simple calculus to determine when it will show best.

Wholesalers and retailers can face tricky challenges with both availability and demand. They need to keep on top of seasonal fluctuations in order to sell all their wares in tip-top shape and keep the product moving to satisfy both ripeness and freshness requirements and cash-flow ones. Buyers need to know the vicissitudes of each and every type.

The unfortunate long-term consequence of cheeses being sold too early (or too late) is they can give their entire class a bad name. One dried-up, soapy Berkswell or Spenwood, allowed to languish in less-than-perfect conditions, could turn an enthusiastic buyer off to one of the world's greatest cheese types. If you are that customer and a supposedly superior cheese disappoints you, do not hesitate to voice your opinion and ask what could be wrong. Your cheesemonger should be able to get to the bottom of it.

SERVICE

Further to what you should expect in a shop:

TASTING—Any self-respecting cheesemonger should volunteer tastes to browsing customers; if not, all you should have to do is ask. The only possible exception is with cheeses that have to be sold whole (e.g., Époisses, smaller-format chèvre styles, *torta*-style Iberians such as Queso de la Serena), though some stores with rapid turnover are able to offer halves of these cheeses, shrink-wrapping the unsold halves for subsequent sale.

CUTTING—A fresh little wedge out of a 40-pound drum or wheel of a perfectly aged big-boss British cheese the likes of Kirkham's

ROQUEFORT

A CHEESE FOR ALL SEASONS?

France's most famous and majestic blue is a prime example of a famous cheese whose tremendous popularity has made it susceptible to market pressures. As discussed in his *French Cheese Book*, Patrick Rance detected problems back in the 1960s and early '70s, and we still have to be on the lookout for them nowadays.

It all started with lactation cycles of the Lacaune ewes, whose milk, within a well-delineated zone, is the only permissible raw material for genuine Roquefort. The Lacaune have a 5-month gestation period. They give birth beginning in December, their greatest milk output is in April, and the milking season ends by late July. Roquefort cheeses require a minimum of 3 months' aging, which means they will be at peak from April until not much past the end of December.

Apparently, the Roquefort producers figured out a little trick. To guarantee year-round sales, they relegated a significant portion of their cheeses to cold storage *before* they were fully aged in order to freeze the ripening process—literally and figuratively—and thereby ship them out at later intervals. Roquefort ages in the caves of Combalou at 46 to 48 degrees F and around 96 degrees F humidity; cold storage is about 40 to 42 degrees F, with much lower humidity. Major Rance noticed a decline in Roqueforts that had endured cold storage and/or arrived at his shop during the suspect period of January to April: They lacked balance and had defects such as dryness, excess acidity, excess sharpness, and soapiness. (I would add oversalting to that list.) I can attest from personal experience that well-aged Roqueforts at peak are sublime, and that it's smart to be wary when buying these cheeses out of season.

Lancashire or Montgomery's is divine. We should all be so lucky as to be on hand when a shop is opening up one of those and offering tastes. Regardless, any partial chunks, large or small, should be kept in top shape and cheeses must be cut with efficiency and extra care.

From the cutter's viewpoint, the key tactic is to find the center point of the cheese in order to slice evenly shaped radial sections. With some of the bigger cheeses—Comté and other Alpine giants that come in wheels over 2 feet in diameter(!)—this is a step-by-step process, starting with a big half-moon knife or wire cutter. When a large half of cheese has been whittled down and/or is no longer symmetrical, the cutter should still find the imaginary center point and slice accordingly, leaving a tidy leftover chunk for the next cut. When carving up bigger cheeses, wedges for sale should always be cut from the smaller of the two halves, leaving the larger for display. Meanwhile, if the cut surface of the larger half starts to harden up and discolor—any hard cheese will naturally start to form its own rind with exposure to air—it should be periodically scraped to reveal fresh paste.

Well-cut cheeses at the Artisanal Premium Cheese Center.

JUSTIFYING (OR AT LEAST EXPLAINING) PRICES

Real cheese is not inexpensive because artisanal production is labor intensive and can be quite costly. First of all, the high-quality (all-natural, organic) milk necessary to make fine cheeses is expensive to produce, and it constitutes the largest cost factor in handmade cheeses. As a rule of thumb, it takes about 10 units of milk to make 1 unit of cheese. Artisans don't compromise their standards or principles, including TLC for the animals, quality of and components in the milk, and wages and benefits for their workers. The costs add up quickly.

Also, the often-fragile nature of fine cheeses makes transportation and fulfillment logistics difficult, to say the least. Finding the ideal packing, shipping, and handling methods is a challenge. At the cheese center, we frequently consult with artisan producers about ways to streamline the process and improve various details.

Unfortunately, waste is an unavoidable and significant cost in the customer-oriented business of cheesemongering. For cheeses to be carefully trimmed and attractively displayed and sold only in tip-top condition, and for customers to be offered plenty of tastes, there has to be about a 7 percent waste factor figured in to the equation.

These are just some of the many costs that contribute to the high prices of the cheeses we love. No excuses, just a few explanations. When you stop to consider all that goes into artisanal cheesemaking—from feeding the animals right through to hand-selling the final product (fine-cheese shops earn their markup, too)—its prices begin to make more sense. There is no doubt in my mind that a great artisanal cheese is worth paying for. The intensity of flavors and aromas, the concentration of good biological raw materials, the expression of *terroir*—all the attributes we hold in such high regard—are worth a premium. Beyond that, we have an obligation, a collective responsibility, to support and sustain traditional artisan food manufacturing as a counterweight to all the ills of large-scale industrial practices. Fast food versus Slow Food—there's no question which is better for you (and for the earth). So pay your cheese farmer a little more now or hang on to it and pay your doctor later. End of sermon.

A wall of cheese at Patricia Michelson's La Fromagerie, London.

WRAPPING—Your cheeses should be wrapped in good, cheese-friendly paper that is semipermeable to protect against grease or butterfat spreading while allowing the cheese to breathe. The paper—as opposed to the plastic—surface of the wrapping should be in contact with cheese so no plastic residue sticks to the cheese. This is one reason why shrink-wrapping is only acceptable for expedience in high-turnover situations and preferable only for the harder, aged, more stable cheeses.

YOUR CHEESE CONNECTION

As a customer, when I walk through that door of the cheese shop, I want to know I'm stepping into a realm of connoisseurship well beyond what's available from a brief stop in front of the cheese case in my local supermarket. I want my cheesemonger to connect me to the land, the animals, the *terroir*, and the artisan producers.

Most of the time, the buyer is not the same person who's behind the counter hand-selling the product. At Neal's Yard Dairy, the head cheese Randolph Hodgson is seen on the front lines, but certainly not every day. (How often are you greeted by the executive chefs at your three-star restaurants?) His aesthetic, however, his long experience and profound connoisseurship, permeate the entire operation and trickle down to even the most novice of employees. This is largely because Randolph trains his cheesemongers by the Socratic method, tasting with them and asking questions: "What do you think about this one? How about that one?"

ACCOMPANIMENTS

Many retailers sell plenty of other specialty foods alongside their cheeses, making us cheese purists a little itchy under the collar. (Sometimes I think it's a pity they can't survive on cheese alone, but business is business.) While a great cheese *requires* no accompaniment other than perhaps a good, fresh piece of crusty baguette, there are a few other foods your shop may sell that can pair quite well. Some of the options:

BREAD—For the milder and/or more complex cheeses, choose breads that are fairly neutral. For some of the stronger-flavored, more rustic cheeses, look for complementary breads. A plain baguette can highlight the texture contrasts and balance the flavors of the triple crèmes, the bloomy rinds, and many of the more unobtrusive washed-rind types. A Cheddar, harder and with more volume of flavor, might take a hardier bread, perhaps leaning toward a whole wheat or rye type. A blue would classically pair with raisin-walnut bread: The sweetness of the raisins balances the bite of the blue; the crunchy nuts provide a texture contrast with its creaminess; the inherent oils and complex flavor profile of the nuts harmonize with similar traits in the cheese. Other bread options include sourdough, rye, multigrain, olive loaf; Tuscan rounds or other peasant-style breads; focaccia (plain or with onions, herbs, tomatoes, even grapes); wheat or rye crackers; flatbreads; or thin slices of toast for texture contrast.

JAMS AND CHUTNEYS—The classic is *membrillo,* or quince paste, which is very sweet (a little bit goes a long way) and balances out the salty, biting flavors and dry, crumbly textures of many cheeses. Cheddar or some other big-boss British cheese alongside various

"The main thing [customers] should expect is value. In all his books, books that were required reading when I was [in school], Peter Drucker would always talk about innovation and entrepreneurship, but it all came down to perception of value. If the customer no longer perceives value, you will go out of business. What we have to keep in mind is it's not what we think of as valuable, it's what [the customer] thinks of as valuable."

ROB KAUFELT,
MURRAY'S CHEESE SHOP

STORAGE CONDITIONS

BLUES: 42 to 46 degrees F, 85 to 95 percent humidity

SOFT RIPENED: 50 to 52 degrees F, 80 to 90 percent humidity

WASHED RIND: 50 to 55 degrees F., 90+ percent humidity

HARD, AGED: 55 to 50 degrees F, 80+ percent humidity

CHEESE AND OTHER FOODS

In matching cheeses with other foods, use the same principles as with beverage pairings—contrast, balance, and complement.

Contrasting flavors and textures should be balanced against each other, so things don't tilt too far in any one direction. Among the fundamental contrasts are sweet versus sour; sweet versus salty; bitter versus salty, hard versus soft, crunchy versus smooth; dense versus aerated; and wet versus dry.

Some of the more interesting, complex components in a cheese's flavor profile can find complements in a partner. Floral, fruity, or nutty aromatics may seek harmony with similar characteristics in a partner. Minerally or earthy flavors may do the same. A rough, rustic mouth feel in a cheese may go well with the same trait in its food partners.

Depending on the character and traits of each partner, these basic principles may be applied all at once or to differing degrees. For example, if a cheese's dominant traits are a strong, sharp, biting flavor, it may be looking for a sweet, mild partner.

Regional affinities may hold more sway in food pairings (as opposed to beverage matchups), particularly in the case of breads. After all, didn't the creameries and bakeries exist side by side down through history? In fact, they were probably pretty much under the same roof in feudal and monastic times. Tuscan peasant bread with a fine aged local Pecorino . . . Baguette freshly baked on the outskirts of Paris to accompany the soft-ripened cheeses of Normandy and the Île-de-France . . . It doesn't get much better than that.

ABOVE: A Parisian fromagerie.

OPPOSITE TOP TO BOTTOM: Honeycomb, a nice match for salty, dry cheeses; jams and chutneys are good potential cheese partners; if you have a chance, learn what you can from a cheese's label. This is Pecorino delle Balze Volterrane, the revival of an ancient type from Caseificio Pinzani (see also page 319).

chutneys is another classic. Small dollops or drizzles of high-quality honey, super-smooth and sweet, provide another complement to the drying, salty textures of cheeses. Fruit jams and preserves as well as relishes offer similar contrasts. Tomato preserves with chèvre-style cheeses are a good example of the double whammy of flavor and texture contrasts (sweet vs. salty; sweet vs. acidic; and smooth vs. chalky) that can be achieved with well-thought-out cheese-food pairings.

FRUIT—High-pectin fruits provide a good platform; they also supply the two main nutrients missing from cheese: vitamin C and fiber. Ripe figs, apples, grapes, peaches, pears, or melons work well. Other fruit possibilities include dried figs, Catalonian fig cake, plum cake, and dates.

VEGETABLES—Raw, very lightly steamed, or blanched vegetables can work well with cheeses, perhaps as a large appetizer plate or a light meal for lunch or supper. Think of all the potentially delicious contrasts, starting with raw versus fermented and juicy versus dry. Other interesting combinations are Pecorino or some other hard, aged sheep's milk cheese with freshly shelled fava beans (a traditional Tuscan snack); pickled vegetable salad, marinated (sweet and/or hot) peppers, and/or assorted olives with cheese and bread. As always, be sure that none of the accompanying flavors over-whelm your cheeses.

NUTS—Raw or toasted nuts can also offer complementary flavors and contrasting textures for many fine cheeses. The possibilities include almonds, Brazil nuts, cashews, hazelnuts, pecans, and walnuts.

MEATS—Hearty cheeses can stand up very nicely to many rustic and/or sophisticated cured meats, including Italian prosciutto, sorpressata, capicola, or salami; Spanish *jamón serrano* or chorizo; German Speck; or Virginia ham. Be sure to exercise some restraint here, too, since there are a lot of potentially strong, salty, gamey flavors competing for attention.

HOW TO SHOP FOR CHEESE: MAXIMIZING YOUR BUYING EXPERIENCE

Following is some practical advice for buying fine cheeses. Always remember to sample plenty and be sure of what you're getting. Be adventurous: If you're buying more than a couple of cheeses in a good shop, leave at least some of your requests open ended; this way, you have a chance of discovering something new and excit-ing every time you go shopping.

Reading Labels

Here are a few tips to help you decipher labels when browsing.

CHEESE NAME—If you have any difficulties with pronunciation, your cheese retailer should be able to help. Note instances where the cheese name is also a place-name. American artisanal cheeses, generally being more recent arrivals on the scene, tend to have more fanciful, made-up, and sometimes even "cutesy" names as opposed to European ones, which are more often associated with the cheese's place of origin.

PROVENANCE—Apart from the name, the label should state spe-cifically where the cheese comes from—its country, region, village, and so forth.

TYPE OF CHEESE—Is it categorized on its label? For example, the label should specify whether the cheese is fresh and/or aged under 60 days; bloomy-rind; hard, aged.

The Neal's Yard Dairy label represents a quality brand.

GUIDELINES FOR HOME

- Never serve cheeses too cold; it masks all their wonderful flavors and aromas. This is the biggest mistake cheese novices make. In general, if they're in the fridge, give them at least 1 hour out of it to make sure they come to room temperature.

- Blue cheeses may get bluer quite fast, so they can be given less than an hour out of the fridge before serving.

- For soft, ripe, gooey, runny cheeses, provide a separate plate onto which they can melt and expand.

- Sharp steak knives and/or small- to medium-sized kitchen knives are all you need to cut cheeses.

- If you're using a board for cutting or presentation, be sure it is made out of an inert material: hardwood works well as do different types of nonreactive plastic and glass or stone surfaces.

- Cut all cheeses fresh; don't precut.

- Consider keeping separate knives and other utensils for each cheese or cheese type.

- Keep utensils clean by wiping them with a clean cloth napkin or thick paper towel immediately after cutting each cheese.

- Slice harder cheeses into smaller, thinner pieces.

- Slice semisoft cheeses in long wedges.

- Slice soft cheeses in shorter, thicker wedges.

- Include a portion of the rind (if applicable).

- Serve cheeses on dinner or salad plates with dinner knife and dinner (or salad or dessert) fork; add a spoon if they're gooey.

- Rewrap cheeses as they were wrapped in the store, with semipermeable paper touching the cheese and plastic wrap encasing the package; use a zip-locking bag or some scotch tape if necessary.

- Storing most cheeses, particularly firm to semisoft types, at cool room temperature conditions, away from any sources of heat or light, is fine for probably longer than you would imagine.

- For refrigerator storage, treat your cheeses like bread or any other fragile food you don't want to dry out: Put them in the vegetable drawer—or perhaps the smaller cold-cuts tray—if possible alongside other foods that provide some moisture (vegetables and/or other cheeses).

TYPE OF MILK—Is it made from cow's, sheep's, or goat's milk, or is it a mix? Is the milk raw or pasteurized?

PRODUCER—Who made the cheese and what type of operation is it? Is it a factory, a cooperative, a dairy or creamery, a farmhouse? Each and every artisanal cheese has a story. Most U.S. producers have their own websites, where at least a bit of their history is explained. If you see that cheese comes to you via a co-op, an *affineur*, or a foreign source, by way of an importer, you may find interesting information on these individual companies' sites.

AFFINEUR—Certain operations source their cheeses from very small and/or independent producers whose names are not listed on the cheeses. You are essentially buying the *affineur*'s brand, which becomes your quality guarantee. This is also true of a major cheese such as Parmigiano-Reggiano, which comes from a huge consortium of producers (of all different sizes), each indicated by number only. In the case of Parm, if it is selected and aged under the supervision of a quality *affineur* exporter such as Giorgio Cravero, there is your guarantee. Another good example is Neal's Yard Dairy, which is *the* brand for British artisanal cheeses and which allows for no confusion about the exact origins of its cheeses.

CONTENT—The fat content of cheeses is expressed on their labels as a percentage of "fat in dry matter" or "fat on a dry basis"—in other words, what portion of their solids are fat. (The term is *matière grasse* in French; *grassi* in Italian; *Fett in Trochenmasse,* or F.i.T. in German.) Whole-milk cheeses range from about 35 to 50 percent butterfat; double crèmes are 60 to 75 percent and triple crèmes over 75 percent.

DESIGNATIONS—How is the cheese qualified in terms of official designations of origin such as the European AOC or DOP labels? (See appendix 1, page 363.) Check to see whether there are any other official stamps on the cheese itself or its labels—and if so, what additional qualifications they may indicate. France, for example, has four categories of production.

- **FERMIER (FARMHOUSE):** Raw milk from the farm's own herd is made into cheese there by traditional methods; small-sized operations.

- **ARTISANAL:** This is an individual producer, like the fermier, but milk may be bought from other farms; small-sized operations.

"The designation of origin for agricultural products [comes from] a much more ancient tradition than any kind of commercial trademark. . . Nowadays, the temptation to plagiarize and usurp in the form of brand names is more and more present, even in the case of very traditional products."

JEAN G. BOYAZOGLU, "PRODUCTS OF ORIGIN AND THE INTERNATIONAL CONSUMER," IN CASEUS, 2002

This conversion chart is useful if you are reading European labels or traveling and shopping in stores abroad.

100 grams = 3.5 ounces

150 grams = 5.3 ounces

250 grams = 8.8 ounces

500 grams = 17.6 ounces (or 1 pound, 1.6 ounces)

1 kilo = 2.2 pounds

To convert ounces to grams, divide by 28.35.

To convert kilos to pounds, multiply by 2.2 (or divide by .454).

- **COOPÉRATIVES (OR FRUITIÈRES):** An individual local dairy, to which co-op member farms contribute their milk for cheese-making; small- to medium-sized operations.

- **INDUSTRIEL:** Factory-style dairies, which may receive milk from distant regions; medium-sized to large operations.

Mountain cheeses may have additional qualifications such as *alpage*. (For more on appellations, see appendix 1, page 363.)

CERTIFICATIONS—Cheeses, particularly U.S. artisanal ones, may make other claims and/or have other types of certifications as to whether they are organic, biodynamic, natural, sustainable, and so on. Rogue Creamery's cheeses, for example, have three different third parties certifying them organic, sustainable, and quality assured (for cleanliness and proper sanitary procedures). Since the United States has no appellation designations, these third-party certifications tend to hold more weight. As always, when in doubt ask your cheesemonger.

Know What You're Getting

Beware of "brand confusion," which can happen if you don't read the labels carefully. Sometimes industrial, commercial cheeses may be masquerading as the real thing.

QUESTIONS

WHAT TO ASK IN A SHOP

Test the cheese shop staff's knowledge and information. If you don't know, ask! If they don't have ready answers, they should be able to find them quickly and/or refer you to some good sources of further information.

- What is it? Note name, origin, producer, and type of cheese (rind, texture, species, category).

- May I have a taste?

- Where is it from?

- Who made it? What type of operation are they?

- How old is it? How long was it aged?

- What cheeses are good *right now*? (What's in season?)

- Who is the cheese buyer for the store and is it possible to speak with that person?

- Is it ready for this evening?

- Will it be better tomorrow, the next day, or the next day?

- How long can it last? When is the best time to eat it?

- How should I keep it? Is the rind edible?

- Do you have any organic cheeses?

- Do you have any vegetarian cheeses (i.e., not made with animal rennet)?

- Do you have a good cheese for cooking? I have a recipe that calls for Emmentaler. Do you have any—or anything similar?

How Much to Buy

The rule of thumb I follow is about 1 ounce of cheese per person for a tasting of 5 to 8 cheeses. If you're presenting more cheeses, you can reduce that to around ¾ ounce per person. For a main course or a deluxe after-dinner plate, you'll want to figure on as much as 1½ ounces per person. If you're organizing a cheese-centered event—particularly, a tasting or a dinner where a plate of special cheeses with more than a couple of wines is the main focus—you may want to increase it to as much as 2 ounces per person.

Generally speaking, with softer cheeses you can increase the quantities. For blues, I increase it by about 20 percent per serving; for the bloomy rinds and other softer selections, I'll go up as much as 50 percent. With washed-rind cheeses and some of the bloomy-rind ones, there is going to be a certain amount of waste, so you need to figure that into the equation: First of all, people are not necessarily going to eat the smelly and slimy (should we say "fragrant and moist"?) rinds. For your cheese eaters to get their money's worth in this case, again you should probably figure on between 25 and 50 percent more—about 1¼ to 1½ ounces if you want them to consume 1 ounce and so forth.

Parmigiano-Reggianos spend several months in the Cravero aging facility, Bra, Italy.

"Buy what you like, have some fun with the people behind the counter. Don't be afraid to experiment. Don't take it too seriously: It's only cheese. It's not the presidential election, it's not a life or death issue, it's not about the future of the Republic."

ROB KAUFELT,
MURRAY'S CHEESE SHOP

BRINGING THEM HOME AND KEEPING THEM HAPPY

One of the biggest FAQs I get both in classes or seminars and during restaurant service goes something like this: "I really love these cheeses; how can I put together this kind of plate at home?" When people first discover the wonderful world of real cheeses, they're often in such a state of euphoria, they have a hard time believing the experience could be replicated in their own homes. It certainly can. There are a few simple guidelines you can follow to make it happen.

As a moist, living thing, cheese respires and can expire because of smothering, lack of air exchange, or drying out. (When the temperature of air drops, it holds less humidity, which is why refrigeration can be bad for fine cheeses.) The moderately low temperatures and fairly high humidities used to store cheeses in professional settings are difficult to achieve, which is why it's recommended you store fine cheeses as little as possible at home. The mantra is "Buy less, but buy often."

FROM TOP: Idiazábal and Kunik.

Cheese for Sale

CHEESEMONGER CHECKLIST: WHAT TO LOOK FOR IN A SHOP

- Atmosphere and ambience (lighting, temperature, sound, size)
- Ownership/History
- Information and education
- Feedback
- Selection and condition of cheeses
- Substitutions/Alternatives
- Display and organization
- Descriptions
- Care and handling
- Service: cutting, tasting, and wrapping

☐ Plastic can leave some residue on the surface of the cheese that negatively affects its flavor—not to mention the effects of suffocation owing to prolonged shrink-wrapping.

☐ Hard cheeses are better able to survive poor storage conditions and other abuses, including shrink-wrapping to the point of suffocation.

☐ Cheesemongers must stay on top of the natural ebb and flow of real cheeses and master the challenges of seasonal availability and demand.

☐ The staff of any good cheese shop should offer accurate basic facts, including specific knowledge and useful practical advice—in an appropriate, unobtrusive manner.

☐ Great cheeses are not inexpensive; artisans work hard to produce them and have high costs. A little bit goes a long way.

☐ Know what you're getting: Beware of "brand confusion," read the labels carefully, and avoid industrial cheeses and usurpers of real-cheese names.

CHAPTER 10

CHEESE IN RESTAURANTS: WHITE LINEN, SILVER SERVICE, AND THREE STARS

OF ALL THE WAYS TO PUT AN EXCLAMATION POINT AT THE END OF A fine meal, I can think of none better than a cheese course. As you can imagine, the subject of cheese in restaurants is one very near and dear to my heart. From the beginning of the program at Picholine in 1994, I spent from 7 to 12 hours a day (sometimes more), mostly on my feet, 6 days a week, practically year round, caring for and serving cheeses. A much smaller percentage of my working hours was divided between sitting down at the computer and/or talking on the phone to procure the finest selections available, and tasting, tasting, and tasting some more.

Since the Artisanal Premium Cheese Center opened in 2003 and I was appointed its Dean of Curriculum, my duties have shifted a bit. I still perform cheese service occasionally as well as help manage inventory and train other cheese servers. And, as mentioned, I teach plenty of classes to amateurs and professionals, including restaurant people. (In the fine-cheese realm, the importance of education, of spreading the good word about the curd, cannot be stressed enough.)

Pouring Champagne into a hollowed-out Langres—a festive touch for a special occasion.

The cheese board at Picholine during assembly: Quite a selection of cheese artistry.

THE RESTAURANT ADVANTAGE

Naturally, I'm a little prejudiced in favor of restaurants because that's where I got my start. There are a few clear advantages to cheese service in this milieu. Although they have more limited resources and generally smaller selections than stores, restaurants do have more captive audiences and greater focus. As a *Fromager* at a fine-dining destination, I have an edge over the retail cheese-monger similar to the enhanced perspective a Sommelier has over a wine retailer.

Our restaurant customers taste cheeses at their leisure in an intimate, relaxed setting. Most retailers offer tastes, but the ensuing conversation is almost always more curt, less expansive. A large percentage of customers in a retail shop already know what they want; they walk in ready to state their needs and preferences. They may not browse as much or want to take the time to taste, reflect, and expound while in the store. I find restaurant customers are more likely to be open to suggestions and certainly more willing and able to carry on a dialogue.

HOW MANY CHEESES (AND HOW MUCH CHEESE)?

When we first put together our cheese board at Picholine in 1994, we had fourteen of the best cheeses we could corral. That number quickly grew past twenty, then thirty, and on, until it hit as many as seventy cheeses on the ordering list, sixty in the cave, and up to fifty on the trolley at a time. We set the standard for serious restaurant programs in the United States. As part of this effort, we created the first dedicated restaurant cheese cave in North America: A back office was converted into a small private dining room and a refrigeration unit, like the ones used in flower shops, was installed in its closet, transforming that into the cheese-storage unit. (The door is fairly airtight and we also spray down the walls, as needed, to keep up the humidity.) Since 1994, I'm proud to say over 50 tons of fine cheeses have passed through that little cave. Spread over the years, it may not seem like a lot but when you divide it up into ½- or 1-ounce chunks, that's cutting a lot of cheese.

From very early on, every day there was dining service, we put together two identical cheese boards, with more than half of the in-house stock arranged in an eye-catching display. The board destined for show in the dining room was wheeled out on a *guéridon* or food trolley we set up (now manufactured as specialty items by restaurant supply firms) while the other "production board" was kept in back to fulfill orders.

I realize a Picholine-sized cheese program may be way more than is practical or even desirable for most restaurants. For some places, a preselected daily offering of three to five is all that's possible. In any case, a little bit of real cheese is far better than none at all. The most concise advice I can give for the expedient route to a good small program is to choose from among "Max's Picks," which appear throughout part III of this book, selecting the top cheese from each major category and/or country. By the way, all cheese plates—including a limited, preselected one—should be fresh cut to order; they should never be precut or preassembled.

THE HIGHEST STANDARDS

If you aim to start a restaurant program of, say, twenty cheeses, there are plenty of great ones—not just very good but great—from which to choose, leaving no room for mediocre or lackluster selections. If you've only got five spots on your roster, it should be pretty easy to select five really superlative world-class cheeses. Another way of looking at it: Limitations force you to raise your standards, which is the positive aspect of having only modest resources available to devote to fine cheeses.

Artfully and purposefully arranged together on a board, artisanal cheeses form an irresistibly alluring display of edible sculpture.

OWNING THE TROLLEY

One question to be answered very early on is who's in charge? Someone has got to "own the cheese." Often it's the Chef, Maître d', or a Sommelier who starts out in this position. Cheese prep may be delegated to an assistant chef or *Garde Manger,* often the person in charge of the salads and other cold plates.

Whether the cheese program is assigned to a front-of-the-house or a back-of-the-house employee is a crucial decision. I'm a firm believer in strong front-of-house involvement. The reason is many assistant chefs tend to lose touch with what's going on in the dining room. Too often the person who's assembling the plate is stuck toiling in the back, unable to see people enjoying cheese. To me, it's imperative that the people responsible for a restaurant program interact with diners on a regular basis to learn firsthand how people respond to the selection.

To be a strong cheese server, you have to collect plenty of feedback. The *Maître Fromager* and his or her assistants need to know exactly "where their customers are" cheese-wise. I've been doing it long enough and we have enough regular cheese customers that I have a good idea of many of their personal likes and dislikes. In conversation, I can share some inside knowledge with my diners and they can clue me in on what the public wants. I've found some of the best leads on new cheeses–and on successful wine pairings— come from our patrons who travel. Customers can really help drive a good restaurant program. If we take our time, listen to each other and share our love for cheese, everyone benefits.

WHAT TO LOOK FOR IN A RESTAURANT

Whether you're judging a retail program (as in the previous chapter) or a restaurant one, it's good to establish and maintain high standards. Here are the main criteria.

Selection: Themes and Rotation

The largest restaurant cheese menu will rarely equal even a smaller cheese shop's roster. (In its heyday, Picholine had a bigger one than a small retailer, say, Saxelby Cheesemongers, but this is the exception.) The question becomes how a restaurant applies its more limited resources and scope to the wealth of great cheese choices now available. A restaurant should choose some themes and determine, within those, how to cover an impressively broad range of cheese types and expressions of *terroir*. It should also establish a rotation (i.e., how often cheeses will go on or off the list, how many changes will be made and for what reasons).

How does a restaurant's particular style of cuisine relate to its cheese selections? Does a Spanish restaurant feature Spanish or Spanish-style cheeses and if so to what extent? The options seems endless. Take Italy, for example: You have the northern mountain cheeses, with subcategories of *tomme* (actually *toma*) styles; the Robiola family (delicious little patties, with some fascinating mixed-milk types); and blues. Then you have the Tuscan farmhouse cheeses, mostly variations on Pecorino. You've got the obligatory chunk of genuine Parmigiano-Reggiano, and then you can move on to the lesser-known ancient, rustic types of Sardegna and/or the south. And that's just Italy! One or more seemingly narrow themes can open the window to a surprisingly wide selection, but with limitations it's important to find a clear focus.

Sharing cheese talk with customers is a maître fromager's pleasure; listening carefully to their preferences is his duty.

Display and Presentation

Artfully and purposefully arranged together on a board, artisanal cheeses form an irresistibly alluring display of edible sculpture. There is so much variation in texture, shape, and color, so much delectable detail. While most restaurants offer cheese in the form of a preselected dessert-alternative plate, the elite few are able to present a spectacular cheese board, the presentation of which can be a memorable, theatrical moment. (It happened more than once at Picholine, but the first time a diner remarked how our display reminded them of the Manhattan skyline portrayed in cheese it forever changed my way of looking at—and arranging—the board.) A good organizational plan is key for a successful cheese board. Cheeses should be arranged in clear, logical order—by animal types, by country and/or some other coherent scheme—making them easier for diners to recognize and for servers to pick out and serve quickly and efficiently.

With artisanal cheeses, we can't forget aesthetics. My main instruction to my assistant *fromagers,* beyond organization, is to make sure it looks great. ("You're the conductor and your customers are the audience," I'll tell them. "Arrange your cheeses like members of an orchestra, with everybody looking front and center.") Cheeses are easier to see and better highlighted if they're presented on a dark, contrasting background. At Picholine, we

SOME OF THE CHEESES ARE TOUCHING (AND THEY DON'T MIND)

To make the most of limited space on the board, keep the air exposure to a minimum, and avoid excessive drying, we would lean some cheeses against each other. This worked with some of the harder, aged cheeses, particularly the sheep's milk ones, some of which are round-edged and have a difficult time standing up on their own. (I thought of them as a nice little flock . . .) The goat cheeses, on the other hand, being capricious, tended not to fit together as snugly as the sheep.

used several slabs of dark green marble, slightly veined, which were quite flattering. Other viable surfaces include lighter-colored marble or smooth, dark hardwood.

Keeping it clean is not the last nor the least of our concerns: The board should remain pristine, appealing, and attractive, even when cheese service is in high gear. The cheeses themselves should be "faced," the surface of exposed paste trimmed and cleaned, scraping it lightly or slicing off just the outer layer. Every cut should be a fresh one and the board should be kept free of scraps.

Menus and Lists

How the cheese selections are listed, and the information about them presented, is of utmost importance. Do they get a separate menu or a separate section of either the main or dessert menu(s)? How much information does it offer and how useful or desirable is it? At the very least, a menu should correctly list the names and provenances of cheeses, their producers, and a short description, with animal species, cheese type, and perhaps a few descriptive words about flavors and textures. Cheese lists should be thoroughly checked for accuracy and frequently updated as the roster changes. (Remember another mantra: "Cheese is a moving target.") An especially nice touch is to print a separate cheese menu and offer it as a take-home item. Not only can this be a great introduction to cheese connoisseurship, but also a good marketing tool for the restaurant.

Regardless of how detailed a menu is offered, it won't have the space to include all the information available on every cheese. Cheese servers need to be ready, willing, and able to discuss and explain their offerings with additional helpful details. I always try to read my customers quickly in terms of how much of a conversation they're willing or able to have when I'm serving them. Exchanging cheese banter with my dining customers is one of the best parts of my job as *Maître Fromager*. I hope it's just as enjoyable for them.

Service

Of course, the best establishments make attentive, efficient, polite, unobtrusive service a high priority. In a restaurant, not only is the interaction between customer and server more immediate and intimate than in a shop, it is also often more formal. Intelligent and discreet but enthusiastic is the attitude I'd want my servers to project.

As for the practicalities, I train them to cut fine cheeses very carefully and precisely. Whether the cheese is cut in front of the guests or somewhere behind the scenes, the knife (and fork or other cutting utensil) must be kept clean at all times. I can't stress this enough! Beyond practical considerations, cutting cheeses to order, with great care, in front of diners demonstrates attention to detail and instills confidence in the entire cheese program.

When the cheeses are presented, they should be in the proper sequence, from mildest to strongest, with alternating texture, milks, rind types, and so forth. (See chapter 11 for everything you need to know about assembling a progression.) Servers should offer clear recommendations and subtle reminders about the logic of a sequence and the potential consequences of not following it. Naturally, people get excited and may eat cheeses out of order, which is their prerogative. All we need to do is alert them to the risks.

Though cheeses may be very close or even touching in the display, once plated they should have enough space in between so each can garner plenty of individual attention. We began serving our Picholine cheese courses on white china, which works fairly well to highlight colors and textures. (I recall one regular patron with poor eyesight who used to bring in her own dark blue plate so she could admire her cheeses more easily.) On round plates, we originally placed the mildest cheese at the six o'clock position, closest to the diner, with the order proceeding around the plate clockwise, finishing with the strongest cheese at around five o'clock. This is somewhat in defiance of convention, which would be to start at the noon position, but it has worked well for us. Later, we began serving cheeses on olive wood boards, ordered from left to right, an effective and aesthetically pleasing alternative.

CHEESE DEMOGRAPHICS: REQUESTS AND PREFERENCES

There is really no accounting for personal preferences; people have their prohibitions, they have their dietary restrictions, their beliefs and prejudices, and for the most part they come by them honestly. We in the business must honor these preferences, while at the same time, as appropriate, encouraging diners to expand their cheese horizons.

TO EAT OR NOT TO EAT

Diners to whom I've served cheese have been peppering me with questions since day one. Among the most common FAQs I've heard in the restaurant is, "Is it okay to eat the rind?" The short answer: "Yes, as long as it tastes good." A conscientious cheese server may feel obligated to add a few caveats for the uninitiated: Rinds may harbor a fair amount of bacteria and molds, which may be harmless but can be funky-tasting. And although a rind may be eminently edible, its textures may not be particularly delightful and it is more likely to clash with potential wine partners.

CUTTING & SERVING

A FEW SMART STRATEGIES

Following are some further guidelines I follow and stress in training *fromagers*.

- Present each cheese with a small portion of its rind—as long as it has one. This has a practical purpose: It's a convenient handle, making soft and semisoft cheeses easier to pick up. It also helps as a reference and mnemonic device, adds an interesting visual and textural element, and allows for tasting.

- Very hard and/or very strong cheeses should be cut thin. Sbrinz, somewhat of an extreme example, needs to be shaved nearly paper thin.

- Softer, melting cheeses ought to be served in nice, plump chunks.

- Semisoft to semihard cheeses should be served in wedges, thinner than the soft ones.

- If a cheese is flaky or crumbling, the server is obliged to keep the portion neat and self-contained. This may take some discreet rearranging by way of digital dexterity.

- When cutting soft, collapsing, runny cheeses such as Époisses, servers should use a fork to support the rind.

- Before cutting into a cheese, it's important to consider the size, shape, and appearance of what will be left—the remaining chunk. The *fromager* should assess how many slices can be had, especially from a relatively small cheese. With a cheese the size of Wabash Cannonball for example, which is a little 3-ounce spheroid about 1½ to 2 inches in diameter, do you expect to get three slices or will you try for four or more? If you're aiming for five slices from a small, soft, and/or oozing cheese, the first cut should be smaller than one-fifth of the entire cheese. Take your time and be conservative with your "eyeball estimates"; if you make too large of a first cut, you may come up short on the last slice.

My cheese-eating customers have often expressed preferences in terms of dislikes. Among the most common of these is "No matter what, no goat cheese," which continues to surprise me and appears to be based on the misconception that all goat cheeses taste goaty (for more on this, see chapter 22). On the flip side of the goat cheese prohibition, some people may prefer them because they believe they're somehow less fattening.

The second most common prohibition is against blue cheeses. Some people just don't like that sharp bite of the blue. They feel it overwhelms all the other flavors and just won't go away. (To some extent, this is true, but it's also a matter of tolerance.) Others don't feel comfortable eating something so closely associated with spoilage and decay (the molds). People who need to follow a gluten-free diet may want to avoid the blues, since there could be traces of gluten from the propagation of the molds in bread (as is the case with Roquefort).

Some other frequent requests I've heard over the years have

been for a particular style or type of cheese, for a density or texture, for the cheeses of a particular country or region or simply for "something new and exciting." Some people say they like harder cheeses, others softer ones. The public seems to be split right down the middle on this one. Just as there's a percentage wanting to bypass the blues, there are people who want to stay away from the "stinkers." Some aromas can be overwhelming or borderline noxious.

As for national or regional preferences, there was a time when many of my Picholine diners would have dismissed American-made cheeses, not realizing how well they were measuring up to their European counterparts. Fortunately, this doesn't happen much anymore. I recall one diner who was interested in trying any cheeses as long as they weren't British. This was during a serious outbreak of foot-and-mouth disease on many farms in the United Kingdom and Belgium. Little did this customer know the virus responsible for this disease is not transmitted through cheese. (She didn't mention Belgian cheeses either, perhaps assuming we had none on the cart.) This is exactly where the server's ability to allay fears, address concerns, and answer FAQs comes in handy.

Another category of requests is for cheeses that pair especially well with someone's favorite wine. Depending on the wine, this can lead to serious limitations in the choice of cheeses. Various recommendations and perhaps even flights (see page 202) can address this challenge. (Much more about all this in chapter 12.)

STORAGE

Beyond the issue of maintaining attractive and reasonably sized portions for your beautiful open-air display—which is the model, albeit perhaps not the norm—storing the larger remaining chunks properly is crucial. At Picholine, we always turned over a lot of cheese, which helped alleviate concerns about storage and inventory flow. We were continually able to display cheeses at their best. Restaurants need to ensure freshness as savvy cheese connoisseurs will notice if everything is not in tip-top shape.

Cheese maintenance in the restaurant setting should not be taken lightly. It is demanding work: The cheeses need the same precise and individual care as they receive at retail. A restaurant offering up to thirty cheeses does not require a large cave, but proper temperature and humidity levels must be maintained.

PUSHING THE ENVELOPE

True cheese lovers never tire of the quest to venture beyond what they've already tasted. Once a cheese program has its legs, there will be no shortage of requests from customers for cheeses to equal or top old standbys: An established cheese program, recognized for its quality and diversity, should never disappoint its patrons. The goal is always to keep things exciting and to push the envelope. Regulars often bring in friends, eager to turn them on to real cheese; they exercise their connoisseurship and their appreciation, almost always requesting a few old favorites along with recommendations for exciting new discoveries.

"THE PROFIT IS IN THE BOTTLE"

I recall a memorable occasion in the early days of cheese service at Picholine: It was a busy evening and a table of four had just finished a good meal. We would have been happy for them to request their check so we could seat the next party, which was waiting for the table. But the first party asked to see the cheese menu and ordered a modest selection for one shared plate. They had about a third of a bottle of a pricey California boutique Cabernet Sauvignon left over, and we figured there wasn't much potential for an additional beverage sale. The party's host asked for a recommendation to pair with the cheeses—perhaps a dessert wine? It was blatantly evident to me that this plate of cheeses *screamed* for a Château d'Yquem Sauternes. We had half bottles of this "nectar of the gods" in a somewhat older vintage priced at $495, so I mentioned it, somewhat sheepishly. Lo and behold, our quiet party of four ordered the half of Yquem without a flinch, increasing their bill by about thirty times the price of their cheese plate. It's amazing to see to what heights real cheese can elevate a dinner.

PRICING

In critiquing a restaurant's cheese program, you'll want to note portion sizes and prices, and compare them with what you might find elsewhere. Fine cheeses are expensive at wholesale, and restaurants try to maintain a set percentage of ingredient cost per dish so they can achieve a reasonable profit margin. Cheese may not satisfy those requirements and may need to be treated as an exception. Held to standard margins, it may end up pricing itself right off the menu.

There's a lot of behind-the-scenes work that goes into maintaining a proper cheese program—from sourcing and selecting to maintenance and presentation—but it is not a major profit center for a restaurant business. It's well known that in restaurants almost all of the profit is in the bottle, meaning, from a cheese perspective, wines and other beverages for pairings.

My arguments in favor of real cheese—when the owners, managers, and accountants were all hollering at me, "Max, the cheese is costing us too much money and we aren't selling enough of it!"—are all about how a serious program represents special added value for the whole dining experience, stimulates beverage sales, generates publicity, and in general puts us at the cutting edge of the fancy food business. At times, it might seem difficult to argue in favor of real cheese—especially if you expect it to be a big moneymaker—but the tangential benefits are hard to dismiss.

Asking a *fromager* to seriously limit his or her selection is like demanding a chef give up a whole rack of his or her ingredients. (I take it personally . . .) From a cheese lover's perspective, the wider the selection the better. From a business/profit perspective, fewer cheeses means limited potential for patrons to experience those euphoric cheese moments and to savor those cheese-and-wine (or other beverage) "marriages made in heaven."

PORTIONS

Cheese servings must represent sufficient value and offer enough enjoyment to keep the customers satisfied and coming back for more. Portions shouldn't be too small; neither should they be too large, in which case the cheeses are perceived as less precious, and either diners get too full or cheese is wasted. Price considerations aside, a reasonable restaurant portion is about half an ounce. (Even at this amount, I can recall plenty of enthusiastic cheese lovers who've consumed plates of nine selections and then asked for another nine!)

With triple-crème or smaller-format soft cheeses (washed rind and so forth), there is quite a bit more waste so portions should increase. If a cheese is unctuous and melting, the portion may increase by as much as 1½ ounces. As mentioned in connection with cutting, it's a matter of careful estimation and precise dividing up. An 8-ounce melting Époisses cannot easily be sectioned into eight 1-ounce portions. It should be cut into sixths at most. The *fromager* has to allow enough leeway, especially when dividing a runny cheese.

Some cheeses, such as Roquefort, contain quite a bit of excess water. Others have inedible rinds: They may be waxed, cloth-bound, leaf wrapped, or bark bound; they may also have yeasts, molds, or bacteria that people may not want to eat. Small increments of waste can add up fast. From the business manager's viewpoint, if this becomes chronic, it can be a real problem. On the other hand, cutting hard, aged cheeses such as Gruyère or Comté into clean, discreet (nonwasteful) portions of a half-ounce is quite easy—and that's where we pick up the slack and keep our business managers happy.

WINE RECOMMENDATIONS

Another huge advantage restaurant service has over retail is it can offer all the delicious promise of beverage pairings. Pairings are a prime example of added value; often, both partners are elevated by the matchup.

From the beginning at Picholine, word went out from the business office to all of us cheese servers to sell a glass of Port every time we sold a cheese plate. Something was going to have to help pay the salary of the full-time cheese guy (me). It didn't take long for me to realize the beverage wasn't always going to be that glass of Port. People often had wine left over in a bottle from their main course or they wanted something other than Port. It was up to me to figure out how to dovetail cheese service with beverage imperatives. It's beneficial to build your own library and to have exceptional pairings at your fingertips. (For more on this topic, see chapter 12.)

Portions should be not too big, not too small.

WHAT TO ASK IN A RESTAURANT

- How are the cheeses displayed? Is the presentation sufficiently eye catching and mouth-watering?

- Is the service neat, clean, and precise?

- How are the cheeses offered? What are the options?

- Is information about the cheeses offered in a comprehensive, comprehensible, and entertaining way? Can the cheese server carry on an intelligent discourse about his or her cheeses? Tell a few fun stories?

- Are the cheeses in good shape and at peak ripeness?

- How are the plates composed? Do the progressions work?

- Do the cheese servers fulfill your requests? Do they expand your horizons without making you feel dumb?

- How good are their recommendations—for cheeses alone and also with beverage partners? Do they meet (or exceed) your expectations?

Flights

Cheese-and-wine flights are an easy way to take the risk out of the cheese course experience while also injecting some adventure into it. They are also a great way to introduce neophytes to the magical pleasures of "marriages made in heaven" (outstanding pairings). From both the diner's and the restaurant's viewpoint, flights mean less delay and more assurance. As a *fromager,* I would never misrepresent my restaurant's cheese savvy, or risk its reputation, by recommending a less-successful pairing for a flight.

Flights can take on some fun and interesting themes: they can be regional or national, loosely defining *terroir;* or they can be somewhat whimsical. A couple of examples follow.

TASTING PLATES

French Flight

LOIRE VALLEY GOAT CHEESE (SAINTE-MAURE, SELLES-SUR-CHER, VALENÇAY) WITH SANCERRE (SAUVIGNON BLANC)

BRIE (OR BRIE STYLE) WITH CHAMPAGNE

OSSAU-IRATY WITH MADIRAN (TANNAT)

MUNSTER WITH ALSATIAN GEWÜRZTRAMINER

CANTAL WITH A RHÔNE VALLEY RED (CORNAS, CÔTE DU VENTOUX, GIGONDAS, HERMITAGE)

Spanish Flight

MAJORERO WITH ALBARIÑO

QUESO DE LA SERENA WITH RIBERA DEL DUERO (TEMPRANILLO)

MAHÓN WITH JUMILLA (MONASTRELL)

CABRALES WITH PEDRO XIMÉNEZ SHERRY

ACCOMPANIMENTS

Though a "composed" cheese plate is something many chefs can't seem to resist—they drizzle fine cheeses with honey, for example, pair them with elaborate pastries, or make them into tortes and logs with fruit—this is not what real cheese (to me) is all about.

That said, there are certain simple food pairings, appropriate in restaurants, that can amplify or contrast the flavors of fine cheeses, adding value and elevating the partnership in the same way a successful beverage pairing does. A good crusty baguette-style white bread is the premier choice; there are other good bread choices as well as fruits, jams, and chutneys. (For more on accompaniments, see page 181.)

Occasionally, there is a request for butter with the cheese course. This is an old French custom that has its advantages as some butter on bread accompanying the cheese can take the sting out of a "sharp" cheese. It can also stimulate and lubricate the tongue, enhancing its ability to absorb a cheese's flavors.

CHAPTER REVIEW

Cheese in Restaurants

☐ Restaurants possess an advantage over retailers because the cheese experience is more focused, leisurely, and personal.

☐ Most of the same criteria for selection, care, and presentation applied to retailing are relevant to restaurant cheese programs, except the resources are generally more limited and the customer-interaction is more formal (neither of which is necessarily a disadvantage).

☐ Restaurants can also offer the added value of wine and other beverage pairings.

☐ "The profit is in the bottle" and the enhancement effect of pairings are good arguments to support an extensive real-cheese program in a restaurant.

☐ The cheese course can be offered for any meal and at any time during the meal.

WHAT TO LOOK FOR IN A RESTAURANT

- Selection: rotation and theme(s)
- Display and presentation: organization, aesthetics, keeping it clean
- Menus and lists: good information
- Service: manners, cutting, progression, plating

FOOLPROOF LOGIC AND PERFECT PROGRESSION: PUTTING TOGETHER CHEESE TASTINGS

OF COURSE, THE TITLE OF THIS CHAPTER IS A TRIFLE FACETIOUS BECAUSE nothing in the world of real cheese is truly foolproof or perfect. In fact, every "truth" is open to a certain degree of debate and interpretation—just as every supposition is based not only on ironclad logic but also a good helping of inspired guesswork. The rationale of how we put together cheese plates is quite simple and straightforward. Putting it into practice soon opens the door to many more themes and variations than could possibly be enumerated in these pages. Once you master the fundamentals, the possibilities are endless, and you can have a lot of fun experimenting.

THE PRINCIPLES OF PROGRESSION

Whether you're putting together a selection for a small, medium, or large plate or even assembling a deluxe cheese board with twenty or more cheeses, it needs to demonstrate a clear sense of organization and progression. By the way, a plate can have as few as three cheeses and as many as you like; the composed restaurant and tasting-class plates I put together generally have five, six, or seven selections. For a theme plate of all one type—blues, goats, strong smelly cheeses (see chapters 19–22)—four or five cheeses is probably enough; if you're looking to cover a wide spectrum of flavors, aromas, textures, and types it's going to be tough with less than seven to nine choices.

A nine-cheese plate, demonstrating the principles of progression: From the bottom: Piper's Pyramid; Azeitão; Manchester; Abbaye de Tamié; Pecorino Stagionato; Barely Buzzed; Kuntener; Gruyère; Smokey Oregon Blue. (See page 211 for tasting notes.)

FUNDAMENTAL PROGRESSION GUIDELINES

- Milder to stronger
- Younger to older
- Simpler to more complex flavors
- Softer to harder (or vice versa)
- All else being equal, goat, then sheep, followed by cow
- Natural rind, bloomy rind, washed rind
- Pasteurized milk followed by raw milk
- Blues always last

The usual order is fresh, mild, and simple to aged, strong, and complex. There is also a component of soft to hard, but since some soft and semisoft cheeses can be very strong (and hard ones quite mild), the ordering principle with regard to density or consistency is usually to alternate. The same is true of texture: generally speaking, you want to alternate smooth and rough cheeses with unctuous and crumbly ones, the thick and the rich ones with the mellow and the liquid. You also want to alternate milk types (goat, sheep, cow), rind types, regions, countries, and/or whatever other features might be helpful in distinguishing or contrasting one cheese from the next.

When tasting a progression, inevitably some people will jump right ahead to the blue or some other "end game" cheese. This is fine, but I do worry they may miss out on the nuances of some of the milder cheeses if, for example, their taste faculties are full of strong blue flavors. What a shame not to be able to pick up on all the fresh, milky aromas and flavors of the former for the simple reason that you ate some cheeses out of order. So, if I had to insist, I would recommend trying a progression in its "proper order" once, and then do whatever you like on the second pass.

More often than not, a progression will start with a goat cheese. One rationale for this is goat cheeses are generally not only milder but easier to digest since the fat globules in goat's milk are relatively smaller. The rationale is these "easier" cheeses help prepare the stomach for digesting the ones with larger globules. The enzymes introduced by the easier cheeses stimulate our digestive juices. Also, goat's milk cheeses are in general relatively young compared to cheeses made from other milks, meaning they will naturally appear earlier in a progression; sheep's milk ones are generally aged a bit longer than goat's and cow's a bit longer than that. Rarely do you find a goat cheese aged past a year, although there are always exceptions to every cheese rule: A 2-year-old goat cheese, Capricious, from Acadinha Goat Cheese Company in Sonoma, California, which won a Best in Show award at the American Cheese Society contest in 2002, comes to mind.

Another reason goat cheeses frequently lead off progressions is they tend to marry best with lighter, brighter wines. Sheep's milk cheeses tend to harmonize more successfully with fuller-bodied wines, while most cow cheeses are best matched with the bigger, bolder wines. (This is not to say the sweeter dessert wines cannot work wonders with some of the younger, milder goat cheeses.)

Pasteurized-milk cheeses precede raw-milk ones because, all other factors being equal, they simply do not present the depth and complexity of flavors. Older cheeses follow younger ones because not only do they become harder but their flavors become more focused and concentrated (even if the aromas of some of the harder ones may fade).

TASTING HORIZONTALLY AND VERTICALLY

Horizontal and vertical progressions are concepts borrowed from the wine world that don't necessarily apply so much to amateur cheese tasting but can be used to create some fun cheese plate variations. They can also be useful when illustrating specific points such as the differences between similar cheeses (in the case of a horizontal tasting) or the stages of ripeness of a cheese (in the case of a vertical tasting). In putting together these sorts of plates, you'll want to follow the basic principles of progression and also pay attention to the stages of maturation for each individual cheese under consideration.

For a horizontal tasting, you might pick a family such as the hard, pressed sheep's milk cheeses in the Ossau-Iraty style and compose a category plate including Roncal, Berkswell, Spenwood, Vermont Shepherd, and Piedmont. Another possible horizontal: the "challenging" category of washed-rind goat's milk types, beginning with Aracena, Chevrotin des Aravis, Mont St. Francis, and Manchester, and perhaps adding a Wimer Winter. Along these lines, you'll find the previously mentioned all-smelly, all-blue, and all-goat, tasting plates in chapters 19, 21, and 22, respectively.

Don't forget: Once you've planned a sequence, taste the cheeses and shuffle your lineup in case one or more is "showing differently."

For vertical tastings, you might select a type wherein there's an assortment of cheeses sold at different ages: A good possibility is the Italian Pecorinos, beginning with the Tuscans and also including a Sardo and other variations. Shifting the focus north to the Alps, you might try a number of Comtés from different producers and *affineurs*, aged from about 5 months to up to 2 years.

One important piece of advice: Once you've settled on a sequence for a tasting, applying your best-educated guesses about how the proposed cheeses will harmonize and proceed in a most stimulating order, don't forget to try them one by one. Tasting them before serving is the best guarantee of putting them in the proper order. A particular cheese's stage of ripeness may affect its place in the sequence and necessitate some shuffling. Sometimes cheeses can

Putting together a cheese board or cheese plate for entertaining at your house or for a potluck somewhere else is easy to do (with help from this book) and makes you look like a hero.

fool you. Strong mold-imparted flavors, for example, may not be obvious because the cheese may not display any of those dark-colored veins or heavy greenish blue pockets. I've seen this with Monte Enebro, where the mold looks fairly intense on the exterior—close to black—while the paste appears innocently pure and white; if the mold's effects have penetrated the paste, though, the cheese can be quite strong.

TASTING PLATES

To demonstrate the principles of progression outlined above, and to give you a workable template, we felt it would be helpful to assemble a couple of real-life tasting plates. Learning the theory and practice of progressions is really the anchor of connoisseurship as I've learned it. Composing a plate is a powerful tool for analysis, description, and enjoyment. Remember, it is easier to discern any cheese's character when there is a comparison, when you can start to say, "This one's stronger, this one's creamier, this one's saltier," and so forth. Try these plates, following them verbatim or using them as templates and substituting alternatives.

Seven-Cheese Plate

ROVES DES GARRIGUES

EVORA

ROBIOLA TRE LATTI

IDIAZÁBAL

BOURBOULE

MONTGOMERY'S CHEDDAR

STICHELTON

GENERAL COMMENTS—This first tasting is an all-European affair, which has a historical logic, if you will; it represents each of the major Old World gourmet–cheese-producing countries, except Switzerland, which is well served in the following selection of nine. It has balance—as well as alternation—of textures and consistencies, and it proceeds from goat to sheep to cow, from fresher and younger to more complex and more aged. A fresh goat cheese and an elegant blue are the bookends. (More often than not, my composed cheese plates begin and end with these types, but it's good to be on the lookout for viable exceptions to this rule.)

ROVES DES GARRIGUES—We open with a young goat cheese from the south of France—the ROVES, which I've considered a superstar since the day I first tasted it. This superior example of its type features two wonderful taste accents—one breed-based and the other emanating from *terroir*. First, you can taste the fresh, pure Roves goat's milk, which gives this cheese a thick, rich texture. The *terroir* (also reflected in the cheese's Provençal place-name, Garrigues) is reflected in a gentle hint of fresh wild herbs emerging from its mellow, welcoming flavor profile.

A well put-together, properly sequenced, and nicely arranged cheese plate.

EVORA—When I taste EVORA, which is from Portugal, it makes me think of a fine extra-virgin olive oil (albeit tasting like sheep's milk) more than almost any other cheese—at least any Iberian one. This provides a fitting contrast to the clay-like mouth feel of the ROVES DES GARRIGUES. The Evora is also saltier, nuttier, pleasantly sheepy, and firmer yet still moist. Let's just say it does not lack for moisture, but presents it in a very different package.

ROBIOLA TRE LATTI—We return to a fresher format and a semi-soft consistency, from northern Italy. The ROBIOLA is nimble and light on its feet, offering a refreshing antidote to the oily Evora. With a mix of three milks, it has additional flavor complexity as compared to the prior two cheeses, making it a logical next step in this progression. Robiola's DOP allows for up to 85 percent cow's milk; even with a version at that threshold, there is enough of a buffering effect from the goat and sheep components to offer a smooth transition to the rest of this plate. If you wanted to shorten this sequence from seven to five cheeses, by the way, you could skip the first two cheeses and lead off with the Robiola.

IDIAZÁBAL—Next up is the 100 percent raw sheep's milk Spanish treasure IDIAZÁBAL, which is harder and grassier than the preceding cheese and also has an extra flavor kick from smoking. Without this added treatment, its flavor profile would be virtually identical to RONCAL. The Idiazábal is emblematic and exemplary: Its smoky flavors are gentle and well-integrated; its consistency is akin to a farmhouse Cheddar. Somewhat surprisingly for an Iberian sheep cheese, I've heard it likened to a genuine Parmesan, a recurring compliment cheese lovers give to many of their favorite harder, aged types. Either way, when a cheese can evoke these sorts of comparisons, you know it's a high-class character.

BOURBOULE—With this selection, we revert to a semisoft, fairly dense consistency and a more rustic character, not dissimilar to the Alpine *tomme* styles. BOURBOULE represents an ancient

Cheese	Milk	Country/Region	Texture/ Consistency	Type/Style
Roves des Garrigues	Goat	France/Provence	Semisoft	Fresh, rindless
Evora	Raw sheep	Portugal	Firm	Thistle renneted
Robiola Tre Latti	Pasteurized, mixed goat, sheep, and cow	Italy/Piedmont	Semisoft	Fresh, mixed milk
Idiazábal	Raw sheep	Spain	Hard	Pressed, lightly smoked
Bourboule	Raw cow	France/Auvergne	Semisoft	Lightly pressed, lightly washed
Montgomery's Cheddar	Raw cow	England	Hard	Scalded, cheddared, pressed
Stichelton	Raw cow	England	Firm	Blue

French cheese type, essentially a smaller version of Saint-Nectaire, whose unique, special ripening molds and bacteria give it full, milky flavors. (Saint-Nectaire was the subject of in-depth study by the famous dairy microbiologist Mother Noella Marcellino, aka "The Cheese Nun.") The Bourboule expresses its *terroir* not only via these indigenous microflora but also with hints of the minerally, volcanic soil of its Massif Central origins.

MONTGOMERY'S CHEDDAR—From an old, somewhat rough-edged character out of France's south-central highlands, we shift to a couple of refined English country gentlemen to give us a smooth but nonetheless majestic finale. Randolph Hodgson of Neal's Yard has a hand in both MONTGOMERY'S CHEDDAR and Stichelton; he selects and helps ripen the former and is the creative force behind the latter. Monty's is harder and more toothsome in consistency, more mature and composed, less earthy and rustic than the BOURBOULE. You'll note a similar transition from the KUNTENER to the GRUYÈRE in the nine-cheese lineup that follows. Montgomery's delivers a complex, deep, round symphony of flavors that makes it a perennial candidate among cognoscenti (and indeed at contests) for the world's greatest cheese. (Do I hear any Sbrinz, Parmesan, or Spenwood fans piping up?) With the Monty's, it's all about the wholesome Holstein-Friesian milk, those lush pastures in ancient Camelot, and the masterful aging touches of its makers.

STICHELTON—Our final cheese here is another new-old invention, the imaginative recreation of old-fashioned raw-milk Stilton under the name of that cheese's original home village. Randolph Hodgson and cheesemaker Joe Schneider developed this cheese over a period of about two years and first unveiled it in late 2007. Stilton took over 300 years to evolve and, even though it's now pasteurized, is still a profoundly delightful cheese. So imagine the excitement when Stichelton hit the market. As of this writing, it's a great blue cheese—and it only promises to get better. If you're looking for a beautifully balanced finale with a generous accent of blue and a luxuriant, drawn-out finish, this is your best choice.

Nine-Cheese Plate

PIPER'S PYRAMID

AZEITÃO

MANCHESTER

ABBAYE DE TAMIÉ

PECORINO STAGIONATO

BARELY BUZZED

KUNTENER

GRUYÈRE

SMOKEY OREGON BLUE

GENERAL COMMENTS—Among other cogent points, this sequence demonstrates that you don't always have to progress from softer to harder. You do alternate, however; for example, a somewhat harder, milder-tasting cheese is often followed by a somewhat softer, stronger-tasting one. This plate includes four American cheeses from four different corners of our country: the Midwest, the East, the West, and the Northwest, respectively. The remaining cheeses are from four very different regions of Europe. There are two mountain cheeses, albeit very distinct in character, and two Swiss, from similar milk but otherwise diverse.

The strength and complexity of flavors, the length and persistence of finishes, follows more or less a steady crescendo. The progression starts with a goat and ends with a blue; there are two goats and two sheep, with the rest (all cows) bunched toward the end. There is one pasteurized cheese, which makes up for this presumed shortcoming with an unexpected, even slightly bizarre, twist. The plate follows our fundamental guidelines, with no conspicuous rule breaking. It nonetheless represents an impressive sampling of the prodigious charms and wide variation among fine artisanal cheeses.

PIPER'S PYRAMID—We start with a distinguished American original goat cheese, which is Judy Schad's answer to the Loire Valley's Valençay and certainly no run-of-the mill imitation *chèvre* (far from it). The truncated PYRAMID (in the same shape as a Valençay) has a dusting of paprika on top and the occasional blue-tinged mold on its rind, giving it some nice subtle accents in a generally very smooth, fresh, clean flavor profile—the classic way to open a multicheese tasting plate.

AZEITÃO—Next comes one of my favorite Iberian cheeses (and cheese names): The AZEITÃO is softer and more buttery than the PIPER'S PYRAMIDE and signals a complete change of gears, flavorwise, since it's made of sheep's milk and is also thistle renneted, giving it that familiar, pleasant bittersweet note.

NINE-CHEESE TASTING PLATE SEQUENCE CHART				
Cheese	**Milk**	**Country/Region**	**Texture/ Consistency**	**Type/Style**
Piper's Pyramid	Raw goat	U.S./Indiana	Semisoft	Surface ripened
Azeitão	Raw sheep	Portugal	Soft	Thistle renneted
Manchester	Raw goat	U.S./Vermont	Firm but moist	Pressed, washed rind
Abbaye de Tamié	Raw cow	France/Haute-Savoie	Semisoft	Lightly pressed, washed rind
Pecorino Stagionato	Raw sheep	Italy/Tuscany	Firm	Pressed
Barely Buzzed	Pasteurized cow	U.S./Utah	Firm	Coffee and lavender rubbed, cheddared, pressed
Kuntener	Raw cow	Switzerland	Semisoft	Lightly pressed, washed rind
Gruyère	Raw cow	Switzerland	Hard	Cooked, pressed, Alpine
Smokey Oregon Blue	Raw cow	U.S./Oregon	Firm but moist	Smoked, blue

MANCHESTER—This cheese, from the valley of Lake Champlain, ushers us back into the realm of goat's milk, this time in a washed-rind format with a firmer but still moist consistency. Its thin, pinkish rind (from *Brevibacterium linens*) foretells gamier, more pungent aromas with some distinctly outdoorsy and perhaps cabbage-like notes; its profile also includes fruitiness and hints of mushroom.

ABBAYE DE TAMIÉ—A famous monastery cheese from the mountains of the Haute-Savoie, the ABBAYE, like the MANCHESTER, has a thin skin of *B. linens*–inhabited rind as a launching pad for its ripening agents, which include *Geotrichum candidum* mold. The Abbaye's consistency is softer than the Manchester; its flavor profile contains more fruit as well as beefier, meatier elements, and perhaps hints of sulfurous compounds. You can definitely taste the high-altitude pastures in this, the first cow's milk cheese in the lineup.

PECORINO STAGIONATO—We move on to a sheep's milk cheese, one of the many variants of the classic and very ancient Pecorino Toscano type. This cheese is much firmer than its two predecessors, saltier (yet still nicely balanced) and oilier; it introduces some nuttiness in the profile and hints of sweetness. It is more persistent and has a longer finish than the Abbaye and preceding cheeses. In fact, by now, the crescendo of this progression should have become quite apparent. So perhaps it's time to take a short break for a palate-cleansing sip of water and/or a small bite of plain baguette.

BARELY BUZZED—The sixth selection is the second cow cheese in this tasting. Whatever aspects of its Salt Lake *terroir* may be masked by pasteurization—the milk is pure, clean, and buttery but somewhat of a blank canvas—are made up for by a special treatment of rubbings with a blend of ground coffee and lavender in oil. It sounds like trickery, the kind of gimmick I don't usually endorse. But trust me, it works and bespeaks of real cheesemaking skill. The Pecorino and the BARELY BUZZED have some textural likeness—it's the only firm-to-firm transition in the tasting—but that's where their similarities end. Their differences highlight some nice sheep versus cow and Old World versus New World contrasts.

KUNTENER—Buttery Jersey milk is also the medium for this number, which features a completely different expression of *terroir*. It hits your palate with a strong first impression of untreated raw milk from lush Swiss pastures. But even before that, you pick up the stinky aromas of the KUNTENER's washed rind: fertile, barnyardy, vegetal, and garlicky, with a wafting of ammonia. This rustic cheese sustains the plate's flavor crescendo with a broad, deep, mouth-filling, meaty, slightly mushroomy profile. Kuntener is a strong cheese but not necessarily a sharp or biting one. Its texture is fairly dense yet still pliable (i.e., not hard or crumbly). It features very persistent flavors and a long finish, with good balance and no oversalting (which you may see in cheeses of similar profiles). Even after a piece of Kuntener has physically left your mouth, its flavors are still solidly parked there—and that's a good feeling.

GRUYÈRE—Where do we go after a big, stinky cheese like the KUNTENER? A 16-month-old Rolf Beeler–aged GRUYÈRE is the answer. This is another masterful raw cow's milk expression of exquisite Swiss *terroir,* but in a more mature, smoother guise. It's quite dense, considerably firmer than the Kuntener, with less pliant texture, and will often exhibit some crystallization. Compared to the Kuntener, the Gruyère is much less of a country bumpkin, yet it has in no way lost touch with its roots. Its barnyardy aspects have receded, leaving a broad, deep, balanced profile highlighting essential grassy and fruity elements as well as underlying sweet ones. This is a noble, sophisticated cheese, with a very long finish, ready to stand up and be saluted on the international stage (and also, incidentally, to pair with a variety of wine partners).

SMOKEY OREGON BLUE—I selected this new American classic because I knew it would be a slam-dunk, even after an elegant well-aged Gruyère, which could easily have had the last word. The SMOKEY OREGON is firm but moist, softer than the Gruyère, buttery, creamy, salty (but its salt is in balance), and has just enough of a moldy bite to accent the flavor of its raw milk, which shines through brilliantly and deliciously. So why smoke it? Isn't this an unnecessary embellishment to an already beautifully balanced cheese? No, I'd have to say cheesemaker Cary Bryant has ensured it's a well-integrated component and a distinguishing feature that helps make this unique cheese an excellent anchor for this exceptional lineup.

SELECTING CHEESES BY CATEGORY

The following list—by no means complete or exhaustive—is simply meant as a broad and representative sampling organized by species then type to facilitate putting together cheese progressions.

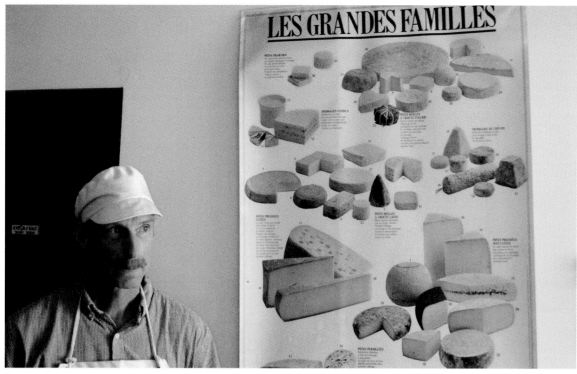

Pierre Kolisch, Oregon artisan cheese pioneer, with a poster of categories.

• Goat •

FRESH
Cabecou de Rocamadour
Cabecou Feuille
Hoja Santa
Mothais-sur-Feuille
Nocetto (or Caprino Nocetto)
O'Banon
Roves des Garrigues
Thym Tamarre

CHÈVRE STYLE/SURFACE RIPENED
Bonde de Gâtine
Bonne Bouche
Chabichou de Poitou
Clacbitou
Coupole
Crottin de Chavignol
Garrotxa (or Queso de la Garrotxa)
Humboldt Fog

Julianna
Otentique
Pouligny Saint-Pierre
Purple Haze
Piper's Pyramid
Sainte-Maure de Touraine
Selles-sur-Cher
Valençay
Wabash Cannonball

WASHED RIND, SOFT/SEMISOFT
Aracena
Le Cabri Ariègeois
Casinca Chèvre
Chevrotin des Aravis
Hölzige Geiss
Mont St. Francis
Pau (a Sant Mateu)
Wimer Winter

WASHED RIND, FIRM/SEMIFIRM
Tessiner Geisskäse

FIRM, PRESSED, AGED/TOMME STYLE
(Tumalo Farms) Classico
Elk Mountain
Hillis Peak
Ibores
Majorero
Old Kentucky Tomme
Persillé de Tignes
Pondhopper
Redmondo

BLUE
Blaue Geiss
Classic Blue
Harbourne Blue
Monte Enebro

FRESH
Brin d'Amour
Fleur du Maquis
Summer Tomme

SURFACE RIPENED, SOFT/ SEMISOFT
Pérail

THISTLE RENNETED, SOFT/ SEMISOFT
Amanteigado
Azeitão
(Queijo) Evora
Mondegueiro
Nisa
Pecorino delle Balze Volterrane
(Queso de la) Serena
(Queijo) Serpa
(Queijo) Serra da Estrela

(Queijo) Terrincho Velho
Torta del Casar
Tortita de Barros

WASHED RIND, SOFT/SEMISOFT
Carruchon
Fium'orbu Brebis
Stanser Schaf Reblochon (aka
    Innerschweizer Schafchäs)

WASHED RIND, SEMIFIRM/FIRM
Flixer
Peña Blanca
Stanser Schafchäs

FIRM/PRESSED, AGED
Abbaye de Bellocq
Autumn Oak
Berkswell
Idiazábal

Ossau-Iraty (family of cheeses)
Pecorino Foja de Noce
Pecorino di Fossa
Pecorino Sardo
Pecorino Toscano
Roncal
Spenwood
Trade Lake Cedar
Vermont Shepherd
Zamorano

BLUE
Beenleigh Blue
Bleu des Basques
Ewe's Blue
Crozier Blue
Roquefort

FRESH
Banon

BLOOMY RIND, SOFT/SEMISOFT
Barat
Brie de Nangis
Camembert de Normandie
Chaource
Constant Bliss
Coulommiers
Fougerus
Tomme Vaudoise
Triple crèmes (family)

WASHED RIND, SOFT/SEMISOFT
Abbaye de Tamié
Ardrahan
Bergfichte (formerly known as
    Krümmenswiler Försterkäse)
Bourboule
Brescianella Stagionata
Durrus
Époisses (de Bourgogne)

Innerschweizer Weicher (aka
    Stanser Röteli)
Küntener
Langres
Munster
Pont l'Évêque
Saint-Nectaire
Stanser Chua Fladä
Stanser Röteli (aka Innerschweizer
    Weicher)
Taleggio
Winnimere

WASHED RIND, SEMIFIRM/FIRM
Beermat (aka Aarauer Bierdeckel,
    see above)
Chimay
Grayson
Gubbeen
Hooligan
Maroilles
Ogleshield
Tomme Fermière d'Alsace
Val Bagner

FIRM, PRESSED (INCLUDING TOMME STYLE, CHEDDAR STYLE, AND TRADITIONAL ENGLISH FARMHOUSE STYLE)
Aspenhurst
Tomme des Bauges
Bra
Caerphilly
Cantal
Cheddar
Cheshire
Double Gloucester
Gabrielson Lake
Laguiole
(Kirkham's) Lancashire
Lincolnshire Poacher
Matos St. George
Monterey Dry Jack
Le Moulis
Orb Weaver
Salers
Single Gloucester

HARD, COOKED, PRESSED AGED
Abondance
Alp Dräckloch
Appenzeller
Beaufort
Comté
Doddington
Fontina Val d'Aosta
Gouda (Goudse Boerenkaas or
    aged Dutch farmhouse Gouda)
Grana Padano
Gruyère
Mahón

Parmigiano-Reggiano
Piave
Prattigauer
Sbrinz
Tarentaise
Toggenburger
Vacherin Fribourgeois

BLUE
Bayley Hazen
Berkshire Blue
Bleu d'Auvergne
Bleu de Gex

Bleu de Laqueuille
Bleu de Termignon
Blu del Moncenisio
Blu del Re
Cashel Blue
Fourme d'Ambert
Gamonedo
Gorgonzola
Great Hill Blue
Rogue River Blue
Stichelton
Stilton

• *Mixed Milk* •

FRESH
Caprino Noce
Robiola Castagna
Robiola Fia
Robiola Incavolata
Robiola Vite

BLOOMY
Hudson Valley Camembert
Kunik
Robiola Due Latti
Robiola Tre Latti

SEMISOFT/FIRM
(Queijo) Amarelo da Beira Baixa

BLUE
Cabrales
Echo Mountain
Gamonedo
(Queso de la) Peral
Valdeón

CHAPTER REVIEW:

Foolproof Logic and Perfect Progression

- [ ] The fundamental principles of progression—mild to strong, young to old, soft to hard, and so forth—are helpful as guidelines but do not always need to be followed strictly.
- [ ] Always have a planned sequence.
- [ ] Taste your cheeses in sequence first and adjust the order if necessary.
- [ ] Suggest your guests try them in order once, then anything goes.
- [ ] Goat cheeses usually go first, followed by sheep then cow.
- [ ] Blues go last.
- [ ] Textures, consistencies, milk types, rind types, countries, and regions alternate

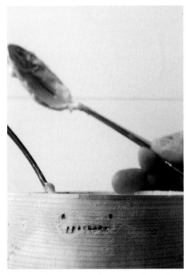

Ripe, melting party cheeses such as the Vacherin Mont d'Or pictured here often require a spoon for scooping.

CHAPTER 12

WINE AND CHEESE: IN SEARCH OF THOSE MARRIAGES MADE IN HEAVEN

AS HINTED IN CHAPTER 2, IT WAS PROBABLY AS MANY AS 10,000 YEARS ago when our human ancestors discovered how to harvest and preserve mammalian milk in the form of nutritious, tasty cheese. Wine emerged as an equally stimulating and delicious way of preserving the fruit of the vine—or, more accurately, the juice of that fruit. When paired well, these two ancient products of the miracle of fermentation dovetail spectacularly. They find what I call a marriage made in heaven, forming a magical partnership that's as close to nirvana as you're going to get in the world of gastronomy. It really is a "wow," and when you try some of the better ones you'll sense this instantaneously.

On a most fundamental level, when we're hungry and thirsty the cheese-wine combination supplies just what our bodies crave—ideal sustenance, balanced nutrition, physical and psychic energy, and a satisfying fulfillment of our anticipation.

A little basic organic chemistry suggests several reasons why cheese-wine partnerships can flourish. The wine helps denature the proteins in the cheese, breaking them down into more elemental amino acids. The fats in cheeses and the acids in wines complement each other; indeed, the acids in both (they're higher in wines but also present in cheeses) can happily coexist. The sugars in the wines balance the salts in the cheeses. The aromatics in each intermingle; they can either neutralize each other, harmonize and elevate both partners, or—in the worst-case scenario—clash and reflect badly on both.

Blue cheeses and dessert wines are a standby of pairings; in this case, it's Spanish Queso de la Peral with a late-harvest blend from Southern Oregon.

Vacherin Fribourgeois and two of its wine partners, Sauternes and Red Bordeaux.

HOW I BECAME A CHEESE MATCHMAKER

The trajectory of my professional life started to get really interesting around 1995, when I began what became a lifelong quest to find all the best cheese-and-wine pairings. At the time, I was launching the cheese program at Picholine. Our sophisticated clientele was looking for specific recommendations, but the science and art of cheese-wine pairings had not advanced very far. Most of the conventional wisdom I could find was focused on that "big red" from the entrée course and/or was *terroir* based: Either have them wash the cheese down with whatever was left over or simply recommend a wine from the same region as the cheese. I knew there had to be more. My curiosity was piqued. I started to experiment with pairings and began compiling tasting notes.

Very early on, it became obvious that any wine with residual sugar was going to be a good candidate for a cheese pairing. With a handle like that, I could begin to push the envelope in different directions, always referring back to some confirmed standards. I knew if a wine had the sweetness or fruitiness to counteract a salty cheese, all its other flavor components nevertheless needed to be in balance. I also knew there is a rather long list of varietals and blends capable of achieving this sort of equilibrium.

THE 5-POINT SCALE AND DEVELOPING A CATALOG

After a few years of keeping handwritten notes on paper, I realized I would have to find a more practical method of recording my data. I needed to have a catalog of foolproof pairings at my fingertips so I could make solid recommendations. I devised a 5-point rating scale from –2 to +2, with 0 in the middle indicating a "neutral" pairing. I began keeping my catalog on my personal computer at home—successful cheese-and-wine matchups and a cross-referenced list of successful wine-and-cheese ones. (My handwritten notes included all pairings—the positive ones but also the neutral and negative ones. The electronic catalog listed only the +1s and +2s, allowing me to focus on the successes and watch for patterns.) As soon I bought my first PDA, in 1997, I transferred the pairings catalog to it and carried it in my suit pocket, which was very convenient for nightly restaurant service.

My pairings catalog lists cheese-based pairings and wine-based ones, i.e., with the varietal or, as applicable, the dominant varietal in a blend. This allows me to approach the question from either direction. For example, a conversation might start with, "I'm drinking Pinot Noir. What cheeses would you recommend?" Of course, the proper response would be to pose the next question: "What kind of Pinot Noir?" Was it from California, Burgundy, or somewhere else on the world wine map? What was its style, condition, vintage, and when was the pairing tried? I recorded all of these variables in my notes—and the equivalent ones for matching cheeses. After a while, trends started to emerge. As my catalog expanded, one thing became increasingly clear: Certain cheese types showed a preference for certain varietals, regardless of their provenance.

Over the nearly 15 years since I began tasting and recording cheese-wine pairings, I've accumulated thousands of individual tasting notes. Of all the work I've done on cheese over the years, exploring pairings has probably been the most fun. It has also been a surprising and at times puzzling endeavor due to its unpredictability. Furthermore, I believe the catalog is a tremendous resource because, as far as I know, there's isn't another one like it.

Many of my recommended pairings, by the way, have been created for Cheese & Wine 101 seminars, which means they've been tested and confirmed by a variety of palates—not just mine. This is important, of course, because taste and personal preference do factor into the equation. Nevertheless there is a great deal more objectivity in judging cheese-wine pairings than in assessing either partner on its own, as some styles inevitably clash.

A word about consensus: As I get older and more crotchety, I become less generous with handing out +2 ratings. If I feel a given pairing merits a +1 but there are enough students in a class convinced it's a +2, I'm at least willing to listen. By the same token, if I look out into the crowd and see a preponderance of frowning faces, with a little cheese and wine still mulling around in their mouths, then I know it's time to acknowledge there is something wrong with that particular pairing. My veteran cheese-and-wine palate should hold some sway, but so should the will of the people.

CONCEIVING THE PAIRINGS: A HOLISTIC APPROACH

It would be nice to be able to say matching cheeses and wines is not so complicated and that you could follow a few easy rules such as "Cheese goes with red wine," or "It always works with wines from its region." But it's much trickier for the simple reason that there are so many variables to consider.

> **THE 5-POINT RATING SCALE FOR PAIRINGS**
>
> **+2:** very positive/outstanding
>
> **+1:** positive/good
>
> **0:** neutral
>
> **−1:** negative/poor
>
> **−2:** very negative/clashing

If you have a wine with apples, honey, orange, pear, lead pencil, or any other number of aromatics, what is it about each and every one of their opposite numbers—the equivalent aromatics in a cheese—that may pair or clash? When it involves cheese-wine pairings, there is almost no accounting for every aspect of (literal and figurative) chemistry. This said, let's examine some of the truths I've uncovered based on sifting through huge mounds of empirical evidence, i.e., years of tastings.

Aside from consulting my vast trove of notes, the way I try to formulate a matchup is to create an integral or holistic picture of a cheese and its potential wine partner; in other words, I try to consider all the different traits of each and determine which of these may indicate harmony. I base this analysis on three main criteria: *terroir*, sapidity, and organoleptic profile. The concepts underlying this Big Three of pairings are actually quite straightforward and will lead quickly to much more advanced tasting and assessing—and tons of cheese-and-wine fun.

Terroir

As discussed in many wine tomes and also earlier in these pages with respect to cheese, *terroir* is everything about the soil, water, climate, location, and geography of a vineyard, which, combined with other factors such as the grapes themselves, the growing methods, and the winemaking recipe, give a wine its unique character. The soil and the water feed the vines that bear the fruit that yield the juice to make the wine. As we learned in chapter 4, the cheese equation includes a few extra variables, which is why we tyrophiliacs feel we can boldly argue it may be even more complex than wine: The soil and water feed the plants that feed the animals that yield the milk to make the cheese; the animals also drink that water, which provides over 80 percent of their milk's volume.

One pitfall to avoid is the assumption that regional pairings automatically work. It may seem logical, but there are far too many other more significant factors to make it a good predictor. Don't get me wrong: Regional pairings are worth looking into, but they are only a starting point.

Any proposed pairing—including a regional one—needs to be broken down and analyzed in terms of *terroir*. In other words, try to figure out how the *terroir* is expressed in the wine and the cheese;

then determine whether there is any basis for believing they might find bliss together.

Let's try this with one of my favorite mountain cheeses—or rather family of cheeses: the Ossau-Iratys of the Basque and Bearn Pyrénées. They are rustic, yet their flavor profiles are fairly aristocratic—multifaceted, complex, and beautifully integrated. If you're looking for a regional wine to match an Ossau-Iraty, you need go no further than the nearby Madiran appellation of extreme southern France. This powerful Tannat varietal—dark, dense, and with a solid one-two punch of fruit and tannins—shares much of the direct, earthy appeal of the Ossau-Iraty cheeses. Their respective *terroirs* lend them solid enough credentials but with an apparently unsophisticated veneer. Don't be fooled by their humble appearances, they are artifacts of intriguing personality and profound character who also happen to form a most impressive partnership.

The holistic approach is about looking at the bigger picture and trying to take into account all of the numerous components of a potential pairing. If *terroir* is a specific, objective, and chemically based criterion, then there is also a more subjective or ephemeral aspect you could call spirit of place. This notion that a cheese or wine embodies the unique character, spirit and personality of its appellation does hold some weight in trying to predict pairings.

Another aspect of *terroir* is what I call the "being there" factor. Tasting a cheese, a wine, or a pairing when you are in their element—the picturesque outdoor café in the medieval walled city surrounded by vineyards—is an added treat. The intellectual and romantic appeal of being in the very place that imbues a cheese, a wine or a cheese-wine partnership with its essential spirit can certainly enhance the experience. This phenomenon can work both ways: If it's only a so-so pairing, the "being there" factor can inflate it into something it's not.

I remember a trip to Portugal when I was excited to visit the Azeitão region, just south of Lisbon, which produces the eponymous cheese, one of my favorites. I had a ripe Azeitão with one of the local wines made from the Castelão grape in a quaint little bistro. Local cheese, local wine, beautiful spot—everything was copacetic. I marked it down as a very successful pairing. Some time later, back in my "lab" in New York City, I tasted the same pairing and it didn't rate nearly as highly. In fact, subsequent tastings led me to recommend quite a few other matches for the

Terroir *is among the main considerations in taking a holistic approach to pairings; pictured here is a corner of Ancient Heritage Farm in Oregon.*

The holistic approach is about looking at the bigger picture and trying to take into account all of the numerous components of a potential pairing. If terroir is a specific, objective, and chemically based criterion, then there is also a more subjective or ephemeral aspect you could call spirit of place. This notion that a cheese or wine embodies the unique character, spirit, and personality of its appellation does hold some weight in trying to predict pairings.

OPPOSITE: A triple-crème such as Brillat-Savarin can find some good cheese partners (Blanc de Noir Champagne, pictured here; White Burgundy/Chardonnay) but beware of its rind-causing clashes.

Azeitão: with an Alvariño from northern Portugal or a Spanish Albariño (same grape, different place); a Sangiovese from Tuscany; or a Chenin Blanc from the Loire Valley. In the harsh light of objectivity, a regional pairing perhaps considered automatic by residents and visitors alike turned out to be a relative dud.

Sapidity

Dave's old Webster's college dictionary defines *sapid* as "having a pleasing taste, being savory," and "agreeable to the mind, interesting or engaging." I use the term *sapidity* in a broader sense. My definition refers to the fullness, the persistence, and the length of flavors in a cheese or a wine. It's about what kind of impression they leave, or, in other words, how big of a personality they have.

Almost all of the fine cheeses I would recommend have sapidity. The issue is not whether they're attractive, savory, or engaging—they all are—but rather how much of this quality they possess and at what volume they broadcast it. How loudly do they announce themselves when they walk in the room? Are they the larger-than-life Bill Clinton type or are they more along the lines of a Truman Capote or an Andy Warhol, quiet, understated, shy but nevertheless brilliant. Big cheeses like Clinton command a bigger stage; littler ones perform in more intimate settings. Bigger, by the way, isn't necessarily better. In fact, many connoisseurs prefer the lower-volume, more discreet types.

The cogent point here is that each partner must be matched with another of appropriate size. A big, bold, assertive cheese demands a big, bold, assertive wine; otherwise, the cheese dominates, the wine recedes, and there goes the balance. At times, the wine in a partnership may have higher sapidity than the cheese, but this is the exception not the rule. Ideally, the cheese and wine should be pretty close in size. For a full-flavored Vacherin Fribourgeois—strong, profound, lingering yet not overpowering—I'd look for a wine partner with some fruit, a good deal of character, its own full personality. So my first try would probably be a Claret or some other Bordeaux-style Cabernet Sauvignon blend. With a subtler cheese of lesser sapidity, say a Fleur de Maquis, which is soft, mild, aromatic, and herb coated, I'd try a cleaner, lighter, gentler style of wine such as an Italian Pinot Grigio or an Alsatian Pinot Blanc.

Chèvre-style cheeses like Juniper Grove's Ottentique can pair well with Sauvignon Blancs—both Old World and New.

Complexity

Complexity is another matter, by which I mean I don't consider it one of the main criteria of cheese-wine pairings but rather a combination factor that follows from the above-mentioned three. Once we've taken the size of a wine or cheese into account, we can start to piece all of its traits together and get an idea of its complexity, that is, of how sophisticated and multifaceted it may be.

Now, just because the wine is an '82 Château Lafite-Rothschild does not mean it will stand up to any cheese. In fact, I've often found a complex, "aristocratic" wine goes better with a humble, unassuming "workaday" cheese. By the same token, a cheese of multifaceted character or complex personality demands a simple—albeit always well made—wine. Queijo Amarelo da Beira Baixa, for example, a sheep–goat blend from eastern Portugal, with humble origins yet a complex and expansive flavor profile, finds some of its better matches in an ordinary California Pinot Noir or a straight-forward Sancerre (Sauvignon Blanc/Loire Valley), whereas it might clash with a sophisticated first-growth Bordeaux.

Sometimes, wines considered fairly insipid on their own hold up quite well to big-flavored cheeses. The simplest Beaujolais-Villages can match some of the great British farmhouse Cheddars very well. This unpretentious wine provides just the fruity berry flavor these big-boss cheeses require of their beverage mate. This, by the way, is one of my favorite facets of cheese-and-wine pairings: They can flatter and elevate many less fancy (and less expensive) wines.

An important aside: Pasteurized-milk cheeses are less challenging to wines than raw milk ones. They have less complexity and fewer attributes, which means they yield "simpler" pairings; for example, salty versus sweet; dry versus wet (what I call "cheese as food" vs. "wine as beverage"). Of the positive pairings, pasteurized cheeses yield more of the good (+1) ones and less of the outstanding (+2) ones. Put another way, there's less risk but, naturally, less reward.

Organoleptic Profiling

Organoleptic is defined in Webster's as "affecting or involving an organ, especially a sense organ as of taste, smell, or sight" and "responsive to sensory stimuli." With respect to fine cheeses and wines, the point is that every one of them creates an overall, composite impression by its combined effects on all the senses.

The organoleptic profile of a cheese or a wine begins and ends with its aromas. We start out by smelling the cheese and then taking a whiff of the wine, creating a preview of what their respective aromatics will offer. (Remember, there are about 10,000 possibilities.) As we've learned, some wines and cheeses have very light aromas, while others have everything from delicious floral or fruity notes to startling barnyardy ones. We're generally looking for a complementary relationship between cheese aromas and their wine counterparts. A couple of examples: a Pinot Noir, with its mouthwatering ripe cherry-like aromas might work well with the meaty, somewhat gamey aroma of a thistle-renneted sheep's milk cheese such as Torta del Casar; the yellow citrus aromatics of a Sauvignon Blanc might find harmony with a classic milky-tart, pleasantly soured mild goat cheese from the Loire Valley.

A pairing's first impression (aka its attack) involves the five basic flavors of the tongue, along with emerging and developing retronasal aromas and sensations of texture. Just as when we taste a cheese alone, the pairing delivers taste and mouth feel by way of its numerous components, texture included. You can preview a cheese's texture by giving it the old Pillsbury Doughboy poke and/or crumbling or breaking a piece between your thumb and forefinger. To do the same for a wine, slosh it around up to the edge of the glass, then watch how its "legs" drip. The more viscous the wine, the more slowly and unctuously it will slide back down. An interesting and related aspect of mouth feel, by the way, is astringency, which is the drying-type effect certain cheeses and wines may have on the tongue.

The basic goal of organoleptic profiling for pairings is to delineate how the partners' textures play off each other to create an overall mouth feel and complete the full sensory impression. It's fascinating to experience how the aromas of a pairing, along with its flavors and textures, present themselves and develop, as they migrate from the tongue, spread across the palate, and create a full retronasal imprint. You won't have a verdict until you let the two partners inhabit your mouth together for a while, do their partnership dance, and see how they finish together.

LOOKS COUNT (AND APPEARANCES CAN BE DECEIVING)

A few other factors come into play with regard to pairings, including the visual (part of the organoleptic profile). When tasting foods

A pasteurized cheese such as Piper's Pyramid can be a less challenging, more versatile partner for beverages.

and wines, we usually get an initial impression from their appearance. If it's an appealing little package—say a soft, smooth off-white triple crème with a fuzzy, undulating, barely pinkish rind—we're already predisposed to enjoying it. Same thing with, say, a pink Champagne—pale, dazzling, and romantically bubbly in low evening light. Both partners look great; you're itching to try them. On the other hand, if the cheese looks splotchy, slimy, and stale, and smells like a barnyard on a hot, humid day, and if the wine is a dull, dense shade of brownish purple ... well, we might be put off by what could be a fantastic pairing. The point is not to avoid prejudgments, but to just beware of any biases and try not to let them cloud your assessment of a pairing.

BALANCE AND HARMONY

Great pairings ought to have a balance of sugar and salt, tastes that correspond to fruity and savory flavors, respectively. The saltier the cheese, the sweeter the wine needs to be, which is a bit of an oversimplification because often what we're really looking for is a wine with well-integrated sugars.

The first wines to consider matching with cheeses are those in the sweet (either fortified or botrytized) dessert category that have substantial residual sugar. Beyond that most obvious counterpoint, we can begin to explore wines with some underlying fruitiness. Even without residual sugar, a "dry" wine can balance the saltiness and savory qualities of a cheese via its *inherent* fruit flavors.

Another key factor to consider is the relative sourness or acidity of potential partners. Since both cheeses and wines contain acid, it's not so much a question of balance as it is of compatibility and harmony. On the 14-point pH scale where 0 is pure acid and 14 pure base, wines are in the 3 to 3.5 range, which is fairly acidic for a foodstuff, while cheeses are still acidic but less so, usually in the 5 to 6.5 range. A more acidic cheese will generally demand a more acidic wine. Two good examples: a Sauvignon Blanc with Cheshire, a nicely textured traditional British farmhouse cheese, moderately salty and with full-bodied tang; or the same wine alongside a good chèvre, with its delicious just-sour goat's milk flavor.

After the acids in wines, which we know can help cut fats and strike a nice balance (hence the concept of "food wines"), the next consideration is tannins. The flavor of these compounds, which are present in developing reds, can be considered another hybrid

SUGAR AND SALT

A FEW PLEASANT SURPRISES

Just as the fruity flavors in many wines can either complement or contrast similar flavors in cheeses, conversely, a salty cheese is often capable of bringing out the fruit in a wine. This is one reason why some of the fruit-forward New World wines can be more successful with unlikely cheese partners. An example is Pinot Noir, which normally would have a disdain for blue cheeses; yet a few of the fruiter Pinots—from California, Oregon, Australia, and New Zealand—harmonize well with assertive blues. Checking my catalog, I found two such pairings for Bleu de Laqueuille, an ancient and rustic blue type from the rugged Auvergne, in south-central France, one with a Pinot Noir from Martinborough, New Zealand, and another with a Pinot from California's Russian River Valley; Valdeón—another rustic blue but leaf-wrapped and from a mountainous part of northwestern Spain—found a surprising match with a Napa/Carneros Pinot Noir. (By the way, it's interesting to note both of these blues are made from pasteurized milk, which no doubt tames them just enough so they're more accepting of a wine like a Pinot Noir.)

Another exemplary pairing along these lines is a big California Zinfandel with the Beenleigh Blue, an herbaceous artisanal sheep's milk type with sweet, caramelly undertones (and, again, pasteurized). This one might raise some eyebrows. For one, a Zin is, frankly, not most connoisseurs' notion of a sophisticated wine. Secondly, the idea of matching a blue with a big red wine might seem quite risky. But the Zinfandel has strong underlying fruit, and this can be an ideal pairing, where the sugars and salts find beautiful balance and harmony.

taste to be classified under "chemical feel," as is *umami*. Tannins offer astringency in their mouth feel along with a flavor somewhat akin to the greenness of chewing on a "raw" (still slightly green) branch (i.e., nonlignified wood). The butterfats in some cheeses can soften the mouth-puckering effects of some of the more astringent, tannic wines. A good example of this would be a young Cabernet Sauvignon, not quite mellowed to full maturity, with a nice buttery Vacherin Fribourgeois.

RETRONASALS AND THE FINISH

So far, we've found complementary aromas, matched personalities, balanced sugar and salt (sweet and savory), and harmonized acidities. Once all these aspects of a pairing have been accounted for, it's time to wait for the finish before recording your conclusions.

Trying to come up with foolproof cheese-and-wine pairings can be a humbling exercise. If I can recall two instances of a perfect match, I can recall a couple hundred more in which all the factors predicting a marriage made in heaven were aligned, but it all fell apart so quickly when the retronasals came into play. This endgame is precisely where things get interesting.

If a pair doesn't work out, you can't necessarily blame either partner. Ultimately, you have to conclude that they just aren't meant for each other.

Let's assume the aromas, flavors, and mouth feel of both the cheese and the wine have dovetailed smoothly in the attack and development. Now the lingering aromas make their way gradually up to the olfactory apparatus, creating the final impression. There are three possible results: the mix of retronasal aromas is sublime, and the pairing elevates both partners and declares a "marriage made in heaven"; the event is neutral, with the retronasals neither amplifying nor diminishing the pairing; or the retronasals clash and the whole house of cards comes crashing down. The latter is no great tragedy, but it does illustrate how this science of cheese-and-wine pairings is more than a simple one-dimensional equation.

SURPRISES, SURPRISES (PLEASANT AND OTHERWISE)

In my research, it became clear very quickly that there are no guarantees when it comes to predicting pairings. Your best bet is to base them on reliable recommendations or on your own experience. If you're starting from scratch, you can use the previously described criteria—*terroir*, sapidity, and organoleptic profile—to create overall impressions of cheeses and wines and predict possible matches.

A couple of examples: If you like the Brut style of Blanc de Blanc Champagnes and also moldy blue cheeses such as Fourme d'Ambert, you might imagine the refreshing aspects of the former (along with its reputation for versatility in matching with many salty foods) would complement the persistent character of the latter. But they don't pair up well: The Brut Champagne just doesn't have enough sugar to balance even the most benign of blues, and the Fourme can be pretty strong. Likewise, you might think a typical well-ripened Loire Valley-style chèvre—mild, delicate, and chalky—would go well (via contrast *and* complement) with a big-bodied, bold red wine, but the reality is this is almost always a disappointing pairing.

I always stress it's important not to make too many assumptions or to automatically rule out some pairings you might feel are risky. Don't hesitate to experiment and don't be discouraged if your first few guesses yield dull matches or even clunkers.

CLASHES

You'll know right away when you've hit on a clash; it's as distinctive as any other unpleasant taste or bad smell, as a cheese gone

OPPOSITE: *Cabrales and Pedro Ximenez sherry—a classic salt-vs.-sugar pairing.*

A WORD ABOUT ORDER

The order in which cheeses are tasted with a wine (or wines) can affect your perceptions and assessments of the pairings. One lingering pairing impression can have an influence—often negative or distracting—on the next. There is also a cumulative effect; things tend to get fuzzy, especially when you're adding alcohol to the mix. In a Cheese and Wine 101 class at the Artisanal Premium Cheese Center, I normally present three wines and seven cheeses; that's twenty-one pairings to taste, contemplate, and sort out, which is a lot. Taking notes is absolutely *not* required, but if you're tasting more than just a few pairings, it can help you remember them. It can also serve as a handy reference in case you plan to organize future tastings.

Another interesting phenomenon I've observed when tasting a sequence of cheese-and-beverage pairings is the first one has a natural advantage. There are several reasons for this: first, you're likely to be hungrier and thirstier; second, there's more anticipation; and third, you have a clean palate. Because of its built-in advantage, the first pairing should probably be "handicapped" down.

Some additional benchmark pairings: Chabichou de Poitou with Sauvignon Blanc; Gorwydd Caerphilly with Syrah; and Monte Enebro with Moscato d'Asti.

south or a corked wine. One of the most common signals is a metallic flavor, familiar from the well-known dissonance between red wines and certain vegetables, particularly spinach, asparagus, or artichokes. By the way, in mastering wine (or other beverage) pairings, I recommend you intentionally set up some clashes and taste them in order to establish a sense of the bottom line.

A note of caution: The paste (interior) of a cheese determines the success of a pairing. If a clash occurs, however, it is often as a result of the rind interfering. So beware of funky rinds messing up a potentially happy marriage.

HOW TO TASTE PAIRINGS: SOME BASIC ADVICE

PAY ATTENTION TO SERVING TEMPERATURES: The cheese must, of course, be at room temperature, whereas the wine must be at the optimal temperature for its type. In general, red wine should be served a touch cooler than room temperature and white wine not so cold—with the exception of Champagne, most of which is best enjoyed cooler. Some white wines, particularly sweeter ones, are better colder than others; for example, I'll take my Riesling chillier than my Chardonnay. In any case, excessive temperatures—too-cold cheese, too-warm red wines, or too-cold whites—can mute flavors, distort textures, and impair marriages.

SMELL: First, take some time to savor the aromas of both cheese and wine separately.

TASTE: Next, taste the wine with a neutral palate, and then clear your palate and taste the cheese. Then taste the two together. Give them a chance to commingle in your mouth and bathe your palate in their aromas and flavors.

WAIT FOR THE FINISH: Whether in the preliminary, separate, or mixed tastings of cheese and wine, make sure to note not just the attack but also the finish. Give the flavors and aromas time to evolve and visit your entire tasting apparatus.

REFRESH YOUR PALATE:

WATER—Cheese has its salt and wine has its own special way of clouding things up, so I recommend you quench your thirst with some water. Too much wine can dull your taste buds, drowning out the subtleties and complexities of the best pairings. I prefer still water when tasting pairings since sparkling can speed up the assimilation of alcohol. It also adds a potentially distracting texture to the mix.

BREAD—Consider eating a little neutral-flavored bread to soak up the residue from the previous pairing before you're ready to move on. You don't want to miss out on the finer nuances of any cheese-and-wine pairing because you have leftover particles from a previous one still clinging to your mouth or tongue.

FOLLOW THE ORDER: Taste in the prescribed pairing sequence and note your first impressions, which are usually correct. Then don't hesitate to go back and try the pairings again, this time not necessarily in the "correct" order.

REFLECT: Give yourself plenty of time not only to taste the full impact of a pairing, from attack to finish, but also to reflect on it and perhaps make comparisons to other pairings.

"BENCHMARK" PAIRINGS

So now let's move on to some cheese-wine tastings, beginning with a few exemplary pairings to demonstrate what it's like when things really work.

SELLES-SUR-CHER or WABASH CANNONBALL, a soft-ripened chèvre-style cheese, chalky, pleasantly tart, and refreshing with a SAUVIGNON BLANC wine—Pouilly-Fumé, Sancerre, or California. The citrus in the wine dissolves nicely into the creamy, clayish goat cheese, making a nice *beurre blanc*–like mix on your palate.

A triple crème such as BRILLAT-SAVARIN or PIERRE-ROBERT with CHAMPAGNE (or a comparable sparkling wine). This popular cheese type does not find so many easy wine pairings, largely because its rinds have a slightly metallic taste that creates potential conflicts. The Champagne—best if not of the bone-dry Brut style—uses its effervescence to lift up the butterfats in the triple crème and swirl them around deliciously so they don't sit too hard on your palate; the wine's hints of fruit meet the cheese's salt evenly and its acidity cuts through those butterfats.

A semihard, aged raw sheep's milk classic such as MANCHEGO, ZAMORANO, SPENWOOD, BERKSWELL, or VERMONT SHEPHERD alongside a RHÔNE VALLEY SYRAH blend (or other comparable New World SYRAH or SHIRAZ). The nutty flavors of these balanced, wine-friendly cheeses find harmony with the raisiny qualities of Syrah wines. Not too tannic, these wines promise a pleasing finish as the partners fade slowly and gracefully together.

A rich, meaty washed-rind raw cow's milk cheese such as TALEGGIO or (more extreme) ÉPOISSES with a WHITE BURGUNDY (or other comparable CHARDONNAY). The crisp apple and/or pear notes in these wines play off the savory butterlike cheese, creating a flavor mélange reminiscent of grandma's sweet homemade apple pie with just a sprinkle of salt on top.

British farmhouse CHEDDAR, CHESHIRE, or LANCASHIRE (or the American equivalents FISCALINI BANDAGE CHEDDAR or CABOT CLOTHBOUND) with a PINOT NOIR (from California, Washington, or Burgundy), or, for an exotic touch, an ALSATIAN GEWÜRZTRAMINER (SPÄTLESE). In the first pairing, these big-boss cheeses find a complementary bit of cherry, with perhaps a nice hint of sourness, in a Pinot Noir wine, which helps melt their harder textures and highlight their well-developed flavor profiles. For the second, the cheeses' buttery textures and flavors (tang included) work well with the spiciness and well-integrated fruit in this wine.

ROQUEFORT with SAUTERNES—*Mais oui!* This is among the first and most fundamental of all cheese-wine pairings, demonstrating a classic balance of salty and sweet. A well-aged Madeira or Tawny Port is a less-expensive alternative to the Sauternes.

RESPECT FOR GAMAY: ONE WINE AND EIGHT CHEESES

A wine of so-called humble pedigree such as Beaujolais-Villages shows good pairing versatility and gives me a strong, newfound respect for the Gamay grape. Use a top-quality Beaujolais such as Moulin-à-Vent, Morgon, or Julienas.

Six countries are represented in this eight-cheese lineup, a fairly standard mild-to-strong, alternating-texture sequence.

GARROTXA—This is an easy milky, creamy cheese, which plays off the Gamay nimbly. Think berries and cream.

SERRA DA ESTRELA—This cheese's buttery, vegetal flavors don't deal well with higher-tannin reds. In this pairing, though, you can taste both partners right through to the finish.

FOUGERUS—Its opulent, delicious butterfats fold right into the Gamay, no questions asked. It's a straightforward wine, showing no difficult layers of complexity or issues of compatibility with such a rich cheese.

ZAMORANO—A nuttier-textured *and* -flavored cheese, the Zamorano finds just the right notes of berry in the juicy Gamay.

DURRUS—This cheese's flavor profile is very broad, and if it wasn't so full of *umami* we might have a conflict here. Yet it's also buttery enough with just enough sour and salt to be a willing partner for many reds, including this one.

CHESHIRE—A rustic British traditional with a unique signature taste, which I call the maritime tang. Go inland and continental for your berry-full Gamay and you have a nice contrast, no disclaimers necessary.

UPLANDS PLEASANT RIDGE RESERVE—You might expect this noble cheese to put up a firewall, as it does for many wines with too much attitude. Yet it accepts the invitations of the more humble Gamay. Like a Hollywood star signing an autograph for an adoring adolescent, the two get along admirably.

VALDEÓN—Even though it's made with pasteurized milk, this is no wallflower. Rather bossy, it can overwhelm many a red wine. This good little Gamay acquiesces to its intensity, though, and no feelings are hurt.

Great pairings ought to have a balance of sugar and salt, tastes that correspond to fruity and savory flavors, respectively.

TASTING PLATE

A Round-Robin: Four Wines and Eight Cheeses

The following round-robin (or is it a marathon?) requires a really game group of cheese lovers who are ready to focus and get down to some serious tasting. For these sessions, I have to be especially concise with my introductory remarks because tasting up to four wines with up to eight cheeses takes some time. Here is the lineup, with wine-by-wine tasting notes and my score sheet from that evening.

THE CHEESES

SAINTE-MAURE DE TOURAINE

AZEITÃO

BRILLAT-SAVARIN

BERKSWELL

CASINCA CHÈVRE

GORWYDD CAERPHILLY

HOCH YBRIG

BAYLEY HAZEN

THE WINES

POUILLY-FUMÉ (SAUVIGNON BLANC)

DRY CREEK VALLEY (CALIFORNIA) CHARDONNAY

BARBARESCO (NEBBIOLO)

DRY CREEK VALLEY (CALIFORNIA) ZINFANDEL

SAINTE-MAURE—This regional goat cheese–Sauvignon Blanc pairing (from the Loire Valley) might have had a +2 rating if not for the oak in the wine, which was a bit too heavy for this lighter cheese. The Pouilly is elegant but also fresh and crisp enough for this cheese. Most expressions of Chardonnay go well with many goat cheeses and the Californian in this lineup is no exception. The tannins in the Barbaresco create enough of a clash with the acids in this goat cheese to recommend against the pairing. The Zin, bigger (at 14.5 percent alcohol) and fruitier, was unable to find much common ground.

AZEITÃO—Like many thistle-renneted sheep's milk cheeses, the Azeitão works well with the Sauvignon Blanc's acidity. The wine cuts through, softens, and melts down the cheese's rich butterfats. The Chardonnay has nice complementary fruit, but its acidity recedes enough not to elevate that pairing. With the Barbaresco, you have your berry flavors working nicely with your buttery

The Chardonnay's column showed versatility and consistency with all of these cheeses, scoring a strong 8. The Zinfandel, with its well-integrated sweet fruit seeking out the salt in the cheeses, was also a consistently good partner, achieving a composite score of 9 and recording two of the four outstanding (+2) matches.

OPPOSITE: The cheeses: Center, Sainte-Maure de Touraine; Center, right, Azeitão; clockwise, from top, Brillat-Savarin; Berkswell; Casinca Chèvre; Gorwydd Caerphilly; Hoch Ybrig; Bayley Hazen. The wines: Counter clockwise from bottom right, Pouilly-Fumé; California Chardonnay; Barbaresco; California Zinfandel.

sheep's milk. The Zin offers even more fruit and the Azeitão stays right with it, its salt playing off the wine's sweeter notes.

BRILLAT-SAVARIN—This luxurious cheese parked itself on the palate and the Sauvignon Blanc couldn't find a place to blend in; texturally, this relatively fat wine (remember the oak) could not distinguish itself enough from this relatively fatty cheese. The Chardonnay, rich and round, but with good freshness and acidity, found a "like meets like" textural pairing with the Brillat. Flavorwise, it was like a good meeting of apples and butter. The clash with the Barbaresco was not so obvious on the attack, but the finish really fell apart: The wine's lingering aromatics struck a dissonant chord with that touch of mold in the cheese's rind. The Zinfandel didn't clash as badly: Its fruit tried to harmonize with the salt in the Brillat, but the result still could not be called beautiful music.

BERKSWELL—A noble, reliable cheese with fairly prominent salt but nevertheless good balance. This hard sheep's milk type—like MANCHEGO and VERMONT SHEPHERD—generally does very well with Sauvignon Blancs, which cut through their buttery nuttiness nicely. Perhaps the Berkswell was a tad too big for this particular

CHEESE AND WINE 101: SCORE SHEET				
	Marc Deshamps Les Champs de Cri Pouilly-Fumé 2003 (Sauvignon Blanc)	Sbragia "Home Ranch" Dry Creek Valley 2003 (Chardonnay)	Michaele Chiarlo Barbaresco 2003 (Nebbiolo)	Dashe Dry Creek Valley Zinfandel 2003
SAINT-MAURE DE TOURAINE	+1	+1	−1	0
AZEITÃO	+1	0	+1	+1
BRILLAT-SAVARIN	−2	+1	−2	+1
BERKSWELL	+1	+1	+2	+2
CASINCA CHÈVRE	0	+1	0	+1
GORWYDD CAERPHILLY	0	+1	+1	+2
HOCH YBRIG	−1	+2	+1	+1
BAYLEY HAZEN	−2	+1	0	+1

wine, though: I recorded the pairing as "merely good." The fruity, apple-y California Chardonnay finds a pretty good soul mate in the grassy, nutty Berkswell, and their sweet-salty contrast worked, too. The sophisticated Barbaresco was flattered by the Berkswell, like a handful of berries with nuts. Not at all surprisingly, this suave British immigrant—salty and nutty yet substantial and smooth—settled in happily with the big, jammy, friendly vibe of the California Zinfandel—two very different but well-rounded characters able to complement each other.

CASINCA CHÈVRE—Washed-rind goat's milk cheeses are challenging on their own so you would expect them to be difficult wine partners. The New World wines, with their fruit-forward qualities, balanced the saltiness of this cheese. It was a little too funky and assertive for the Pouilly-Fumé, which, in fact, was pretty much finished as a partner for the rest of this lineup. The Chardonnay, on the other hand, was full and fruity enough to continue holding its own well past the Casinca. The Barbaresco was perhaps a bit too subtle for the Casinca, but the Zin, predictably, had enough zest to meet this cheese on its own terms.

CAERPHILLY—The Sauvignon Blanc was "only okay," merely managing to wash down the Caerphilly. This cheese's buttery, semi-firm texture and heft was on equal footing with the big buttery flavor of the Chardonnay. The Barbaresco offered good red berry flavor: Think cheese 'n' cherry pie. The Zinfandel takes the fruit iteration to its next level—thicker and more concentrated—creating a pairing reminiscent of butter and jam on toast.

HOCH YBRIG—This big Swiss cheese easily overshadowed the Sauvignon Blanc. A solid Chardonnay paired with a long-finishing, hard Alpine classic, on the other hand, is a good bet. Hence the +2 score with the Dry Creek Chardonnay. This wine's full apple and pear aromas, backed up with a touch of citric acid and a little vanilla from the oak barrels, stood up well to the complex flavors of the Hoch Ybrig. The Nebbiolo grape likes its balanced sheep cheeses, but it can also work with the broader profile of a bigger cow cheese, accounting for the successful Barbaresco pairing here. Hoch Ybrig is a well-aged, mature cheese, its saltiness fully integrated and settled down, allowing it to meld smoothly with both the subtler Old World Italian red and also the up-front Californian that followed.

Hoch Ybrig is a well-aged, mature cheese, its saltiness fully integrated and settled down, allowing it to meld smoothly with both the subtler Old World Italian red and also the up-front Californian that followed.

BAYLEY HAZEN—*Penicillium roqueforti* mold can be a killer for wines. Bayley Hazen is a demanding cheese, sprightly and salty enough to dance with the fruity American wines here, but way too much for the Loire Valley white and meeting plain disinterest from the Barbaresco. Bayley Hazen does find some good pairings with apple-and-pear Chardonnays, with some medium-dry Kabinett-type Rieslings, some Sangioveses, and not at all surprisingly, Zinfandel, which is a known partner for certain blues because of its inherent fruit sugars.

One of my favorite tools to use when tasting pairings is a grid where you can record individual scores and then tally them to look at composites by adding a cheese's numbers across the wine columns or a wine's total down the cheese rows. This reveals some

HAPPY PARTNERS

WHAT MAKES CHEESES WINE-FRIENDLY (AND VICE VERSA)

- Cheeses with balanced flavor profiles find greater pairing success with wines and other beverages. By balance, we mean that none of their basic flavors—salt, sweet, sour, bitter, and *umami*—are out of whack. If they are, there isn't a lot a wine can do to bring them around.

- Because their flavors are more focused and they are more stable, hard cheeses find more successful pairings with wines. Younger, softer cheeses are less predictable.

- The saltier the cheese, the fruitier or sweeter the wine

should be; salty cheeses flatter the fruit in a wine.

- White wines find more successful marriages with cheeses than reds do (which might convert some red-wine fans to the white camp, a good thing).

- Sweeter dessert wines find more successful pairings with cheeses than any other type.

- Mixed-milk cheeses pair well with a wide variety of wines.

- Goat's milk cheeses prefer white wines, though there are some fine pairings to be found with some red varietals. Examples: Zinfandel, Primitivo, Sangiovese, and occasionally Tempranillo.

- Simpler wines can be elevated by cheeses. Examples: Beaujolais Villages; "everyday" Chardonnay.

- Big-flavored and persistent cheeses prefer wines with depth. Some prime examples: British farmhouse Cheddar with classified Bordeaux

(Montgomery's and Château Margaux); or Carles Roquefort with older vintage Sauternes, especially Château d'Yquem.

- Bloomy-rind cheeses can be especially difficult to pair successfully with wines; effervescence or extra sweetness in the wine can help.

- The tannins in red wines can be softened by the butterfats in cheeses.

- A cheese with a healthy dose of *umami* can pair well, even with wines outside of its anticipated pairings. (Bergfichte with Tempranillo wines is a good example.)

- Washed-rind cheeses, with their complex aroma and flavor profiles, tend to work better with wines that have floral, aromatic, fruity (apple, pear, apricot) qualities. Examples: Gewürztraminer, Muscat, Riesling, and Grüner Veltliner.

interesting trends and starts to give a sense of a cheese's wine friendliness and a wine's cheese friendliness.

Among the cheeses in this tasting, Berkswell scored the highest composite, with a 6, confirming a very positive trait of aged, hard sheep's milk types: Magnificent and elegant, quite worthy of standing on their own, they are also very accepting of many wine types. Goat cheeses tend to prefer white wines and sheep cheeses tolerate reds better. Checking across the Berkswell's row, we may have an illustration of that principle or merely of this cheese's compatibility with these specific wine types. Perusing the Sainte-Maure's row supports the goat cheese–with–white wine generalization.

The Chardonnay's column showed versatility and consistency with all of these cheeses, scoring a strong 8. The Zinfandel, with its well-integrated sweet fruit seeking out the salt in the cheeses, was also a consistently good partner, achieving a composite score of 9 and recording two of the four outstanding (+2) matches. The Sauvignon Blanc, on the other hand, demonstrated a steadily deteriorating ability to stand up as the cheeses got stronger and more complex. It started with good compatibility vis-à-vis the first four cheeses, although it was a clunker opposite the triple crème, which illustrates another truth about pairings: Clashes often seem to arise arbitrarily, where logic and trends might suggest a good match. The Nebbiolo, a very classy wine, was not such a willing cheese partner, as evidenced in its varying scores and middling total of 2; perhaps it was too individualistic or aloof to find harmony in a pair.

One final comment on this round-robin: The two American New World–style wines were more successful with the cheeses than were the two Old World ones, confirming the general notion that more inherently fruity wines find better synergy with cheeses than nuanced traditional European types.

These generalizations and guidelines are compiled from my expanding library of pairings and are meant as handy references anytime you're looking to put together a cheese course or plate with matching wines.

CHEESE-FRIENDLY WINES

I like to say for every cheese there is a wine and for every wine there is a cheese. I almost always start with the cheese(s) and go looking for wine partners; but if you're starting with the wine(s), you can use the following guidelines to search for their cheeses of choice.

In considering cheese-friendly wines, it's refreshing to see some of the lesser-known and even relatively obscure local or regional wines cropping up and providing very successful pairings. They include such wines as Txakolina from Basque country and Schiava/Vernatsch from Alto Adige/Sudtirol.

Now let's run down a list of some of my favorite cheese-friendly wines, highlighting their traits that are relevant to cheese pairings and noting some trends regarding how they relate to cheeses. The main traits we're looking for in judging whether a wine will match well with a given cheese is its weight or body, its flavors and aromas, and whether it's acidic or tannic.

AGLIANICO—Full-bodied, robust red from southern Italy with good acidity. Versatile; prefers goat and sheep, less successful with blues.

ALBARIÑO—Floral, aromatic, citrusy light-bodied, and, at times, slightly effervescent white from northwestern Spain and northern Portugal (where it's known as Alvarinho). Prefers sheep and most goat cheeses; washed-rind, semisoft cow can work, but not blues.

BARBERA—Full-bodied, full-flavored red, with berry notes and good acid, originally from northern Italy, especially Piedmont. Versatile but prefers cow or sheep cheese; if goat, it should be an aged cheese; young washed rinds are less successful.

CABERNET SAUVIGNON—Full-bodied, tannic (especially when young), elegant red with layers of flavors. Prefers cow cheeses; not as fond of goat or sheep unless they're blue.

CHAMPAGNE—Effervescent white from northeastern France (*département* of same name), made either from Chardonnay, Pinot Noir, and/or Pinot Meunier. Prefers cow or goat, soft to aged; bloomy or washed rind are fine but usually not blues unless it is a sweeter Champagne.

CHARDONNAY—Medium- to full-bodied, fruity, elegant white, with medium acidity. Does well with goat, soft to aged washed-rind cow cheeses, and blues; not as reliable with bloomy rinds.

CHENIN BLANC—Light- to medium-bodied, floral, honeyed white, with good acidity. Versatile, especially the fruitier expressions; prefers goat and sheep, particularly thistle renneted; can do well with cow, too.

GAMAY—Light- to medium-bodied, low-tannin, berry-flavored red, with refreshingly high acidity. Versatile; finds favor with many cheeses; it's hard to go wrong with this varietal.

GEWÜRZTRAMINER—Light- to medium-bodied spicy, aromatic, fruity, floral white. Prefers washed rinds, especially cow.

GRENACHE (OR GARNACHA)—Fairly light- to medium-bodied, spicy, peppery, herbal red. Versatile; does quite well with blues; less successful with washed-rind cow.

GRÜNER VELTLINER—Light-bodied, fresh-flavored, vegetal white, native to Austria. Versatile; prefers cow cheeses and most washed rinds; disappoints with the blues.

LAGREIN—Light- to medium-bodied, berry-flavored red. Prefers washed, pressed cow and sheep; also blues.

MALBEC—Full-bodied, low-acid, tannic, complex red with deep, balanced flavors. Prefers harder cheeses and works well with the thistle-renneted sheep cheeses.

MERLOT—Soft, medium-bodied, fruity, berry-flavored red. Prefers sheep and cow, preferably pressed and/or cooked; blues usually work well, too.

MUSKAT (OR MOSCATO)—Medium-bodied all the way to viscous, very fruity, very aromatic white, with nice citrus notes. Versatile with cheeses, from the driest to sweetest styles.

NEBBIOLO (as in Barolos and Barbarescos)—Full-bodied, concentrated, intense red, dark-flavored and tannic but with a good balance of acidity. Prefers cow, natural, or washed rind, pressed and often cooked; can work well with goat and some sheep; less successful with blues.

NERO D'AVOLA—Medium- to full-bodied peppery-flavored red from southern Italy. Versatile; less successful with younger, fresh cheeses.

PINOT BLANC (PINOT BIANCO)—Light-bodied, floral, gentle white with low acidity. Prefers washed-rind sheep and goat.

PINOT GRIS (PINOT GRIGIO)—Light-bodied white, spicier than Pinot Blanc, with apricot notes. Versatile, especially in its fruitiest expressions.

PINOT NOIR—Medium- to full-bodied, berry flavored (cherry, strawberry) red, with medium tannins. Prefers sheep and cow; less successful with goat, washed rinds, and blues. Often melds well with the softer thistle-renneted sheep cheeses.

PRIMITIVO—Medium- to full-bodied, spicy, rustic red from southern Italy. Versatile with cheeses, like its descendant Zinfandel.

Muscat, in its many incarnations, is a great example of how a simple, non-noble varietal can be friendly to cheeses and versatile in pairings.

Tasting pairings with Spanish cheese maestro Enric Canut (see also page 306) at Tutusaus in Barcelona.

RIESLING—Medium-bodied, honeyed, floral white, with layers of flavor and good acidity. Versatile with many, though it can disappoint with the blues.

SANGIOVESE—Light- to medium-bodied, moderately tannic, berry-full, earthy red, originally from Tuscany. Successful with a broad range of cheese types—goat, sheep, cow, or mixed—though may fall short with the more assertive cheeses.

SAUVIGNON BLANC—Light- to medium-bodied, flinty, occasionally grassy white, with citrus flavors. Prefers goat and some sheep; less successful with cow cheeses and blues.

SCHIAVA (AKA VERNATSCH)—Medium-bodied, low-tannin, berry-flavored red, best known in the Alto Adige/Sudtirol. Prefers medium-aged cows' milk.

SÉMILLON (in Sauternes and other wines)—Light-bodied all the way to viscous (in the dessert wines), honeyed white, with low acidity and hints of high-pectin fruits such as peach and apricot. A natural for blues and washed rinds.

SYRAH—Full-bodied, intense, tannic yet balanced red, with dark berry and pepper flavors. Prefers sheep (especially the thistle renneted) and aged cow cheeses.

TANNAT (as in Madiran)—Full-bodied, strong, tannic red, with dark berry flavors. Prefers pressed and/or washed-rind sheep and cow cheeses; also works well with thistle-renneted sheep.

TEMPRANILLO—Medium- to full-bodied, berry-flavored, fruity, spicy red, with low acidity. Versatile and very friendly with goat, sheep, and cow cheeses, and the occasional blue; uncooked, pressed, and aged. Usually less successful with the washed rinds.

TXAKOLINA—Light-bodied, floral white, with good acidity, made from the Folle Blanche grape in Basque country. Prefers relatively mild goat and sheep cheeses.

VERDEJO (OR VERDELHO IN PORTUGAL)—Light- to medium-bodied, aromatic, honeyed, nutty-flavored white, with gentle acidity. Prefers goat or sheep cheeses.

VIOGNIER—Full-bodied, highly aromatic, floral white, with peach flavors. Prefers goat and washed-rind cow; less successful with aged cheese of any kind, sheep cheeses, and blues.

VIURA—Light-bodied, floral white from eastern Spain with good acidity and tart green apple flavors, used primarily for Macabeo wines. Prefers goat, sheep, and aged cow cheeses.

ZINFANDEL (SEE ALSO PRIMITIVO)—Full-bodied, fruity, spicy red, with black currant and brambly notes. One of the more versatile of cheese-friendly reds, with few clashes.

CHAPTER REVIEW:

Cheese and Wine

- ☐ Cheese-and-wine pairings can be surprising and unpredictable; the number of variables adds complexity to the equation.
- ☐ The three main criteria for analyzing and predicting pairings are *terroir,* sapidity, and organoleptic profile.
- ☐ Sapidity is about answering the question "How big of a personality does a wine or a cheese have?"
- ☐ The components of a cheese's organoleptic profile are aroma, flavor, texture, and temperature.
- ☐ For a successful pairing:
  - The partners should be appropriately sized for each other.
  - Aromas should be complementary.
  - Salt and sugar (savory and fruity) should be in balance.
  - Acidities should be harmonious.
- ☐ Aromas mark both the beginning and the end of a cheese-wine pairing.
- ☐ In tasting a pairing, note the attack but wait for the finish (retronasal effect) before passing final judgment.
- ☐ Regional pairings can be a decent starting point, but they don't always work.
- ☐ Visual and other preferences may represent bias—positive or negative; there's nothing wrong with this, just be cognizant of it.
- ☐ White wines often work better with cheeses than you might imagine.
- ☐ Harmonious pairings can elevate both partners; clashes bring out the worst qualities (and even faults or defects) in each.

CHAPTER 13

BEER AND CHEESE (BEYOND THE PLOWMAN'S LUNCH)

IT'S MY DISTINCT IMPRESSION THAT THE SCIENCE AND ART OF BEER-and-cheese pairings is about where wine-and-cheese couplings were when I first started looking into it seriously in the mid-1990s. If you take a look at Garret Oliver's *Brewmaster's Table,* for example, you'll find about a two-page passage devoted to cheese-and-beer pairings, which as far as I know is all that's been printed on this subject. Oliver cites the two traditional British pairings, which are Stilton with barleywine and the plowman's lunch of a hardy cheese such as Cheddar, Cheshire, or Lancashire with a pint of pale ale. Well, at least it's a start . . .

At the Artisanal Premium Cheese Center, the main beer expert we've consulted with was Jon Lundbom, a specialty importer who is familiar with many national and international craft brews. Jon began conducting beer-and-cheese tasting classes at the center in 2005.

BEER BASICS: A SHORT COURSE IN FLAVOR PROFILES

As with wine pairings, the starting point is the flavor profiles of the beers. (For the purposes of this book, when we say "beer" we mean fine craft brews, made in many different traditional European formats—and quite a few new styles —largely here in the United States but also back in their old countries.) Craft beers have a lot of flavor variation and subtlety, which make them excellent potential partners for fine artisanal cheeses. In fact, they have as much range as wines, which is why beer pairing is such an exciting new frontier.

Fine craft beers and artisan cheeses often find beautiful partnerships; pictured here is Kirkham's Lancashire with an India Pale Ale.

While these brews are somewhat comparable to the wines we began matching with cheeses in the previous chapter, there are a few big differences. The most important distinction between wine and beer is that while wine is a fermented agricultural product beer is a brewed drink. Wines are all about growing the grapes and fermenting their juice; beers are about several basic ingredients and the recipe for preparing and combining them—that is, the craft of brewing.

WHAT'S IN BEER?

Beer is to Germany as wine is to France, so naturally that's where we go for fundamental definitions. Germany has a famous old piece of legislation called the Reinheitsgebot, which was first written up in 1487 and ratified in 1516. Originally a consumer protection act in reaction to some poisonous herbs being included in beers, it sanctifies and protects the purity of the country's national drink. The Reinheitsgebot states four permissible ingredients for beer: malt, hops, water, and yeast. Once you understand how each of these are treated in a recipe, you can get a handle on the flavor profile of a brew and then come up with some pairings.

The brewing process involves boiling up a concoction of malt and water, which is called the wort. Yeast is added to ferment the sugars in the wort, transforming it into the mildly alcoholic brew that becomes beer. Hops are added for their flavor and preservative effects. Other ingredients may be added to spice things up and then the brew is aged briefly before being shipped out in bottles, barrels, or kegs for consumption.

Craft breweries are often very inventive and adventurous not only in concocting their brews but also in sourcing ingredients. The final product reflects both the brewing steps and the nature of the carefully sourced ingredients. To make a barleywine, for example, brewers add a relatively large amount of sugar, which in turn requires a substantial dose of yeast to ferment it. The resulting brew has at least 9 percent alcohol and a good deal of sweetness in its profile. Brewers often go far afield to acquire their malt, hops and yeast. Sixpoint Craft Ales, a prominent Brooklyn brewer and a local favorite in the New York area, uses malt from Scotland, hops from the Pacific Northwest, and a yeast strain that is most definitely not indigenous to any of the five boroughs or the tri-state area. In contrast, ancient traditional brewers—the Trappist monks of Belgium among them—frequently use indigenous yeasts, which is where *terroir* enters into the equation. (The malt and the hops are also often regional, if not strictly local.)

Malt

Malt is the term used to refer to a specially treated type of grain, usually barley. The grain is soaked and then roasted, which converts its starches to sugars. (The process is called malting.) The yeast in turn converts those starches into alcohol and many other tasty by-products.

Malting is analogous to the roasting of coffee beans. The longer a grain is roasted, the darker it becomes and the stronger and deeper its flavor. There are many different types of malts, which are selected by brewers according to their desired effects. Malt gives flavor characteristics to beer in a spectrum from lightly caramelized, sugary, and honeylike (for lighter beers) to dark, "roasty," and reminiscent of chocolate (for porters and stouts). One of the most famous malts is pilsner, which originated in the area around Pilsen in the Czech Republic and defines that particular style of beer.

Hops

Hops is a plant pod believed to be closely related to cannabis. Its predominant flavor is bitterness, but it can also add floral, citrus, grassy, and even piney elements to a beer's profile. In the terminology of craft brewing, if a beer has very up-front bitter and/or acidic (citrus) flavors it's called *hop forward*.

How and when the hops are added helps determine flavor. The more hops you add and the longer they stay in the wort, the more bitterness creeps into the beer. If the hops are added at the end of the process, they contribute mostly aroma; if they're added *after* the beer is already fermented, which is called dry-hopping, they lend just a hint of aroma.

Yeast

The yeasts responsible for fermentation can also add flavors to the final brew. Many of them are neutral and don't add much, which is the scenario for the lighter, milder lagers popular in the United States and Canada. The yeasts in traditional Belgian brews and also in Bavarian wheat beers are much more prominent. They deliver those familiar "yeasty" flavors of raw dough or baking

The Reinheitsgebot states four permissible ingredients for beer: malt, hops, water, and yeast. Once you understand how each of these are treated in a recipe, you can get a handle on the flavor profile of a brew and then come up with some pairings.

bread; they can also provide fruity and floral aromas, with hints of banana and/or clove. Generally speaking, the fruity notes come from esters and the bubble-gummy ones from phenols. (Sound familiar? See chapter 4.)

Other Ingredients

The only other ingredients that are major potential contributors to a beer's profile are additives such as spices or fruit flavors, which can be found in such "exotic" brews as Belgian *wit* beers. Coriander and orange peel are two prime examples.

Mouth Feel and Weight

Mostly because it's carbonated, mouth feel is also an important part of a beer's profile. The size and quantity of the bubbles is one factor, and the weight of the beer—how heavy and alcoholic it feels on the palate—is another. Alcohol content in beers is indicated by "Alcohol by Volume (ABV)" on its labels and ranges from under 5 percent to around 9 percent. In extreme brews, it can range from 15 to 25 percent. Brewers keep track of the specific gravity of their wort. This is a measure of the sugar content of a solution relative to water and is often referred to as merely gravity. The more sugar a beer starts out with, the "heavier" it will be and ultimately the more alcohol and/or residual sugar it will have. (So if we overhear beer connoisseurs discussing a drink that's brewed with a lot of gravity, now we know what they mean . . .)

GENERAL PAIRING PRINCIPLES

The general principles of pairing beers with cheeses are pretty much the same as the wine-and-cheese guidelines. You're looking for balance, where neither partner overwhelms the other, and you want to consider both complement and contrast. Once you've sussed out a beer's profile, you can start to look for similar, overlapping, or contrasting flavors, textures, and aromas in a cheese, just as we did with wine in the previous chapter. An important note: Just as with artisanal cheeses, there is variety from batch to batch in craft brews, so you should taste test each one first before turning your attention to its possible matches.

As with wine pairings, there will be surprises—matchups that should work but don't and vice versa. Among the more challenging partners for beers are the Iberian cheeses; their gamey, sour qualities are generally incompatible. Given that the Iberian peninsula doesn't have a particularly strong beer tradition, perhaps this should come as no surprise.

Both wines and beers have fruity or sweet flavor components, which are among the first considerations to help clue us in on possible pairings. I've found wines tend to rely more on finding complements to their flavor components (i.e., harmony), whereas beers seem to be looking more for balance—it's more of a seesaw effect. The beer pairing balance is more about bitterness, in that bitter (hoppy) beers tend to go well with more sour cheeses and vice versa. (Beer, at 3.7 to 4.1 on the pH scale is significantly less acidic than wine, which ranges from about 2.5 to 3.5 and therefore relies much more on its acid levels to find happy pairings.) Cheddars, which have good acidity, are classic partners for various types of beers, from English ales to Belgian *wit* styles.

Salt content is also of prime importance when considering cheese-and-beer pairings. Oftentimes, when you pair a cheese with beers its salt can come to dominate, even with types you don't think of as very salty. What's happening is the other flavor components in the two partners are balancing each other out, leaving the cheese's salt to come too far to the fore.

In a beer-and-cheese lineup, as with a tasting of wine pairings, you'll want to proceed from the lighter, milder lager, pilsner, and pale ale styles to the deeper, richer, heavier, darker, more complex-flavored styles of brew.

Just as with artisanal cheeses, there is variety from batch to batch in craft brews, so you should taste test each one first before turning your attention to its possible matches.

SOME CHEESE-AND-BEER PAIRING GUIDELINES

Both beer and cheese are indigenous to the Belgian, German, and English cultures, just as wine and cheese are to the French. So traditional Belgian- and English-type cheeses with the traditional brew styles of those countries is a good starting point for pairings.

- Bigger cheeses such as aged farmhouse-style Goudas can be good partners, but you need a big beer to stand up to them. The full, long-lasting flavors of hard Alpine cheeses can work well with bigger beers.

- Washed-rind cheeses often make excellent beer partners as long as the latter are big and bold enough. A hoppy ale is a good choice; delicate, subtler-tasting brews likely won't stand up.

- Another strong pairing is triple-crème cheeses with stouts.

BREW STYLES

"LAGERS & PILSNERS & BOCKS—OH, MY!"

The two main categories of beers are lagers and ales. Lagers are made using bottom-fermenting yeasts that perform their magic at colder temperatures and yield lighter, milder, drier brews while ales are made with top-fermenting yeasts for sweeter, stronger, more complex brews. Lagers are aged—the word *lager* means "store" in German—sometimes for months; ales are sold sooner, often within weeks. In general, lagers are the beers we think of as popular mass-market quaffing types whereas ales are the craft beers we prefer to match with artisanal cheeses. Beer types generally get heavier and stronger as they go from lighter to darker (i.e., as the malts are more roasted and toasted); the exceptions are some strong light-colored ales that are considered much more substantial than some darker-colored lagers.

A couple of notes: The beer types are listed below in order of strength, from lighter to heavier (although there can be exceptions), to assist you in selected lineups for cheese tastings.

LAGERS

American, Canadian, and Australian Lagers—These are basic, light commercial brews for the mass market.

Pilsner—Simple, light, refreshing, and very tasty, this type was defined by the original brand, Pilsner Urquell, which some still swear by as the *only* one. In any case, this is the most popular beer style on the planet.

Oktoberfest and Maerzen—Virtually identical seasonal German lagers, which are balanced and light, without the more breadlike character of British lagers or German Bocks. They get their respective names from the fact that they're brewed, often in March, for the Munich beer festival in October.

Bock—This is an ancient German, bready, yeasty, darker lager style with various subcategories such as Dopple (stronger, more alcoholic) or Maibock (brewed in May), ranging from lighter and milder to darker and heavier.

ALES

Wheat Beer—Also known as *Weiss* (white), this looks like a lager but it's not. Bavarian *hefeweizen* is brewed using at least 50 percent wheat as its malted grain. There are also northern German (Berlin) styles and Belgian, called *wit,* as well as American ones. The latter are delicate and very fizzy-effervescent in mouth feel, acidic, citrusy, and yeasty tasting.

Pale Ale—An old British style that is malty, albeit with more slowly roasted and thus lighter malts than other ale styles. This includes the subcategories bitter and ESB (for extra special bitter). American pale ale styles are hoppier than their British cousins.

India Pale Ale—This pale ale, made with extra hops (for their preservative effect), allowed it to survive shipping to India and other faraway British colonies.

Amber Ale—Made with amber-colored malts, this is a darker version of British ale.

Brown Ale—This is a sweeter, heavier, darker version of traditional British pale ale.

Lambic—A relatively strong wheat beer from Belgium, it is often flavored with fruit additives.

Belgian Blonde—This fairly strong but light golden-colored ale is exemplified by the oft-imitated Duvel, which pioneered the category.

Saison—This is a farmhouse-style, bottle-conditioned pale ale from Wallonia, the French-speaking part of Belgium.

Flemish Red Ale—Defined by the Rodenbach brand, this is a moderately strong brew with a distinct sour taste.

Belgian Abbey or Trappist Ales—A strong, heavy sweetish but complex and balanced reddish-brown to dark brown ale brewed in the ancient monk style. Subcategories are *dubbel* (for double) and *tripel* (for triple), which are progressively bigger and higher in alcohol.

Porter—A traditional roasty and toasty brew, it is very dark and similar to stout but milder and not as big, bitter, or complex.

Stout—Like porter but with higher gravity and brewed with black roasted (albeit unmalted) barley. Stouts have a lot of additive options, including coffee, oatmeal, and chocolate.

Barleywine—A heavy, complex, relatively high-alcohol brew that is the beer world's equivalent to fine, ageable red wines—one of the stronger, sweeter styles on record.

Knowing as we do that Champagne and triple crèmes work well together, this might be a bit of a surprise. When you've got a rich, buttery cheese in your mouth, a big dark beer that is also dry, bitter, and roasty is a nice complement, forming a "desserty" combo, like ice cream and chocolate cake.

- Some mellow middle-of-the road cow cheeses pair well with more acidic beers such as the Berliner Weisse style (northern German wheat beer), which can be quite delicate and contain a good amount of lactic acid.

- Blue cheeses pair well with stouts and barleywines, which have the heft and inherent sweetness to provide balance.

- Generally speaking, sweeter blue cheeses go better with more bitter beers while more bitter blue cheeses go with sweeter beers.

"BENCHMARK" PAIRINGS

The FISCALINI BANDAGED CHEDDAR, which is quite acidic, bright and fruity, would pair well with a British-style ale, one with enough body to stand up to this fairly big cheese and not too much acidity to tip the scales: ITHACA'S NUT BROWN is a good example. The Fiscalini also goes nicely with DUVEL, a signature Belgian light ale with hoppy, spicy, and citrusy components.

MONTGOMERY'S CHEDDAR, on the other hand, probably the most elegant and balanced of its class, might pair better with a hoppier beer, with perhaps some contrasting citrus fruitiness, such as the Belgian-style BARNSTORMER TRIPLE ale from Heartland Brewery.

CABECOU FEUILLE, a little jewel of a goat cheese from south of France, pairs with an interesting range of brews from the hearty, rich BOURBON BARRELS STOUT (also from Heartland Brewery) to the meadlike MIDAS TOUCH GOLDEN ELIXIR (from Dogfish Head) and the *saison*-style OMMEGANG HENNEPIN.

HOJA SANTA, a reliable American goat-cheese favorite—fresh, simple and with a nice note of sassafras or root beer from its leaf wrapping—pairs with an even wider range across the beer spectrum, making it one of the most versatile partners: Bayrischer Bahnhof's BERLINER WEISSE; Heartland Brewery's GRATEFUL RED LAGER; Kelso's HOP LAGER; THE MIDAS TOUCH GOLDEN ELIXIR; Ithaca's NUT BROWN LAGER and PALE ALE; Dogfish Head's RAISON D'EXTRA and Captain Lawrence's SMOKED PORTER.

GOOD PARTNERS

CHEESE-FRIENDLY BREWS

Here are some fine craft brews, representative of significant types, that have found more and better matches with cheeses:

GRATEFUL RED LAGER
(Heartland Brewery)

HOP LAGER
(Kelso of Brooklyn)

INDIAN BROWN ALE
(Dogfish Head)

LIQUID GOLD
(Captain Lawrence)

MIDAS TOUCH GOLDEN ELIXIR
(Dogfish Head)

PALE ALE
(Captain Lawrence)

ITHACA
(Pale Ale)

MAREDSOUS DUBBEL

SMOKED PORTER
(Captain Lawrence)

A 4-year-old DUTCH FARMHOUSE GOUDA works with several substantial brews: GRATEFUL RED LAGER, Dogfish Head's INDIAN BROWN ALE, and Captain Lawrence's PALE ALE; GRUYÈRE also finds harmony with INDIAN BROWN ALE as well as the even bigger BARNSTORMER TRIPLE.

STILTON with WORLD WIDE STOUT (Dogfish Head) is a prime example of a profound blue cheese with a substantial, sweeter, "desserty" style of beer.

HARBOURNE BLUE, on the other hand, is a sweeter blue that finds a willing partner in a more bitter beer, for example the CAPTAIN'S RESERVE from Captain Lawrence Brewing Company.

A stolid MORBIER, which, although it has a washed rind and can be stinky, offers a dense, mellow aged profile not entirely unlike some *tomme* types or less rustic Cheddars is a confirmed partner for three good wheat beers: Bayrischer Bahnhof's BERLINER WEISSE; the 1809 BERLINER WEISSE, from Professor Fritz Briem; and the OMMEGANG WITTE.

CRAFT BREWS AND THEIR CHEESE PARTNERS

Here is a rundown of some interesting craft brews and their cheese partners; follow it specifically or simply use it as a guide to the types of beers and cheeses that go well together. The pairings listed have all been tested and rated either good (+1) or outstanding (+2).

90 MINUTE IPA (DOGFISH HEAD)—A bigger, maltier, hoppier IPA with 9 percent alcohol. Comparable to a Sauvignon Blanc. Matching cheeses: Époisses, Harbourne Blue, Pleasant Ridge Reserve.

BARNSTORMER TRIPLE (HEARTLAND BREWERY)—Golden in color with fragrant aroma of English noble hops and spicy Belgian yeast, this one has a crisp, dry finish. Matching cheeses: Gruyère, Lancashire, Montgomery's Cheddar.

BERLINER WEISSE (BAYRISCHER BAHNHOF)—This soft, light, and delicate interpretation of the Berliner Weisse style (only 3 percent ABV) is bright and acidic. Matching cheeses: Hoja Santa, Morbier, Purple Haze.

1809 BERLINER WEISSE (PROFESSOR FRITZ BRIEM)—Professor Briem's historic interpretation of the Berliner Weisse style has loads of tartness from lactic acid bacteria and a complex, fruity profile to balance. Matching cheeses: Comté, Morbier.

XTREME BEER

AMERICAN CRAFT BREWS

Most of the craft breweries have eye-catching and entertaining websites, full of colorful verbiage, including tasting notes that mimic the grocery lists we've grown accustomed to for wines over the years. In fact, these notes often come with a wine equivalent, which can be very helpful for conceptualizing a brew's flavors and proposing cheese pairings.

Like our American winemakers, who early on churned out heavily oaked Chardonnays and big fruit-bomb Pinot Noirs, our U.S. craft brewers gravitate toward the extreme. Dogfish Head, a well-known microbrewery out of Rehoboth Beach, Delaware, typifies this trend, offering a lineup studded with curious and exotic brews, many of which have alcohol contents well above 10 percent and/or are super-hoppy or extra chocolatey. Perusing some recent Dogfish tasting notes, we came across an interesting assortment of components: candied orange, brandied fruitcake, raisiney, honey, saffron, papaya, biscuity, molasses, ginger, Raisinets—and, of course, plenty of coffee and chocolate references. Imagine all these flavors in beer . . . Comparable wines cited ranged from Shiraz and Amarone to Sauvignon Blanc and Sauternes.

A few other U.S. craft breweries worth checking out (and matching their brews with fine cheeses): Bell's, Blue Point, Lagunitas, New Belgium, Ommegang, Rogue (from Oregon, like the creamery we love; see chapter 14), Russian River, Stoudt's, and a few local New York favorites—Kelso of Brooklyn and its sister operation Heartland Brewery, along with Ithaca Beer Co. and Captain Lawrence Brewing Co.

BOURBON BARRELS STOUT (HEARTLAND BREWERY)—Notes of vanilla and bourbon from the barrels are tempered by espresso and chocolate flavors. Matching cheese: Cabecou Feuille.

CAPTAIN'S RESERVE (CAPTAIN LAWRENCE BREWING COMPANY)—This is a big, hoppy Double IPA. Matching cheeses: Harbourne Blue, Monte Enebro, Prattigauer, Valdeón.

CASCAZILLA (ITHACA BEER COMPANY)—A red ale with a significant dose of Cascade hops (contributing their signature bitter citrus flavor), it also has a taste of caramel malt. Matching cheeses: Époisses, Mont St. Francis, Wensleydale.

DUVEL—This Belgian classic, which claims to be a category of one, Strong Golden Ale, looks like a pilsner but is really a Belgian ale (8.5 percent ABV). Matching cheeses: Brillat-Savarin, Fiscalini Bandage Cheddar, Lancashire.

GOLDEN ERA (DOGFISH HEAD)—This Imperial pilsner-style lager has been dry-hopped for 8 weeks. Matching cheese: Serpa.

GRATEFUL RED LAGER (HEARTLAND BREWERY)—This amber lager, the color of burnt sienna, is malty with light, sweet notes and

Pairing abbey-style cheeses such as this Hooligan with traditional Belgian and English brew types is a good place to start your beer-and-cheese adventure.

a nutty finish. Matching cheeses: Brillat-Savarin, Comté, Gouda (4-year-aged Boeren Kass), Hoja Santa, Isle of Mull Cheddar.

HOP LAGER (KELSO OF BROOKLYN)—This pale lager is made with German hops and British barley for a full mouthfeel; it has a mildly spicy palate and crisp finish. Matching cheeses: Époisses, Fiscalini Bandage Cheddar, Hoja Santa, Ibores, Pont l'Évêque.

INDIAN BROWN ALE (DOGFISH HEAD)—This ale has characteristics of a Scottish ale and an IPA, both hoppy and malty. Matching cheeses: Appenzeller, Beermat, Berkswell, Cabecou Feuille, Gouda (4-year-aged Boeren Kass), Gruyère, Pleasant Ridge Reserve.

JAN DE LICHTE (DE GLAZEN TOREN)—An imperial white ale (7.5 percent ABV) from Flanders in the Belgian *wit* beer style, it is brewed from barley, wheat, oats, and buckwheat with coriander and other spices added (7.5 percent ABV). Matching cheeses: Gorwydd Caerphilly, Fiscalini Bandaged Cheddar.

LIQUID GOLD (CAPTAIN LAWRENCE BREWING COMPANY)—Brewed with German malts and American hops, it has grassy, spicy, and orange notes. Matching cheeses: Ibores, Monte Enebro, Purple Haze, Wabash Cannonball.

MAREDSOUS DUBBEL—This dark brown Belgian abbey ale is malty, roasty-toasty, and strong. Matching cheeses: Beermat, Krümmenswiler Försterkase, Kuntner, Mont St. Francis, Pleasant Ridge Reserve.

MIDAS TOUCH GOLDEN ELIXIR (DOGFISH HEAD)—This mead-like brew is made with barley, white Muscat grapes, honey, and saffron, from the most-ancient fermented drink recipe known; it is comparable to Sauternes. Matching cheeses: Cabecou, Hoja Santa, Hooligan, Stilton, Valençay, Winnimere.

NUT BROWN (ITHACA BEER COMPANY)—This is a malty, moderately dark ale. Matching cheeses: Fiscalini Bandage Cheddar, Wensleydale.

NUT BROWN LAGER (KELSO OF BROOKLYN)—Made in the style of German Dunkel, it has a full-toasted flavor from lightly kilned Munich malts. Matching cheeses: Hoja Santa, Ibores.

OMMEGANG RARE VOS—This amber ale has notes of orange blossoms and caramel malt; it has a dry, hoppy finish. Matching cheeses: Ibores, Lancashire, Pecorino Foja de Noce, Yarg.

PALE ALE (CAPTAIN LAWRENCE BREWING COMPANY)—This ale features American West Coast hops and citrusy, piney aromas. Matching cheeses: Azeitão, Berkswell, Cabot Clothbound Reserve Cheddar, Époisses, Gouda (4-year-aged Boeren Kass), Mimolette.

PALE ALE (ITHACA BEER COMPANY)—This is a balanced hoppy golden-colored ale. Matching cheeses: Berkswell, Cabecou, Fiscalini Bandage Cheddar, Hoja Santa, Pleasant Ridge Reserve.

RAISON D'ETRE (DOGFISH HEAD)—This complex mahogany ale brewed with Belgian yeast is compared to Amarone della Valpolicella. Matching cheeses: Brillat-Savarin, Hoja Santa, Pleasant Ridge Reserve, Stilton.

REISSDORF KOELSCH—Koelsch is a style of golden ale from Cologne, Germany, light and clean tasting, with a beautiful malt character and a dry finish. Matching cheese: Gorwydd Caerphilly.

RODENBACH GRAND CRU (FLEMISH RED ALE)—This style brew has a signature sour taste owing to the presence of pertannomyces, a bacteria that causes a defect in wines; there is often a good deal of residual sugar to balance the high acidity. Matching cheeses: Bayley Hazen, Beenleigh Blue.

SMOKED PORTER (CAPTAIN LAWRENCE BREWING COMPANY)— A dark brew featuring the old-time flavor of German smoked malt. Matching cheeses: Cabot Clothbound Reserve Cheddar, Fougerus, Harbourne Blue, Hoja Santa, Hooligan, Valdeón.

WORLD WIDE STOUT (DOGFISH HEAD)—A strong stout (15 percent alcohol), it claims comparisons to Tawny Port. Matching cheese: Stilton.

Nutty flavors abound in craft brews and artisanal cheeses.

A ROUND ROBIN: THREE BEERS AND SIX CHEESES

With this progression, we cover a fairly broad spectrum of cheese types, and, although they only number three, an equally broad range of brews. Since we already know that mild goat cheeses are potentially versatile beer partners, I didn't include any in this tasting, wishing to explore other less-charted territory. There's one sheep's milk cheese, from a family often associated with ales: the washed-rind stinkers. The other cheeses that follow are also associated with ale-producing regions so we might reasonably assume we'll have some good matches.

The beers: From the left, Pilsner Urquell; Dogfish Head 60 Minute IPA; and Rogue Chocolate Stout. The cheeses: Clockwise from bottom center, Stanser Schaf Reblochon; Durrus; Fiscalini Bandage Cheddar; Pleasant Ridge Reserve; Aged Dutch Gouda; and Cashel Blue.

TASTING PLATE

THE CHEESES

STANSER SCHAF REBLOCHON (AKA INNERSCHWEIZER SCHAFCHÄS)

DURRUS

FISCALINI BANDAGE CHEDDAR

UPLANDS PLEASANT RIDGE RESERVE

AGED DUTCH GOUDA

CASHEL BLUE

THE BEERS

PILSNER URQUELL

DOGFISH 60 MINUTE IPA

ROGUE CHOCOLATE STOUT

STANSER SCHAF REBLOCHON (aka Innerschweizer Schafchäs)— This particular cheese was quite stinky, so you might have thought it would overwhelm the pilsner, but it didn't. In fact, this relatively light, not-so-sweet beer, dry and refreshing, paired nicely with the cheese. The Stanser Schaf was not salty enough to stand up to the fairly bitter Dogfish Head. It was more successful with the stout, seeming to bring out that brew's delicious chocolatey flavors.

DURRUS—The pilsner scored a solid +2 here, its highest mark: The Durrus, very meaty, buttery, and with a lot of *umami,* found a refreshing partner in this beer, boosting its character. With the IPA, it was able to strike a good salt-sweet balance. It found a nice enough butter-and-chocolate pairing with the stout, although they didn't quite hit the bull's-eye. The stout should be served closer to room temperature than most beers, in which case its rounder, fuller flavors will come to the fore and jibe better with this or any other potential cheese partner.

FISCALINI—Like many American Cheddar styles, this cheese has a good amount of acidity. It was a pleasant enough match for the pilsner, but was clearly looking for a bigger brew, which it found quickly in the IPA. This was a remarkable pairing, another solid +2, with very good bitter-acid balance. The Fiscalini was also an excellent partner for the stout, perhaps a little surprisingly: The brew recognized and deferred nicely to the size of this cheese.

UPLANDS PLEASANT RIDGE RESERVE—A good act to follow the Fiscalini, the Pleasant Ridge—an Alpine-style, harder cheese, with just as big a profile but a smoother texture—found beautiful harmony with the Pilsner Urquell; it dissolved and melted down very nicely into this classic Czech brew. It was not quite as sharp, focused, or sour enough to score higher alongside the bigger, more bitter Dogfish IPA. The effervescence of the chocolate stout was able to break apart the cheese, dissolving it well. It's not a brew I'd necessarily drink by itself, but the way it harmonized with these cheeses heightened my regard for it. Like a slightly sweetened bar of dark chocolate, it had just the right balance of underlying sweetness to offset its potential for strong, bitter burnt-toast flavors.

AGED DUTCH GOUDA—This was a 4-year-old cheese with plenty of big, bold flavors and an impressive length of finish. You might think it would be more successful with the Pilsner Urquell: A northern European style of beer ought to pair with a northern European style of cheese, no? The beer did wash it down well enough, but they didn't find a lot of flavor compatibility. Perhaps the cheese was a little overwhelming. You had to figure the IPA would match it, but the brew was, surprisingly, not quite up to the task. This cheese is big and strong, with very focused flavors, without being smelly or sharp. Just as I was pondering what the ideal beverage for this Gouda would be—"Coffee, that's what I like it with," I thought—it was time to taste it with the stout. Sure enough, they hit it off. This rich, dark brew played a wonderful duet with that concentrated, thick mouthful of a cheese.

CASHEL BLUE—The salt and the bite of this blue were too much for the pilsner, although there was no obvious clash meriting a negative rating. The IPA found more success: The salty cow's milk flavors of the Cashel balanced the bitterness and also the underlying sweetness of this big brew. They went quite well—if not perfectly—together. The strength of this cheese found equal strengths in the stout, illuminating a warm, classic pairing, a resounding desserty +2 to end this highly satisfying encounter between three very different beers styles and some stalwart cheeses.

For this round-robin, I chose cheeses I thought would be beer friendly and paired them with three popular brew styles, hoping to highlight a few good pairings. We got more than we'd bargained for: The high overall scores spoke very well for the general prospects of beer with cheese. The pilsner, which was light, clean, and delightful, did well with the washed-rind cow's milk cheeses

CHEESE AND BEER 101: SCORE SHEET			
	Pilsner Urquell	Dogfish 60 Minute IPA	Rogue Chocolate Stout
STANSER SCHAF REBLOCHON	+1	0	+1
DURRUS	+2	+1	+2
FISCALINI BANDAGE CHEDDAR	+1	+2	+2
PLEASANT RIDGE RESERVE	+1	+1	+1
AGED DUTCH GOUDA	+1	+1	+2
CASHEL BLUE	0	+1	+2

because it freshened them up a bit, dialing down some of their pungency. The IPA, an American-style version of this type—big, hoppy, and fairly bitter but with enough sugar for balance—promised to work well with the salt in cheeses and also their sourness. The lowest pH (highest acidity) cheese was the Cheddar and so it was no surprise it racked up a high score with the IPA. The chocolate stout, with its nice round toasty profile, complexity, and sweetness did well with all of these cheeses. Its cheese compatibility made me appreciate this beer type much more than I might have imagined. Probably my favorite match of all was the stout with the Fiscalini Cheddar, which gave the impression of a big slice of chocolate cream pie. Remember that taste from growing up?

Traditional Tuscan sheep cheeses from Caseificio Pinzani: From top to bottom, Marzolino; Pecorino al Tartufo (with truffles); and Pecorino al Pepe (black pepper-studded). In general, sheep's milk cheeses find many pleasant pairings with wines and beers.

CHAPTER REVIEW:
Beer and Cheese

- ☐ If wine is all about growing the grapes and fermenting their juice, beer is about selecting the basic ingredients—malt, hops, water, and yeast—and brewing them accordingly to a finely tuned recipe.
- ☐ Modern craft brews, mostly based on traditional European styles, offer many interesting, complex texture and flavor profiles with a great deal of cheese-pairing potential.
- ☐ The principles of pairing beers and cheeses are very similar to those of wine pairings; beers, however, seem to rely more on finding balance with cheeses as opposed to seeking out complementary, harmonious flavors.
- ☐ Brews with bitter, hoppy flavors work well with the more acidic cheese types.
- ☐ Cheeses with bigger, bolder profiles and persistent flavors seek out bigger, heavier beers.
- ☐ Strong, salty cheeses—especially the blues—can work well with heftier, sweeter brews.
- ☐ Barleywines with Stilton, IPAs with Époisses, and *triple crèmes* with stouts are three of the best beer-and-cheese pairings uncovered thus far.

Sainte-Maure de Touraine, a highly recognizable Loire Valley classic.

CHAPTER 14

TAKING THE WORLD STAGE: AMERICA'S ARTISANS

BY FAR THE BIGGEST STORY IN THE WORLD OF REAL CHEESE SINCE THE turn of the millennium is being written in America. Beginning in the 1970s, all across the United States small family dairy farms began to go under. A handful of determined farmers have been able to stick it out. Artisanal cheese-making can be a vehicle for rescuing operations destined to fail. Some modern American cheese artisans went back to the land after successful careers elsewhere. Some of them started from scratch; others rejuvenated existing farms or dairies. Many were already breeding animals that produced high-quality milk. So the question inevitably would arise, "What should be done with all that good stuff?" And the answer came in the form of cheese.

For every real cheese—and cheese farm—there is a story. America is now blessed with an impressive group of artisans whose individual and collective efforts have put us on the world cheese map. In our first two books, we would have featured many more home-grown cheeses, but honestly they weren't quite there yet. Before the year 2000, there were only around twenty U.S. cheesemakers who I felt deserved mention alongside the world's greats. Within 8 years, there were nearly four times that number. American farmstead cheeses artisans have truly arrived.

The rebirth of real cheese in America is astonishing because it has occurred within a quarter century—and accelerated tremendously since the year 2000. Most of the Old World cheeses many of the Americans emulate took several centuries, if not an entire millennium, to perfect. The trajectory of our U.S.

Elk Mountain Tomme from Pholia Farm, Oregon.

Winnimere from Jasper Hill Farm, Vermont.

artisans traces a dizzying ascent. To kick off our exploration of the world's finest cheeses, we're going to highlight some of these cheese whizzes in this chapter and then move on to a few more key artisanal regions. For a more complete listing of U.S. producers and their cheeses, see appendix 2.

THE NORTHEAST

As we learned in chapter 2, New York State and Vermont were the cradles of American cheesemaking beginning in the late eighteenth century. Then the pioneers moved west, the Industrial Revolution arrived, and farmstead cheeses began to disappear. The modern artisanal cheesemakers of the Northeast are among the few survivors—and "revivers"—of a precious cottage industry. Its epicenter is still Green Vermont, with ripples up and down the Hudson and Connecticut River valleys.

Max's Picks: Northeast Artisans

CATO CORNER FARM—The first time I tried this Connecticut farm's signature Hooligan around 2002, it tasted just like its name—wild, erratic, somewhat wacky, and out of balance—but they've harnessed it since. With washed-rind, semisoft, relatively young types of this ilk, it is very difficult to turn out a consistently excellent cheese. (For much more on Cato Corner, see chapter 8.)

CONSIDER BARDWELL FARM—Owner and cheese farmer Angela Miller, who also happens to be our literary agent, turns out some fine cheeses from this western Vermont spread. Angela hired Peter Kindel and then Peter Dixon as cheesemakers, which in itself ought to put you on the world cheese map. Consider Bardwell's cheeses started out "just nice," but they've come a long way. Their Manchester, a washed-rind goat's milk cheese, is a real keeper. It's buttery, a little salty, smooth, savory, and not goaty, which can happen with this type unless you master it. I also love their fresh goat's milk Mettowee; when Peter Kindel was working there, he made one I remember tasting to this day, it was so close to perfection. Consider Bardwell's cow's milk cheeses (see Dorset in "Twenty-first-Century U.S. Rock Stars," page 289) are made with milk from Lisa Kaiman's Jersey Girls dairy in nearby Chester, Vermont.

GRAFTON VILLAGE CHEESE COMPANY—This is a fairly commercial operation, but it is producing a clothbound reserve Cheddar,

UNIQUE CHEESES

AMERICAN ORIGINALS

One sure sign U.S. cheeses have earned their place on the world stage is how many of them have attained the status of "unique American originals," meaning they are beyond comparison with their Europeans predecessors. Jasper Hill Farm's Aspenhurst is a fine example. This Vermont cheese was inspired by a British classic, Doddington, and is made by a similar recipe. It also shows some similarities to certain Cheddars. When you first taste an Aspenhurst, you frame your impression in terms of comparisons: "What does this remind me of?" But then you stop yourself and quickly come to realize it really stands on its own, occupying a category of one.

Pleasant Ridge Reserve, from Uplands Cheese Company, is another outstanding American original, this one patterned after Gruyère. The Pleasant Ridge comes from a quintessentially American melting pot of a herd (very mixed) and packs plenty of Wisconsin *terroir* (see also page 287).

Some more unique American originals: Vella Cheese Co.'s Dry Jack, a true pioneer still going strong; Rogue River Blue and Smokey Oregon Blue, new super-stars from Rogue Creamery; Elk Mountain and Hillis Peak from Pholia Farm; Hoja Santa from the Mozzarella Co. in Dallas; Square Cheese from Twig Farm; Old Kentucky Tomme from Capriole; and Tumalo Farms' Pondhopper and Classico.

aged at Jasper Hill Farm, to compete with the best British farmhouse brands. It has very good texture and is well balanced: a true and fruitful collaboration between producer and *affineur*.

JASPER HILL FARM—The Kehler brothers took over an old farm and in less than 10 years became a major force. Jasper Hill's blue, Bayley Hazen, is a winner: You can really taste the milk, and it's neither too salty nor too blue. (As a proud ambassador of American curdistry, I've packed it in my suitcase on a Friday afternoon, taken the overnight flight to Nice and served it on a cruise ship off Sardegna on a Monday evening to a chorus of "oohs" and "aahs.") The Bayley Hazen, and their bloomy rind, Constant Bliss, are perhaps more widely known, but I really like the Kehlers' washed-rind Winnimere: It has an excellent, thick, butterlike texture and a well-balanced profile, virtually oozing skillfully ripened butterfats. Take one look at the gorgeous pastures where their Ayrshire cows graze, and you think, "No wonder they can make such fine cheeses."

MAJOR FARM—Their Vermont Shepherd was one of the first American artisanal cheeses I fell in love with and remains a solid favorite. It's herbaceous, silken yet granular in texture, well balanced, and sublime. Vermont Shepherd is an American original that's been as good as any Ossau-Iraty cheese for a long while.

Cheeses aging in the cave at Jasper Hill Farm.

> *"Cheesemaking is essentially a vehicle for us to present our milk in different formats. We never quite got the point of making a blue cheese where the blue is all you can taste. We're looking for the milky, nutty flavors."*
>
> MATEO KEHLER, JASPER HILL FARM

MECOX BAY DAIRY—This Hamptons (Long Island) cheese farm has improved its cheeses dramatically since 2005 and shows great promise. It's good to see committed raw-milk cheese artisans exploiting all kinds of interesting pockets of *terroir*, including this lovely seaside spot in eastern Long Island. Of their cheeses, I'd single out the Mecox Sunrise, with its pleasant acidic tang.

NETTLE MEADOW FARM—While bloomy-rind, pasteurized-milk cheeses don't always get me excited, I must give this farm's Kunik, a cow-goat blend, its props. This is not a cheese that will pucker your cheeks or cause your palate to palpitate, but it's wonderfully soft, smooth, and accessible—a popular cheese that deservedly finds its place on many a tasting plate.

ORB WEAVER FARM—Like Major Farm's Vermont Shepherd, this farm's eponymous cheese is another long-time favorite among fine American farmstead originals. It's extremely satisfying, reliable, and consistent. Made from cow's milk and somewhat Colby-esque, Orb Weaver is perhaps America's answer to Le Moulis and Bethmale, although it's not as open textured.

SHELBURNE FARMS—Some cheese people say they haven't preferred Shelburne's reserve Cheddars since master cheesemaker Mariano Gonzalez left for Fiscalini Farms in California. But Shelburne's Brown Swiss cows grazing on the shores of Lake Champlain still deliver some exceptional milk, and the farm still turns out some very fine cheeses. They have balance, subtlety, and restraint and none of that very pronounced "sharp" accent so typical of run-of-the-mill Vermont Cheddars.

THISTLE HILL FARM—John and Janine Putnam's signature Tarentaise, which peaks at about 1 year, is golden in more than just its color. It has a wonderful tang—and in fact is one of the cheeses that tempered any skepticism I might have harbored about Jersey milk cheeses—and some intriguing, fruity, orange flavor notes. Its golden-hued paste, from the carotene in fresh plant fodder, reminds me of its roots in those lush green Vermont pastures. I can think of no other cooked, pressed cow's milk cheese like it. When I tasted a Tarentaise with top Spanish cheese expert Enric Canut, we agreed it was a great Alpine-style cheese but at the same time a true American original that could not be replicated elsewhere.

TWIG FARM—Emily Sunderman and Michael Lee opened for business in 2005. Their Square Cheese is excellent. It is reminiscent of Garrotxa but very much an American original. Slightly chalky in consistency, tending toward claylike, I've heard it called semisoft, but I prefer to think of it as "firm but moist." Its flavors are smooth, gentle, milky, and refreshing with a slightly peppery bite on the attack, good middle-palate flavors, and a creamy finish, leaving a gentle, accessible impression, even with 80 days of aging.

WESTFIELD FARM—Westfield's Classic Blue is another consistent favorite, this one from north-central Massachusetts. A surface-ripened blue goat cheese, with the *Penicillium roqueforti* on the outside only, it constitutes a category of one, well worthy of its name. Classic Blue was invented by Westfield founders Bob and Lettie Kilmoyer, who retired in 1996 and handed the reins to Bob and Debby Stetson. It has a nice creamy mouth feel and refreshing flavors, with just enough of the blue penetrating to jazz things up without overwhelming the milk.

VERMONT BUTTER & CHEESE COMPANY—Allison Hooper heads this stellar artisan operation, which uses goat's and cow's milk from 17 farms around Vermont. Two of its cheeses, Coupole and Bonne Bouche, are established American classics, which you'll find at fine shops and restaurants all over the United States. They are milky, smooth, delicate and delightful. I think of the Coupole as a more elemental, fresh type, akin to a Chabichou du Poitu; the Bonne Bouche, on the other hand, is a more traditional somewhat aged chèvre type, a bit chalky and closer to a Selles-sur-Cher.

FROM TOP: John and Janine Putnam of Thistle Hill Farm, Vermont, with their Tarentaises; Allison Hooper and one of her employees of the month; Jersey cows at Cato Corner Farm, Connecticut (featured in chapter 8).

WILLOW HILL FARM—Since 1996, Willa Smart has shown her expertise making excellent farmhouses cheeses from the milk of her East Friesian ewes (and also a couple of Dutch Belt and Brown Swiss cows) at her farm in Milton, Vermont, north of Burlington, close to Lake Champlain. Willa's relatively recent invention Paniolo, which is Hawaiian for "cowboy" (her family owns a ranch there), is a beautiful washed-rind cow's milk cheese comparable to Stanser Röteli or Durrus, though a bit more restrained. Her Summer Tomme is also highly recommended. I knew Willa and her husband David were serious the minute I visited their farm in the late 1990s and saw they had built their own aging cave into a hillside—one of the first of the new artisan operations to do so.

THE KEHLER BROTHERS OF GREENSBORO, VERMONT

Ever since they burst onto the scene in 2002, Mateo and Andy Kehler have been at the forefront of the American artisanal movement. Cheese farmers with a clear mission and higher purpose, they've built their own little fiefdom in the Northeast Kingdom of Vermont, where they practice sustainable food farming at its best and promote grass-roots cheese politics for what ails the world.

The Kehlers brothers grew up in Bogotá, Colombia, and their family summered on the shores of Vermont's Caspian Lake for five generations. (Two of their cheeses, Aspenhurst and Winnimere, are named for lakeside communities.) When things got dangerous in Colombia in the 1980s, the family moved full time to Pomfret, Vermont, right over the hill from Thistle Hill Farm where the Putnam family makes Tarentaise. The Kehlers bought Jasper Hill Farm in 1998, the same year five other small farms in the Greensboro area failed. They made a commitment to saving the property, choosing cheese-farming as their vehicle. Mateo went to Europe for 3 years to learn cheese-making and *affinage*. He studied all the French cheesemaking texts he could get his hands on; visited around sixty cheesemakers; served apprenticeships with the makers of

Ticklemore, Berkswell, and Doddington; and worked in the caves at Neal's Yard Dairy.

Within a few shorts years—5 to be precise—the Kehlers began to establish an American equivalent to Neal's Yard, an artisanal brand based on the highest standards of cheese-making, selection, and *affinage*. In fact, Neal's Yard is an investor in Jasper Hill's ripening facility, and the two operations share goals and philosophies, albeit approaching the equation from opposite ends.

As with any farmstead cheese outfit, Jasper Hill's success depends largely on superior milk quality. Mateo is in charge of cheesemaking; Andy is the herd manager. Says Mateo: "It starts in the barn, it starts with the milk and that's where Andy has left his mark on our business." In 2007, Jasper Hill won Vermont's Best Standard Plate Count award for the third consecutive year, which means they're producing the cleanest raw milk in one of our nation's best dairy states.

Jasper Hill Farm reached its production capacity toward the end of 2007 and into early 2008. They made about 30,000 pounds of cheese in 2006, increased to 63,000 in 2007, and topped off at roughly 75,000 in 2008. From there on, any business growth would have to occur by promoting the work of other Vermont artisans—that is, by providing services as ripeners.

The seeds for Jasper Hill's *affinage* operation were planted early, in 2003, when they contracted to ripen select clothbound Cheddars for Cabot. In 2007, the Kehlers started construction on a 22,000-square-foot aging facility with space for the

cheeses of forty to fifty farms their size. They dug out an entire hillside and created underground vaults of poured concrete with floors 27 feet below grade. The facility, completed in early 2008, has different cave zones with five separate temperature and humidity levels. Not only is this a great business boon for them, but the Kehlers aim bigger—hoping to populate the surrounding countryside with cheese artisans. They encourage fledgling young cheesemakers to join them for internships and they work with newcomer farms in the area to build their own plants. Their *affinage* business creates economies of scale and provides logistical support for other artisans.

As of mid-2008, Jasper Hill had fourteen employees, including the Kehler brothers and their wives, Victoria and Angela, and was aging cheeses for thirteen independent artisanal producers, including Twig Farm, Dancing Cow Farm, Crawford Family Farm, Grafton Village Cheese Company, Lazy Lady Farm, Plymouth Cheese Company, and Crowley.

One of the questions I've often pondered is what motivates these otherwise apparently sane and intelligent people to work such long, tough hours and tie themselves so thoroughly down to raising animals and making cheese, 24/7/365. What are the hidden motivators? People like the Kehlers, who began in their early 30s, and Cary Bryant and David Gremmels, who began a little later, after successful previous careers, begin to provide some answers. They're reinventing the sustainable family farm and they're reviving a cottage industry that was threatened with extinction, all the while becoming famous and making

The Kehler brothers, Mateo, left, and Andy.

a lot of people very happy by manufacturing great cheeses. They are tackling physical and intellectual challenges, discovering the psychic and spiritual rewards of living off the land, creating delicious expressions of *terroir*, and contributing significantly to their communities. Some of them may even be making money.

Can the Kehler brothers' efforts salvage the farm economy of the Northeast Kingdom from utter depression? Perhaps not single-handedly. But they can make a difference, both in real dollars and also symbolically, demonstrating what can be done with hard work, commitment, smart farming, and deft cheese artistry.

Jasper Hill's Cheeses

ASPENHURST—When he worked at England's Doddington Dairy for one of his apprenticeships, Mateo fell in love with their eponymous cheese, a traditional British farmhouse type, made to a Leicester recipe and generally aged at least 18 months. The model for Aspenhurst, Doddington is somewhat Cheddar-like, but with a more subtle and nuanced flavor profile as a result of gentler acidification. The Doddington and Aspenhurst curds are not actually cheddared, meaning they cool more quickly and have a shallower acidification curve.

BARTLETT BLUE—This is a Stilton-style cheese made in the summer; Winnimere (see below) is made with the same milk in the winter. Although I'm a little partial to their other cheeses, I want to stress that Jasper Hill's blues are excellent and have very deservedly made their impact in the market. They bring out their pasture quality and milk character wonderfully; compared to Stilton, they're sweeter and have that fuller aroma typical of well-made raw milk cheeses.

BAYLEY HAZEN—This is mellower and, again, somewhat sweeter than most blues—a blue for non-blue lovers—which is attributable, according to Mateo, to its relatively low moisture content, its natural rind, and to a very proteolytic strain of *P. roqueforti*.

CONSTANT BLISS—Jasper Hill's signature bloomy-rind cheese is made by a Chaource-type recipe but without added cream; that is, it's not a double- or triple crème. They introduce small amounts of *Geotrichum candidum* and *Penicillium candidum* into the milk and age the cheese 60 days. "If *you* could sell it at 21 days, that would be easy," Mateo told us. "Aging it 60 days has, in a way, forced us to be better cheese-makers." Several times a year, they make a wilder version of Constant Bliss called Naked Bliss, wherein they allow the milk's inherent microflora to completely take over and do their crazy magic.

MOSES SLEEPER—Moses Sleeper and Constant Bliss were both Revolutionary War scouts killed by the redcoats while guarding the local Bayley Hazen Road in 1781—a nice tribute and strong statement about these cheeses' native roots. The Moses Sleeper is a Camembert-style disk, although Mateo refuses to liken it to that French classic because, he says, "it's pretty different and we're not trying for that model."

WINNIMERE—This cheese was inspired by a Krümmenswiler Försterkase Mateo once tried at Picholine. It features a triple expression of *terroir*: First, it's made from raw milk of the farm's pasture-fed herd; second, it's wrapped in strips of bark from local spruce trees; and third, it's washed in a lambic-style beer brewed right on the farm using ambient yeasts. The cheese is aged 70 days and made December through June. I must say it's an exceptional cheese that's gotten better by the year and packs more flavor than just about any of its type.

THE WEST COAST

The big story on our left coast is the Northwest—Oregon and, to some extent, Washington. This is no knock on California, where great American cheesemaking continues to thrive—if perhaps not as much as one would hope for from a state the size of the world's greatest ancient cheese nation (France) and one that encompasses the most productive agricultural zones on the planet.

First, let's look at some outstanding California curdmeisters. With gorgeous countryside, rolling hills, diverse microclimates, progressive politics, and a penchant for adventurous, outdoor lifestyles, the Golden State offers much fertile ground for artisan dairy farming.

Max's Picks: California's Artisans

BELLWETHER FARMS—In the rolling hills of Sonoma County, not far from Tomales Bay and also Bodega Bay, this family farm, founded by Cindy Callahan in 1986 and now run by her son Liam and his wife, Diana, turns out some excellent farmstead cheeses. I especially like their Carmody Reserve, made to a Doddington-type recipe with raw Jersey cow's milk from a nearby farm, and the San Andreas, a firm, pressed type made from the raw sheep's milk of their own herd.

COWGIRL CREAMERY—By early 2008, Peggy Smith and Sue Conley had relocated their cheesemaking facility to Petaluma, where they continued to produce a lineup that includes Red Hawk, an organic, washed-rind, semisoft triple crème which, when in top form, is truly excellent. (It would be great to taste a raw-milk version.) Red Hawk is pretty and blush with *Brevibacterium linens* and has an appropriate amount of "stink." Its texture and consistency deliver a mouth feel with the potential to bowl you over when it's good and ripe. Cowgirl and its sister company, Tomales Bay Foods, are major forces in U.S. retail and also in sustainable food farming in the wild west of Marin County.

CYPRESS GROVE CHÈVRE—Mary Keehn began selective breeding of Alpine dairy goats in the 1970s, and in 1983 she began selling her own cheeses from their milk. Her signature item is Humboldt Fog, which has won multiple first-place awards at the American Cheese Society (ACS) convention and also a gold medal at the World Cheese Competition in London. Beyond this established American original, Mary and her staff make nearly twenty other cheeses, many of them variations on basic chèvre types. All of Cypress Grove's production reflects the foggy, remote *terroir* of Humboldt County, a beautiful slice of northern California not to be missed on your cheese plate.

FISCALINI FARMS—Its bandaged Cheddar is exceptional—another legitimate American rival for the great British farmhouse Cheddars. You go right down the checklist and it has all the requisites for its type: balance, fruity and grassy notes, good texture, rustic yet elegant, and restrained character. Its maker, Mariano Gonzalez, is definitely among the elite of American cheesemakers; Fiscalini is located in the Central Valley, near Modesto.

MATOS CHEESE FACTORY—The Matos family immigrated to Santa Rosa, Sonoma County, from São Jorge in the Azores, and their St. George cheese emulates their native island's eponymous cheese. Actually, St. George reminds me more of Kirkham's Lancashire than anything else: It's firm, moist, crumbly, milky, smooth, mellow, and very approachable—in fact, so much so that it might be considered as a sandwich or melting cheese, though I'd recommend it as a stand-alone.

RUMIANO CHEESE COMPANY—Its excellent Dry Jack is comparable to Vella (see below), whose Special Reserve Dry Jack is the standard-bearer of this unique American category. The company was founded by three Italian brothers, who immigrated to the States in the early twentieth century and worked as miners; it's located in Crescent City, in the heart of northern California's redwood country, not far south of the Oregon border.

VELLA CHEESE COMPANY—If you are looking for a truly indigenous American original, a piece of our cheese history still vibrant and intact, you need look no further than the Vella family's artisanal factory in Sonoma and its Dry Jack. Tom Vella invented it in the 1930s and his company continues to make it under his son, Ig. Their distinctive Special Reserve Dry Jack brings out the best in its milk, has a mouthwatering texture, and a highly stimulating mouth feel.

THE PACIFIC NORTHWEST

The main geographical feature of this region relevant to cheese is that its western parts are lower in elevation, greener, and wetter, whereas in the east it's drier and more barren—much of it high desert, with grassy plains, badlands, and volcanic areas. The

FROM TOP: Maureen Cunnie, cheesemaker at Cowgirl Creamery, California; Cowgirl proprietors Peggy Smith, left, and Sue Conley.

Elle Obringer in the milking room of Ancient Heritage Farm, Oregon.

Cascade Mountains run down the middle, dividing the region along a north-south axis. The wetter west is cow country while the drier east is the land of goats and sheep. The extreme western parts of Oregon and Washington have coastal mountain ranges, with plenty of niches defining interesting microclimates.

Both states, particularly Oregon but also Washington, are very much on board with the Slow Food movement. The political and bureaucratic climate is right for real cheese.

Oregon

Along with Vermont, Oregon has become perhaps the world's best laboratory for developing artisanal cheeses. What makes Oregon such fertile ground for fine cheese? It is home to a forward-looking, ecologically aware population. There is a small but gifted group of cheese artisans and a history of high-quality dairying. The state has vast natural resources and a government committed to protecting them. Its *terroir* features lush and varied pasturelands, four distinct seasons with a relatively mild winter, and plenty of good water from clean ground sources and regular rain.

Until 2002, there were only two traditional artisanal creameries in Oregon making cow's milk cheeses, Rogue and Tillamook, and Juniper Grove Farm was the only one making goat's milk ones. The turning point for Oregon, and indeed the entire Pacific Northwest, was the year 2002, in which Cary Bryant and David Gremmels bought the Rogue Creamery. Oregon's artisan cheesemakers won twenty-two awards at the ACS convention in August 2007, a stunning showing that solidified the state's place on the world cheese map.

Max's Picks: Oregon's Artisans

ANCIENT HERITAGE FARMSTEAD—By all appearances, this farm, located in Scio, a seemingly remote yet quite cosmopolitan area about 20 miles south of Salem, is the quintessential early twentieth-century dairy operation. Kathy Obringer, an artist with no formal training in cheesemaking but an obvious yellow thumb, and her husband, Paul, who worked in the corporate world, are the owner-operators. Their Ayrshire cows and Friesian sheep provide the cheesemaking milk. There aren't enough fine artisanal sheep's milk cheeses being made in the United States: Ancient Heritage helps fill the gap, producing masterfully crafted, unique-tasting cheeses,

ARTISAN SUPPORT

A TEMPLATE FOR THE BENEFIT OF ALL: THE OREGON CHEESE GUILD

This exemplary organization, begun in 2006, was founded in the wake of the Oregon Cheese Festival, which has been held in the parking lot of the Rogue Creamery each March since David Gremmels started it in 2004. Gremmels made the guild's template—business plan, founding guidelines, website map, bylaws, and so forth—available to anyone wishing to launch a similar group. Among those who took him up on the offer were California and Wisconsin and also the Raw Milk Cheesemakers' Association (RMCA).

Education is such an important part of the real-cheese movement, and professional guilds like this one take the role of offering knowledge to the public. Its website and other outlets offer valuable information—especially safety and quality assurances. Guilds also perform a lot of important advocacy functions: They demand strict professional qualifications for membership; they help establish and maintain the highest standards in raw materials, production, and aesthetics; and they offer strength in numbers to small producers, which helps them enhance their marketing and publicity efforts and tackle logistical challenges. Behind the scenes, if members of a guild can communicate frankly and offer honest, constructive criticism to each other, everyone's cheesemaking improves.

none of them loud but all broad ranging and distinct. I particularly like their Odessa Blue; a raw sheep's milk cheese with gentle bluing which debuted in 2006. It kind of reminds me of Beenleigh Blue but (thankfully) without the pasteurization. It's a relatively gentle blue, with a creamy, smooth, thick cheesecake-like texture that has hints of granularity; its flavors are subtle, grassy, and a little sweet, although not quite as sweet as the Beenleigh.

FERN'S EDGE GOAT DAIRY—Andhi Reyna is a maverick proponent of organic and biodynamic raw-milk dairy goat farming. Her mother-in-law, Shari, has been an expert goat breeder for more than 30 years; they began cheesemaking as a way to sustain their farm, located in Lowell about 20 miles southeast of Eugene. They are dedicated to the health and well-being of their animals and to making wonderful unpasteurized fresh chèvre-style cheeses.

FRAGA FARM—Janice and Larry Neilson are healers (massage therapists to be precise) who found themselves a beautiful piece of property in the town of Sweet Home, west of the Cascade range between Eugene and Salem. In the early fall, their does—a really happy, healthy-looking group of animals—enjoy feasting on the Himalayan blackberries which grow on long vines along the banks of the nearby Santiam River. The Neilsons make a fine goat Feta and also a Cheddar.

Andhi Reyna of Fern's Edge Goat Dairy.

JUNIPER GROVE FARM—Pierre Kolisch was an attorney with a passion for cheese. In 1985, he traveled to France, explored cheese *terroir*, learned about cheesemaking, and returned to found Oregon's first goat-cheese dairy (in 1987). Juniper Grove, near Redmond, in the central part of the state, east of the Cascades, has since become a household name in artisanal production. (More lawyers should become cheesemakers, don't you think?) Pierre's Redmondo has long set the standard for raw goat's milk *tommes* in America. At peak, it still has plenty of fresh, milky flavors and never turns "goaty." That he can so successfully age such a cheese is a testament to both his cheesemaking and *affinage* skills. Too bad he's not allowed to make young raw chèvre types; I bet they'd be great.

OREGON GOURMET CHEESES—Proprietors Brian and Lori Richter are small-dairy entrepreneurs in Albany, about 25 miles south of Salem, utilizing New World cheesemaking techniques Brian learned during apprenticeships in Australia. They are the first producers of both pasteurized and raw-milk Camembert-style cheeses in Oregon. I recommend you get hold of some on their sixty-first day—when they're barely legal, but perfectly aged. For me, their most successful cheese is the washed-rind Sublimity, made in several versions, including one with peppercorns and another with Herbes de Provence.

PHOLIA FARM—I really love Gianaclis Caldwell's cheeses—their flavors are so well knit together—but I worry they might be a bit misunderstood, all their nuances not sufficiently appreciated. Not to say anything negative about it, but you can hardly tell they're made from goat's milk; there is nothing goaty or gamey about them. The milk of Pholia's Nigerian Dwarf goats—concentrated, flavorful, and fresh tasting—stands out for its wonderful nutty qualities. Oregon's Rogue River Valley *terroir* is so well expressed through these masterfully bred, forest-browsing little animals. Gianaclis and husband Vern operate their farm off the grid and this alone, apart from their fabulous cheeses, is an inspiration. I highly recommend their Elk Mountain, which is featured in our U.S. rock-stars tasting plate (page 289). Its sister cheese, Hillis Peak, is washed in a honey-wheat ale as opposed to simple brine. Their Wimer Winter, a younger washed-rind number with firmish texture, is another thoroughly delicious cheese. It reminds me of a cross between a Lancashire and an Amarelo da Beira Beixa, and it ages out beautifully at 4 months. Pholia Farm is in Rogue River, in the southwestern corner of the state, not far from Grant's Pass and Central Point, the location of Rogue Creamery.

SILVER FALLS CREAMERY—A third-generation dairy farmer, Shawn Hannowell is an expert herdsman and breeder whose award-winning Nubian, Alpine, and Toggenburg goats produce equally acclaimed chèvres. He's slightly breaking the mold of his Dutch heritage by branching out into goats, perhaps bringing a frown to the faces of his cow-dairying ancestors. The family-owned Hanohaven Farm is situated in Monmouth, in the Willamette Valley near Silver Creek Falls, not far from Salem.

SISKIYOU CREST GOAT DAIRY (BOONES FARM)—Owner Mookie Moss and his partner, Stu, bring an energetic, creative approach to sustainable farming. They employ ancient techniques and take advantage of pristine wild habitats, namely the beautiful forests all around Jacksonville, in the foothills of the Siskiyou Mountains, bordering on the southern Rogue River Valley. They built a collection pond for their natural spring and a straw bale cave in an old timber barn to help nourish their herd of foraging goats. They began making cheese in 2007, with fresh pasteurized types as well as aged raw-milk ones, using their own purpose-built aging cave. Mookie is a cheese farmer with clear and admirable intent; watch for great things from him in the future.

THREE RING FARM (RIVERS EDGE CHÈVRE)—Pat Morford, owner/cheesemaker, is a former chef who likes to tinker and create fabulous original cheeses. Instead of using the standard ash in the center of a cheese, for example, she might try a flavor accent such as a little Spanish paprika. Up In Smoke is a stand-out in her fluctuating lineup of twenty or so cheeses, all worth investigating. Three Ring occupies a lovely spot outside of Logsden, west of the Cascade range, near the Pacific Ocean. The crystal-clear stream running out back provides yet another reminder of the crucial importance of water in the cheese-farming equation.

ROGUE CREAMERY—Located in Central Point beside the main road, which runs parallel to the railroad tracks, Rogue has the unassuming look of a small dairy plant, unchanged since it was founded as one of the state's first cheese co-ops in the 1920s. Some

FROM TOP: Oregon Gourmet Cheese's Camembert; Gianaclis Caldwell, Pholia Farm, with an Elk Mountain Tomme.

FROM TOP: Visiting with Shawn Hanowell at Silver Falls Creamery; some of Pat Morford's paprika-rubbed cheeses at Three Ring Farm; Classicos aging at Tumalo Farms.

great milk has gone into this little factory during all those years and some great cheeses have come out. Its new owners, Cary Bryant and David Gremmels, have done a great job perpetuating the legacy started by Tom Vella in the mid-1930s and continued by his family, including son Ig, for the remainder of the twentieth century. Cary and David's Rogue River Blue, a modern American artisanal great, is a direct descendant of Tom Vella's blue cheese creations of the 1950s. See sidebar, page 280.

TILLAMOOK COUNTY CREAMERY ASSOCIATION—This is the original Oregon cheesemaking co-op, founded in 1927, in Tillamook, by the ocean, about 60 miles east of Portland. Tillamook is quite large, yet it represents a group of producers dedicated to the right values—sustainability and a legacy of making delicious, healthy, natural cheeses of quality and consistency, with good aging potential. Its products may qualify as supermarket cheeses, but they are outstanding and some are even made from unpasteurized milk.

TUMALO FARMS—It's somewhat surprising Flavio DeCastilhos's goat cheeses can deliver such depth and complexity of flavors, given that Tumalo's pastures are smack-dab in the middle of the central Oregon high desert (near Bend, east of the Cascade Mountains), without a lot of green vegetation apparent. His cheeses are fully developed and masterfully balanced, exhibiting excellent consistency and mouthfeel—even though they're made from pasteurized milk and waxed. There is some real cheesemaking skill being exercised here. (Flavio's state-of-the-art plant, by the way, is impressive, a model for other artisan manufacturers.) The high quality of the local water certainly comes into play as does Flavio's selection of dry feed and cultures. Classico is their award-winning signature cheese (see page 359). I also recommend the Pondhopper, which is washed in beer, and the Fenacho, flavored with fenugreek—one of my few picks among flavored cheeses.

WILLAMETTE VALLEY CHEESE COMPANY—Rod Volbeda is a second-generation dairy farmer, who was part of the Tillamook County Creamery Association co-op. He and his wife, Melissa, farm the family spread near Salem; their cheeses come from the milk of their Jersey cow herd and reflect both Rod's father's Dutch heritage and his mother's Italian lineage. Their Brindisi, a Fontina-inspired cheese, reminds me of Le Moulis. Their aging cave is an adapted refrigerated truck trailer—artisanal ingenuity at work.

A CHEESEMAKER'S SMORGASBOARD

When we visited Pat Morford at her Three Ring Farm in late November, she put together a lovely smorgasbord of her creations and laid it out for us on her dining room table—*tortes*, rounds, buttons, *crottins*, bloomies, washed rinds. Every little cheese was a dish in itself. Pat paired each one with a different wine, most of them whites. I spied one pretty little bloomy-rind round, encased in fuzzy white *candidum* mold (which I later determined was the one she calls "The Mayor of Nye Beach"). Well aware of how these types can disappoint, I thought, "Well, maybe this one won't make the cut." Pat knows her medium, though, and she had captured a lovely balance of gently fermented goat's milk under that rind; the cheese was very much alive.

I always approach "specially treated" cheeses with some skepticism, but Pat's Up In Smoke is hard not to love. It's a hand-shaped small chèvre-style cheese wrapped in smoked maple leaves that have been spritzed with some bourbon; the cheeses themselves are also lightly smoked prior to being wrapped. I remember tasting a smoked goat ricotta at the Slow Food convivium in Bra, Italy, one year; it caught me off guard—in a good way—and was one of the more interesting cheeses I'd ever tasted. Up In Smoke elicited the same reaction. Any cheese that makes you stop, reconsider your personal prejudices, and contemplate its potential for greatness is worth a detour.

Smoked goat's milk ricottas at the Slow Food Convivium, Bra, Italy.

Washington State

Washington has larger populations of both humans and cows than Oregon, with a bigger dairy industry and more cheesemakers, although perhaps not as many who qualify as farmstead or artisanal.

Probably Washington's most prominent artisan pioneer is Sally Jackson, whose family farm in the high-and-dry north-central part of the state, very close to the Canadian border, has been turning out small amounts of very fine cheeses for the better part of 3 decades. One other notable Washington State pioneer is the Quillisascut Cheese Company, Rick and Lora Lea Misterly's outfit in Rice, which is in the northeastern corner of the state. Quillisascut has been operating since the early 1980s; the Misterlys turn out exclusively raw goat's milk cheeses and they also have a farm school.

The Skagit Valley region, near Bellingham (north of Seattle), is a beautiful pocket of traditional bovine dairy country. Prominent among a handful of small cheese farm operations there is veteran George Train's Pleasant Valley Dairy in Ferndale; his daughter, Joyce Snook, is cheesemaker. There is also a group of island-based cheese artisans cropping up around Washington, including Port

Beautiful high-desert terrain at Tumalo Farms in central Oregon.

ROGUE CREAMERY

AN AMAZING TRAJECTORY

When two guys named Cary Bryant and David Gremmels met for a snowboarding lesson at Whistler-Blackcomb Resort in the year 2000, who knew it would come to be regarded as a turning point in modern U.S. cheese history? Their initial plan was to open a wine bar together, but they stumbled on something even better. Through a combination of savvy, good fortune, and hard work, they were able to take over an artisan creamery and rocket to the top of the cheese world.

Cary Bryant, left, and David Gremmels.

Don't let the sweet smile, low-key manner, and measured elocution fool you: David Gremmels is a force to be reckoned with. He speaks convincingly and in grand terms, with a mix of altruism and chutzpah, modesty and pragmatism, confidence and audacity. Neither Cary nor David had any cheese experience prior to buying Rogue Creamery in 2002. Cary is a microbiologist by training

and was a successful entrepreneur, with his line of decorative refrigerator magnets (including the dress-him-up of Michelangelo's *David*). David was vice president of product design for the mail-order fruit purveyor Harry & David. Naturally, David became Rogue's "marketing guy," though he keeps his hands in the business—literally—helping out daily with cheesemaking, which is Cary's job.

Many people, including the director of Oregon's Department of Agriculture, Katy Coba, credit the Gremmels-Bryant team with creating the artisanal cheese movement in the state. While that may be a slight exaggeration—Pierre Kolisch, for example, was an Oregon pioneer back in the 1980s—it's not entirely invalid. By 2004, within a couple of years of taking over the business, not only were they turning out a line of award-winning world-class cheeses, but they had founded both a festival and a guild; David was vice president of the American Cheese Society and Cary was heading the Raw Milk Cheesemakers Association of America.

Some Rogue History

Much of Oregon's cheesemaking history is told in the story of Tom Vella and the Rogue Creamery. It connects a traditional family business, started by a Sicilian immigrant named Tom Vella and continued by his son Ignazio ("Ig"), to the new artisanal movement of the late twentieth and early twenty-first centuries.

Young Tom Vella arrived in California in 1923 and founded his own Vella Cheese Company, in Sonoma

in November, 1931. Tom developed Dry Jack, a harder version of Monterey Jack, based on demand from his Italian compatriots for a gratable cheese. In the late 1930s, Tom's younger brother, Francesco, back in Italy, warned of impending war. Tom realized all the Bay Area milk would be taken up by the war effort so he convinced an industrial cheese magnate by the name of Kraft (you may have heard the name) to help finance his takeover of a failing local co-op dairy up in Central Point (population 400 at the time), in the Rogue River Valley.

During the World War II years, Tom turned out 5 million pounds of mostly Cheddar types from the little Central Point plant. After the war, he was contracted by Borden to produce butter, cottage cheese, and blue cheese. Recalls Ig: "My father told my mother, 'We're going to Roquefort.' She asked him why and he said, 'Because we're going to make blue cheese and the best place to learn is where the hell it started.' That's the way my father did things."

Tom and his wife Zolita, mother of Ig and his three siblings (Carmela, Maria, and Zolita), spent the summer of 1956 in Roquefort-sur-Soulzon. The 28-year-old Ig was left in charge of the family outfit back home. In October 1957, the Vellas began shipping out a new cheese called Oregon Blue, perfected based on what Tom had learned in France. Tom brought back *P. roqueforti* cultures, which, many, many generations later, are still used in some Rogue cheeses. He also built Rogue's cave, where its cheeses still age today.

Over the final two decades of the twentieth century, small dairies and creameries throughout the west gradually disappeared, but the Vella operation survived. Tom and Ig ran it together until the elder Vella's death in 1998 at the age of 100. Ig continued to run both the Vella Cheese Co. and Rogue Creamery, dividing his time between Sonoma and Central Point as his father had done. He wasn't getting any younger, though, and in 2002, he decided to sell Rogue. There were four bona fide offers from buyers who would shut it down and use its brands and formulas elsewhere. Along came a fifth, from Cary Bryant and David Gremmels, who believed they could save the business and keep it independent. The deal was done with a hand-shake on the front porch.

"I wouldn't have sold it to anybody else," says Ig. "It fulfilled what my father wanted to do, which was to stay in the Rogue River Valley and be an economic asset. When he came up here there was nothing. It was *tempo di miseria* (a time of misery), the middle of the Depression. He left a lot of blood here. If they were going to close it down, then the hell with it—*I'd* close it down!"

The Creamery Today

Rogue's credentials include many awards and firsts. It was one of the very first U.S. cheese producers to be featured at Slow Food's semiannual festival, Cheese, in Bra, Italy, in the fall of 2007. Rogue River Blue won the Best Blue in the World award at the 2003 World Cheese Awards in London, an American first.

"Before we shook hands, I said, 'Let me tell you one thing: This business is spelled W-O-R-K.' Every once in a while, they say, 'You warned us.' And I say, 'Yeah— I warned you.'"

IG VELLA

Ig Vella

In early 2008, Rogue became the first American cheese producer to export its raw-milk cheeses to the European Union, culminating a 27-month collaborative effort from an assemblage of enlightened advocates, including one of Oregon's U.S. senators, a U.S. congressman, a local state senator, Oregon's governor, and various federal officials. (Lotta paperwork there!) Both Randolph Hodgson of Neal's Yard Dairy and Cathy Strange of Whole Foods Markets got in on the act; their respective stores in London would be among the first to carry Rogue's pioneering exports. Meanwhile, Hodgson was getting

ready to send his own creation, Stichelton, to the United States. The mere thought of two great raw-milk blues crossing each other's paths high above the Atlantic is enough to send me into cheese ecstasy—or at least lift my spirits if I'm ever feeling glum about the future of real cheese.

Rogue was also among the first U.S. cheese producers to obtain multiple third-party certifications. Its cheeses are certified organic by Oregon Tilth; sustainable by Food Alliance, another Oregon-based group; and for safety and quality by the Steritech Group, a "brand protection company."

Busy small producers may be put off by all the time and trouble of obtaining certifications. Gremmels sees it as a valuable extension of one's marketing efforts, reinforcing via specific standards and independent judgments that a company is truly representing its claims. The fees are comparable to booth and association fees at a farmer's market, another typical marketing outlay for artisan dairies and creameries.

Rogue's Cheeses

Whenever a cheesemaker is able to use a single milk source to turn out such a stellar lineup of distinctive cheeses, you have to credit his or her skill. Of course, it all starts with *terroir* and milk quality, and Cary Bryant has both of those in spades at Rogue. Cary's choices of cultures and his clever recipe manipulations are equally important. The milk all comes from the Rogue View Dairy in Grants Pass, Oregon, where the herd is a naturally raised mix of Brown Swiss and Holstein cows.

(CONTINUED)

They graze on native grasses, clover, orchard grass, rye grass, and wild hops as well as Himalayan blackberries growing along the river and fence lines.

Let's take a look at how all these unique assets and carefully selected raw materials play out in the flavor profiles of Rogue's cheeses. Beyond all the main traits you look for in a blue, they feature a broad spectrum of extra, underlying notes. They have a component of *umami,* a nuttiness hinting of Brazil nuts, some berry flavor, hints of citrus, and, particularly in the fall, an earthy trufflelike note. Some of them have pearlike fruity notes. Rogue cheeses also have a signature buttery consistency and mouth feel, with occasional hints of crystalline texture. Here's a rundown:

CRATER LAKE BLUE—With a nod to a famous nearby geographical landmark, this cheese delivers a range of fairly daring flavors, even including metallic hints.

ECHO MOUNTAIN BLUE—Only about 300 wheels of this 80–20 blend of cow's and goat's milk cheese are made. It has an earthy profile with some grassy and citrus notes; its mouthfeel is buttery, with some granularity. The goat's milk portion comes from the Peaceful Mountain dairy farm in Applegate Valley.

OREGON BLUE—A contemporary version of Tom Vella's original, this is creamy, has hints of fruit, approachable blue flavor, and a nice long finish.

OREGONZOLA—Rogue's most approachable blue, this one is balanced, sweet, savory, with a dose of *umami* and a very buttery finish. Ig Vella believes every generation of Rogue Creamery cheesemakers should have his or her own commemorative blue; he created this cheese in honor of his father Tom. It is made from a Gorgonzola mold strain, obtained from Italy via air mail.

ROGUE RIVER BLUE—This has become Rogue's most celebrated cheese and is among America's greatest artisanal champions. It's made with the same Roquefort mold strain as Oregon Blue, but wrapped in pear brandy–soaked Syrah grapevine leaves, thanks to a suggestion from Judy Schad of Capriole, Inc. The planning cycle for this cheese begins a year before its release when the pear eau-de-vie is purchased from Clear Creek Distillery. Carpenter Hill Vineyard, in the Rogue Valley nearby, provides the leaves. About 60,000 of them are selected and washed by hand, then soaked in the eau-de-vie. The cheeses are wrapped about halfway through their aging process, after the *B. linens* have already taken up residence and given the natural rind a golden orange hue. This is a labor-intensive cheese: it's quarter-turned daily and frequently tasted. It is closely monitored from day 120 on and sold only when ripe and ready, usually beginning around 9 months of age. Sacrificial cheeses are reserved for core sampling and rewrapped to keep pace with the rest of a batch. In some years, it takes as long as 13 months for the Rogue Rivers to reach maturity and in others much less; in any case, the cheeses are released only when they're good and ready.

SMOKEY OREGON BLUE—This is a variation of the Oregon Blue subjected to 16 hours of smoking over smoldering hazelnut shells, followed by an additional 30 days of aging, which allows the smoke accent to meld completely with the cheese's other flavors.

CHEDDARS—Rogue makes three Cheddars—medium, sharp, and extra sharp—in pasteurized and raw-milk versions.

Madison Farm on Bainbridge Island, across Puget Sound from Seattle; Sea Breeze Farm on Vashon Island, also near Seattle; and Quail Croft Goat Cheese in Friday Harbor, San Juan Island, farther north, near Bellingham.

Max's Picks: Washington State's Artisans

BEECHER'S HANDMADE CHEESE—Located in Seattle's world-famous Pike Place Market, Beecher's is a force in U.S. cheese. Kurt Dammaier, a Washington State University grad (like many Northwest artisans), launched this cheesemaking operation in 2002. Kurt designed Beecher's Flagship cheese in the style of his school's Cougar Gold. The clothbound Flagship Reserve is a unique American original: a Cheddar type that, when aged out, achieves some of the caramelly depth of a farmhouse Gouda as well as the dryish texture and tangy notes of a British farmhouse Cheddar. Beecher's, which is also a cheesemonger, makes other cheeses, including No Woman, a jack cheese with Jamaican jerk spices, which I find interesting. Brad Sinko is their cheesemaker.

Kelli Estrella, left, and Mother Noella Marcellino trading cheese lore at the Seattle Cheese Festival.

ESTRELLA FAMILY CREAMERY—Northwest cheese expert Tami Parr calls Kelli Estrella's lineup of raw cow's milk (with some goat's milk) cheeses "truly world class," adding that if she could mention only one cheesemaker in the Northwest, it would probably be Kelli. The Estrellas have six children, adopted from all over the world, and everyone pitches in on their family cheese farm in Montesano, west of Olympia, at the base of the Olympic Peninsula.

SALLY JACKSON CHEESES—The Jacksons' family farm is in Oroville, way up north, and Sally makes great cheeses by very traditional methods. When I first tasted them in the mid-1990s, they left a big impression. They were refreshing, and really tasted of the milk and the land. Here were cheeses from a small family farm in an isolated part of our country that could compete on the world stage; Sally was the first true American cheese artisan about whom I could say this. Because she doesn't do any advertising, doesn't make massive quantities of cheese, and sells mostly in the Northwest, Sally has acquired a reputation as somewhat of a recluse—a bit of a misperception, since she's traveled as far as Bangladesh to share her cheesemaking savvy. Sally has helped define what real cheesemaking in America is all about for many years. She works wonders with raw milk, and recently she's highlighted leaf-wrapped types, aged 2 to 3 months.

The Rest of the Northwest

ALASKA—The climate is so harsh it's quite amazing they can sustain any kind of dairying, but there are a few hardy artisans in our

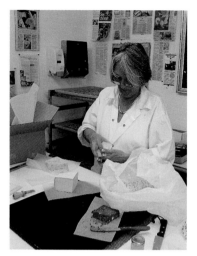

Judy Schad wrapping cheeses at Capriole.

forty-ninth state, including Matt and Rhonda Shaul. Their Cranberry Ridge Farm is a goat-cheese operation in Wasilla. Gary and Carla Beu have also found success in Alaska's extremes with their Windsong Farm in Palmer, a cow's milk cheese dairy.

IDAHO—This is traditionally a highly industrialized cheese state, with very large dairies, actually the third-biggest dairy-producing state after California and Wisconsin. Consequently, it is somewhat behind the curve in terms of the artisanal revolution. Since the early 1990s, Charles and Karen Evans of Rollingstone, in Parma, in the Snake River Valley, have been making regular, aged, and also flavored chèvres that have won several awards, including one at the ACS convention.

UTAH—Utah State University, in Logan, has a creamery and cheesemaking classes. It is not quite as influential in the artisanal community yet as Washington State, but it's up-and-coming. Like Idaho, Utah is a highly industrial cheese-producing zone with perhaps much unfulfilled farmstead potential and a long way to go before it catches up with Oregon and Washington. Two Utah producers worth checking out: Rockhill Creamery, a small cow dairy in Richmond, in the extreme northern part of the state, and Beehive Cheese Company, an artisanal dairy located in Uintah, just south of Ogden, which makes Barely Buzzed, a somewhat Cheddar-like cheese rubbed in espresso coffee and lavender (see page 213).

Max's Picks: The Best of the Rest

Because there are pockets of rich farmland and dairying culture all over our land and because people everywhere are jumping on board the Slow Food wagon, you'll find the vast American heartland is home to more real-cheese artisans than you might imagine. Without the infrastructure and support available in places like Vermont and Oregon, it can be difficult; yet there are quite a few inspiring pioneers who've stuck it out and quite a few newcomers making a go of it.

BITTERSWEET PLANTATION DAIRY—Chef John Folse's success with his Lafite's Landing Restaurant led him to become an international culinary ambassador of Cajun cuisine. This dairy, in Gonzalez, Lousiana, southeast of Baton Rouge, is part of his multi-pronged operation, which includes a cooking school. They make Fleur-de-Lis, a triple-crème-style cheese, which, when I first tasted it, I mis-

MORE THAN JUST A BLOG

TAMI PARR'S PACIFIC NORTHWEST CHEESE PROJECT

Tami Parr is one of our new American cheese heroes. She grew up milking cows and doing chores during summers at her uncle's dairy farm in southern Wisconsin. Originally a writer with literary aspirations and holding a Ph.D. in English, she went to law school and got a day job as an attorney. In July 2004, her love for cheese led her to start a blog called "The Pacific Northwest Cheese Project" (PNCP), which became her full-time occupation when she quit the law firm in early 2007. Tami's forum for personal cheese musings soon morphed into one of the best sources on what's happening in the world of real cheese in America.

Some people, including Tami, may still call the PNCP a blog, but I think that does it a disservice. The PNCP is well-written, informative, and comprehensive, covering all the important trends and issues. Tami offers breaking news and developing stories: In December 2007, for example, there was a big flood in Washington State that damaged a lot of dairy farms. Black Sheep Creamery, a prominent artisanal cheese operation, was one of the hardest hit. Tami got the word out through her PNCP, galvanizing recovery assistance.

Even such valuable sites as PNCP don't always pull in a lot of money, especially considering the service they do for our industries. One way you can support Tami's efforts is to click the Google ads on her site because she gets paid per click.

took for a Pierre-Robert. It was a dead ringer, a fine American version of a French classic. They also make Feliciana Nevat, a mixed-milk (cow and goat) version of a famous Catalan cheese.

CAPRIOLE—Judy Schad is an American pioneer with a great vibe and strong energy; she established Capriole in the 1980s and was the first U.S. artisan who won me over with her utter joy at cheese-making. Capriole occupies a bucolic site in southeastern Indiana, amid beautiful rolling hills. You can tell there's a lot of love that goes into their impressive lineup of cheeses. Wabash Cannonball, a wonderful little fresh *crottin*-style ball, which I think of as Judy's original signature cheese, started out very good and has been getting steadily better for years. Her O'Banon is better than the European original, Banon. Milky, clean, raw, refreshing, Judy's Old Kentucky Tomme is a cheese that makes me happy. Her pasteurized Piper's Pyramide is a versatile partner for wines and beers, and her Mont St. Francis is a fine American representative of a challenging type—semisoft washed-rind raw goat's milk. I think it was Judy herself who said it was more than a match for any Munster. She's right. The Mont St. Francis is best at between 60 and 75 days, having developed some good meaty, funky flavors.

Tami Parr, PNCP founder

Paula Lambert of The Mozzarella Co., Dallas

EVERONA DAIRY—Pat Elliott is one of my favorite cheesemakers, very dedicated, focused, and consistent. From her farm in the Piedmont region of central Virginia, she turns out raw, pressed sheep's milk cheeses. They are smaller-format versions of the Ossau-Iraty or Pyrénées types, requiring a month or two less aging to reach ideal maturity. Piedmont, her signature cheese and a fine expression of *terroir*, is nutty and a little sweet, with a nice break and very good mouth feel. (What a stroke of luck it was for the real-cheese world that Pat needed a herd of sheep to keep her Border Collie occupied.)

FROMAGERIE BELLE CHÈVRE—Northern Alabama (Elkmont to be exact) is another place you wouldn't normally associate with fine artisanal goat cheeses, for the heat and humidity alone. How does anyone survive summers down there? Liz and Tom Parnell founded their farm in 1989 and made very fine cheeses until 2008, when they turned the business over to Tasia Malakasis, Culinary Institute of America grad with a passion for cheesemaking. Their chèvres are pasteurized but darn good.

LAKE ERIE CREAMERY—Yet another highly encouraging sign: Real cheese from the shores of Lake Erie, right in good, old Cleveland, Ohio. Lake Erie's Blomma was the favorite of an eight-judge dairy panel at the 2008 Gallo Family Vineyards awards in competition with such acclaimed cheeses as Jasper Hill's Winnimere. *Blomma*, which means "flower" in Swedish, is a bloomy-rind pasteurized goat's milk type—tasty, refreshing, and creamy, a little tart and with a rind just thick enough to keep it together without sending it over the top.

LOVETREE FARM—You don't necessarily think of the Midwest in general and of Wisconsin in particular as a hotbed of artisanal cheese production. Mary and David Falk's family farm is an outpost amid rolling hills and lakes by the shores of Trade Lake in the western part of the state only about 60 miles north-northeast of the twin cities of Minneapolis and St. Paul, Minnesota. Mary is a dedicated, skilled raw-milk artisan. Her signature Trade Lake Cedar is a little different every time I taste it, but it's consistently a top American Pyrénées-style sheep cheese.

MEADOW CREEK DAIRY—From a lovely spot 2,800 feet up in the mountains of southwest Virginia, dairy farmers Helen and Rick Feete began making their mark in 1980 and have become prominent and respected American cheese artisans. Their Grayson is a distinguished washed-rind raw cow's milk cheese, well made and delicious, with the right amount of rind and just enough washings for an appropriate amount of *B. linens* growth. It's a well-balanced cheese, the salt is in check, and its texture qualifies as "squidgy" in the best sense of the term. They also make Mountaineer, a slightly harder, Alpine-style cheese.

THE MOZZARELLA COMPANY—Paula Lambert is real dynamo and a significant player in the U.S. artisan movement. She's an author, promoter, prominent ACS member and officer, and creator of many cheeses, including the famous Hoja Santa—her flagship cheese. At the cheese center, we take delivery of about 400 Hoja Santas a month. It's a perfectly nice cheese when fresh. (The leaves of the Hoja Santa plant, aka *yierba santa* or Mexican pepperleaf, have not yet contributed their intriguing hint of sassafras-like flavor and the fresh, pure milk hasn't delivered on its potential yet.) Give it some time in our goat-cheese aging cave, and you've got a cheese to be reckoned with, able to stand up to such a leaf-wrapped, aged French goat delicacy as genuine Cabècou Feuille. Paula also makes a very nice pungent raw-milk, washed-rind cow cheese called Blanca Bianca.

The Feete family of Meadow Creek Dairy, makers of Grayson: From left, Jim, Kat, Helen, and Rick.

SWEET HOME FARM—Another pioneering Alabama artisan, Sweet Home's Alyce Birchenough is sought after for advice and counsel and has inspired many American cheesemakers. She has the experience, having practiced sustainable, all-natural dairy farming since the mid-1980s, and the touch, as demonstrated with her full line of cow's milk cheeses. I like the Perdido, a Morbier-style cheese made from the milk of her Guernsey cow herd and dusted with herb ash. Sweet Home Farm is located in Elberta, Alabama, near the Gulf Coast and close to the Florida Panhandle.

UPLANDS CHEESE COMPANY—This Wisconsin farmstead operation began in 1994, in Dodgeville. Mike and Carol Gingrich focus on only one cheese and stick to artisanal methods. They very consciously chose to base their seasonally made Pleasant Ridge Reserve on genuine French Gruyère. Pleasant Ridge Reserve is aged 8 to 12 months, with a limited extra-aged edition going up to 18 months. When it's young it can be reminiscent of Piave. After about a year, it undergoes an interesting transformation and begins to show a deeper, more complex profile, recalling a Swiss

Alpine cheese such as Appenzeller or perhaps Hoch Ybrig. It is also comparable to another distinguished American, the Tarentaise from Vermont. Both are full flavored and clearly come from the fresh, select milk of pasture-fed cows. The Pleasant Ridge is nutty, a bit sweeter and milder, with more balance and a long, smooth finish.

OPPOSITE: U.S. rock stars: Clockwise from top, Constant Bliss; Dorset; Tarentaise; Rogue River Blue; Adelle; and Elk Mountain Tomme.

TASTING PLATE

Twenty-First-Century U.S. Rock Stars

ADELLE
(Ancient Heritage Dairy, Scio, OR)

CONSTANT BLISS
(Jasper Hill Farm, Greensboro, VT)

ELK MOUNTAIN TOMME
(Pholia Farm, Rogue River, OR)

DORSET
(Consider Bardwell Farm, West Pawlett, VT)

TARENTAISE
(Thistle Hill Farm, North Pomfret, VT)

ROGUE RIVER BLUE
(Rogue Creamery, Central Point, OR)

This seven-cheese lineup reflects the best of the new American artisanal explosion and features the two "bookend" regions where things are really happening: Vermont and Oregon. Incidentally, while the U.S. government has been decidedly lacking in sympathy toward raw-milk cheesemaking, these two states' agriculture departments and dairy bureaucrats have been quite supportive.

Our rock-stars tasting starts with a mild sheep's milk cheese, progresses to some interesting cow's milk variations, and ends with an outstanding blue. Every one of these cheeses has been created since the year 2000, and each and every one of them is a "wow."

Our opening act is a mellow, fresh chèvre style—think Crottin de Chavignol—but in the sheep's milk medium, produced by Kathy and Paul Obringer at their Ancient Heritage farmstead and dairy. The Adelle has a smooth, creamy mouth feel with gentle milk flavor; as compared to a standard goat's milk opener, it's not as tart or claylike and is more rich and buttery.

The next cheese is Constant Bliss from the Kehler Brothers, who probably epitomize the rock-star moniker more than any other twenty-first century U.S. cheese farmers. Constant Bliss is one of only two American raw-milk bloomy-rind cow cheeses I know of—not an easy act to pull off gracefully. I've tasted the milk of Jasper Hill's Ayrshire herd and I've tasted this cheese; the latter is about as close to capturing the essence of the former as you can get. For a relatively young cheese, Constant Bliss has a complex profile with big, bold flavors and a memorable impact on the palate. All of this said, it is also supple, subtle, restrained, and sophisticated enough to take the second spot in a tasting. I detect a slight hint of smokiness, which I attribute to the milk as it reflects this Vermont farmstead's typically pristine and all-natural pastures.

Pholia Farm's Elk Mountain ushers the progression into the raw goat's milk realm in an aged format, with strong West Coast credentials. I first tasted it as a judge at the 2005 American Dairy Goat Association contest when it was still in the amateur category. Elk Mountain's mouthwatering consistency is similar to a European *tomme* but chalkier and somewhat crumbly; for this reason, I'd also compare it to Spain's Ibores. Elk Mountain's flavors are fairly assertive and forward, with a sweetness and a round nuttiness to its profile, which could easily cause it to be mistaken for a sheep's milk cheese. It lingers to a brilliant, clean, not at all gamey finish—none of which is easy to achieve in the goat's milk medium and all of which places it firmly in the third spot in this sequence.

Next, it's back to Vermont for Consider Bardwell's washed-rind Dorset, which I'd venture to say is quickly becoming America's answer to Ireland's Durrus and/or France's Tomme de Savoie. The region around Lake Champlain in western Vermont has plenty of early American dairy farms—or the remnants thereof—and Angela Miller has revived this one's cheesemaking traditions masterfully. Old soil, rich vegetation, and avoidance of herbicides and pesticides are the norm in these parts. Dorset is a bit softer—or rather, more moist and buttery, with that recognizable Jersey milk heft and tang— than the Elk Mountain and thus a logical next step.

Tarentaise has quite a few similarities to Dorset, including raw Vermont pasture-fed cow's milk, but a few key differences. Tarentaise is more of a mountain style, reflecting its higher-elevation *terroir*. It is cooked and pressed, giving it a firmer texture with more undertones of sweetness. Although it was inspired by Beaufort and Abondance, Tarentaise's granularity and complex flavor profile also give a nod to British farmhouse Cheddars such as

Cheeses ripening at Tumalo Farms.

Montgomery's and Keen's. I recommend you get a year-old Tarentaise, which, for me, offers a more captivating and complete flavor profile than its younger incarnations.

We end with another blue that has quickly become an international envoy not only for Oregon but for the entire American artisan movement. When I first tasted Rogue River Blue, in 2006, it was one of my most memorable cheese encounters to date. How, I wondered, did such a fabulous cheese come seemingly *out of nowhere*? It packs an Oregon *terroir* triple whammy: raw milk from the Rogue View Dairy where the cows graze close by the river itself; local Syrah grapevine leaves to wrap the cheeses; and local pear brandy to soak those wrappers. Rogue River Blue looks a lot like its European antecedent, Valdeón, but it's a much more interesting cheese with fruity undertones, a fine balance of salt and bite, and crumbly yet with moist consistency. All the qualities you look for in an outstanding blue cheese are present here in abundance. It would be hard to argue against it as the closing act for a tasting of modern American superstars.

CHAPTER 15

"THERE IS NO SWISS CHEESE": SWITZERLAND'S BEST

FROM A FINE-CHEESE PERSPECTIVE, SWITZERLAND IS A TRUE GIANT. FOR a fairly small country with relatively few cheeses—compared to, say, France's 300 (or 700, depending on whose count you endorse)—Switzerland hits the mark more than any other. Its artisanal cheeses represent unsurpassed expressions of *terroir*, the apotheosis of the real-cheese aesthetic.

Along with the excitement brewing since the turn of the twenty-first century in U.S. artisanal production, my favorite trend in fine cheese is the emergence on the world stage of a strong roster of traditional and modern Swiss classics. Perhaps genuine Swiss modesty or lack of a powerful international marketing arm delayed their debut in our consciousness. But since the year 2000, we can say they have definitely arrived, thanks in large part to the efforts of Caroline Hostettler and Rolf Beeler, both of whom are profiled in this chapter.

In an interview for our second book, it was Caroline who made the memorable statement, "There is no Swiss cheese, but there are Swiss cheeses." What in the world did she mean by that? The basic message is that the American concept of Swiss cheese—shrink-wrapped, vacuum-packed, plasticized, rubbery pasteurized sandwich slices with cookie-cutter holes—is so far from the reality of her country's genuine artisanal cheeses as to be completely irrelevant. Switzerland turns out arguably the greatest of the pure traditional farmhouse and mountain-made cheeses. The best of them are sublime, unique and often irresistibly funky.

Genuine Swiss cave-aged Gruyère from Rolf Beeler Selections: It doesn't get any better than this.

THE SWISS ALPS

When I think of Swiss *terroir*, I envision pristine high-altitude pastures with a backdrop of breathtaking mountain views. I hear few sounds breaking the profound silence of unpopulated nature: Perhaps the faint clanking of cow bells, the rustle of grasses in the breeze, and the occasional gentle snort from a big, slow-moving quadriped, happily munching her lush grasses and lovely pastel-colored wildflowers. I see little huts with smoky wood fires under old copper cauldrons where wool-clad herdsmen stoop to stir curds brimming with rich butterfats and grassy proteins. I imagine large, heavy wheels of old-fashioned raw-milk cheese—weighing upward of 175 pounds—aging on sodden wooden planks in the dank cellar of an ancient stone fortress. How often can you eat something so good it paints such pretty pictures in your mind?

GEOGRAPHY AND *TERROIR*

Switzerland spans about 180 miles from west to east at its widest and roughly 100 miles from north to south at its tallest, covering a little less than the combined square mileage of Connecticut and Massachusetts. It has several climates and numerous microclimates, delineated by hills, mountains, and valleys. As Caroline Hostettler explains it, "You're either on the mountain or off the mountain; there are not really any flat places."

What makes Swiss cheeses superior? To begin with, the country has many untouched areas where for more than 2,000 years small-scale dairying was the only industry able to survive the long, cold winters and the isolation. Like Italy, Switzerland was not unified until the mid-nineteenth century. Its government is a federation, and the country is divided into twenty-six cantons, which arose from the independent city-states of the Middle Ages. Each canton maintains pride in its local customs, traditions, and artisanal products, including (of course) cheese. You'll recognize some significant cheese names among the place-names of the Swiss cantons, including Appenzell, Friboug, Neuchâtel, and Jura.

Another significant Swiss geographical designation is the alp, which is really any place on a mountain where people and animals settle during the summer. Each alp represents a unique locale, with its own microclimate and *terroir*. An alp is a very small singular settlement, like a village but sometimes even smaller, perhaps just one or two buildings or a small shack or other shelter. One mountain can contain a number of different alps. Alps developed hand in hand with *transhumance*, which is another important phenomenon contributing to the greatness of Swiss cheeses—or for that matter any mountain cheese. This is the traditional seasonal migration of grazing animals and their herdsmen from their valley homes in the spring to the high mountain pastures in mid- to late summer and back down to the valleys in the fall and winter. (As we've learned in previous chapters, summer pasture-fed animals produce milk with depth and complexity of flavors, which can translate into superb cheeses.)

The Alps cut a big, rocky swathe across southern Switzerland, covering almost half the country. The Jura Mountains, not quite as imposing as the Alps but equally significant for Swiss cheeses, provide a border with France and define Switzerland's western

QUALITY CHEESE

THE NAME SAYS IT ALL

Caroline Hostettler has been my main source for the finest Swiss cheeses since she began importing them to the United States in the late 1990s. Caroline is proof you can take the girl out of the country, but you can't take the country out of the girl. She grew up in Biel (aka Bienne), a small town about 20 miles west of Bern, on the border of the German and French-speaking parts of Switzerland. The home turf of several great Swiss cheeses, including Emmentaler, Gruyère, and Vacherin Fribourgeois, was close by. Her father shopped at all the best farmer's markets and dairy shops, bringing home 5-pound portions of the good stuff. "Just like some people always put bread on the table when they sit down to dinner, we always had a hunk of cheese," she recalls. "Every day at every meal."

Caroline is *the* ambassador for fine Swiss cheeses in America; she's the one who brought us the elite cheeses selected and ripened by Rolf Beeler and others, who wore out her shoes and racked up serious frequent-flier miles convincing wholesale buyers they were worth their premiums. Curiously, in the 1990s, Caroline landed in Fort Myers, Florida, a place from which you might not expect anyone to launch one of the more significant campaigns in the Great American Cheese Rennaisance. Together with her husband, Daniel, who manages the numbers end of the business and helps mind the store, Caroline has raised the bar for Swiss—and thereby all—fine cheeses, first with their import and wholesale firm and later with their retail operation, 55 Degrees: Cool Cheese and Wine.

In 1998, Caroline started their import business and called it, in typical no-nonsense fashion, Quality Cheese. Her initial investment was in two coolers (one small hand carrier and the other larger, on wheels), 100 pounds each of three sample cheeses, and a 2-week sales trip to five American cities she deemed gourmet hotbeds. Almost all her potential customers were restaurants. She called on Daniel Boulud in New York, Charlie Trotter in Chicago, Thomas Keller in Napa Valley—and yours truly at Picholine. Caroline's first order of business was to convince hardened food professionals—albeit sophisticated palates—the likes of those top chefs that her cheeses were superior: "They would say, 'I can get a Gruyère for a third of your price.' I'd say, 'Taste this one.' If you're a sommelier, you don't just buy red wine; you need to say what kind, what quality you want. It's the same thing, for example, with chocolate. A pastry chef or a chocolatier who makes truffles here in the U.S. doesn't just buy *any* chocolate as his basis. The toughest part was to convince these people that cheese is not just cheese, and that the phrase 'cave aged' in the cheese business is the most overused and abused term. It was a very slow process."

It took Quality Cheese nearly 5 years to achieve profitability; the real run-up happened after the turn of the millennium. In 2002, the Hostettlers set up a warehouse in Fort Myers and by 2004 they had a full-scale nationwide wholesaling operation. Thanks to a deal with the big specialty wholesaler-distributor Crystal Food Imports, Quality Cheese's Swiss selections, featuring Rolf Beeler's lineup, are now available in every state and Puerto Rico.

region, which angles from Basel in the north down to Geneva in the southwest. Both the Jura region and Emmental, which is just to the east of Bern in the center of the country, are hilly—though not necessarily mountainous—and offer lush, diversified summer pastures comparable to the higher Alpine ones.

THE GREAT SWISS CHEESES

Use common sense and take a look at the map; try to locate the region, the canton (like a province), the locality, even the alp, where the cheese was made.

Swiss cheeses very often have place-names, and in fact two virtually identical cheeses from nearby villages or adjacent regions can be called something completely different. A Hoch Ybrig from western French-speaking Switzerland, for example, goes by the name of Jura Montagne. By the same token, a cheese type may have its provenance added to the name, so, for example, a Chua Fladä (yes, that translates as "cow patty") from the Stans area becomes Stanser Chua Fladä; a Röteli ("little red thing") from the same area is called Stanser Röteli. Swiss cheeses also often have "alp," "alpage," or other mountain designations added to their names to indicate they are the traditional artisanal versions of given types.

The ancient Swiss cheeses are large, hard, cooked Gruyère- or mountain-style types. In a rugged landscape with ample dairying and scattered infrastructure, these types were the most practical way to preserve, transport, and market excess milk.

Until recently, there were no blue cheeses made in Switzerland. The vast majority of Swiss cheeses are in the aforementioned hard, aged cow's milk category. Adhering to the traditional approach and emphasizing exacting craftsmanship, a few Swiss artisans have turned out some notable new—and at times surprising—cheeses, quite a few with sheep's and goat's milk.

The Swiss do not promote their cheese exports the way, for example, the Spanish, the Italians, or the French do. There seems to be an ingrained modesty or reluctance as part of the national character. The government-supported Swiss cheese marketing association was disbanded and anyway it was based on subsidies, so sagging numbers could be made to look artificially sound. What's left of the Swiss promotional effort, an office of Swiss Cheese Marketing (U.S.A.), Inc., in Valley Cottage, New York, does not promote artisanal cheeses; it's owned by a few large producers, including the conglomerate Emmi, and focuses on mass-market cheeses.

Very few Swiss artisanal food products are name protected; some of its best cheeses are—as of this writing, there are ten, with four others pending—but many are not.

Max's Picks: Switzerland's Artisans

JOSEF BARMETTLER—A distinguished dairy farmer and producer of Stanser Schafkäse, Schaf Reblochon (aka Innerschweizer Schafkäse), Stanser Chua Fladä, and Stanser Röteli (formerly known as Innerschweizer Weicher), among other top cheeses. (Barmettler is in the town of Stans, Canton Schywz—hence the appellation "Stanser" for several of his cheeses.) These soft-ripened types aren't easy to make consistently; Barmettler pulls it off with great artistry. The Röteli is a real winner.

ROLF BEELER—Switzerland's number-one selector and *affineur*. Consider his label a virtual guarantee. (See sidebar, page 298.)

SEPP BRÜLISWILER—A master cheesemaker based near Baden, in Canton Aargau, Brüliswiler makes the Aarauer Bierdeckel and the Kuntener Reblochon, which Rolf Beeler holds in high regard. Brüliswiler's more recent creation is the mini-Urchruter, a soft, aromatic 1-pound cheese washed in a solution including a mix of Alpine herbs.

MARIO COTTI—Cotti is a farmer who makes Flixer in Alp Flixer, Graubünden, eastern Switzerland. He only makes this little round cheese when he is "on the alp" during summer and sells his entire output to one local dairy, from which the Hostettlers obtain it.

RUEDI FÖHN—A very traditional cheesemaker whose cheese is Alp Dräckloch (see page 299) and whose last name is also the name of a strong, feared wind in specific regions of the Alps.

UELI MOSER—Moser's cheeses are among the softer, bloomy-rind types not part of Beeler's selection. He makes Riesling x Sylvaner, Buure Weichchäsli, Huus Chäs, Bio Nusskäse, a cheese called just Chardonnay, and others, including Crublanc, a raw-milk Camembert-style cheese. Moser's cheeses fill in for some of the French types that have been compromised and/or aren't readily available here in the United States. In fact, after his apprenticeship in Switzerland, Moser spent time working in France, learning its techniques. His creamery is in Canton Berne, near Biel (Bienne).

Willy Schmid, maker of Bergfichte and other distinguished cheeses.

WILLY SCHMID—Formerly of the Diriwachter and Schmid partnership, which made such stunning cheeses as Wildmannli and Krümmenswiler Försterkase, Schmid now makes a Krümmenswiler-type cheese under a different name, Bergfichte; the Wildmannli has been discontinued. Schmid, whose cheesemaking operation is located in Canton Thurgau near Toggenburg, is also making a goat's milk version of the Krümmenswiler called Holzige Geiss ("wooden goat"). It is not unlike a Vacherin Fribourgeois (except from goat's milk); it also reminds me of the "holy grail" cheese from the French Pyrénées, Le Cabri Ariègeois, which has become rare if not extinct. Schmid also makes Jersey Blue, Toma, Cesto, Mülistei, and Blaue Geiss (see page 300).

Max's Picks: Selected Swiss Favorites

Hoch Ybrig and Appenzeller were two of my early favorites from among the Swiss for best cheese in the universe. Talk about the essence of gorgeous high-mountain pastures and pure, unadulterated milk . . . But cheeses tend to suffer and, ironically, are often diminished by their popularity. Bit by bit, as market pressures

ROLF BEELER

THE POPE OF SWISS CHEESES

Rolf Beeler's name has become synonymous with the finest Swiss artisanal cheeses. His charisma, charm, and enthusiasm are backed by all the hard work he's done to improve the cheeses and bring them to market locally then internationally. Like all great real-cheese businesses, he's built his from the ground up—or should we say the underground up?.

True to his wares, Rolf is a rustic character with a down-to-earth personality. A former schoolteacher, he is patient, naturally an important quality for an *affineur;* but when the subject of real cheese arises, his passion flares, his opinions emerge fast and furious.

The business is run out of the Beelers' one-family house in Nesselnbach, a village in Canton Aargau, about 20 miles outside of Zurich. Its basement is a natural cave, with rough-hewn stone walls and cool, moist conditions but not a great deal of space. For this reason, he leaves a large percentage of his cheese selections at the dairies where they're made and has a

regular weekly route of scheduled cheese visits. The Beeler selection is limited to around twenty cheeses.

Rolf works so closely with his cheesemakers as to have almost become one himself: At any given moment, he's up-to-date not just on the aging status of every batch but also the condition of his producers' pastures, the health of animals, what cultures and rennets they're using, and which recipe tweaks they may need to consider. Producers of high-quality milk come to him for cheesemaking advice. Cheesemakers aspire to qualify for his roster.

We asked Rolf to explain what makes a great cheese; he listed what he feels are the most important factors and ingredients, which included one surprise: He believes Jersey cow milk, with its higher fat content, makes better cheeses—even of the harder, aged types he prefers.

ROLF BEELER'S KEYS TO GREAT CHEESE

Raw Milk: *"With raw milk, you have the full aromas of the grasses the cows have eaten. Pasteurized milk gives a bitter taste to the finish of a cheese."*

Pastures: *"You have to have a good grazing area, with different types of grasses. In Switzerland, we have the Alps where you have a lot of grasses and wild herbs you don't find down in the valleys and the towns."*

Rolf Beeler brushing a wheel of Gruyère.

Proper Aging: *"The other really important thing for the taste is the affinage—whether you mature a Gruyère, for example, for only 6 or 7 months or for 18 months, like I do. Also, how you do the maturing? If you apply brine for too long, for example, it can be a problem."*

Some years ago, a journalist writing for Blich, the Swiss tabloid whose title means "the glimpse," dubbed Rolf Beeler "the Pope of Swiss Cheeses." If you want to catch your own glimpse of the Pope, or perhaps buy some of his selections directly, you can find him selling from his cart at the outdoor market in Wettingen, near his home base in Aargau on Fridays and the one in Lucerne on Saturdays.

mount, they start to shed their unique charms. Both of the aforementioned favorites are now made in cooperative dairies from multiple milk sources. Both have been knocked off their pedestals by Toggenburger. Perhaps by the time this book reaches your hands,

Toggenburger will have been taken down a notch by a resurgence of these cheeses—or by the advent of a new Swiss champion. They're all great; some of them are just a little greater than the others.

AARAUER BIERDECKEL—Made by Sepp Brüliswiler, this cheese is washed in wheat beer and turns pinkish red from a healthy growth of *Brevibacterium linens*. The Aauraer looks a lot like a Red Hawk (from California's Cowgirl Creamery) but is much more intense. A little bit of the Aaurauer hits you right in the middle of the tongue and offers a really big flavor. Its aroma is pungent and meaty, with plenty of *umami*, like a big slab of top-quality buffalo tenderloin.

ALP DRÄCKLOCH—Both Caroline Hostettler and Rolf Beeler insist if there's one place in Switzerland you should see it's this alp in Muothatal in Canton Schwyz as it's one of the most beautiful spots in the land. Alp Dräckloch producer Ruedi Föhn is a fifth-generation cheese man who works in a one-room hut with a copper cauldron over a wood fire. The cheese is cooked, pressed, all-natural, and as old style as you can get. An Alp Dräckloch's consistency is hard, its texture quite dense, but it retains its moisture well. It gives a subtle initial impression but its flavors unfold dramatically, offering toasty aromas and hints of dark chocolate, tobacco, wild game, wild grasses, wildflowers. A truly remarkable and thoroughly artisanal cheese, it brings to mind the phrase "inconsistency celebrated," by which I mean each and every wheel has a different story to tell. Yet the heft, the intensity, and the fullness of flavors will always show through. Making the most of lush pasturage (not a thought of herbicides or formula feed), the Dräckloch is an Alpine masterpiece, not to be missed.

APPENZELLER—This great cheese is delicious and a model of balance, with just the right amounts of salt and of sweetness. I suspect some of the subpar Appenzellers circulating in the market may be pasteurized versions. I leave it up to Rolf Beeler to locate and ripen the good ones—or supply us with an alternative, whether it's Toggenburger or some other equivalent local type.

BERGFICHTE— Swiss German for "mountain fir," this is the new name for an old Swiss favorite, Krümmenswiler Försterskase. Schmid himself cuts the bark from the trees to encircle this cheese, forming a girdle to prevent it from spilling out when it melts, and the bark also imparts a subtle woodsy flavor. The Bergfichte is best when not too soft; it needs some palpable texture and consistency

Rolf Beeler with a couple of his selections.

"Rolf and I were joking about how Fort Myers was a desert: there was nothing but chain restaurants, supermarkets, and prepacked cheese. I told him, 'I need to bring your cheeses in here.' Somehow the idea stuck in my head."

CAROLINE HOSTETTLER,
SWISS CHEESE IMPORTER

I love the crystalline texture in a fine Gruyère, the way it seems to sparkle across the palate. Eat a thin sliver and you'll feel you've done your body some real good.

If they were putting on the blindfold and I was down to my last cheese, it might have to be Sbrinz.

to deliver its best potential mouth feel. Despite being a quirky washed-rind cheese, it is very versatile with wines, clearly attributable to its remarkable balance.

BLAUE GEISS—Also from Willy Schmid, this is an amazing cheese, highly atypical and distinct, the only Swiss cheese of its type and the most successful unpasteurized veined goat's milk blue made. A little of this "blue goat" goes a long way. The Blaue Geiss is scary looking but not nearly as mean and dastardly tasting as, for example, a mature Cabrales. The closest cheese I can think of to a Blaue is a Harbourne Blue, also highly successful but pasteurized and not as strong.

FLIXER—A lovely sheep's milk cheese made in an Alpine cow's milk style, I liken Flixer to a sheep version of Appenzeller (although its flavor profile is not as deep) or perhaps an alpine version of an Ossau-Iraty. It is subtle and unique, mild yet exquisite, a good example of an underappreciated delicacy. It comes in relatively small wheels and is good both young, at around 3 months, and old, up to 1 year.

GRUYÈRE—A Gruyère selected and aged 16 to 18 months by Rolf Beeler is a showstopper and hard to beat; I can't think of a serious competitor, including perhaps the very best Comté. I love the crystalline texture in a fine Gruyère, the way it seems to sparkle across the palate. Eat a thin sliver and you'll feel you've done your body some real good. Its flavor profile includes nutty, slightly sweet notes, along with hints of mushroom and a pleasant mustiness. In a full Picholine selection of 40 to 60 cheeses, this is one of two or three "mandatory" items.

HOCH YBRIG—This is another I've long thought of as among the greatest of the Swiss greats. For people who may not be predisposed to the notion of great Swiss cheeses, the Hoch Ybrig is a very good starting point. It's a bit sweeter and nuttier than Gruyère, and really there's nothing not to like about it. Whether it's as superb as it once was is another question. If the Hoch Ybrig lost some of its luster, perhaps it was because increasing demand forced it to be made with milk from outside its original *terroir*.

KUNTENER (REBLOCHON)—I wish they wouldn't attach Reblochon to the name of this cheese because it's not really a relevant comparison; its Swiss place-name should be sufficient. The Kuntener, compared with a genuine French Reblochon, has a lot more *B. linens*, showing much more of an effect from its washings. Made from Jersey cow's milk, it has deliciously soft texture and assertive raw-milk flavors. It is much more intense than a French Reblochon, and may be just too stinky for some people.

PRATTIGAUER—Of all the classic Swiss mountain cheeses, this one has the deepest flavor profile; its impact is much more thunderous than, say, its neighboring cheese, the Appenzeller. Prattigauer comes from southeastern Switzerland and is very much a high-elevation cheese: it has a depth and persistence of flavor wherein you can really taste the diversity of those mountain pastures. Secret recipes for washes have been passed down through generations of local cheesemakers. Prattigauer is intense, robust, and nuttier than Appenzeller and similar types, with a longer finish. It is funkier and more artisanal, so some holes, fissures, and even a few cracks should be no cause for alarm.

SBRINZ—If they were putting on the blindfold and I was down to my last cheese, it might have to be Sbrinz. For me, there is no match for a thin shaving of this ancient delight—a serious rival of genuine Parmigiano-Reggiano for the best old cheese in the universe. Sbrinz is strong yet very balanced, dryish yet mouthwatering. The butterfats in the whole-milk Sbrinz give it a smoother, nuttier, less salty profile than a Parmigiano-Reggiano. (Incidentally, Sbrinz is also more wine-friendly than the Parmigiano, which is made from skim milk.) The Sbrinzes we see are aged around 2 years, but they can last 8 years or longer.

VACHERIN FRIBOURGEOIS—This labor-intensive, ladled delicacy is sold after 7 to 9 months of careful aging, including regular turnings and changing of its cloths. (Rolf Beeler leaves his select Vacherins at their dairies and visits them weekly.) A top-of-the-line Vacherin Fribourgeois can be spectacular: It has very meaty flavors, with a lot of *umami;* its texture is dense yet smooth and melting, slightly elastic but nevertheless delightful.

VAL BAGNER—I remember a specific Val Bagner from the year 2001 that may have been the best cheese I had put in my mouth to that point (in fact, it's pictured on page 50 of my first book, *The Cheese Plate*). In recent years, the Val Bagners have edged toward something younger and more akin to Fontina Val d'Aosta. This

A CHEESE WORTHY OF CONTEMPLATION (AND KIDS LOVE IT, TOO)

Sbrinz is a cheese that commands attention. Because it's dry and very strong and requires careful shaving to create an appropriate serving, it might be off-putting. I had always thought of it as kind of an *hors catégoire* cheese. This is why I didn't push it on my customers at the restaurant, only slipping it in occasionally for those I knew would appreciate its lip-smacking intensity. That is, until I took a scrap home to my daughter Scarlett, who was very young at the time. I put a small taste on her plate, she tried it, sat up from her chair at the kitchen counter, and said, "Daddy, I want another bite!" I realized then if my innocent, unprejudiced child could appreciate this cheese, then I should never dismiss it again—for myself or anyone else. Am I saying even a little kid can recognize a great cheese? Yes, I guess that's what I'm saying.

THE REAL DEAL VERSUS A CLAIMANT

As Caroline Hostettler stated somewhat indignantly, CAVE AGED is one of the more abused terms in the cheese world. If you would like a true illustration of the difference between the genuine article and a commercial imitation, try a Rolf Beeler–selected, 16-month-old Gruyère alongside one from a big industrial producer such as Emmi, which makes similar claims. (Another cheese mantra to keep in mind: "Tasting is believing.")

Some notes: This is like comparing Wonder Bread to an organic, whole-grain rustic peasant loaf. There are worse things you can put in your mouth than a mass-market, "industrial" Gruyère-type cheese; it will have a hint of the taste and character of an authentic one but nowhere near the length and depth of flavors. The real deal delivers a full symphony of flavors and textures that go on and on. Its aromas are quite subtle and sweet, but they are most definitely present in the Beeler select cheese—and not in the supermarket one.

may be another example of market pressures dumbing down a cheese, eroding its standards. It's perfectly fine and edible when a bit young, but if it's aged out properly to a harder, drier texture—around 10 months—it becomes exquisite. I've heard Val Bagner is used as a raclette cheese, but I have to question why anyone would melt anything this good on top of potatoes.

TASTING PLATE
But There Are Swiss Cheeses
TOMME VAUDOISE
FLIXER
STANSER RÖTELI
VACHERIN FRIBOURGEOIS
SBRINZ
BLAUE GEISS

This plate features some of the more modern Swiss artisanal delights—mostly cow, one sheep, and one very intriguing goat—in ascending order of complexity and persistence of flavors. Conspicuously absent is a Gruyère type, but we figured we had that covered elsewhere, particularly in chapter 11's exemplary nine-cheese tasting. Certainly, a well-aged 2-year-old Gruyère has the heft to offer the last word in many a progression and could be substituted for the Sbrinz. I feel compelled to feature Sbrinz here. And how could I resist including one of Switzerland's newest and most arresting artisanal cheeses: "The Blue Goat."

We start with Tomme Vaudoise, which you could call the Swiss equivalent to France's Brie de Meaux. The Tomme has a bloomy rind, soft consistency, gentle texture, and a balanced, welcoming profile. The dominant flavor impression is of fresh, raw milk. The Flixer that follows has a much harder consistency, which I'd term toothsome, and some nice nutty flavor notes. Comparing the Flixer to another superior sheep cheese, Spenwood, it's got some surface *B. linens*, which may explain why its flavors are more meaty than its English cousin. Although relatively mild for a sheep's milk cheese, the Flixer has a pleasantly lingering finish, a characteristic you'll note in many great Swiss cheeses.

Stanser Röteli brings us back into the cow's milk arena; it has just enough *B. linens* from washings to develop its flavors into one

OPPOSITE: A taste of Switzerland: Clockwise from the left, Tomme Vaudoise; Flixer; Stanser Röteli; Vacherin Fribourgeois; Sbrinz; Blaue Geiss.

of the best-balanced, broadest, and most satisfying of any semisoft (and semi-stinky) cheese I can recall. The Röteli's texture is not unlike a fine Robiola Pineta. The Röteli has smooth, buttery, full, plump consistency and flavor without excess salt and really anchors the center of this plate, inviting you to taste it repeatedly at your leisure. Among other delicacies, I might compare it to L'Ami du Chambertin, a French artisanal cheese we don't see much in the United States anymore (it's essentially a variation of Époisses); the Röteli is similar to L'Ami but is a bit larger and not quite as stinky.

The next item, Vacherin Fribourgeois, falls more into the category of pressed mountain-style cheeses, even though it's made in a relatively low-altitude part of the country, near Lake Geneva. Its consistency is firm yet moist, along the lines of Fontina Val d'Aosta; more frequent washings, however, encourage more bacterial growth in the Vacherin and give it more pungent aromas, leading to some really attractive deep, warm, savory flavors. The Vacherin is truly an artisanal cheese—with a fair amount of variation in textures and flavors, none of them displeasing—and for this reason I worry about its survival. Speaking of artisanal variability, it sometimes harbors mites, but we take care of those by simply scraping them off.

There are few cheeses with the volume and persistence of flavors to follow a Sbrinz. It's hard, crumbly, and strong, which is why it's presented in very thin slices. It magically disintegrates into mouthwatering shards and then a smooth, buttery-nutty blanket on your palate. Potentially arresting on the attack, a Sbrinz always seems to mellow gracefully and deliver a wonderfully elegant finish.

Among the Swiss elite, there's really only one cheese I would think of introducing after Sbrinz and that is the unique, modern creation Blaue Geiss, a trailblazer in the sense that Switzerland is famous for neither its blues nor its goat cheeses. The Blaue's attack is quite intense and broad across the palate, as you'd expect from a relatively young goat's milk blue, but it fades to a fairly gentle, pleasant finish and, coupled with its persistent moisture, ends this tasting of great Swiss cheeses on an appropriately polite, yet nonetheless memorable, note.

OPPOSITE: *Blaue Geiss: One of the world's scariest-looking, and most delicious, cheeses.*

CHAPTER 16

THE CHEESES OF IBERIA: RUSTIC, REAL, AND READY

THIS IS A SPECIAL REGIONAL CLASS I HOLD CLOSE TO MY HEART. WHAT defines the character and personality of Spanish and Portuguese cheeses? What is it about them that defines such a distinct and special category? Iberian cheeses are strong, outgoing, unabashed—most definitely not shy. The ones I love haven't caved to market pressures. They are what they are; they're happy about it and so am I. Many of them are made from sheep's milk—another big plus—and much of that milk is left unpasteurized. The Iberian thistle-renneted cheeses form a unique subcategory—one not perfected, let alone developed much, in other parts of the world.

GEOGRAPHY AND *TERROIR*

The Iberian Peninsula is neatly divided from France and the rest of Europe by the Pyrénées mountain range, which stretches from Basque country in the west, home of the great Ossau-Iraty family of hard, pressed, aged sheep's milk cheeses, eastward to Catalonia and its capital, Barcelona—a cultural and gastronomic hub and thus a major source of artisanal cheeses. (I have fond memories of tasting great Iberian cheeses with wines at the bistro-restaurant-deli Tutusaus there, with the Spanish cheese maestro Enric Canut.)

Green Spain, in the northwest, with its wetter climate and lower average elevation, yields more cow cheeses. The high and dry central plain, which looks more like Utah than you might expect (and perhaps accounts for the conquistadores' affinity for the American West), accounts for the preponderance of sheep cheeses.

Peña Blanca, with one of its wine partners, Rioja.

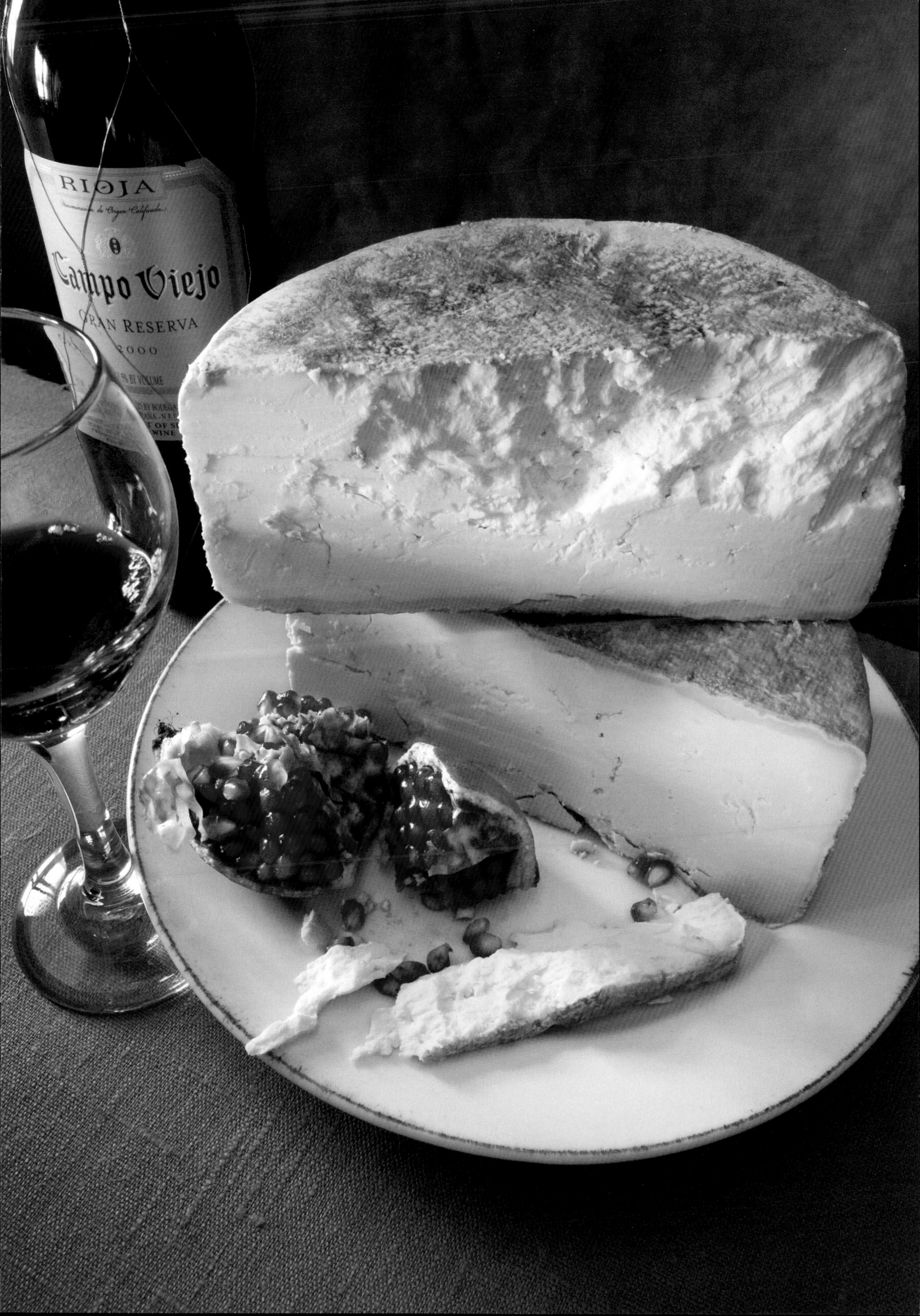
RIOJA
Campo Viejo
GRAN RESERVA
2000

Aracena, a complex and classy Iberian.

Three great mountain ranges—the aforementioned Pyrénées, the Picos de Europa in Asturias, and the Serra da Estrela of Portugal—yield outstanding cheeses. Several island subregions, thought of as summer resorts and not much else, are actually fertile ground for some very interesting and *terroir*-expressive indigenous types: The Balearic Islands of the Mediterranean give us Mahón, the Canaries Majorero and Palmero, and the Azores São Jorge.

Max's Picks: Great Spanish Artisan Cheeses

Almost all of the historically well-known Spanish cheeses are Manchego types, most of them from sheep's milk with few if any ancient survivors among cow and goat's milk. What you'll note from the following picks is a refreshing trend on the modern Spanish cheese scene: Nowadays many charmingly rustic artisanal types have arisen, among them the *torta* styles Serena and del Casar, the slightly flattened goat's milk log that is Garrotxa, and the eye-opening washed-rind goat's milk Aracena, which quickly went on my top favorites list when I "rediscovered" it (and was relieved to find out it had not gone extinct).

ARACENA—A washed-rind raw goat's milk cheese from Andalusia in Spain's southwest where sheep cheeses are much more prevalent, Aracena to me personifies real, organic, rustic character. Like many washed-rind goat cheeses—a potentially difficult type—its rind can be gamey or goaty. Aracena's paste, however, is creamy and very approachable, with firm yet moist consistency and pleasantly earthy flavors.

(QUESO DE LOS) BEYOS—Although pasteurized, the Beyos is a unique cheese. It comes in cow's, goat's, and mixed-milk versions; I feel the former works much better. If well aged, the Beyos becomes quite chalky, which is unusual in a cow cheese: a sliver of the paste melts beautifully on the tongue, releasing its wonderful dry yet buttery character. (Skip the rind on this one; it's too moldy.)

CABRALES—Spain's most famous blue, Cabrales is unfortunately no longer leaf-wrapped, but it still delivers a classic flavor profile. Try to get it young. An older Cabrales can be really mean; it becomes more of a curiosity and less eminently edible. I like to be able to taste the milk, not just sharp, salty, harsh mold. If you do decide to go for an extreme old Cabrales, try washing it down with an outstanding sweet, raisiny Pedro Ximénez Sherry.

GAMONEDO—This is one of the last of the naturally blued blues. Rustic and delicious, Gamonedo is gently smoked and takes on a subtle hint of apple wood. The purist in me is drawn to the fact that its smoking is an integral part of the ancient manufacturing process, where it helped dry the cheeses inside the mountain huts where they were made.

(QUESO) IBORES—A wonderful cheese with a dryish, pleasantly chalky texture, Ibores presents goat's milk at its best—pure, white, and refreshing. The Ibores flavor profile includes a good deal of *umami* and it is a very versatile partner for wines, without relying on excessive salt to do the trick. I prefer the version rubbed with *pimentón* (Spanish paprika), which gives it a subtle peppery zest.

Majorero Pimentón and La Peral

IDIAZÁBAL—A sheep's milk cheese from Navarra, reminiscent of Roncal but lightly smoked. Artisanal and subtle, you can taste the milk. Like Zamorano, Roncal and Manchego, Idiazábal has firm texture and rich, nutty flavors—but with a slightly smoky accent.

(QUESO) MAHÓN—This is very much a *terroir* cheese in the sense it reflects its origins on the Mediterranean island of Menorca quite literally, with a very evident taste of the sea. It has the same maritime tang quality you find (somewhat curiously) in a genuine English Cheshire. Aged from 3 to 8 months, a raw-milk Mahón can be excellent. Past that point, it can become too much of a salt lick.

(QUESO) MAJORERO—The *pimentón*-rubbed raw-milk version of this pressed goat cheese from the island of Fuerteventura in the Canaries is the one to get. It has a wonderful minerally quality, which I couldn't possibly place on first tasting. It all makes sense, though, when you find out about its volcanic island *terroir*.

MONTE ENEBRO—One trick to make a successful blue goat cheese is to use the mold for surface ripening only. This is how Monte Enebro is made. At 3 to 5 weeks of age, it can be fabulous, with just the right amount of flavor development from external *Penicillium roqueforti*. The mold adds zing—a distinct, brilliant accent all the way through to the cheese's core—but there's no hint of interior veining. Get your Monte Enebro while it's young, though; as it ages, the mold can take over, making the cheese wet and slimy, injecting a somewhat noxious chemical taste and feel.

PEÑA BLANCA—This is a very unusual if not unique raw-milk cheese made in both goat and sheep versions, though the goat

Monte Enebro

version has become rare. It benefits from *Brevibacterium linens* growth but manages to avoid the potential gaminess of many washed-rind non-cow cheeses. The Peña Blanca launches a full-frontal assault, but it mellows quite gracefully in the finish. It has a nice, somewhat open texture, and is not oversalted.

PERAL—A modern, relatively mild blue cheese, invented just over 100 years ago, Peral is now made from pasteurized cow's milk with added sheep cream, a distinguishing twist. It can be feisty and variable. A good one is balanced, neither too salty nor too blue; you can taste its cow's milk and sheep cream distinctly, which I find utterly fascinating.

RONCAL—A primordial Spanish cheese, worthy of its fame, and the first to receive DOP status, Roncal has been made pretty much the same way for at least 3,000 years. It is a transhumance cheese, so you should be able to taste those summer mountain pastures. Oily, high in both butterfat and protein, it ages very well; expect it to peak between 5 and 10 months.

(QUESO DE LA) SERENA—This and the Torta del Casar are Spain's entrants in the wonderful subcategory of sheep's milk *torta* styles, which I like to think of as "party cheeses." A close comparison almost always reveals the Serena to be the "nicer" (i.e., more accessible) of the two. Thistle renneting and their extremely high-quality sheep's milk create an unusual flavor profile, with a fascinating and distinct bittersweetness.

TORTA DEL CASAR—This is a smaller production cheese, a bit more rustic and potentially stronger in comparison to its sister, Serena; when the Torta is good, though, you simply can't top it.

(QUESO DE) VALDEÓN—This has been such a consistently good cheese—a staple of my offerings—for so long sometimes I take it for granted and forget how fine it can be. Although the Valdeón is now pasteurized, it can be made with goat and/or sheep's milk and is still wrapped in the traditional *plageru* (sycamore) leaves, as Cabrales once was, which lend a nice vegetal note.

(QUESO) ZAMORANO—Another primordial Spanish sheep's milk type, probably closer to Manchego (i.e., a bit less rustic) than Roncal is. Zamorano is also more place specific, coming only from the area around Zamora, and more versatile in wine pairings. Otherwise, it is quite similar to Roncal.

Max's Picks: Great Portuguese Artisanal Cheeses

Portugal is home to more than just a handful of cheesemakers who really stick to their old ways; herds of sheep are allowed to range free in the mountains and transmit many wonderful aspects of the country's *terroir* to the cheeses.

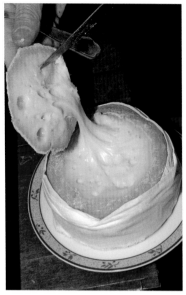

Queijo Serra da Estrela, showing us why it's a party cheese.

(QUEIJO) AMARELO DA BEIRA BAIXA—The Amarelo is made of a mix of goat's and sheep's milk, not necessarily always in the same proportions, which yields some interesting variations. While almost every other Portuguese cheese is thistle renneted, the Amarelo relies on animal rennet, accounting for its meatier character. Usually well balanced, it can be potentially flawed by both gamey flavor and oversalting.

(QUEIJO) AZEITÃO—This has long been one of my favorite cheeses and one I recommend as a good entry point into the realm of thistle-renneted types. It provides great buttery flavor, clearly announcing its origins in the rich milk of free-grazing ewes. Azeitão's texture and consistency can range from soft and unctuous to firm and chewy. It should be eaten at around 3 months; aged 4 or 5 months, it starts to dry out too much.

(QUEIJO DE) EVORA—This is a fairly sheepy cheese in appearance—and on first whiff and the attack. I've often noticed people taste it then hesitate, but those who take the time to savor it inevitably take on a happy expression. Evora, like Azeitão, is another small-format cheese that keeps quite well. It's firmer in texture than Serra or Azeitão, thick and buttery yet with no hint of greasiness; it has a robust, meaty flavor without being extra salty.

(QUEIJO DE) NISA—A highly recommended cheese, although a little bit goes a long way since it is a more concentrated, drier cheese than most of the other thistle-renneted Iberian types. Nisa tastes grassier, a little saltier, with more of a roasted chestnut flavor and a more clay-like, sandier texture.

(QUEIJO) SÃO JORGE—I think of this great DOP cheese from the Azores as a cross between a Cheddar and a Sbrinz. Its native *terroir,* situated almost 1,000 miles west of Lisbon, is full of wide open pastures and is reminiscent of Scotland. São Jorge has a beautiful golden paste packed with delicious butterfats. It has some Cheddar-like sharpness and is not quite as sweet as some of the Alpine cheeses, but it delivers a comparable depth of flavor.

(QUEIJO) SERPA—Another fine Portuguese artifact, Serpa is to Serra (da Estrela) what a Torta del Casar is to (Queso de la) Serena: A Serpa can be as soft as a Serra but generally speaking is more rustic. Serpa is very traditionally manufactured (with hand pressing) and it does fluctuate; it is best consumed during the summer.

(QUEIJO) SERRA DA ESTRELA—This is the quintessential Portuguese cheese, the grandaddy of them all. Its history extends back more than 2,000 years and is the one I'd likely recommend as most exemplary of its *terroir* and traditions. Serra, which gets its name from Portugal's tallest mountain range, is a little sheepy and rustic, yet at the same time elegant and beautifully balanced. Because of staggered lactation, it is now available in good form year round. Most of the Serras I serve are aged 3 to 5 months; at this stage, they're soft and easy to love. Serra is a party cheese with good, solid butterfats that will melt to an unctuous—but not liquid—state.

(QUEIJO) TERRINCHO—A traditional cheese, which, by the time it reaches the United States, is quite firm, meaty and insistent. It comes from an isolated region (far northeastern Portugal).

TASTING PLATE
A Taste of Iberia
ARACENA
(QUESO) IBORES
(QUEIJO) AMARELO DA BEIRA BAIXA
(QUEIJO DE) NISA
GAMONEDO
PEÑA BLANCA (SHEEP'S MILK VERSION)
VALDÉON

This plate consists of cheeses only from the peninsula—none from the islands—and naturally features strong representatives of different rustic goat and sheep types. They range from the far south of Spain (Aracena, from Andalusia); to Asturias in the north (Gamonedo and La Peral) and over to the east-central countryside of Portugal, not far from Spain's Extremadura (Amarelo and Nisa).

The plate starts with a washed-rind goat's milk stinker—the Aracena—albeit one with an inviting, mild, milky, creamy interior. Aracena has an interesting seasonal variation: It's semisoft, smoother, and I think better, in the winter months; during the warmer season, it turns a bit crumbly.

OPPOSITE: An Iberian tasting: From the bottom, Aracena; Ibores; Amarelo da Beira Baixa; Nisa; Gamonedo; Peña Blanca; and Valdeón.

We progress to a harder cheese, the Ibores, but still Spanish and of goat's milk. I prefer the *pimentón*-rubbed versions but in any case Ibores is more of a year-round cheese, with consistently chalkier texture at any stage than its predecessor here. It doesn't have the funky aromas or creamy consistency of the Aracena but it's zesty, more toothsome, and has a bigger flavor profile.

Next comes a captivating, very artisanal Portuguese mixed-milk cheese, the Amarelo, made from raw goat's and sheep's milk using traditional animal rennet, which adds a layer of meaty flavor. I love this cheese, nearly as much as I do the Azeitão; it smells a little gamey and tastes a little funky. It has a good amount of salt, which is counteracted by the oily qualities of the sheep's milk.

I think of the Nisa, made from raw sheep's milk and decidedly artisanal, as a Portuguese answer to the Ibores. Nisa is similar to (but saltier than) Evora. It is harder and nuttier tasting than all other thistle-renneted types, and generally is drier than the Amarelo while maintaining a good olive oil–like quality to its butterfats and a nice toothsome texture. Although it's quite rustic, the Nisa's open-textured paste lends a delicate aspect to its mouth feel, which paves the way for the Gamonedo. This Asturian delight is gently smoked by apple-wood fires and has a hint of natural bluing, giving it attractive flavor accents and a unique profile. Gamonedo's rules permit the use of all three milks. Its crumbly, dry texture and mouth feel, which can approach brittleness in longer-aged versions, offers good contrast to the Nisa before it and the Peña Blanca that follows.

The Gamonedo is followed by a pair of very lively Iberians, beginning with the Peña Blanca. The first impression from the Peña Blanca is a cheesecake–like texture, semisoft but quite thick in consistency. This can fool you because it spreads itself out quickly on your palate and lays down a pronounced sheep's milk profile, with a fairly strong attack, whereas you might expect something sweeter and milder out of this texture. The Peña has more *umami* and zest compared to the meaty, oily qualities of the other Iberian sheep's milk cheeses on this plate.

Our closing act here is another quirky Iberian, Valdéon, which is made from cow's milk along with some goat's milk, usually. Tantalizing, bold, and refreshing, it's a bit of a show-stopper. The leaves in which Valdéon are wrapped are a reminder of the history of this type of cheese—at one time this was the way that many artisanal cheeses were wrapped and transported.

OPPOSITE: Many Iberian cheeses are made with sheep's milk.

ITALY: A BOOTFUL OF GREAT CHEESES

A SHORT OVERVIEW CANNOT POSSIBLY DO JUSTICE TO THE VAST AND variegated cheese landscape of the Italian peninsula. The more I delve into it, the more it occurs to me there may very well be nearly as many cheeses in Italy as there are in France. The cheese *types* of an ancient culture are easy enough to delineate, but if you want to list every single cheese—with all its variations and place-names, reflecting every nook of *terroir*—the task of quantifying becomes virtually impossible. In Italy, you see various major types divided up and defined as individual cheeses depending on how they're elaborated locally. Suffice it to say that in the United States we see a fraction of the variety and range of cheeses actually produced in Italy.

Perhaps just as decades ago, when Italian wines were thought of as nothing more than simple, rustic food partners represented by either bad Chianti in straw-encased bottles or cheap Asti Spumante, we are just beginning to uncover the tremendous breadth, depth, and sophistication of Italian cheese. It will be many more years before I—or any other cheese expert from America—can say, "I have tasted my way through all of them." Just consider such typical Italian "cheese families" as the Pecorinos or the Caprinos: Here in the United States, we see quite a few of the former, though not nearly the full range, and relatively few of the latter, since goat's milk cheeses are not automatically associated with Italy. There are many fine goat cheeses from northern and central Italy, but they simply don't travel as do the other types.

From bottom: Caprino Noce, Pecorino Sardo, Taleggio, Parmigiano-Reggiano, Gorgonzola Piccante.

GEOGRAPHY AND *TERROIR*

Geographically and culturally, Italy, which was not unified from its medieval city-states until the late nineteenth century, has always been divided into two very different regions, the north and the south. For cheese purposes, I might divide it roughly into five zones: the northern mountainous regions, mostly the Alps; the northern plains, beginning at the foothills of the Alps and extending across the Po Valley; Tuscany and the central hills down to Rome; the mountainous south; and Sicily, with its distinct island *terroir*.

Northern Italians take a more Germanic approach, tending to tinker and invent more, expanding their product lines, creating more—and more adventurous—variations on traditional themes. In general, there is more elaboration and more cow's milk cheese, mostly owing to the Alpine *terroir*. In central and southern Italy, cheesemakers emphasize traditional, rustic cheeses and there are more sheep's milk types. The southern cheeses are simple, unassuming, sturdy, and very old, Sicily's Ragusano providing a good example.

Like many ancient cheesemaking cultures, steeped in local character and bound by tradition, Italy tends to keep some of its best types to itself. A wonderful delicacy such as Fontina is thought of as *the* cheese from the Val d'Aosta, and its authentic artisanal versions, properly aged, can be superb. Yet there may be a better, more interesting local cheese, which the natives refuse to let go. For example, you might be surprised to find another DOP cheese, Valle d'Aosta Fromadzo (named in the local dialect), or a non-DOP "unnamed" local type, that may surpass a genuine Fontina.

Another important characteristic of many Italian cheeses is they are sold at various stages of ripeness. In the process of going from a fresh, young state to a hard, aged one, they may change so much as to become a different cheese. In general, with some age, their flavor profiles become deeper and more rounded. Yet while I'm always looking for sophistication and development, there are advantages to selling cheeses younger: It widens their audience to include people who may prefer milder versions of given cheese items.

Max's Picks: A Few Key Italian Players

CORA—This family business located in Monesiglio, Piedmont, about 20 miles south of Bra, is one of the anchors of northern

FROM TOP: *A fancifully designed rustic cheese on display at the Slow Food Convivium, Bra, Italy; raw-milk Pecorinos from Caseificio Pinzani.*

Italian artisan production. I have a great deal of respect for their painstaking, labor-intensive elaboration of so many small-format cheeses. Their leaf-wrapped Robiolas are gorgeous little works of art. The various types of leaves used for wrapping (including grapevine, chestnut, fig) lend catchy flavor accents to the fresh, pure, mild, milky flavors of these cheeses that are often made of mixed milks.

CRAVERO—A fifth-generation cheese man, Giorgio Cravero manages the family operation started by his great-great-grandfather in 1855. Its headquarters is in Bra, the birthplace of the Slow Food organization. The Craveros finish their Parmigianos in an old stone and stucco warehouse with no apparent temperature control system other than natural cooling and ventilation.

GUFFANTI—Giovanni Guffanti Fiori and his father Carlo represent the current generations of this family *affinage* firm on the shores of Lake Maggiore, northwest of Milan. The operation, called Luigi Guffanti 1876 after Carlo's great-grandfather and the year he founded it, positioned its ripening facility literally across the street from the lake. Its basement caves benefit from constant seepage through the building's cracked old rock foundations. Guffanti's catalog contains nearly 200 cheeses from producers all over the boot; it reads like an encyclopedia of fine Italian cheeses.

CASEIFICIO PINZANI—The Pinzani family are modern Tuscan artisans who turn out a range of traditional Pecorinos and related cheeses. Their office, welcoming center, and tasting room is in an ancient stucco-walled, tile-roofed farmhouse, once the family's country home that is situated not far from San Gimignano. The Pinzanis collect milk from 30 local shepherds whose herds of between 2,000 to 3,000 sheep roam the highlands and forests surrounding the medieval town of Volterra. Father Guido and daughter Giulia run the operation and they've been highly successful at promoting and marketing these traditional Tuscan food artifacts. An exciting recent project was their revival of an ancient Pecorino type, which they call Pecorino delle Balze Volterrane. Made with cardoon thistle-renneted raw milk, it is aged in oak barrels for 60 days and it has a rind formed by rubbings of oak and olive wood ash, which imparts a unique green olive flavor. The Pinzanis filed for its European Union PDO status and were awaiting approval at the time of this writing.

FROM TOP: *Parmigiano-Reggianos aging at the Cravero facility, Bra, Italy; on the road to Caseificio Pinzani in Tuscany.*

More Italian artistry: A smoked goat's milk ricotta.

Max's Picks: Great Italian Artisanal Cheeses

BRA—A fine representative of Piedmont, from the area around Cuneo and Bra in Barolo country, this cheese is sold at several stages of ripeness. *Tenero* (tender) is 45 days to 4 months old; *duro* (hard) is around 6 months; *nostrale* (rustic or farmhouse style), the most aged version, turns hard and grainy like Grana Padano. I find a well-aged Bra most interesting at about 6 months.

CALLU DE CABREDDU (OR CABRETTU)—Rewind your cheese clock about 6,000 years when you sample this Sardinian goat's milk cheese that is ripened in a dried kid's stomach. It is focused and intense; in one of the Italian cheese references I found, it was dubbed *fortissimo ed esplosivo* (very strong and explosive) and I can vouch for that: it indeed explodes on your tongue with a flavor burst that can be even stronger than Cabrales.

CANESTRATO PUGLIESE—The name of this cheese translates roughly as "the basketed one from Puglia" (Apulia), which is the province encompassing the spur and heel of the boot. This is a fine example of rustic, artisanal production, with the draining-basket imprints on its rind and its hearty flavors. I consider this cheese Italy's prime entry in the ancient sheep's milk category. It's grassy, oily, firm, and has good underlying sweetness.

ERBORINATI—The term *erborinato* is the Italian equivalent of *persillé* (parsleyed) in French, meaning the cheese is blued, either by piercing or inoculation with molds. One notable member of this family is the Erborinato di Pecora, a sheep's milk version from Bolzano and nearby pastures in the Dolomites. Another worth checking out is the raw cow's milk Erborinato di Artavaggio, from the foothills of the Alps north of Milan.

FONTINA VAL D'AOSTA—The is the quintessential Italian Alpine cheese; its best DOP artisan versions bring to mind the beauty of this northwestern valley corridor to Switzerland and the high Alps. Its flavors are mild, very smooth, milky, and approachable, but it really develops some length and depth to its profile, leaving a rich, substantial, sumptuous overall impression. An important note regarding care: Be sure to carefully store a Fontina well because any exposed surfaces can turn dry and crusty.

GORGONZOLA—Historically one of Italy's most famous and important cheeses and its original blue, a product of herds of cows migrating from the valleys of Lombardy up through the foothills and into the Alps for summer pasturing. Unfortunately, in the past 15 to 20 years, I've found many Gorgonzolas, as a type, to be disappointing on occasion. The aged, or *piccante*, versions are the ones to look for. (I'm not at all partial to the *dolce*, younger, sweeter versions.)

GRANA PADANO—You could call this "Parmigiano Lite" and not be far off. It's the less specifically defined, more widely produced and younger (aged up to 2 years) version of Italy's granddaddy of all cheeses, and it's a less expensive alternative to genuine DOP Parmigiano-Reggiano.

PARMIGIANO-REGGIANO—A perennial candidate for the world's greatest cheese, it is also always under market pressure to become more industrialized and commercial. Giorgio Cravero selects and ripens some of the best genuine. Generally speaking, Parmigiano-Reggiano is ready to ship at 18 months to 2 years.

PECORINO TOSCANO—Pecorino is a generic term indicating sheep's milk cheese, literally translated as "little sheep." It only becomes a legitimate cheese name when its *terroir* is specified. The Tuscan version of Pecorino is among the world's greatest sheep's milk cheeses, bar none. Pecorino di Pienza, from the beautiful hilltown of that name in south-central Tuscany, is an excellent subcategory. Many aged Pecorinos of this type are rubbed with olive oil and/or tomato paste. The best of the Tuscan Pecorinos for my money is the Pecorino delle Balze Volterrane, which is made from organic raw milk, rubbed with olive oil, and aged 4 to 6 months. It's firm, tending toward a Roncal-like texture, oily, with fairly subtle taste yet great depth of character. There are so many different brands and producers of genuine Tuscan Pecorino, I strongly suggest you close your eyes and take a taste before committing to buy. Your best bets are aged (*stagionato*) DOP Pecorino Toscanos from Societá Cooperativa Val d'Orcia, Caseificio Il Fiorino, Fattoria Corzano e Paterno, or an equivalent producer.

PECORINO SARDO—This is another important ancient cheese whose DOP versions are made from raw milk. As you might expect from the rugged, stone landscape, Sardinian Pecorino is a little harder, more crumbly, saltier, and less smooth and subtle than the Tuscan version. I like the Sardo when aged about 6 months.

A pecorino from Caseificio Pinzani in Tuscany.

Parmigiano-Reggianos aging at Cravero's facility.

PIAVE—Comparable to Parmigiano, but more of a mountain cheese and not as granular, Piave has great balance and stability. If Grana is "Parm Lite" then Piave could be "Sbrinz Lite." True to its Italian origins, Piave has sweeter, fruitier flavors than the similar Centovalli Ticino from the Swiss side of the border. Piave *fresco* is aged less than 3 months; *mezzano,* 3 to 4 months; and *stagionato,* 6 to 8 or more months. I recommend it around 6 months.

RAGUSANO—A wonderfully unpretentious, rustic *pasta filata* aged Provolone-style cheese authentically transmitting its Sicilian *terroir.* Ragusano and other similar southern Italian types have a distinct flavor component of what seems to be borderline rancidity, the product of advanced degradation of butterfats, which translates into a lip-smacking, mouthwatering taste.

ROBIOLA—This is a wonderful and distinguished family of small, fresh, cheeses from Piedmont that are often made with mixed milks, many of them made by the Cora family firm, the Caseificio dell'Alta Langa and other distinguished producers. When in Italy, be sure to get your hands on a genuine DOP Robiola di Roccaverano, aged just 3 to 4 weeks, and savor its lush flavors. The Tre Latti version (from all three milks) is legal here and highly recommended.

TASTING PLATE
A Taste of Italy
CAPRINO NOCE
PECORINO DELLE BALZE VOLTERRANE
BRA TENERO
PECORINO SARDO
TALEGGIO
PARMIGIANO-REGGIANO
GORGONZOLA PICCANTE

Our Italian tasting naturally starts with a relatively fresh, mild cheese. The Caprino Noce, made by the Cora family from goat's milk with some cow's milk added, is wrapped in black walnut leaves, which gives it a nutty and ever-so-slightly bitter accent.

Next up is a member of the Tuscan Pecorino family, the Balze Volterrane. It is pressed, olive oil-rubbed, balanced, subtle, mild yet memorable—and probably as close as anything to the ancient style of cheeses made in the region, when they were still known as the *cacio* (an alternative word for "cheese"). The Bra Tenero, made from all cow's milk and aged 2 to 3 months, can gracefully follow. This younger Bra is heavier than the Pecorino but it's still a mild-tasting cheese, very satisfying, with great buttery texture and flavors, aptly representing its Piemonte *terroir*.

We cycle back to another Pecorino, this one the harder, saltier, more intense one from Sardinia, aged about 4 months. The Pecorino Sardo provides interesting contrasts with the Tuscan one, geographically and also in terms of flavor development.

For the next cheese, Taleggio has a washed rind, and its profile is yeasty, meaty, and chock-full of *umami*. Raw milk artisan versions can be excellent; pasteurized ones are still good. If you leave a ripe Taleggio out at room temperature for a couple hours, it very gradually bulges, collapses, and eventually melts. Don't be alarmed; just enjoy it in its "relaxed" form. I don't recommend eating the rind, because it can be gritty with salt from the evaporated remnants of its brine baths. Guffanti carries good authentic Taleggios; Jean-Battista Arrigoni also produces a fine one.

What gastronomic tour of Italy would be complete without a taste of real DOP Parmigiano-Reggiano? I recommend one aged at least 2 and up to 3 years. It will be dense, dry, slightly granular, hard but thoroughly moist and dissolvable, a little crumbly, providing a nice contrasting mouth feel to the Taleggio but with formidable and long-lasting flavors. The Parmesan should offer well-rounded and lingering fruity, sweet, and grassy flavors. No wonder the Russian cosmonauts took it to outer space.

On to the finale: a high-end Gorgonzola Piccante. Regardless of whether I've occasionally been down on some Gorgonzolas in the past, you should seriously consider ending any first tasting of Italy with this representative blue. It is sweeter, less intense, and less salty than a Roquefort but still makes a strong impression.

ITALIAN TERMS

STAGES OF RIPENESS

FRESCO—fresh

TENERO—tender

DOLCE—sweet

DURO—hard

STAGIONATO—seasoned (aged or matured)

VECCHIO—old

STRAVECCHIO—extra old

CHAPTER 18

REMEMBRANCE OF THINGS PAST: WE'LL ALWAYS HAVE FRANCE

NEXT STOP ON OUR TOUR OF THE ARTISANAL CHEESE LANDSCAPE IS France, where they get quite a few things right, especially wine and cheese. Long ago, the French elevated cheese to an art form. They insisted on further elaboration, consequently achieving greater diversity and providing the world with more and better cheeses than any other cheesemaking nation. Any conversation about great cheeses has to include a large number of French—or at least French-*style*—cheeses.

The fundamental point regarding France is that over the centuries it has evolved an unparalleled understanding and respect for food production. France is historically a nation truly concerned about the health of its populace (first) and the aesthetics of food (a close second); both of these principles lay the foundation for producing superior farmstead milk and great artisanal cheeses.

Although our regulations governing raw-milk cheeses seem to have targeted specific French cheeses (and also French styles), and although U.S. prohibitions may have placed a damper on traditional cheese production in France, there are still a lot of great French cheeses. I would not counsel you to smuggle in the "illegal" ones, if for no other reason than the very practical one that they're delicate and are meant to be consumed within a day or two of purchase. Such fragile young cheeses don't travel well, particularly buried inside your suitcase. I would urge you to go to France and try some of its old-style authentic treasures; short of that, go to your local cheesemonger and try some of the cheeses recommended in this chapter.

Roquefort and Sauternes: A flawless French duet.

AROUND FRANCE

CHEESES BY REGION

AUVERGNE—Limousin (Massif Central)—Bleu d'Auvergne, Cantal, Fourme d'Ambert, Laguiole, Salers, St. Nectaire

EAST (including Alsace, Burgundy, and Franche-Comté)—Bleu de Gex, Époisses, Comté, Morbier, Munster-Géromé

NORMANDIE/ÎLE-DE-FRANCE—Brie (de Meaux and de Melun), Brillat-Savarin, Camembert, Livarot, Pont l'Évêque

NORTH—Bergues, Boulette d'Avesnes, Maroilles, Mimolette

RHÔNE-ALPES—Abbaye de Tamié, Abondance, Beaufort, Bleu de Termignon, Chevrotin des Aravis, Persillé de Tignes, Reblochon, Tomme de Savoie

SOUTHEAST (including Corsica and Provence)—Banon, Brin d'Amour, Fium'orbu

SOUTHWEST (including Aquitaine, Pyrénées, and Languedoc-Rousillon)—Bethmale, Blue des Causses, Le Moulis, Ossau-Iraty, Roquefort

WEST (includes the Loire Valley, and Poitou-Charentes)—Bonde de Gâtine, Chabichou de Poitou, Crottin de Chavignol, Mothais à la Feuille, Sainte-Maure de Touraine, Selles-sur-Cher, Valençay

With its 60-day rule and periodic import bans against French cheeses, the U.S. government has erected a formidable barrier. This "modern problem" makes it difficult, if not impossible, to obtain many of France's great cheeses on our shores. It also places market pressures on the French to compromise their artisanal cheese heritage. Looking at France in the context of cheese history, some of the biggest questions are: whether industrialization of such iconic cheeses as Brie can be offset by a rebirth of artisanal cheesemaking, to what extent real-cheese traditions survive in France, and will any of its cheeses reach U.S. tables?

GEOGRAPHY AND *TERROIR*

It is estimated that fully one-fifth of the area of France, western Europe's largest country, is occupied by permanent pastureland, which bodes well for milk and cheese production. The geographical truism of a cooler, wetter, more lush north (cow country) and a warmer, drier, more sparse south (the land of sheep and goats) applies to some extent. Likewise, the world's preeminent cheese nation has quite a few well-defined and distinct regions, each with its typical cheese types. As a result of the revolution and for political reasons, the old medieval and renaissance provinces of France were divided up into smaller departments; however, the original geographical and cultural divides are still far more relevant and reflective of cheese types.

The plains and rolling hills of northern France, encompassing the Île-de-France region around Paris and extending to the west toward Normandy, produce some very famous cow's milk cheeses. Normandy and nearby zones in the northwest are traditionally the source of rich, creamy milk and therefore simple, soft, ladled farmhouse cheeses in the Brie and Camembert—and also Pont l'Évêque—styles. The extreme north, along with the northeast, closer to Belgium, Holland, and Germany, and encompassing the border land of Alsace, tends to produce stinkier, washed-rind monastery types, Munster and Maroilles being prime examples.

France shares two major mountain ranges, the Alps and the Pyrénées, which border Switzerland and Italy (the former) and Spain (the latter). The French Alps, in the southeastern regions of Rhône-Alpes and Alpes Côte d'Azur, produce typical cow's milk mountain styles such as Beaufort. The Pyrénées, on the other hand, yield indigenous sheep's milk types such as the Ossau-Iraty

A LOVER'S LAMENT

When I think of French cheeses these days, many of those thoughts are sad because so many of the great types are rare or extinct. Unfortunately—tragically, even— many of my favorite French cheeses are either no longer seen in these parts or have fallen precipitously from their previous heights. Some of them are compromised and others provide merely a glimpse of their former glory. Many of the best raw-milk French cheeses are contraband here in the United States. This is a depressing thought. The Saint-Marcellins and the Saint-Féliciens aren't the same as they used to be. The Chevrotin des Aravis is no longer technically legal, although you do see a real one occasionally. The Banons are often insipid; I'd much rather have an O'Banon from Capriole in Indiana. We don't see Le Cabri Ariègeois anymore; it's probably barely hanging on. Nor do we see the Bonde de Gâtine, L'Ami du Chambertin, Reblochon, Truffe de Valensole, Tétoun de Santa Agata, or Taupinière. The Valençays, Selles-sur-Chers, and the Sainte-Maures we do see in the States are pasteurized and don't really represent their maximum potential. Though you may not have the chance to taste these fine cheeses in all their glory here in the United States, familiarizing yourself with such French classics is an important step in achieving mastery.

family and Abbaye de Bellocq as well as similarly made (pressed, not cooked) goat and cow *tommes*. Each have their equivalents among the Swiss, Italians, and Spanish, and in fact these types are more indicative of climate and geography than any national proclivities. France also shares a smaller mountain range, the Jura, with Switzerland, in the Franche-Comté region, which produces another prominent mountain type, Comté.

While you might think the green pastures of the Loire Valley would sustain the cow-dairying dominance of Normandy and other points north, it is goats that rule there owing to their introduction by the Saracens during the early Middle Ages. The chèvres of this region, exemplified by such cheeses as Valençay and Selles-sur-Cher, have since become among the world's most recognizable cheese types, most closely identified with their place of origin.

Once the most active volcanic region on earth, the vast rocky plateau of the Massif Central, in the south-central part of France and encompassing the Auvergne, is what I think of as primordial dairy country. It is home to some of the country's most ancient and respected cheeses, notably the Cantal and Salers, and the old blues Fourme d'Ambert and Bleu d'Auvergne. Roquefort is a product of a special place on the southern flank of the Massif, closer to the southern regions of the Languedoc (to its west) and Provence (to its east). The Rhone Valley divides the Massif Central, to its west,

Sainte-Maure de Touraine

from the Alps, to its east, and carves out the zone of Burgundy, home to another of France's most famous cheeses, Époisses. Corsica, the big, rugged island off France's southeast coast, is an extension of rocky sheep and goat country, and thus home to those types, notably Brin d'Amour and Fium'orbu Brebis.

Max's Picks: Some Key French Players

JEAN D'ALOS—Jean is one of my favorite cheesemongers and his shop is among France's premier retail locations. This mecca of great cheeses is located in Bordeaux. Jean's selection is outstanding, with a broad range and a focus on the southwest of France, and his merchandising is done in the proper, old-fashioned way. His Pyrénées sheep's milk selection is exceptional. If you can't make it to Bordeaux, please note he supplies some of his cheeses to the Cowgirl Creamery shops here in the States.

ROLAND BARTHÉLEMY—In terms of both *affinage* and retail sales, I consider Barthélemy the successor to the great French cheese expert, retailer, and author Pierre Androuët. Barthélemy's shop in the center of Paris is an important site to visit on your cheese tour of France. As befits a serious cheesemonger in the capital city, he selects cheeses around the entire nation, from the Pyrénées all the way up to the extreme north.

PASCAL BEILLEVAIRE—This father-son producer-*affineur*-distributor-retailer team has done excellent work with traditional goat's milk cheeses. I associate him with ancient types such as Bonde de Gâtine and Couronne Lochoise—rustic, no-nonsense, nothing fancy, just well made and skillfully aged classics. The Beillevaire shop is in Nantes, at the base of the peninsula of Brittany, and their creamery is in Machecoul, outside of the city.

FROMAGERIE P. JACQUIN ET FILS—Historically, Jacquin has been *the* name for production, selection, and *affinage* of Loire Valley chèvres. He and his sons see that their cheeses are made right, treated well, aged properly, and distributed to a wide cheese-loving public. Their selection is very broad—and I only worry if too many pasteurized-milk types seem to enter the lineup. Always looking to improve how their cheeses present, they listen to customer feedback and implement suggestions. They also experiment consistently and successfully with packaging. (Jacquin is located in La Vernelle, close to Selles-sur-Cher.)

CHANTAL PLASSE—Based outside of Lyons near the Beaujolais region, Chantal is a respected veteran selector and distributor. I especially admire all the hard work she's put into marketing the Corsican cheeses. Whether or not you consider this island part of France proper, its cheeses are wonderful—mostly goat's and sheep's milk, rustic, primordial, full of distinction and character.

DENIS PROVENT—From his two Laiterie des Halles shops (one in Chambéry, the capital of the Savoie region, and the other in nearby Aix-les-Bains), this distinguished *affineur* runs an operation very much like Rolf Beeler's in Switzerland, focusing on the best of the artisanal mountain types of the region, including Tome des Bauges, Beaufort, Bleu de Termignon, and Persillé de Tignes.

Max's Picks: Great French Artisanal Cheeses

You've heard my lament about French cheeses diminished by commerce and denied entry by the U.S. border authorities. Because I want nothing more than for our readers to enjoy the best of what France still has to offer, for the following picks I'm focusing on cheeses available in the United States at the time of this writing. Cheese mastery, by the way, does not require a trip to France to try its "illegal" cheeses, but it would be a great idea if you could manage it some day. Meanwhile, try some of the following.

ABBAYE DE TAMIÉ (see also page 213)—This is a venerable and ancient mountain-monastery cheese and the closest thing we can get legally here in the States to a real French Reblochon. The Abbaye de Tamié has a nice eggy aroma and an appealing, eminently approachable, mild, buttery flavor profile. It has a relatively short peak window of about 3 weeks somewhere between the 60- and 80-day marks; a ripe one should have a little give to the touch, just short of spongy, and its rind should have a good uniform light pink shade.

BEAUFORT (see also page 78)—Among French Alpine cheeses, this is usually my top choice, alongside an aged Comté. A Beaufort can easily hold its own with a well-aged Swiss Gruyère: It has sufficient complexity and staying power so that, on a tasting plate, it can perhaps only be followed by an aged farmhouse Gouda or a Sbrinz before the progression moves on to the blues. Beaufort speaks of its high-altitude *terroir* and reminds us that France is about much more than Bries, Camemberts, and chèvres.

FROM TOP: *From top: Bleu de Termignon, a naturally blueing, not-so-blue blue; Brillat-Savarin, the quintessential triple-crème.*

BLEU DE TERMIGNON—Because so many of the cheeses we think of as quintessentially French have either declined or are no longer legal in the United States, I find myself skirting the country and venturing into some out-of-the-way, historically obscure spots for great cheeses. The Bleu de Termignon is a local delicacy made at nearly a mile-high altitude by a single maker with a small herd of cows. For a blue, it's relatively mild, sweetish, and not so salty, which helps its milk flavors stand out.

CASINCA CHÈVRE—One of the more interesting French goat cheeses available, it is essentially the goat's milk version of Fium'orbu Brebis. The Casinca's label claims a "natural rind," which means although it's not strictly in the washed-rind category, it's getting a few baths and growing enough of a layer of *Brevibacterium linens* and other beneficial ambient microorganisms to ripen it deliciously. When I taste a Casinca, I can see the steep, rugged terrain of Corsica and feel its temperate climate. The Casinca is very rustic and has a very forward goat quality to it and a light saltiness in both aroma and flavor. It is firm yet moist and tends to dry a little as it reaches peak shortly after 60 days.

COMTÉ—An enduring impression of my cheese-buying trips to France are the funny looks that cross many a French person's face when you ask for an aged Comté. It's traditionally preferred at the *doux* (sweet or soft) stage, not much more than 5 months old, and used for snacking, cooking, or making sandwiches. The younger Comtés are nice and can be quite fine but a trifle undeveloped. A Comté at 18 months to 24 months becomes stronger, deeper, and more concentrated; its flavors are fuller and it leaves a bigger impression. It's still milder, more graceful, and easy-going, however, than an aged Beaufort, with not quite the volume of flavor.

FIUM'ORBU BREBIS—Made with raw sheep's milk, this funky Corsican washed-rind stinker has a good amount of salt and offers a fair amount of *umami*-type flavors; I consider it the cheese equivalent of a fine organic peanut butter, for both texture and flavor. Encountering a Fium'Orbu is a special experience, starting with its barnyardy aromas, maritime notes, and Mediterranean accent, followed by its assertive first impression, its leisurely evolution over the palate, and lingering but not overly complex finish. Most of my favorite sheep's milk cheeses are in the Ossau-Iraty mold; this one is very different and, I'd say, unique.

LAGUIOLE—Here is a great-tasting French-style big-boss cheese. It's both smoother-flavored and -textured than its British farmhouse Cheddar counterparts; you might call it a cross between a Caerphilly and a Cheddar. The Laguiole's profile is more fresh and milky tasting; its full raw-milk flavors reflect appropriately subtle, restrained influences of cultures and rennets. It is earthier, less acidic, perhaps a bit meatier, and more about the milk than its British counterparts.

LE MOULIS—A one-family dairy cheese from the mid-Pyrénées near the Spanish border, Le Moulis is available in both sheep and goat versions, but the cow's milk variant is the one to get. When aged up to 4 months, it is simple, buttery, and mild with friendly, familiar cow's milk flavors, making it very accessible and easy to like. With more age, it hardens but remains firm-yet-moist; its flavors become funkier, with some barnyardy and sulfurous notes emerging. Compared to similar Alpine cheeses, Le Moulis, which is merely pressed (not cooked), is neither as sweet nor as salty.

OSSAU-IRATY PARDOU ARRIOU—From the Basque country, this has long been one of my favorites in the Ossau-Iraty category (hard, pressed, aged raw sheep's milk), which is perhaps the most reliable—or at least unassailable—cheese type in history. The Ossau-Iratys have inspired many great emulators and imitators, not the least of which are Spenwood and Berkswell in England, and Vermont Shepherd and Trade Lake Cedar in the United States. (The English might contend Spenwood and Berkswell types have been around for centuries, being descendants of ancient British cheeses rather than a family in the Pyrénées.)

PIERRE-ROBERT—The triple crèmes do not necessarily constitute my favorite cheese type; yet they're so important and such a key aspect of French culture, you ought to experience them in their full glory before making any claim to cheese mastery. Over the long haul, I've found Pierre-Robert is the best representative of its class. It is also among the most frequently requested cheeses in my restaurant service. Being just so darn well made, I consider it an emblem of French pride and savoir-faire in artisanal manufacturing. Starting with its very thin (and skillfully crafted) rind, it is silky, subtle, sophisticated, and oh-so-buttery. It rolls everything anybody's ever loved about fine butter and fresh cream into an irresistibly smooth, rich package.

Looking at France in the context of cheese history, one of the biggest questions is whether industrialization of such iconic cheeses as Brie can be offset by a rebirth of artisanal cheesemaking. How much of a real-cheese tradition survives in France and are any of its cheeses reaching our tables?

ROQUEFORT—Arguably this is the world's most historically significant and enduring blue cheese, a true product and expression of its unique and specific *terroir*, and a cheese that has inspired many modern greats. A top Roquefort should present a generous, opulent profile, with enough salt to balance its sweet cream flavors. I like it semisoft throughout, with a creamy texture around the outside and some softening toward its interior, although with a firm heart. Carles has remained my favorite of the Roquefort brands, but I never take this for granted: I'm constantly taste-testing it against other brands—applying the all-important criteria of balance (no oversalting) and complex raw-milk flavor, bite without harshness, and soft buttery consistency. (See also page 352.)

TOME DES BAUGES—Like the Le Moulis, this is a pressed (but not cooked) cheese from the mountains, in this case the Haute-Savoie. The AOC for Tome des Bauges was ratified in 2002 and it includes provisions for using the raw milk of the ancient traditional Abondance, Tarine, and/or Montbeliard cow breeds. Compared with its close cousin, the Tomme de Savoie, the Bauges is more artisanal and a bit milder. The Bauges is graceful, unassuming, buttery, and thick in consistency, with lovely clotted-cream flavors.

TASTING PLATE

A Taste of France

CHAROLAIS

BRILLAT-SAVARIN

ABBAYE DE BELLOCQ

CASINCA CHÈVRE

TOMME FERMIÈRE D'ALSACE

LAGUIOLE VIEUX

COMTÉ (FORT DES ROUSSES)

ROQUEFORT (CARLES)

For our tasting tour of France, we start with a goat's milk Charolais, from Burgundy (there's also a cow version). It's light, creamy, smooth, and not quite as tart or chalky as its cousins, the Loire Valley chèvres. The Charolais is more clay-like.

Next up is the triple-crème Brillat-Savarin, which is really the epitome of a luxury cheese. It is semisoft, buttery, rich, and smooth—and physically quite fragile—for a nice contrast to the characteristic textures and flavors of the goat's milk Charolais.

OPPOSITE: Clockwise from bottom right: Charolais; Brillat-Savarin; Abbaye de Bellocq; Casinca Chèvre; Tomme Fermière d'Alsace; Laguiole Vieux; Comté (Fort des Rousses); Roquefort (Carles).

Roquefort is arguably the world's most historically significant and enduring blue cheese, and a cheese that has inspired many modern greats.

Second only to Pierre-Robert, the Brillat is a "go-to" triple crème as it is available year round, reliable, and very well balanced at peak. Although it's produced industrially and the versions we see here in the United States are pasteurized, when they get it right it approaches true greatness. One quality I really appreciate in the Brillat: It has just enough *Penicillium candidum* growth on its rind to give it a subtle mushroomy flavor note, which is the telltale sign that what you have in your mouth is cheese rather than butter. The Brillat has the rare distinction of having been named by Henri Androuët (father of Pierre) after a famous historical personage: author and gastronome Jean Anthelme Brillat-Savarin (1755–1826).

The Abbaye de Bellocq takes us from the Île-de-France, way up north near Paris where Brillat-Savarin is made, down to Basque country in the extreme southwest. An ancient cheese (as opposed to the Brillat-Savarin, which was created in the 1930s) made from raw sheep's milk in a Benedictine abbey, the Abbaye de Bellocq belongs to the Ossau-Iraty family and, like many of its type, is formidable, reliable, durable, and very approachable. In firm contrast to the triple crème, the Bellocq has full fruity, nutty aromas. It glistens with sheep's milk butterfats at room temperature and is a consistent crowd pleaser.

The Casinca is a Corsican cheese with an orangish washed rind and a light yellowish paste—all uncommon traits among goat cheeses. Comparable cheeses include Judy Schad's Mont St. Francis, Gianaolis Caldwell's Wimer Winter, Chevrotin des Aravis from the mountainous Haute-Savoie in eastern France, and the Swiss Holzige Geiss. Pleasantly tangy and tart, the Casinca announces its Mediterranean roots with a little more salt and a more clay-like texture than the latter two. The Casinca is semisoft at peak, providing a good contrast in consistency to the harder Abbaye, and its flavors are sharper and more focused.

What follows is a trio of noble raw cow's milk cheeses, each from very different regions, with distinct character, and each offering progressively stronger, more complex, and persistent profiles.

The Tomme Fermière, from the lush pastures of Alsace, is a less industrial, more authentic farmhouse cheese than most Morbier types. Like Morbier, it is smear ripened (a lighter form of washing, more like rubbing, is applied) and buttery but is thicker and more dense in texture with fuller flavors in a wider range and with greater persistence. Its finish, reminiscent of lightly salted butter, includes a nice note of spicy fruitiness.

The aged Laguiole, from the Auvergne and adjoining south-central areas, is drier than the Tomme Fermière and somewhat crumbly, for contrasting mouth feel. It has deeper flavors and more tart acidity. Generally regarded as France's ancient cousin of the British farmhouse Cheddars, it has an equally long, delightful finish as the Cheddars but is less fruity and also less acidic; perhaps you could say it's more akin to a Keen's than a Montgomery's.

Next comes France's answer to another great type, the authentic Swiss Alpine Gruyères and Emmentalers. Fort des Rousses, the best brand of aged Comté I've encountered, is outstanding when aged from 18 months to 2 years. Both harder in consistency and smoother in texture than the Laguiole, it conjures an authentically rustic yet nevertheless elegant taste of the French Alps—very approachable, and with a memorably long finish—albeit more restrained, less piquant, and also less sweet than a Rolf Beeler Swiss Gruyère.

No other French blue could be a more appropriate finale for such a representative plate than a fine Roquefort. A top-notch Carles, my favorite brand, is the quintessential showstopper, with piercing, penetrating mold-induced flavors and plenty of complementary salt adding to its hefty profile. But it is seldom if ever oversalted. A substantial, fruity red or a dessert wine such as Sauternes works hand in hand, ending your meal—and your Tour de Fromage—with a resounding, elegant, and balanced chorus of big, bold blue flavors balanced by an equally dignified yet powerful and inherently sweet liquid antidote.

A Langres awaits shipment in its little wooden box. It is a well-known and respected northern French stinky cheese.

CHAPTER 19

STUNNING STINKERS

AS WE LEARNED IN EARLIER CHAPTERS ON CHEESE HISTORY AND understanding cheesemaking, if it weren't for St. Benedict, there may never have been any washed-rind cheeses. He begat the monasteries and the monasteries begat washed-rind cheeses, of which the stinkers are the most remarkable subcategory. Washed rinds may have been invented before the medieval monastic sects began to perfect their recipes, but it was these pious, industrious habit-clad artisans who found the time to elaborate these cheeses and ultimately put them on the map.

Cheese is a butt of jokes largely because it can smell so weird, even downright awful, and yet many people continue to eat it happily. Let's face it, it *is* funny—but also some sort of miracle—that bad-smelling cheese can taste so good. There is more than a handful of delicious cheeses, which, if you let them sit on your kitchen counter at room temperature for a half-hour, can waft their aromas throughout your home. (Anyone stumbling upon such a scenario—"What *is* that smell?—will be relieved to discover it's only cheese.)

As noted in chapter 5 and elsewhere, bad smells often go hand in hand with good tastes. Even pasteurized-milk washed-rind cheeses can get pretty rambunctious in aroma. Yet it never ceases to amaze me how, with the good ones, those mild, milky flavors manage to come to the fore and politely, even gracefully, inhabit and stimulate your palate.

A smelly cheese plate: From left to right, Mont St. Francis; Fium'Orbo Brebis; Taleggio; Bergfichte; (Queso de la) Peral.

Stanser Chua Fladä

The main culprit—or rather our greatest ally—in creating all these marvelously stinky cheeses is our little friend, the *Brevibacterium linens* bug. The chemistry is a bit complex, but suffice it to say, *B. linens* thrive in humid atmospheric conditions, on moist surfaces, at moderate temperature conditions. Their enzymes "eat" their way gradually through a cheese to ripen it while melding, mellowing, and focusing its milk (and milk by-product) flavors. Meanwhile, a somewhat bizarre phenomenon occurs: Volatile complex compounds are emitted from the cheese's surface to be perceived as all kinds of sulfurous (eggy), cabbage-y, cow dungy, garlicky, and other curious odors. The *B. linens* also turn the cheese's exterior slimy and lend it some good-looking shades of orange, pink, and red.

Cow's milk seems to be the most forgiving medium for the stinkers; sheep's milk is harder to handle and goat's milk is the most difficult. The butterfats in the cow's milk are more stable and able to successfully resist the initial assaults of our bacterial friends. All the funky aromas and flavors develop more slowly and synergistically. (Stanser Chua Fladä is a nice example). Higher in solids (more concentrated), sheep's milk seems to develop the most profoundly funky, barnyardy, and at times daunting aromas. (Fium'Orbu and Schaf Reblochon are a couple of good examples). Yet the quickest of the three species milks to develop stinky aromas and flavors is goat; washed-rind goat cheeses have a shorter peak window and they turn gamey more quickly and easily.

Munster is the quintessential historical monastery cheese and among the original washed-rind stinkers. It's originally from Alsace, on the border of France and Germany. The family of Époisses-style cheeses, from Burgundy, is among the best known of the smelly types: it includes Affidélice, Aisy Cendré, and L'Ami du Chambertin. Langres, from northern France, is a cousin. Washed-rind types in the vein of Époisses—or, better, yet their unabashed Swiss neighbors (Bergfichte, Kuntener, etc.)—can be quite putrid smelling. They can also be just a little bit or only occasionally smelly, like Taleggio.

Unfortunately, quite a few sets of the French AOC rules permit the use of pasteurized milk in its classic cheeses, including certain stinkers. This is true for Époisses, and the result is often a cheese that's nice and milky-creamy all right, but its other flavors can't quite stand up to the salt, which ends up dominating.

American artisans have tackled the challenges of making smelly cheeses with a good deal of success, often picking up where the French left off—or where the U.S. Customs and Border Protection barred the door. They've come out with cheeses that hit their prime at the barely legal threshold of 61 days. The best of these types still maintain their fresh-milk profiles but start to develop some pungent aromas and evolved, deep, buttery flavors. Cowgirl Creamery's Red Hawk, Cato Corner's Hooligan, and Dancing Cow's Bourrée are among those; north of the border with Canada, Le Detour's Magie de Madawaska is another worthy stinker.

Max's Picks: The World's Greatest Smelly Cheeses
You'll note that four of the nine outstanding odiferous delicacies in the following listing are American, yet further confirmation of how far our U.S. artisans have come in the past quarter century.

BERGFICHTE—The spruce bark girdle gives this cheese an extra, mildly resinous flavor kick; in this respect it replicates a VACHERIN MONT D'OR, but it is aged to a minimum of 60 days, making it legal in the United States, and is also available year-round. (See also page 299.)

DURRUS—My favorite Irish cheese, a taste of that country's wild western *terroir*. Jeffa Gill is a modern-day cheese heroine for resisting pressure from the pasteurization police. I like a Durrus aged 2 to 4 months but not much beyond, when it may go over the hill. It's very aromatic, with full, meaty, delicious milk flavors yet plenty of good grace and balance.

FIUM'ORBU BREBIS—From Corsica, this is a one-of-a-kind real stinker made by a 2,000-year-old recipe. It's rustic, variable and develops funky aromas that can be off-putting. Although it comes on strong, it exits gracefully.

GRAYSON—From Virginia cheese farmers Helen and Rick Feete, Grayson improved year by year in the late 1990s and early 2000s and achieved world-class status by around 2006. It's full flavored and smelly and perhaps not for everyone; it's meatier and stronger than a mature TALEGGIO but not quite as forceful as a KUNTENER. (See also page 286.)

INNERSCHWEIZER SCHAFKÄSE (AKA SCHAF REBLOCHON)—This has got to be the single stinkiest cheese I've ever encountered. It delivers a strong, sheepy smell prior to unveiling its beautiful, lush, complex, raw-milk, long-finishing flavor profile.

KUNTENER—When it comes to stinkers, the Swiss know how to make 'em, and this, along with the BERGFICHTE, is a prime example. Made with raw cow's milk, the Kuntener is velvety and buttery; it fills the mouth and has a luxuriously long finish. Strength-wise, I'd likely place it after a *tomme*-style cheese and before a stout farmhouse Cheddar. (See also page 300.)

MONT ST. FRANCIS—The only washed-rind goat's milk cheese on this select list, it can smell a little goaty. For a stinker, its flavors are smooth, balanced, and not so sweet; it has some good goat's milk acids and its salt doesn't get in their way. (See also page 00.)

WIMER WINTER—Lighter on its feet, less pungent but not totally dissimilar to a FIUM'ORBU, the Wimer is also the nuttiest-tasting cheese of these picks. It's normally aged 60 to 80 days, which is why it is only mildly smelly. (See also below.)

WINNIMERE—A moderately stinky new American classic; the Kehler Brothers have done a fine job improving this cheese since they invented it soon after the turn of the twenty-first century. (See also page 271.)

TASTING PLATE
Not for the Faint of Heart: A Smelly Cheese Plate
MONT ST. FRANCIS
FIUM'ORBU BREBIS
TALEGGIO
BERGFICHTE (OR WINNIMERE)
(QUESO DE LA) PERAL

I've organized this plate in a classic goat-sheep-cow progression, beginning with the Mont St. Francis, a semisoft raw goat's milk cheese available 9 or more months per year. I like it relatively young (no older than 75 days), when it's off-white, a little smelly, but still fairly mild. Even on the mild side, though, a Mont St. Francis offers a pretty distinct, dramatic and profound flavor and aroma package. It packs a wallop and I'd say it is one of the strongest if not the strongest of the washed-rind goat cheeses.

The Fium'Orbu, which follows and is the only 100 percent sheep's milk cheese in this group, can have a wicked aroma and mount a fierce attack but is mild and balanced on the finish. It's good semisoft and youngish; it can also work well a bit older and drier. I especially appreciate the way a Fium'Orbu ages out, even to the point of becoming firm. It also has soupçon of fishiness or seafood, which you wouldn't normally say in favor of a cheese, but I find quite pleasant and authentic in this Corsican character.

Taleggio is the Italian ambassador to this stinky lineup, reappearing here after a cameo on the Italian plate in chapter 17. Here it shows up in the guise of a somewhat subtle, smooth "mellow stinker" with tremendous appeal at different stages of its development. Taleggio is potentially quite smelly, meaty, and fairly insistent in aroma yet still elegant and normally polite in flavor, albeit big and beefy; try to get a raw-milk version, though a well-made pasteurized one can be fine. Taleggio is smoother in consistency, compared to the Fium'Orbu, which has a stickier, tackier texture. A top Taleggio has a long, slow, penetrating flavor profile backed up with a little bit of salt. The overall effect is like eating the best thick, creamy mashed potatoes you've ever tasted. It's a comfort food cheese to the max.

A close-up of Stanser Chua Fladä

With the Bergfichte, listed as a first choice over the Winnimere only because it's available for a longer period of each year, we start to enter the realm of stronger flavors and longer, more insistent finishes. Bergfichte's consistency ranges from semisoft to almost runny. The spruce bark gives it a resinous, mossy fertile aroma like the forest after a warm rain, and it has a baconlike flavor, as opposed to the Taleggio, which is a bit more on the eggy side. A Winnimere is, in some sense, the American version of the Swiss Bergfichte, and so a good alternative.

Although it's featured more than once throughout this book, let's end this progression with La Peral, if for no other reason than its unique status as both blue *and* stinky but not washed rind. Because the blues are the strongest-tasting cheese category, you might imagine at least some of them would be stinky, too, but they usually aren't. La Peral is the exception. It does smell barnyardy, and you might even detect some roasted garlic in its nose. One of Peral's many distinguishing traits is its firm yet moist texture. Peral's pungent aromas, its touch of the blue and its sheep cream kicker make it stand out over and above the Berfichte. It also has more salt, making it an appropriate finishing act but in no way too loud for this plate of "charmingly aromatic" cheeses.

CHAPTER 20

CHAMPION CHEDDARS

ONE OF THE UNFORTUNATE ANOMALIES OF CHEESE HISTORY IS THE FACT that the name Cheddar was never properly defined or protected. Sometimes I wonder how the English could have been so trusting and innocent to have sat by while opportunistic cheesemakers all over the world copied one of their greatest cheeses and purloined its name. Now, under the aegis of the Slow Food movement, the defenders of genuine English farmhouse Cheddar are making some moves to legislate its legitimacy. Slow Food UK, for example, convened a presidium that defined "Artisan Somerset Cheddar" and admitted the few "real deals" to this exclusive club.

The homeland of Cheddar is Somerset in western England, although there are authentic farmhouse Cheddar types made in other parts of Great Britain and the United States. (Indeed, if there were two major subcategories of real Cheddar, they should probably be, first, English Farmhouse Cheddar and then all other Cheddar types, with subcategories by region, including Vermont and other U.S. zones.) The two greatest authentic English farmhouse Cheddars are Montgomery's and Keen's. They've been joined by Westcombe, relatively speaking the new kid on the block. Quicke's is another distinguished English farmhouse Cheddar, from a bit farther to the west and south than the other three. Reade's (aka Isle of Mull Cheddar), is from the island of the same name in Scotland.

Two fine Cheddars: From the left, Keen's and Fiscalini Bandage.

Montgomery's Cheddars for sale at Neal's Yard Dairy, London.

TWO ENGLISH GREATS (WE COMPARE, YOU JUDGE)

Both George Keen and Jamie Montgomery, who are the heads of their respective dairy farming and cheesemaking operations, emphasize the importance of pasture-fed herds and also of starter cultures. "What the animals eat and what the starter cultures are determine the flavor of the cheese, in that order of importance," says Montgomery. Five different bacteria have been identified in the mother culture used to start each daily batch of Keen's Cheddar, and samples have been preserved in a lab so they'll never be lost. Montgomery's started with four of the same five strains. This may account for some—but certainly not all—of the differences between these two great cheeses.

Montgomery told us he looks to control acidity and also moisture levels in order to bring out the full range of flavors in his milk. Too much of either can be problematic. "For my palate," he says, "excess acidity just knocks out all the other wonderful flavors, including the nuttiness and the fruitiness."

Keen is the more deliberate, understated, and upright of the two; Montgomery is the more worldly, rumpled, and conspicuously enthusiastic. Placing them in U.S. geographical terms, Keen would be an understated and highly successful Midwest farmer, Montgomery a hip California health food entrepreneur. Is it my imagination or are the different personalities of these two master cheesemakers reflected in their cheeses?

Without trying to influence opinions about their relative merits, let's compare these two great cheeses. At a given age, Monty's is more moist and has a more rounded, deeper profile. Keen's is the drier, more dense, more straightforward, traditional cheese. Chances are if you consult an American palate, it will prefer the Monty's. A British palate, on the other hand, will more likely tilt toward the Keen's. We did a comparison tasting with some British friends and they tersely declared their preference for the more stolid Keen's: It was the taste they recalled from childhood.

George Keen himself told us the greatest measure he employs when judging his cheeses is tradition: "When older people try my cheeses and they say, 'Okay, this reminds me of a taste I had when I was young,' I know we're doing our job well. We aim to make cheese the way our grandparents made it."

Jamie Montgomery attributes the difference between his cheeses and Keen's mostly to the way the curds are milled. After cheddaring, the curds have a resilient, rubbery consistency and a striated texture like cooked chicken breast. If you chew them, they actually squeak in your mouth. They're relatively flavorless, with a mild, milky acidity and barely a hint of the depth and complexity they'll develop with age. At this stage, they are ready to be passed through a mechanical chopping device—the mill—before being placed in large cylindrical molds to be pressed and formed, attaining the unique textures and flavors of a real farmhouse Cheddar.

The Montgomery operation uses a traditional "peg mill," which tears the curds and results in a more open-textured or "airy" cheese, whereas at Keen's, they use a newer "chip mill," which cuts the curds into discrete finger-sized pieces and results in a more dense, less friable (meltable) cheese. Lancashire makers put their curds through a mill with even smaller pegs, crushing them and yielding a different texture nuance, helping to distinguish this other British cheese.

The Montgomery's Cheddars selected by Randolph Hodgson and colleagues are already aged for a year at the farm before they're shipped to the Neal's Yard Dairy *affinage* facility in London. Hodgson fully credits Montgomery, though it is very much a collaborative relationship. Hodgson's assessments and advice, the feedback from his early and frequent tastings, are taken into account and often put into practice via recipe adjustments. Montgomery, in turn, credits cheesemaker Bridges, though the buck actually stops at Jamie's desk: He is not only the shepherd who manages the farm's herds but also the captain who steers this entire cheesemaking vessel. Both his family's name and its reputation rest solidly on those cheeses. "I know what I like and what I want from our cheeses," he says. "Steven and I talk about this. He and his assistant cheesemakers know how to deliver."

FROM TOP: A close-up of Ogleshield; George Keen shows a visitor the cheddaring process.

Max's Picks: The Great British Cheddars

KEEN'S—Keen's is a fabulous cheese, scaling the heights of artisanal perfection in similar guise to Monty's but from a slightly different angle. Without evoking the *S* word (sharp), Keen's is an assertive, bold-tasting cheese, stronger, tangier, and slightly more acidic than Monty's.

LINCOLNSHIRE POACHER—An English farmhouse Cheddar type, more brittle and, as its dashing name would indicate, with deeper flavors than its Somerset cousins. The brother team of Simon and

A good portion of the Montgomery farm herd grazes on the slopes of Cadbury Castle, the ancient hill fort nearby believed to be the site of King Arthur's Camelot. It was excavated beginning in the late 1960s; the local pub houses an exhibition of its artifacts.

Tim Jones are its farmer-producers, based in a beautiful rolling hill district of east central England called the Lincolnshire Wolds.

MONTGOMERY'S—Montgomery's is one of those cheeses about which you are compelled to ask, "Is there anything better than this?" And the answer is almost always a resounding no. Montgomery's has become the yardstick by which other Cheddars are measured; in fact, it begs comparison to *all* other candidates for "world's greatest cheese," including Sbrinz, Parmigiano-Reggiano, and Spenwood. I always think of Monty's as having a fruity quality. Texture- and consistency-wise, it's crumbly yet moist, and its flavor profile is rich, complex, and round; it also epitomizes balance.

ISLE OF MULL CHEESE (aka Reade's or Tobermory)—The cows are fed the spent barley from whiskey production, giving this cheese a peaty flavor and offering a taste of the wild Scottish moors. It is often referred to as Isle of Mull Cheddar, though I'm sure the Reade family does not presume to purloin the Cheddar name. I've also heard the Isle of Mull called Tobermory, which is the name of the main town on the island. Whatever you call it, it's a great British (as opposed to *English*) farmhouse Cheddar type—that is, it's made in the classic style but has its distinct expression of *terroir*.

WESTCOMBE—This relative newcomer to the Artisan Somerset Cheddar elite has quickly developed a reputation putting it in the same class as Monty's and Keen's. Tom Calver revived the Westcombe Dairy, where cheese had been made since the late nineteenth century, and with cheesemaker Bob Bramley began turning out a farmhouse Cheddar in the 1990s. The Westcombes I've tasted are a bit sweeter, gentler, and less assertive than others of their type but nonetheless beautifully balanced.

Max's Picks: Outstanding U.S. Cheddars

BEECHER'S—Although it doesn't make use of the Cheddar name, Beecher's Flagship Reserve, from Seattle, is another outstanding American Cheddar-style artisanal cheese. It features a smoother consistency and less crumbly or open texture than the other Americans. To me it has a refreshing West Coast character—very lively, friendly, and approachable, as compared with the more grounded and stolid New Englanders. It does have the American Cheddar tang but its aromatics offer a balancing sweetness.

CABOT—Cabot Clothbound is one of two outstanding Vermont Cheddars with aged special select or reserve versions ripened at Jasper Hill Farm. The Cabot definitely embodies the signature New England Cheddar style: Tasting it, the first thing you notice is that upfront tang. A big part of this cheese's success is the way it melts and crumbles around your mouth as it lays its flavors across your tongue. The Cabot Creamery, a co-op founded in the early twentieth century, is still owned by its farmer-suppliers throughout Vermont and offers tours of its factory in the town of Cabot.

FISCALINI—Probably the most outstanding American artisanal Cheddar is the Bandage Cheddar made by Mariano Gonzalez at Fiscalini Cheese Co., in California's Central Valley. The Fiscalini is as pretty as a Cheddar can be. It is crumbly and more open-textured than the other American farmhouse Cheddars. Its flavor profile is smooth, rounded, and very well balanced, with a notable but restrained component of acidity and a haylike flavor note, which I attribute to fresh grasses in the drier California climate.

GRAFTON—Both Cabot and this famous Vermont village cheese company, also founded as a co-op in the late nineteenth century and now part of a foundation whose goal is to preserve traditional local culture, market a range of lesser, more commercial cheese options. Grafton's limited edition Clothbound Reserve, aged at Jasper Hill, also features the New England tang and in fact may be the most sour of the American farmhouse Cheddars. It also has a very nice long finish and a host of green Vermont pasture flavors.

Whether Vermont Cheddar or American Farmhouse Cheddar or some similar designation(s) will ever be defined and protected—and indeed whether the United States will ever legislate *any* cheese appellations—remains to be seen. This distinguished group of cheeses would be a good place to start.

CHEESE CHECKLIST

WHAT MAKES ARTISAN SOMERSET CHEDDARS GREAT?

- *TERROIR*: The Somerset climate is damp, allowing for lush pasture growth, resulting in great cheese-making milk.
- **FARMSTEAD PRODUCTION:** The milk comes from the farms' own herds, managed by the cheese producers.
- **RAW MILK**
- **STARTER CULTURES:** Bacteria strains are carefully selected for their flavor-giving qualities and preserved as "mother cultures" to start each batch of cheese.
- **ANIMAL RENNET**, the best flavor producer among curdling elements for this type of cheese
- **TRADITIONAL MANUFAC-TURING:** Every step is done by hand, including (and especially) the cheddaring.
- **CLOTHBOUND:** Again, the traditional by-hand method of controlling aging, augmented by lard-rubbing
- Aging a minimum of 11 months and up to 18 months

CHAPTER 21

MIRACULOUS MOLDIES: SINGING (IN PRAISE OF) THE BLUES

REGARDLESS OF THE MANNER IN WHICH THE FLAVOR-INDUCING MOLD is introduced into the curds and/or the forming cheese, the one fundamental and outstanding trait shared by all members of this class is the bite imparted by those blue and green molds. In great blue cheeses, the molds act as flavor enhancers—they are a turn-up-the-volume button—without overshadowing any depth and complexity or overwhelming any attractive components in their profiles. As is the case with hot, spicy, and also very salty flavors, the sharpness of cheese molds is an acquired taste, one based on building up a tolerance. If your palate hasn't been exposed to a good deal of that blue bite, it takes some getting used to. Once you clear the hump, once you have the blue experience under your belt, you can start to judge for yourself whether a cheese is delightful, subtle, well-rounded, and complex—or just blue and nothing more.

The main criterion for a great blue cheese is you ought to be able to taste the milk. The blue should never drown out whatever sweet, grassy, or other plant-based flavors are inherent in the milk—not to mention any other aspects of *terroir*, transmitted as minerally or earthy tastes. The blue should focus all a cheese's other flavors, bringing them to the forefront.

Two blues: From left, Stichelton and Stilton.

A blue cheese in cross-section showing its piercing marks.

Blue cheeses will naturally be saltier than almost any other type (though some of the washed-rind varieties can get pretty salty, too). The blues require more salt as part of their development process, to encourage molds and discourage competing microflora. One hazard of this necessity for salt as a ripening catalyst is even the greatest blue cheeses are susceptible to oversalting. Mastery of the blues involves recognizing all the other flavors they're capable of delivering and also being on the lookout for their two main potential faults: overwhelming bite and excessive salt.

As introduced in chapter 12, their extra salt is why blue cheeses generally cry out for sweeter, fruitier wines and why this pairing model yields many marriages made in heaven. There isn't anything better in the real-cheese world than a strong, biting, complex blue cheese with a sweet yet balanced dessert wine. It's one of the best illustrations of the added value of cheese-wine pairings, of the notion that a matchup can elevate both partners. On more than one occasion in tasting classes, we've observed how the synergy between a cheese and a wine can actually bring out additional flavors—often savory, baconlike ones with a good dose of *umami*—that did not emerge from the cheese or the wine alone.

Until quite recently—really the turn of the twenty-first century—the American audience had not experienced the pleasure of recognizing the diversity of flavors blue cheeses can offer. Most of our native blues were one dimensional, indistinguishable, and better suited for salad dressing. Among imports, there were some respectable Roqueforts and decent Gorgonzolas but not much else. It was a narrow selection within a limited range. Boy, have things changed! The blue cheese frontier has opened up, and there is a wonderful roster of both American and overseas cheeses available. They feature complex raw-milk profiles and sweet, fruity flavors where the blue is often merely the exclamation point and frequently not even the primary component. As much as some cheese connoisseurs might become fascinated, even a little obsessed, with harsh molds that can taste so good, in the final analysis it's all about the milk and how it ripens into delectable cheese.

If any (or all) cheesemakers were looking for my advice—and I don't presume they are—I'd only mention they need not wait for the blue-green molds to develop in an outwardly apparent manner before shipping their cheeses to market. Many of the most delicious moldy cheeses arrive without a lot of color in their pastes.

Carefully selected species and strains of molds have already lent their accents to the flavors of the milk and ripening cheese; the visual evidence, the obvious veining, will follow in due course.

Max's Picks: The Best of the Blues

The quartet of the world's most famous blues consists of Roquefort, Stilton, Cabrales, and Gorgonzola—each of which represents a great cheese-producing nation: France, England, Spain, and Italy, respectively. Whatever quibbles one might have with any one of these historic types, they are the framework, the starting point, for any discussion of blue cheeses.

BAYLEY HAZEN—The Kehlers up at Jasper Hill in Vermont deserve a lot of credit for working hard to make this into a world-class American original. Expressing lush, green Vermont *terroir* and striking a very fine balance, their Bayley Hazen is distinct, complex, and very tasty. (See also page 267 and sidebar, page 271.)

BEENLEIGH BLUE—Made by Robin Congdon in Totnes, South Devon, this English sheep's milk superstar is very poised, sweet, and restrained yet with an expansive flavor profile that spreads enticingly over the entire palate. It is also one of the few cheeses to maintain its superiority after converting from raw to pasteurized milk; this is a tribute to its makers and also to the quality of the milk. Because of its delicate, sweet, and balanced qualities, it would always be among the first cheeses in an all-blue tasting plate.

BLEU DE LAQUEUILLE—Alongside a top Roquefort, this would be my first choice among French blues. It's definitely the outstanding cow's milk cheese of its type. I think of the Laqueuille, which is from the town of the same name in the heart of the Auvergne not far from Clermont-Ferrand, as a more artisanal and place-specific alternative to its two close relatives, Fourme d'Ambert and Bleu d'Auvergne. In some instances, the Fourme may have been commercialized; the Bleu has a wider production zone.

CABRALES—You can't really claim blue-cheese connoisseurship until you've sampled this famous Asturian cheese at different stages of its development. This includes its meanest, nastiest old age, where there is no stronger cheese. Cabrales at this juncture is still among the world's great blues, but approach it with caution—and don't try to sample other cheeses afterward—because its bite lives up to (if not exceeds) its bark. Traditional Cabrales was made from

An impressive display of blues at Neal's Yard Dairy.

A great blue cheese ought to at least give you intimations of sweetness and at least a helping of those inherent well-integrated welcoming, round (buttery, oily, smooth, mouth-coating) flavors and textures.

all three milks, giving it additional balance and complexity, but in modern times it's almost all cow's milk. A mature, ripe Cabrales is semisoft and very creamy in consistency but with somewhat granular texture, salty and strong. (See also chapter 16, page 308.)

GORGONZOLA—Italy's most famous blue comes in younger *dolce* (sweet) and older *piccante* (sharp, spicy, piquant) versions, also formerly referred to as *naturale* and *stagionato*. The sweet, young versions are not all that exciting; the older ones can turn overly "cowy" or barnyardy. A well-selected and perfectly aged *piccante* is your best bet. (See also page 320.)

PERAL—When this one's good, it's great, which is what makes it not only among my favorite blues but favorite cheeses, period. (See also page 310.)

ROGUE RIVER BLUE—The signature cheese in a very strong lineup from Rogue Creamery, it has an impressive volume and brilliant intensity of flavors. Fruity, complex, and with appropriate salt, this is a fine modern American example of how multifaceted a blue cheese can be. Cheesemaker Cary Bryant does a great job balancing it, bringing out the sweetness and creaminess of the milk with judicious use of cultures and molds. Rogue River's Echo Mountain is another outstanding blue, which comes around every so often and is a get-it-while-you-can cheese, made with the addition of some goat's milk. (See also page 355 and sidebar, page 282.)

ROQUEFORT—Carles is my perennial first choice among the various brands of this great cheese. It is salty but not oversalted, zesty, quite strong, and very persistent with a long finish. All of these qualities are kept in balance by the creaminess and heft of its raw sheep's milk. Coulet and Vieux Berger are two other Roquefort labels worth trying. Papillon, one of the bigger producers, makes some fine reserve cheeses, but it also markets several more commercial grades, so be sure to know which one you're getting. (See also page 333.)

STICHELTON—This is perhaps one of the more exciting developments in real cheese over the past decade, a collaboration between Randolph Hodgson of Neal's Yard Dairy and U.K.-based American Joe Schneider, who won the title of Britain's champion cheesemaker. Hodgson and Schneider set out to create a traditional, raw-milk Stilton, harking back to its origins in the eighteenth century. Stichelton bears the original name of the village of Stilton; ironically, it can't be called Stilton because that cheese's legal definitions stipulate it must be made from pasteurized milk. Schneider started making it in late 2006, and it took the better part of 2 years to get it right. Sticheltons can be a little wild but not in a bad way; certainly, they're louder than any stately Stilton. Their full raw-milk flavors are backed up by sweet aromas.

STILTON—Colston-Bassett has consistently set the standard among Stiltons for many years. Even though they use pasteurized milk and are a factory operation, this great blue has balance and a smooth, buttery yet crumbly consistency, making it a fine dessert cheese. I love the way the British make their blue cheeses and I appreciate the reliability of a Colston-Basset Stilton.

TASTING PLATE
A Blue Cheese Plate
BEENLEIGH BLUE
FOURME D'AMBERT
STILTON
ROGUE RIVER BLUE
ROQUEFORT

A Colston-Bassett Stilton waiting to be put on display at Neal's Yard Dairy.

This may be more of an academic exercise because in the real world I almost never get a request for an all-blue lineup. But it can be interesting for comparisons and to illustrate—or, quite literally, taste—the progressions possible and the wide range of flavors available among the various types of blues. All great blues are well balanced; some are sweeter and milder than others. Once your palate gets past tasting nothing but the bite, it's a pleasant surprise to discover how many other interesting flavor notes they can offer, many of them in the fruity and even floral realms of the spectrum.

Our blue plate starts with the Beenleigh, which is made from sheep's milk. It is usually the first one I think of as a "dessert blue." The Beenleigh is sweet, gentle, and moist but crumbly, which is a trait I've found to be typical not only of British blues but of many other types from our ancestral island nation. The French style is much smoother and manifests itself in a much more butter-like consistency, the kind where, using a sharp knife, you get that feeling of gliding right through the paste with scant resistance. The British consistency will feel more solid and chunky by comparison. Of the Beenleigh's numerous other positive attributes, it exudes a sweet almost perfumed aroma usually only found in raw-milk cheeses.

The ancient and formidable Fourme d'Ambert has deeper flavors, is less sweet, and therefore constitutes a logical step after the Beenleigh. The Fourme is not particularly salty or strong for a blue, but it does deliver a healthy ration of cow flavor. It smells and tastes like a cow's milk cheese, which to me reaffirms, for the second cheese in a row on this plate, that there's a lot more to blues than just the blue. Here you have a sweetish sheep's milk blue from the English countryside immediately followed by a very old type from the south central highlands of France, which shares highly recognizable cow's milk flavors with its nonblue compatriots from the same region (Laguiole, Cantal, Salers).

The Stilton, alas also from pasteurized milk yet bold and nobly elegant, is a fitting centerpiece for the two mellower blues before and the two more imperious ones to follow. It packs a much more thunderous flavor punch than the first two but is nevertheless quite smooth and creamy in texture, especially for a British cheese. Perhaps contradicting the previous generalization observed in connection with the Beenleigh but once again proving there are so many shades of blue.

Next is Oregon's Rogue River, with a multifaceted profile and a big enough impact on the palate to equal the Stilton but a creamier texture and more resonant mouth feel. You can detect a fruity note from the pear brandy that soaked the syrah leaves for the Rogue's wrappers, a raisiny flavor from the leaves themselves, and multiple other flavors of *terroir* and vegetation being transmitted by this skillfully manipulated and faithfully nurtured raw milk. The Rogue is refreshingly moist, with a higher water content than the Stilton. It's also a definite step up in terms of depth and range of flavors and thereby continues the momentum of this progression.

We finish where we started, which is with a 100 percent sheep's milk cheese, Roquefort. I think this helps reiterate the point that regardless of how strong and persistent it might be, a great blue cheese ought to give you intimations of sweetness and a helping of those inherent well-integrated welcoming, round (buttery, oily, smooth, mouth-coating) flavors and textures. The refrain for Roquefort is it's a hard act to follow, a strong, piquant, and salty finale for many a variegated plate full of bold, individualistic cheeses. I always like to say the only other place to go might be a Cabrales, should you care to chance an extreme encounter.

OPPOSITE: A blue plate: From top, Beenleigh Blue; Fourme d'Ambert; Stilton; Rogue River Blue; Roquefort.

CHAPTER 22

CHÈVRE BY ANY OTHER NAME (WOULD TASTE AS TART AND FRESH AND CREAMY AND . . .)

OF THE THREE PRINCIPAL DAIRY SPECIES, GOATS MAY VERY WELL provide the best drinking milk, as the old saying goes. All stereotypes, preferences, and prejudices aside, it does give us some truly spectacular cheeses, offering unexpected range and depth of flavor profiles. Sheep's and cow's milk cheeses are more predictable: It's easier to tell where they're headed. Goat cheeses, by comparison, have more potential for intrigue and I've found they deliver their share of very pleasant surprises. Beyond the "standard" chèvres of the Loire Valley and the scores of New World cheeses emulating them, goat cheeses of many different types—particularly aged ones—tend to offer more flavor nuances, more unexpected twists and turns.

As mentioned in our restaurant chapter, probably the most frequent prohibition I get from diners is "no goat cheeses." This aversion is a little surprising to me. Some people say they simply can't stand the goaty flavor of anything to do with goat's milk. Others may have been turned off by the plethora of boring, bland, uninspiring, often soapy or chalky goat cheeses offered in commercial, mass-market venues.

An all-goat tasting: Clockwise from top, Classico; Harbourne Blue; Purple Haze; Manchester.

Majorero: Spanish artistry in pasteurized goat's milk.

Some of the misconceptions about goat cheeses do have a basis in fact. It's true that goat cheeses contain unique acids, which can give distinct, somewhat biting notes to their profiles, especially if they're older and drier. Good (or great) goat cheeses, though, deliver flavors as fresh, subtle, mild, toothsome, and complex as any other cheese. Fine goat's milk cheeses rarely, if ever, taste goaty—and even if they do, whatever barnyardy notes are present will be balanced by other components. Perhaps people feel goat products are somehow unsanitary because the animals themselves are considered far-ranging, wild "garbage eaters." This is just not true, especially with regard to the carefully bred and nurtured dairy goats employed to make cheese. As for the notion that goat cheeses—especially the fresh types—taste bland, I offer the following: Many people have not had their palates caressed by the sublime textures and subtle flavors of well-made raw-milk artisanal chèvre styles. Once they taste the cheeses recommended below, I'm confident they'll change their minds.

Max's Picks: The Great Goat Cheeses

Absent of authentic young French chèvres, which are not available in the United States today and may even be becoming rare in Europe, this is a varied international selection confirming there is a lot more to the category than little white buttons of month-old pasteurized goat-milk curds. It features several of the challenging washed-rind and blue goat types. Clever, ambitious twenty-first-century producers have shown themselves more frequently willing to attempt these types than artisans of the past. I salute them for tackling this challenge.

ARACENA—I had heard about his one for quite a while and was delighted to make its acquaintance in Madrid in 2005, when I was worried it had maybe gone extinct. Aracena is best in the cooler half of the year—fall to early spring. It's organic and biodynamic, and when it's good, it's great—soft, creamy, and even when aged for over 60 days, able to retain its fresh milk flavors. (See also page 308.)

BLAUE GEISS—From one of Switzerland's best artisans, Willy Schmid, who also makes **BERGFICHTE**, this raw-milk "blue goat" is a special cheese and arguably the most successful of its type. I was first introduced to it by Caroline Hostettler in 2007. It looked like some kind of experiment gone awry, an amorphous moist cylinder covered with molds and bacteria in just about every shade of blue, green, brown and gray you could imagine. (Come to think of it, there were some yellows and purples, too.) Flavor-wise, it was electric, a showstopper, much more akin to a classic blue-veined cheese than any of its fellow goats. The Blaue Geiss is fairly rare and expensive but definitely worth a try. (See also page 300.)

CLASSICO—Tumalo Farms' Classico is a waxed, Gouda-style cheese usually made with pasteurized milk. I especially appreciate the limited-edition raw-milk version, but in any case it's a very fine American original. I've tasted Dutch goat's milk Goudas that were creamy and uninteresting by comparison; the Classico is pleasantly chalky and raises the bar higher for its category. Its paste is off-white to cream colored, surprising for a goat cheese. (See also page 361.)

GARROTXA—Surface molds, mostly *Penicillium glaucum,* ripen this cheese, giving it a creamy mouth feel and good depth and complexity of flavors. It's semifirm, refreshing, and offers hazelnut-like notes. Though made from pasteurized milk, a good Garrotxa is always a candidate for greatness.

(QUESO) MAJORERO—A unique firm, dryish expression of its volcanic Canary Islands *terroir,* this rustic delicacy, with its maritime and mineral accents, makes several of my all-star rosters, including the Iberian one (see page 309).

OLD KENTUCKY TOMME—You hear me mention Judy Schad and Mont St. Francis a lot, but this may have become my favorite of her Capriole lineup. Sturdy, pressed, firm but moist, the Old Kentucky has a thin natural rind. It ages out well, tastes creamy and a little salty but is almost always well balanced. It's a unique cheese, not entirely dissimilar to ELK MOUNTAIN TOMME and would give a top Ibores a run for its money.

UP IN SMOKE—As far as I know, this is a unique cheese that delivers a pleasant surprise, demonstrating what can be done when you start with a fresh little pasteurized semi-soft *chèvre* and jazz it up with some gentle smoking. (See also page 277.)

ELK MOUNTAIN TOMME—From Pholia Farm in the Rogue River Valley, Oregon, Elk Mountain is a firm, pressed, brined, raw goat's milk cheese and another rival for one the Spanish great Ibores. (See also page 290.)

Classicos ripening at Tumalo Farms, Oregon.

Happy goats head out to pasture at Fraga Farm.

MONTE ENEBRO—The surface-ripening *P. roqueforti* molds do a great job on this pasteurized-milk cheese. At peak, it can start to turn creamy; it remains graceful but attains some bite, making it assertive enough to take the middle spot in a tasting sequence. (See also page 309.)

NOCCETTO—This is a black walnut leaf–wrapped goat cheese from northern Italy made by Cora. It's semisoft and fresh but no wallflower and can make a pretty bold statement to start a tasting plate. There's a small amount of bitter nuttiness from the wrapper; otherwise you taste pure goat's milk, presented in the same form that was taken to market or used as coin from ancient to medieval times.

HARBOURNE BLUE—This is another of a challenging type that spells a tribute to the skills of its makers, Robin Congdon and Sari Cooper. If you can make a pasteurized goat's milk blue succeed, you are a brilliant cheesemaker. I like the Harbourne at about 5 to 6 months of age. If it's too intense, just wait and try it the next day; it is very likely to have mellowed and improved. Once they start to head in a certain direction, most cheeses—especially blues—will continue that way. Harbourne Blue is a remarkable exception.

TASTING PLATE
An All-Goat Lineup: Expect the Unexpected

PURPLE HAZE

CLASSICO

MANCHESTER

HARBOURNE BLUE

Katie Sharrow, working with the herd at Fraga Farm.

We start with a fun variation on a small chèvre, Purple Haze from Mary Keehn's Cypress Grove Farm; it's fresh-tasting, mild, soft, and delightfully creamy, a refreshing, pure, clean, palate-cleansing platform from which to launch this all-goat plate. It has a lingering but very gentle finish where you can taste subtle traces of the lavender and fennel, with which it's dusted prior to aging.

Next up is the Classico, which still exhibits the clean, fresh flavors you expect from fine goat cheeses, but it has a more chalky consistency, harder texture, and more depth of flavor, with well-balanced inherent sweetness. Even the pasteurized versions have a nice long finish. I really like its precise texture—firm, with a nice clean break—and the way the sweet, creamy flavors of the milk are allowed to shine through.

Consider Bardwell Farm's Manchester is one of the most successful washed-rind goat's milk cheese I can think of. Made from raw milk, it's much fuller flavored than the previous cheeses, with some pungent, barnyardy aromas, meaty flavors, and a good helping of *umami*. Manchester has a much deeper, funkier flavor profile than the Classico and its semifirm consistency is softer, providing contrast. You've got to like your goat flavors to appreciate the Manchester; it's strong and persistent but not bitingly sharp. (Note: The Manchester is best at no older than 4 months.)

Our closer, the Harbourne Blue, illustrates the wide range of goat-cheese flavors. The Harbourne is chalkier than the Manchester, providing good texture variation. It can be a touch desserty sweet like the sheep's milk Beenleigh Blue. Although a bit more variable, which is to be expected from this type, the Harbourne is a pretty sure bet as a graceful finisher for your all-goat plate. It's relatively mild for the blue category, which has very few successful goat's milk entries and certainly none like this one. If you wanted to take a more conservative tack, you might end with the surface mold-ripened Monte Enebro, or for a more outrageous finale, try the slimy, scary-looking Swiss Blaue Geiss.

CHEESE APPELLATIONS

THE FRENCH AOC SYSTEM

The French system is the oldest and most extensive one for protecting, classifying, and designating wines, spirits, and agricultural products. It is definitely the template for all other national and international food designations and therefore worthy of study in mastering cheese. Would that every cheese-nation had such a set of rules and regulations in place; most of the rest of Europe now comes close. Will we ever have an equivalent in the United States? Perhaps we should paraphrase General de Gaulle here: *How can you expect to organize a country with no cheese appellations??*

The French tradition began in the fifteenth century with edicts defining the who, what, and where of Roquefort. Legislation defining and protecting Roquefort was enacted beginning in 1666. The AOC system was put in place beginning in 1919. In 1925, Roquefort became the first product of any kind—including wines—to receive AOC status, although there were other official confirmations later. In 1935, further legislation created the Institut National des Appellations d'Origine (INAO), a branch of the French Ministry of Agriculture now known as the Institut National de l'Origine et de la Qualité.

The AOC rules specify manufacturing region, breeds, animal husbandry, cheesemaking, and *affinage*. As a cheese connoisseur, it's edifying to visit the French government website (www.iano.gouv.fr) and peruse some of the rules and definitions. Naturally, they are rich in place-names. It can be fun to try to sort out some of the system's many quirks. Overall, the French AOC is a great

model. It is remarkably well organized and well documented, if at times a bit overwhelming and complex in its details. As such, it is also a fair reflection of the incredible tapestry of French cheeses.

EUROPE FOLLOWS SUIT

In 1992, when the laws in the European Union went into effect, they added a second tier of food and beverage appellation designations, similar to those already in effect in France, Italy, Spain, and Portugal. The EU system has three fundamental levels, each with its own label: Protected Designation of Origin (PDO), Protected Geographical Indication (PGI), and Traditional Specialty Guaranteed (TSG). (Note: These acronyms tend to change from language to language; in French, Italian, and Spanish, for example, PDO becomes DOP.) The PDO (or DOP) is the most stringent and specific, the TSG the least. PDO designates foods that are grown and made in a defined geographical zone by certain prescribed methods; PGI is similar but only one of the three manufacturing stages—production, processing or preparation—must occur within the area; TSG refers to a traditional product but without specific provenance. You can search the EU website's agricultural section (www.ec.europe.eu/agriculture) for products by country or by category by searching these acronyms.

The national systems—AOC in France, DOP in Italy, DO in Spain and so forth—are coordinated with the EU one. The wheels of bureaucracy turn slowly, so understandably the process of applying for designa-

tions, awaiting reviews, and approvals—nationally or at the European level—can take several years or more. At the time of this writing, for example, Caseificio Pinzani in Tuscany had been waiting more than two years to hear about its DOP application for Pecorino delle Balze Volterrane.

All of the French AOC cheeses have received European DOP designation; several with lesser designations have also received their DOPs, notably Tomme de Savoie, Tomme des Pyrénées, and the Emmentals.

In Italy, the DOC (Denominazione di Origine Controllata) system began in 1963, mostly for wines but also for other agricultural products. In 1992, the Italian system was revised to reflect the European Union's new umbrella designations. The two main designations were renamed DOP and IGT (the Italian version of PGI). Every Italian DOP (or former DOP) cheese is now also officially a European DOP cheese as well.

The Spanish DO (Denominacion de Origen) system is set up a bit differently: it is regulated by local (or regional) counsels, called *consejos reguladores,* one for each major cheese appellation, each with its own website (all worth visiting). Of the European DOP cheeses from Spain, only Valdeón does not have a Spanish DO; it does, however, have an IGP, one level down from DOP and equivalent to the European PGI. As of this writing, the following Spanish DO cheeses were not (yet) on the European DOP roster: Afuega'l Pitu, Arzúa-Ulloa, Cebreiro, and San Simón da Costa.

The downside of appellation

designations is they can institutional-
ize the industrialization of cheeses; in
other words, they may legitimize
nontraditional standards and practices, diminishing specificity and
authenticity. The AOC for Crottin de
Chavignol, for example, permits the
use of frozen curds and only requires
10 days of aging. Some AOCs or
DOPs allow for excessive expansion
of production zones (as happened
temporarily with Roquefort); others
permit pasteurized milk. This may
mean the officially designated
version of a cheese is *less* artisanal
than other local versions. (An
example: Pont l'Évêque, which has
the AOC, and its cousin Pavé d'Auge;
of these two fine washed-rind cheeses
from Normandy, the versions we see
here in the United States of the
former are more industrial while the
latter are more old style and artisanal.) Sometimes recognition from a
body such as one of the raw cheesemakers' guilds is more meaningful
than qualification for a national or
international appellation designation.
It really depends upon how stringent
the criteria and standards are.

*European Union PDO (or DOP)
cheeses*

FRANCE (SEE AOC NOTE BELOW)

Abondance
Banon
Beaufort
Bleu d'Auvergne
Bleu des Causses
Bleu du Haut-Jura, de Gex, de
    Septmoncel
Bleu du Vercors
Brie de Meaux
Brie de Melun
Brocciu Corse or Brocciu
Cantal or Fourme de Cantal or
    Cantalet
Camembert de Normandie
Chabichou du Poitou

Chaource
Chevrotin
Comté
Crottin de Chavignol (or Chavignol)
Emmental de Savoie
Emmental Français Est-Central
Époisses de Bourgogne
Fourme d'Ambert (or Fourme de
    Montbrison)
Laguiole
Langres
Livarot
Maroilles (aka Marolles)
Mont d'Or (Vacherin du Haut-Doubs)
Morbier
Munster (Munster-Géromé)
Neufchâtel
Ossau-lraty
Pélardon
Picodon (de l'Ardèche or Picodon de
    la Drôme)
Pont-l'Évêque
Pouligny-Saint-Pierre
Reblochon (Reblochon de Savoie)
Rocamadour
Roquefort
Saint-Nectaire
Sainte-Maure de Touraine
Salers
Selles-sur-Cher
Tome des Bauges
Tomme de Savoie
Tomme des Pyrénées
Valençay

*Note: All French cheeses on this DOP
list also have French AOC status
except the following: Bleu de Vercors,
Chevrotin, Emmental de Savoie,
Emmental, Tomme de Savoie, Tomme
des Pyrénées*

ITALY

Asiago
Bitto
Bra
Caciocavallo Silano
Canestrato Pugliese
Casciotta d'Urbino
Castelmagno
Fiore Sardo

Fontina
Formai de Mut Dell'alta Valle
    Brembana
Gorgonzola
Grana Padano
Montasio
Monte Veronese
Mozzarella di Bufala Campana
Murazzano
Parmigiano Reggiano
Pecorino Romano
Pecorino Sardo
Pecorino Siciliano
Pecorino Toscano
Provolone Valpadana
Quartirolo Lombardo
Ragusano
Raschera
Robiola di Roccaverano
Spressa delle Giudicarie
Stelvio or Stilfser
Taleggio
Toma Piemontese
Valle d'Aosta Fromadzo
Valtellina Casera

PORTUGAL

Queijo de Azeitão
Queijo de Cabra Transmontano
Queijo de Évora
Queijo de Nisa
Queijo do Pico
Queijo Mestiço de Tolosa
Queijo Rabaçal
Queijo São Jorge
Queijo Serpa
Queijo Serra da Estrela
Queijo Terrincho
Queijos da Beira Baixa (Queijo de
    Castelo Branco, Queijo Amarelo da
    Beira Baixa, Queijo Picante da
    Beira Baixa)

SPAIN

Cabrales
Idiazábal
Mahón
Picón Bejes-Tresviso
Queso de Cantabria
Queso de l'Alt Urgell y la Cerdanya
Queso de La Serena

Queso de Murcia
Queso de Murcia al vino
Queso de Valdeón
Queso Ibores
Queso Majorero
Queso Manchego
Queso Palmero o Queso de la Palma
Queso Tetilla
Queso Zamorano
Quesucos de Liébana
Roncal
Torta del Casar

SWITZERLAND (AOC)
GRANTED
Berner (Oberländer) Hobelkäse/
 Berner Alpkäse

Emmentaler
Formaggio d'Alpe Ticinese
Gruyère
L'Etivaz
Raclette du Valais
Sbrinz
Tête de Moine
Vacherin Fribourgeois
Vacherin Mont d'Or

PENDING
Büendner Bergkaese
Buscium da Cavra
Sauerkäse (aka Bloderkäse)
Tomme Vaudoise
Note: *You can visit the website*
www.aoc-igp.ch for more complete
listings and updates on the status of
Swiss cheeses.

UNITED KINGDOM
Beacon Fell traditional Lancashire
 cheese
Bonchester cheese
Buxton Blue
Dorset Blue cheese
Dovedale cheese
Exmoor Blue cheese
Single Gloucester
Staffordshire cheese
Swaledale cheese, Swaledale ewes'
 cheese
Teviotdale cheese
West Country farmhouse Cheddar
 cheese
White Stilton cheese, Blue Stilton
 cheese

• APPENDIX 2 •

U.S. ARTISAN AND FARMSTEAD CHEESE PRODUCERS

Here are some top artisan producers in the United States. Many of
them offer lineups of multiple
cheeses, which I encourage you to try;
the following list contains cheeses
I've tasted and can definitely
recommend.

A
Achadinha Goat Cheese Company,
 Petaluma, CA—Capricious
Ancient Heritage Dairy, Scio,
 OR—Scio Heritage, Adelle, Odessa
 Blue
Andante Dairy, Petaluma,
 CA—various cheeses, cow, sheep,
 goat, mixed, triple crème

B
Beecher's Handmade Cheese, Seattle,
 WA—Flagship
Beehive Cheese Company, Ogden,
 UT—Barely Buzzed

Bellwether Farms, Sonoma,
 CA—Carmody Reserve, San
 Andreas
Berkshire Cheese Makers, Lenox,
 MA—Berkshire Blue
Bittersweet Plantation Dairy,
 Gonzalez, LA—Feliciana Nevat,
 Fleur-de-Lis
Boones Farm, Jacksonville, OR—*see*
 Siskiyou Crest Goat Dairy

C
Cabot Creamery, Cabot, VT—Cabot
 Clothbound Cheddar
Capriole, Greenville, IN—Julianna,
 Mont St. Francis, O'Banon, Old
 Kentucky Tomme, Piper's
 Pyramid, Wabash Cannonball
Cato Corner Farm, Colchester,
 CT—Hooligan
Cobb Hill Farm, Hartland,
 VT—Ascutney Mountain, Four
 Corners Caerphilly

Consider Bardwell Farm, West
 Pawlett, VT— Dorset, Manchester,
 Mettowee
Cowgirl Creamery, Point Reyes
 Station and Petaluma, CA—Red
 Hawk, St. Pat
Crawford Family Farm, Whiting,
 VT—Vermont Ayr
Crowley Cheese, Healdville,
 VT—Clothbound wheels
Cypress Grove Farm, Arcata,
 CA—Humboldt Fog, Purple Haze,
 Truffle Tremor

D
Dancing Cow Farmstead, Bridport,
 VT—Bourrée, Sarabande

E
Everona Dairy, Rapidan,
 VA—Piedmont, Stony Man
Estrella Family Creamery,
 Montesano, WA—various raw cow's
 and goat's milk cheeses

F

Ferns' Edge Goat Dairy, Lowell OR—Various fresh goat cheeses

Fiscalini Cheese Co., Modesto, CA—Fiscalini Bandage-wrapped Cheddar, San Joaquin

Fraga Farm, Sweet Home, OR—Organic Goat Milk Cheddar, Goatzarella, Feta

Fromagerie Belle Chèvre, Elkmont, AL—Montrachet-style logs

G

Grafton Village Cheese Company, Grafton, VT—Clothbound Cheddar (reserve, aged by Jasper Hill Farm)

Great Hill Dairy, Marion, MA—Great Hill Blue

H

Hawthorne Valley Farm, Ghent, NY—Alpine

Hillman Farm, Colrain, MA—Harvest Cheese, Hilltown Wheel

J

Sally Jackson Cheeses, Oroville, WA—various goat, cow, and sheep's milk cheeses

Jasper Hill Farm, Greensboro, VT—Aspenhurst, Bartlett Blue, Bayley Hazen, Constant Bliss, Winnimere

Juniper Grove Farm, Redmond, OR—Ottentique, Redmondo, Tumalo Tomme

L

Lazy Lady Farm, Westfield, VT—various *chèvre* styles

Love Tree Farm Grantsburg, WI—Gabrielson Lake, Trade Lake Cedar

M

Major Farm, Putney, VT—Vermont Shepherd

Meadow Creek Dairy, Galax, VA—Grayson, Mountaineer

Mecox Bay Dairy, Bridgehampton, NY—Mecox Sunrise

Mozzarella Company, Dallas, TX—Blanca Bianca, Hoja Santa

N

Nettle Meadow Goat Farm, Thurman, NY—Kunik

O

Oakvale Farmstead Cheese, London, OH—Gouda

Old Chatham Sheepherding Company, Chatham, NY—Nancy's Hudson Valley Camembert

Oregon Gourmet Cheeses, Albany, OR—Sublimity, Camembert

P

Pholia Farm, Rogue River, OR—Elk Mountain, Hillis Peak, Winter Wimer

Point Reyes Farmstead Cheese Co., Point Reyes Station, CA—Original Blue

R

Redwood Hill Farm, Sonoma, CA—Camellia, California Crottin, Bucheret

River's Edge Chevre, Logsdon, OR—see Three Ring Farm

Rogue Creamery, Central Point, OR—Crater Lake Blue, Echo Mountain Blue, Oregon Blue, Oregonzola, Rogue River Blue, Smokey Blue

Roth Käse, Monroe, WI—Grand Cru Gruyère

Rumiano Cheese Company, Crescent City, CA—Dry Jack

S

Shelburne Farms, Shelburne, VT—Farmhouse Clothbound Cheddar

Silver Falls Creamery, Monmouth, OR—Plain Chèvre

Siskiyou Crest Goat Dairy (Boones Farm), Jacksonville, OR—various pasteurized fresh and aged raw cheeses

Sprout Creek Farm, Poughkeepsie, NY—Barat, Ouray, Toussaint

Sweet Grass Dairy, Thomasville, GA—Thomasville Tomme, Holly Springs

Sweet Home Farm, Elberta, AL—Perdido

T

Taylor Farm, Londonderry, VT—Gouda

Thistle Hill Farm, North Pomfret, VT—Tarentaise

Three Corner Field Farm, Shushan, NY—Battenkill Brebis

Three Ring Farm (River's Edge Chevre), Logsden, OR—Various chèvres, bloomy-rind and washed-rind goat's milk cheeses

Three Sisters Farmstead Cheese, Lindsay, CA—Serena

Tillamook County Creamery Association, Tillamook, OR—Various cheeses of many types

Tumalo Farms, Bend, OR—Classico, Pondhopper

Twig Farm, West Cornwall, VT—Fuzzy Wheel, Goat Tomme, Square Cheese, Washed Rind Wheel

U

Uplands Cheese Company, Dodgeville, WI –Pleasant Ridge Reserve

V

Veldhuizen Family Farm, Dublin TX—Bosque Blue

Vella Cheese Co., Sonoma, CA—Special Select Dry Monterey Jack

Vermont Butter & Cheese Company, Websterville, VT—Bijou, Bonne Bouche, Coupole

W

Westfield Farm, Hubbardston, MA—Classic Blue, Hubbardston Blue

Willamette Valley Cheese Company, Salem, OR—Brindisi Fontina

Willow Hill Farm, Milton, VT—Autumn Oak, Paniolo, Summer Tomme

Winchester Cheese Company, Winchester, CA—Gouda

Orb Weaver Farm, New Haven, VT—Orb Weaver Vermont Farmhouse Cheese

Woodcock Farm, Weston, VT—Weston Wheel

• APPENDIX 3 •
COURSES, CONFERENCES, CONVENTIONS, AND ORGANIZATIONS

Conferences and Festivals

American Dairy Goat Association—National show every July; annual convention every October; regular regional events.

American Cheese Society Convention—Held annually in late summer at various locations.

Cheese Art Conference—Semi-annual, in Ragusa, Sicily.

Epcot International Food & Wine Festival—Late September to mid-November at Disney World in Florida.

Fancy Food Shows—Three per year, run by the National Association for the Specialty Food Trade (NAFST).

The Great British Cheese Festival—Takes place annually in the fall in conjunction with the British Cheese Awards

Oregon Cheese Festival—Held annually in March at Rogue Creamery.

Seattle Cheese Festival—Held each spring at the Pike Place Market.

Slow Food/Cheese—This is Slow Food's artisanal cheese gathering, held every other fall (odd-numbered years) in Bra, Italy; in even-numbered years, Slow Food holds the Salone del Gusto in Turin

Slow Food/Terra Madre—There are numerous international, national, and local Slow Food gatherings in the U.S. and elsewhere.

Sonoma Cheese Conference—Held annually in the late winter/early spring.

World Championship Cheese Contest—Sponsored by the Wisconsin Cheese Makers Association and held every March.

World Cheese Awards—Organized and sponsored by the Guild of Fine Food; held in London.

U. S. Organizations

American Cheese Society

American Dairy Goat Association

California Milk Advisory Board

Cheese Importers Association of America

Cheese of Choice Coalition

New England Cheese Makers Association

Oldways Preservation Trust

Raw Milk Cheesemakers' Association

SlowFood USA

Vermont Cheese Council

Wisconsin Cheese Makers Association

U.S. Cheese Guilds

California Artisan Cheese Guild

Maine Cheese Guild

New York State Farmstead & Artisan Cheese Makers Guild

Oregon Cheese Guild

Ohio Farmstead-Artisan Cheese Guild

Ontario Cheese Society

Pennsylvania Farmstead and Artisan Cheese Alliance

Société des Fromage du Québec

Southern Cheesemakers' Guild

Washington State Cheesemakers Association

Vermont Cheese Council

U.K. Organization

The Specialist Cheesemakers Association

College and University Programs
UNITED STATES

CORNELL UNIVERSITY—Distinguished dairy researcher Professor David Barbano joined the faculty in 1980 and has headed the Northeast Dairy Research Center, a joint program of Cornell and the University of Vermont, since 1988.

NORTH CAROLINA STATE UNIVERSITY—The main cheese expert there is Associate Professor of Food Science Mary Anne Drake, Ph.D.

VERMONT INSTITUTE FOR ARTISAN CHEESES—Professors Paul Kindstedt and Catherine Donnelly founded the institute in 2004 and it has become a major hub of real cheese education in America. Several other influential cheese experts are affiliated, including Jeffrey Roberts, who wrote *The Atlas of American Artisan Cheese,* and Marc Druart, a consulting cheesemaker.

WASHINGTON STATE UNIVERSITY—WSU has graduated many prominent cheesemakers and has a fine creamery, founded in the early part of the 20th century.

OREGON STATE UNIVERSITY—Professor Lisbeth Goddick has spearheaded the revival of OSU's creamery.

ABROAD

CoRFiLaC—Located in Ragusa, Sicily, it was founded in 1996 and is affiliated with the University of Catania, the township of Ragusa and other public and private organizations.

UNIVERSITY OF GASTRONOMIC SCIENCES—Founded, in 2003, in conjunction with the Slow Food movement, it has campuses in Bra and Parma.

Websites

The Cheese Chick
Pacific Northwest Cheese Project
Cheese by Hand
The Cheese Web
CurdNerds

Miscellaneous

Cheese Connoisseur—A Quarterly magazine.
Cheese Market News—An industry/trade weekly.
The Cheese Nun—A one-hour documentary film about Mother Noella Marcellino
The Cheese Reporter—Another industry/trade weekly.
Culture—A quarterly magazine.
The Milkweed—A dairy industry newspaper
New England Cheesemaking Supply Co.

• **APPENDIX 4** •

AN INDEX TO THE FINE CHEESES OF THE WORLD

The following is a list of cheeses I've tried and can recommend without hesitation. They are real cheeses in Patrick Rance's sense of the term; the majority of them are artisanal; many of them qualify as great. It is neither a superselective nor exhaustive list. But it is quite exacting.

An important note: If a cheese is always made from raw milk—or predominately so—we indicate it as such; and likewise if it is always or almost always made from pasteurized milk. If it comes in both versions, there is no indication.

As I always say, the cheeses show up when they want to; you may have a particular selection in mind, but if it's not at its best (peak ripeness) or if it's not available when you want it, you need alternatives. This is the most compelling reason why each cheese listing includes a similar type.

A

AARAUER BIERDECKEL, aka Beermat (Switzerland)—Washed rind, semifirm, raw cow's milk, similar to Maroilles

ABBAYE DE BELLOCQ (French Pyrénées)—Pressed, hard, raw sheep's milk, similar to Manchego

ABBAYE DE TAMIÉ (eastern France)—Lightly pressed, washed rind, semisoft, raw cow's milk, similar to Reblochon

ABONDANCE (eastern France)—Cooked, pressed, hard, raw cow's milk, similar to Beaufort

ADELLE (Oregon)—Fresh pasteurized sheep's milk, similar to fresh chèvres, only made with sheep's milk.

AFFIDÉLICE (France)—Washed rind, pasteurized cow's milk, similar to Époisses

AFUEGA'L PITU (Spain)—Moist, firm, pasteurized cow's milk, similar to Gaperon or Peña Blanca; version with *pimentón* is preferred

ALP DRÄCKLOCH (Switzerland)—Cooked, pressed, hard, raw cow's milk, similar to Prattigauer

ALPINE (New York)—Cooked, pressed, firm, cow's milk, similar to Pleasant Ridge Reserve

(QUEIJO) AMARELO DA BEIRA BAIXA (Portugal)—Semisoft, raw sheep's and goat's milk, similar to Nisa

L'AMI DU CHAMBERTIN (France)—Soft, wash rind, raw cow's milk, similar to Époisses

APPENZELLER (Switzerland)—Cooked, pressed, raw cow's milk, similar to Prattigauer

ARACENA (Spain)—Semisoft, washed rind, raw goat's milk, similar to Mont St. Francis

ARDRAHAN (Ireland)—Semisoft, washed rind, pasteurized cow's milk, similar to Gubbeen

ASCUTNEY MOUNTAIN (Vermont)—Cooked, pressed, cow's milk, similar to Tarentaise

ASIAGO VECCHIO (Italy)—Cooked, pressed, raw cow's milk, similar to Piave

ASPENHURST (Vermont)—Pressed, raw cow's milk, similar to Doddington or Cheddar

AUTUMN OAK (Vermont)—Pressed, raw sheep's milk, similar to Trade Lake Cedar

(QUEIJO DE) AZEITÃO (Portugal)—Soft, thistle renneted, raw sheep's milk, similar to Serra da Estrela

B

BARELY BUZZED (Utah)—Firm, pressed, pasteurized cow's milk, coffee and lavender rubbed, similar to a flavored Cheddar

BARTLETT BLUE (Vermont)—Firm, raw cow's milk, blue, similar to Stichelton

BATTENKILL BREBIS (New York)—Firm, pressed, raw sheep's milk, similar to Spenwood

BAYLEY HAZEN (Vermont)—Firm, raw cow's milk, blue, similar to Stichelton

BEAUFORT (France)—Cooked, pressed, raw cow's milk, similar to Gruyère

BEECHER'S FLAGSHIP (Washington State)—Hard, pressed, raw cow's milk, similar to Cheddar

BEENLEIGH BLUE (England)—Pasteurized sheep's milk, blue, similar to Roquefort

BEERMAT—*See* Aarauer Bierdeckel

BERGFICHTE (formerly Krümmenswiler Försterkäse; Switzerland)—Semisoft, encircled in bark, washed rind, raw cow's milk, similar to Vacherin Mont d'Or

BERGUES (France)—Washed-rind, pasteurized cow's milk, similar to Maroilles

BERKSHIRE BLUE (Massachusetts)—Moist, firm, raw cow's milk, blue, similar to Fourme d'Ambert

BERKSWELL (England)—Pressed, raw sheep's milk, similar to Ossau-Iraty

BERNER OBERLÄNDER HOBELKÄSE (Switzerland)—Cooked, pressed, raw cow's milk, similar to Appenzeller

BETHLEHEM (Connecticut)—Firm, pressed, raw cow's milk, similar to Tomme de Savoie

BETHMALE (France)—Firm, pressed, raw cow's milk, similar to Le Moulis (cow's milk version)

(QUESO DE LOS) BEYOS (northern Spain)—Semihard, pasteurized cow's milk (goat's milk and mixed-milk versions are also made), similar to Mahón, if cow, or Majorero, if goat

BIANCO SARDO DI MOLITERNO—Firm, pressed, sheep's milk, similar to Pecorino Toscano

BIJOU (Vermont)—Semisoft, pasteurized goat's milk, similar to Crottin de Chavignol

BLAUE GEISS (Switzerland)—Moist, firm, raw goat's milk, blue, similar to Harbourne Blue or Monte Enebro

BLEU D'AUVERGNE (France)—Moist, semifirm, cow's milk, blue, similar to Fourme d'Ambert

BLEU DES BASQUES (France)—Firm, raw sheep's milk, blue, similar to Roquefort

BLEU DES CAUSSES (France)—Moist, firm, raw cow's milk, blue, similar to Fourme d'Ambert

BLEU DE GEX (France)—Firm, cow's milk, blue, similar to Bleu des Basques

BLEU DE LAQUEUILLE (France)—Firm, moist, cow's milk, blue, similar to Fourme d'Ambert

BLEU DE TERMIGNON (France)—Firm, raw cow's milk, blue, similar to Castelmagno

BLOMMA (Ohio)—Semisoft, pasteurized goat's milk, bloomy rind, similar to Camellia

BLU DI BACCO (Italy)—Firm, cow's milk, blue, similar to Blu del Re

BLU DEL MONCENISIO (Italy)—Firm, cow's milk, blue, similar to Bleu des Causses

BLU DEL RE (Italy)—Firm, moist, leaf wrapped, cow's milk, blue, similar to Blu di Bacco

BONDE DE GÂTINE (France)—Semisoft, raw goat's milk, similar to Chabichou du Poitou

BONNE BOUCHE (Vermont)—Semisoft, pasteurized goat's milk, similar to Wabash Cannonball

BOULETTE D'AVESNES (France)—Firm, moist, cow's milk, unique, somewhat similar to Afuega'l Pitu

BOURBOULE (France)—Semisoft, raw cow's milk, small version of Saint-Nectaire

BOURRÉE (Vermont)—Semisoft, washed-rind, raw cow's milk, similar to Grayson

BRA (Italy)—Firm, raw cow's milk, similar to Le Moulis

BRESCIANELLA STAGIONATA (Italy)—Semisoft, cow's milk, similar to Taleggio

BRIE DE MEAUX (France)—Soft, cow's milk (raw if AOC), similar to Brie de Nangis

BRIE DE MELUN (France)—Soft, raw cow's milk, similar to Tomme Vaudoise

BRIE DE NANGIS (France)—Soft, cow's milk, similar to Brie de Meaux or Brie de Melun

BRIN D'AMOUR (Corsica)—Semisoft, herb coated, sheep's milk, unique, comparable to mild Feta

BRINDISI FONTINA (Oregon)—Semifirm, cooked, pressed, cow's milk, similar to Fontina Val d'Aosta

C

CABECOU DE ROCAMADOUR (France)—Semisoft, goat's milk, similar to Mothais

CABECOU FEUILLE (France)—Soft, leaf wrapped, goat's milk, similar to Mothais à la Feuille

CABRALES (Spain)—Firm, moist, leaf wrapped, raw mixed milk, blue, similar to Valdeón

LE CABRI ARIÈGEOIS (France)—Semisoft, bark encased, raw goat's milk, similar to Holzige Geiss

CABRIFLORE CHÈVRE (France)—Semisoft, raw goat's milk, similar to Bonde de Gâtine

CAERPHILLY (Wales)—Firm, moist, raw cow's milk, raw, similar to Wensleydale (Wales)

CAMELLIA (California)—Soft, bloomy rind, pasteurized goat's milk, similar to Blomma

CAMEMBERT DE NORMANDIE (France)—Soft, bloomy rind, raw cow's milk, similar to Brie de Melun

(OREGON GOURMET) CAMEMBERT (Oregon)—Soft, bloomy rind, pasteurized and raw cow's milk, similar to Camembert

CANESTRATO PUGLIESE (Italy)—Hard, raw sheep's milk, similar to Pecorino Sardo

CANTAL (France)—Hard, raw cow's milk (if AOC), similar to Laguiole

CAPRICIOUS (California)—Hard, pressed, raw goat's milk, similar to Elk Mountain Tomme

CAPRINO NOCE (Italy)—Semisoft, leaf wrapped (black walnut), goat/cow's milk, wrapped in Black Walnut Leaf, similar to Nocetto

CARDINAL SIN (England)—Semisoft, washed rind, pasteurized cow's milk, similar to Ardrahan

CARMODY RESERVE (California)—Firm, cooked, pressed, raw cow's milk, similar to Doddington

CARRUCHON (France)—Semisoft, washed rind, sheep's milk, similar to Pont l'Évêque

CASHEL BLUE (Ireland)—Firm, moist, pasteurized cow's milk, blue, similar to Fourme d'Ambert

CASINCA CHÈVRE (Corsica)—Semisoft, washed rind, goat's milk, similar to Mont St. Francis

CENTOVALLI TICINO (Switzerland)—Hard, cooked, pressed, cow's milk, similar to Comté

CHABICHOU DU POITOU (France)—Semifirm, goat's milk, similar to Crottin de Chavignol

CHAOURCE (France)—Soft, bloomy rind, cow's milk, similar to Coulommiers

CHAROLAIS (France)—Semifirm, goat, similar to Clacbitou

CHEDDAR, AMERICAN FARMHOUSE—Hard, raw cow's milk, unique; principal producers are Beecher's Flagship (Seattle), Cabot Clothbound (Vermont), Fiscalini Bandage (California), Grafton Clothbound (Vermont), Shelburne Farms (Vermont); similar to British farmhouse Cheddar

CHEDDAR, BRITISH FARMHOUSE (England)—Hard, raw cow's milk, unique; principal producers are Keen's, Montgomery's, Quicke's, Reade's, Isle of Mull, and Westcombe; similar to Laguiole

CHESHIRE—Hard, raw cow's milk, similar to Double Gloucester (England)

LE CHÈVRE NOIR (Canada)—Hard, waxed, pasteurized goat's milk, unique, comparable to Classico

CHEVROTIN DES ARAVIS (France)—Semisoft, washed rind, goat's milk, similar to Mont St. Francis

CHIMAY (Belgium)—Semifirm, washed rind, pasteurized cow's milk, similar to Morbier

CLACBITOU (France)—Semifirm, goat, similar to Cabriflore Chèvre

CLASSIC BLUE (Massachusetts)—Semisoft, blue-rind, pasteurized goat's milk, similar to Monte Enebro

(TUMALO FARMS) CLASSICO (Oregon)—Semihard, Gouda type, raw or pasteurized goat's milk, similar to Majorero

COMTÉ (France)—Hard, cooked, pressed, raw cow's milk, similar to Abondance

CONSTANT BLISS (Vermont)—Semisoft, bloomy rind, raw cow's milk, similar to Chaource

COOLEA (Ireland)—Hard, Gouda type, pasteurized cow's milk

CORNISH YARG (England)—Semihard, cow's milk, similar to Wensleydale

COULOMMIERS (France)—Soft, bloomy rind, cow's milk, similar to Brie de Nangis

COUPOLE (Vermont)—Soft, ash dusted, pasteurized goat's milk, similar to Humboldt Fog

COURONNE LOCHOISE (France)—Semisoft, goat's milk, similar to Selles-sur-Cher

CRATER LAKE BLUE (Oregon)—Firm, moist, raw cow's milk, blue, similar to Bleu des Causses

CROTTIN DE CHAVIGNOL (France)—Semisoft, goat's milk, similar to Wabash Cannonball

CROWLEY CLOTHBOUND WHEELS (Vermont)—Firm, raw, pressed cow, similar to Grafton Clothbound Cheddar

CROZIER BLUE (Ireland)—Semifirm, moist, pasteurized sheep's milk, blue, similar to Beenleigh Blue

D

DODDINGTON (England)—Hard, scalded, cow's milk, cross between a Leicester and a Gouda

DORSET—Firm, washed rind, raw cow's milk, similar to Val Bagner

DOTZIGER HALFMOON (Switzerland)—Semisoft, bloomy rind, cow's milk, similar to Camembert de Normandie

DOUBLE GLOUCESTER (England)—Hard, cow's milk, British traditional, similar to Cheshire

(RUMIANO) DRY JACK (California)—Firm, pressed, cow's milk, similar to Vella Dry Jack

(VELLA SPECIAL SELECT) DRY JACK (California)—Firm, pressed, cow's milk, similar to Rumiano Dry Jack

DURRUS (IRELAND)—Semisoft, washed rind, cow's milk, similar to St. Nectaire

E

ECHO MOUNTAIN (Oregon)—Firm, moist, mixed raw cow's and goat's milk, blue, similar to Valdeón

ECHOURGNAC (France)—Semisoft, monastery style, washed rind (walnut liqueur), cow's milk, similar to Mont des Cats

ELK MOUNTAIN TOMME (Oregon)—Firm, washed rind, raw goat's milk, similar to Hillis Peak or Ibores

EMMENTALER (Switzerland)—Hard, cooked, pressed, cow's milk, similar to Fontina Val d'Aosta

ÉPOISSES, AKA ÉPOISSES DE BOURGOGNE (France)—Soft, washed rind, cow, pasteurized, similar to Munster

(QUEIJO DE) EVORA (Portugal)—Firm, raw sheep's milk, thistle renneted, similar to Nisa

EWE'S BLUE (New York)—Firm, moist, pasteurized sheep's milk, blue, similar to Beenleigh Blue

F

FIUM'ORBU BREBIS (Corsica)—Semisoft, washed rind, sheep's milk, similar to Stanser Schafchäs

FLADÄ, AKA STANSER CHUA FLADÄ OR CHUAFLADÄ (Switzerland)—Soft, gently washed, cow's milk, similar to Vacherin Mont d'Or

FLEUR DES ALPES (France)—Semisoft, lightly pressed, gently washed, cow's milk, similar to Reblochon

FLEUR-DE-LIS (Louisiana)—Soft, bloomy rind, triple crème, pasteurized cow's milk, similar to Pierre Robert

FLEUR DU MAQUIS (Corsica)—Semisoft, herb coated, sheep's milk, similar to Brin d'Amour

FLEURON (France)—Hard, cooked, pressed, raw cow's milk, similar to Beaufort

FLIXER (Switzerland)—Firm, cooked, pressed, washed rind, raw sheep's milk, similar to the Stanser Schafchäs

FONTINA VAL D'AOSTA (Italy)—Firm, cooked, pressed, washed rind, raw cow's milk, similar to Val Bagner

FÖRSTEKÄSE OR KRÜMMENSWILER FÖRSTEKÄSE—*See* Bergfichte

FOUGERUS (France)—Soft, bloomy rind, cow's milk, similar to Coulommiers

FOUR CORNERS CAERPHILLY (Vermont)—Firm, raw, pressed cow, similar to Cornish Yarg Caerphilly

FOURME D'AMBERT (France)—Firm, moist, cow's milk blue, similar to Bleu d'Auvergne

(FRAGA FARM GOAT) CHEDDAR (Oregon)—Firm, pressed, raw goat's milk, similar to Le Chèvre Noir

G

GABRIELSON LAKE (Wisconsin)—Firm, pressed, raw cow's milk, similar to Le Moulis

GAMONEDO (Spain)—Firm, moist, gently smoked raw cow blue, with occasional mix of goat and/or sheep milk, similar to Smokey Oregon Blue

GARROTXA, AKA QUESO DE LA GARROTXA (Spain)—Firm, moist, mold ripened, pasteurized goat's milk, similar to Persillé de Tignes

GORGONZOLA (Italy)—Semisoft (when *cremificato*) to firm (when *piccante*), cow's milk, blue, similar to Bleu d'Auvergne or Fourme d'Ambert

GOUDA, AKA GOUDSE BOERENKAAS OR AGED DUTCH FARMHOUSE GOUDA (Netherlands)—Hard, cooked, pressed, cow's milk, similar to Leicester

(TAYLOR FARM) GOUDA (Vermont)—Raw, pressed cow's milk, similar to Coolea

(WINCHESTER AGED) GOUDA (California)—Raw, pressed, cow's milk, similar to Dutch Boeren Kass

GRANA PADANO (Italy)—Hard, cooked, pressed, cow's milk, similar to Parmigiano-Reggiano

GRAYSON (Virginia)—Semisoft, washed rind, raw, cow's milk, similar to Taleggio (Virginia)

GREAT HILL BLUE (Massachusetts)—Firm, moist, raw cow's milk, blue, similar to Bleu des Causses

GRUYÈRE (Switzerland)—Hard, cooked, pressed, washed rind, raw cow's milk, similar to Comté

GUBBEEN (Ireland)—Semisoft, washed rind, pasteurized cow's milk, similar to Ardrahan

H

HARBOURNE BLUE (England)—Semifirm, moist, pasteurized goat's milk, blue similar to Blaue Geiss

HARVEST CHEESE (Massachusetts)—Firm, pressed, raw goat's milk, similar to Redmondo

HILLIS PEAK (Oregon)—Semihard, raw goat's milk, similar to Ibores

HILLTOWN WHEEL (Massachusetts)—Firm, pressed, raw goat's milk, similar to Redmondo

HOCH YBRIG (Switzerland)—Hard, cooked, pressed, washed rind, similar to Gruyère

HOJA SANTA (Texas)—Soft, leaf-wrapped, pasteurized goat's milk, unique, comparable to Banon

HOLLY SPRINGS (Georgia)—Firm, pressed, *tomme* style, raw goat's milk, similar to Classico

HÖLZIGE GEISS (Switzerland)—Soft, bark encased, lightly washed, raw goat's milk, similar to Le Cabri Ariègeois

HOOLIGAN (Connecticut)—Semisoft, washed rind, raw cow's milk, similar to Grayson

HUDSON VALLEY CAMEMBERT (New York)—Semisoft, bloomy rind, pasteurized cow's and sheep's milk, similar to Kunik

HUMBOLDT FOG (California)—Semisoft, moist, bloomy rind, pasteurized goat's milk, similar to Wabash Cannonball

I

(QUESO) IBORES (Spain)—Firm, moist, pressed, natural or *pimentón*-rubbed rind, raw goat's milk, similar to Majorero

IDIAZÁBAL (Spain)—Hard, pressed, lightly smoked, raw sheep's milk, similar to Fumaison

INNERSCHWEIZER SCHAFCHÄS AKA SCHAF REBLOCHON (Switzerland)—Semisoft, lightly pressed, washed rind, raw sheep's milk, similar to Fium' Orbu or Innerschweizer Weicher

INNERSCHWEIZER WEICHER, AKA STANSER RÖTELI (Switzerland)—Semisoft, lightly pressed, washed rind, raw cow's milk, similar to Reblochon

J

JULIANNA (Indiana)—Semisoft, surface ripened, herb encrusted, raw goat's milk, similar to Brin d'Amour (albeit goat not sheep)

K

KRÜMMENSWILER FÖRSTERKÄSE— *see* Bergfichte

KUNIK (New York)—Soft, bloomy rind, pasteurized goat's milk with cow's milk cream, similar to Hudson Valley Camembert

KUNTENER (Switzerland)—Semisoft, washed rind, lightly pressed, raw cow's milk, similar to Innerschweizer Weicher

L

LAGUIOLE (France)—Hard, pressed, raw cow's milk, similar to Cantal

(KIRKHAM'S) LANCASHIRE—Firm, moist, milled, pressed, raw cow's milk, similar to Cheshire (England)

LANGRES (France)—Semisoft, lightly washed, cow's milk, similar to Époisses

LINCOLNSHIRE POACHER (England)—Hard, milled, pressed, raw cow's milk, similar to other farmhouse cheddars (*see* Cheddar)

LIVAROT (France)—Semisoft, washed rind, cow's milk, similar to Pont l'Évêque

M

(QUESO) MAHÓN (Menorca, Spain)—Semifirm to hard, cooked, pressed, cow's milk, similar to Grana Padano

(QUESO) MAJORERO (Canary Islands)—Hard, pressed, natural or *pimentón*-rubbed rind, similar to Elk Mountain

MANCHEGO (Spain)—Hard, pressed, sheep's milk, similar to Roncal or Ossau-Iraty

MANCHESTER (Vermont)—Firm, pressed, washed rind, raw goat's milk, similar to Wimer Winter

MAROILLES (France)—Firm, washed rind, cow's milk, similar to Munster

MATOS ST. GEORGE (California)—Firm, pressed, raw cow's milk, similar to São Jorge

MECOX SUNRISE (Long Island, New York)—Firm, washed rind, raw cow's milk, similar to Dorset

METTOWEE (Vermont)—Semisoft, pasteurized goat's milk, similar to Bijou

MIMOLETTE (France)—Hard, cooked, pressed, pasteurized cow's milk, similar to Leicester

MONDEGUEIRO (Portugal)—Soft, thistle renneted, raw sheep's milk, similar to Serra da Estrela (essentially a smaller format Serra)

MONTASIO (Italy)—Hard, cooked, pressed, cow's milk, similar to Piave

MONT DES CATS (France)—Semisoft, washed rind, cow's milk, similar to Époisses

MONTE ENEBRO (Spain)—Firm, moist, *Penicillium roqueforti*-molded rind, pasteurized goat's milk, similar to Classic Blue

MONTEREY DRY JACK (California)—Hard, pressed, cow's milk, similar to Mahón

MONT ST. FRANCIS (Indiana)—Semisoft, washed rind, raw goat's milk, similar to Aracena

MORBIER (France)—Firm, pressed, washed rind, cow's milk, similar to Fontina Val d'Aosta

MOTHAIS-SUR-FEUILLE (France)—Soft, leaf wrapped, goat's milk, similar to O'Banon

LE MOULIS (France)—Firm, pressed, cow's milk (goat's and sheep's milk versions also made), similar to Bethmale

MOUNTAINEER (Virginia)—Pressed, washed rind, raw cow's milk, similar to Val Bagner

MUNSTER (France)—Soft, washed rind, cow's milk, similar to Époisses

N

(QUEIJO DE) NISA (Portugal)—Firm, pressed, thistle renneted, raw sheep's milk, similar to Evora

NOCETTO (Italy)—Soft, leaf wrapped (black walnut), goat's milk, similar to Caprino Noce

O

OAKVALE FARMSTEAD GOUDA (Ohio)—Hard, pressed, cooked, Gouda style, raw cow's milk, similar to Goudse Boerenkass

O'BANON (Indiana)—Soft, leaf wrapped, pasteurized goat's milk, similar to Hoja Santa

ODESSA BLUE (Oregon)—Firm, moist, raw sheep's milk blue, similar to Beenleigh Blue

OGLESHIELD (England)—Firm, pressed, washed rind, raw cow's milk, similar to a raclette style

OLD KENTUCKY TOMME (Indiana)—Semihard, pressed, raw goat's milk, similar to Hillis Peak

ORB WEAVER (Vermont)—Firm, pressed, raw cow's milk, similar to Colby

OREGON BLUE (Oregon)—Raw cow's milk, blue, similar to Bleu des Causses

OREGONZOLA (Oregon)—Firm, moist, raw cow's milk, blue, similar to Gorgonzola

OSSAU-IRATY (France)—A large family of hard, pressed, raw sheep's milk cheeses, similar to Ardi-Gasna and Abbaye de Bellocq

OTENTIQUE (Oregon)—Semisoft, goat's milk, similar to Bonne Bouche

OURAY (New York)—Firm, pressed, raw cow's milk, similar to Lancashire

P

(QUESO) PALMERO (Canary Islands)—Semihard, pressed, raw goat's milk, similar to natural-rind Majorero

PANIOLO (Vermont)—Semisoft, washed rind, raw cow's milk, similar to Durrus

PARMIGIANO-REGGIANO (Italy)—Hard, cooked, pressed, raw cow's milk, similar to Grana Padano or Sbrinz

PAU, AKA PAU A SANT MATEU (Spain)—Semisoft, washed rind, pasteurized, goat's milk, similar to Mont St. Francis

PAVÉ D'AUGE (France)—Semisoft, washed rind, cow's milk, similar to Pont l'Évêque

PECORINO DELLE BALZE VOLTERRANE (Italy)—Hard, pressed, thistle renneted, raw sheep's milk, similar to Evora

PECORINO DI FOSSA (Italy)—Hard, pressed, sheep's milk, ripened underground, similar to Pecorino Fiore Sardo

PECORINO FOJA DE NOCE (Italy)—Hard, pressed, leaf wrapped (black walnut), sheep's milk, similar to Pecorino Sardo

PECORINO SARDO (Sardegna)—Hard, pressed, sheep's milk, similar to Pecorino Toscano

PECORINO TOSCANO (Italy)—Hard, pressed, sheep's milk, similar to Manchego

PEÑA BLANCA (Spain)—Firm, moist, washed rind, sheep's or goat's milk, unique, comparable to Fium' Orbu

PEÑAMELLERA (Spain)—Firm, mostly pasteurized cow's milk, similar to Quesucos de Cantabria

PÉRAIL (France)—Soft, sheep's milk, similar to St. Marcellin

(LA) PERAL (Spain)—Firm, moist, pasteurized cow's milk with sheep cream, blue, similar to Valdeón

PERDIDO (Alabama)—Firm, pressed, raw cow's milk, similar to Le Moulis

PERSILLÉ DE TIGNES (France)—Firm, pressed, raw goat's milk, similar to Elk Mountain

PETITE BASQUE—Pressed, firm, sheep's milk, similar to Tourmalet (*see* Tomme, etc.)

PIAVE (Italy)—Hard, cooked, pressed, cow's milk, similar to Montasio

PIEDMONT (Virginia)—Firm, pressed, raw sheep's milk, similar to Roncal

PIPER'S PYRAMIDE (Indiana)—Semisoft, bloomy rind, goat's milk, similar to Valençay

PLEASANT RIDGE RESERVE—Hard, cooked, pressed, raw, cow, Wisconsin, similar to Comté

POINT REYES ORIGINAL BLUE (California)—Raw cow's milk, blue, similar to Great Hill Blue

PONDHOPPER (Oregon)—Hard, washed curd, pasteurized goat's milk, similar to Classico

PONT L'ÉVÊQUE (France)—Semisoft, washed rind, cow's milk, similar to Pavé d'Auge

POULIGNY-SAINT-PIERRE (France)—Semisoft, goat's milk, similar to Valençay

PRATTIGAUER (Switzerland)—Hard, cooked, pressed, raw cow's milk, similar to Appenzeller

PURPLE HAZE (California)—Semisoft, dusted with lavender buds and fennel pollen, pasteurized goat's milk, unique, comparable to Roves de Garrigues

R

RAGUSANO (Sicily)—Hard, *pasta filata* type, raw cow's milk, similar to Caciocavallo

REBLOCHON (France)—Semisoft, lightly pressed, gently washed, raw cow's milk, similar to Abbaye de Tamié

RED HAWK (California)—Semisoft, triple crème style, washed rind, pasteurized cow's milk, similar to Époisses

REDMONDO (Oregon)—Hard, pressed, raw goat's milk, similar to Hilltown Wheel

RIESLING X SYLVANER (Switzerland)—Soft, bloomy rind, cow's milk, curd washed in wine, similar to Tomme Vaudoise

ROARING FORTIES BLUE (Australia)—Firm, moist, waxed, pasteurized cow's milk, blue, similar to Bleu des Causses

ROBIOLA CASTAGNA (Italy)—Semisoft, leaf wrapped (chestnut), mixed goat's, sheep's and cow's milk, similar to other leaf-wrapped Robiolas and to Banon

ROBIOLA DI ROCCAVERANO (Italy)—Semisoft, mixed raw goat's, sheep's and cow's milk, similar to Robiola Tre Latti

ROBIOLA DUE LATTI (Italy)–Semisoft, mixed cow's and sheep's milk, similar to Saint-Felicien

ROBIOLA FIA (Italy)—Semisoft, leaf wrapped (fig), mixed goat's, sheep's and cow's milk, similar to other leaf-wrapped Robiolas and to Banon

ROBIOLA INCAVOLATA (Italy)—Semisoft, leaf wrapped (cabbage), mixed goat's, sheep's, and cow's milk, similar to other leaf-wrapped Robiolas and to Banon

ROBIOLA PINETA (Italy)—Semisoft, washed rind, cow's milk, pine bough resting on top, similar to Taleggio

ROBIOLA TRE LATTI (Italy)—Semisoft, mixed goat's, sheep's, and cow's milk, similar to Robiola di Roccaverano

ROBIOLA VITE (Italy)—Semisoft, (grapevine) leaf wrapped, mixed goat's, sheep's, and cow's milk, similar to other leaf-wrapped Robiolas and to Banon

ROGUE RIVER BLUE (Oregon)—Firm, moist, (Syrah grapevine) leaf wrapped, raw cow's milk, blue, similar to Valdeón

RONCAL (Spain)—Hard, pressed, raw sheep's milk, similar to Ossau-Iraty

ROOMANO (Netherlands)—Hard, cooked, pressed, waxed, cow's milk, similar to extra-aged farmhouse Gouda

ROQUEFORT (France)—Firm, moist, raw sheep's milk, blue, similar to Bleu des Basques

ROVES DES GARRIGUES (France)—Soft, fresh chèvre style, goat's milk, similar to Mettowee

S

SAINT-FÉLICIEN (France)—Soft, goat's milk, similar to Saint-Marcellin

SAINT-MARCELLIN (France)—Soft, goat's and/or cow's milk, similar to Robiola Rochetta

SAINTE-MAURE DE TOURAINE (France)—Semisoft, goat's milk, similar to Selles-sur-Cher

SAINT-NECTAIRE (France)—Semisoft, lightly pressed, cow's milk (various levels of production, from *fermier* to *industriel*), similar to Durrus

ST. OLGA (Oregon)—Firm, pressed, raw goat's milk, similar to Elk Mountain Tomme

SALERS (France)—Firm, pressed, raw cow's milk, similar to Laguiole

SALLY JACKSON (Washington) Goat Cheeses—Semisoft, leaf wrapped, raw goat's milk, similar to Julianna

SALLY JACKSON (Washington) Sheep Cheeses—Semisoft, leaf wrapped (chestnut), raw sheep's milk, similar to Brin d'Amour

SAN ANDREAS (California)—Firm, pressed, raw sheep's milk, similar to Vermont Shepherd

SAN JOAQUIN GOLD (California)—Semihard, raw cow's milk, similar to Fontina Val d'Aosta

(QUEIJO) SÃO JORGE (Azores)—Hard, pressed, scalded, raw cow's milk, like a cross between Cheddar and Sbrinz

SARABANDE (Vermont)—Semisoft, washed rind, raw cow's milk, similar to Grayson

SBRINZ (Switzerland)—Hard, cooked, pressed, raw cow's milk, similar to Parmigiano-Reggiano

SELLES-SUR-CHER (France)—Semisoft, goat's milk, similar to Couronne Lochoise

(QUESO DE LA) SERENA (Spain)—Semisoft, thistle renneted, raw sheep's milk, similar to Torta del Casar

(QUEIJO) SERPA (Portugal)—Semisoft, thistle renneted, raw sheep's milk, similar to Serra d'Estrela

(QUEIJO) SERRA DA ESTRELA (Portugal)—Semisoft to firm, thistle renneted, raw sheep's milk, similar to Torta del Casar

SHROPSHIRE BLUE (England)—Firm, moist, pressed, pasteurized cow's milk, blue, similar to Stilton

SINGLE GLOUCESTER (England)—Firm, pressed, cow's milk, similar to Cheddar

SMOKEY OREGON BLUE (Oregon)—Firm, moist, smoked, raw cow's milk, blue, similar to Gamonedo

SOUMAINTRAIN (France)—Soft, washed rind, cow's milk, similar to Époisses

SPENWOOD (England)—Hard, pressed, raw sheep's milk, similar to Ossau-Iraty

SQUARE CHEESE (Vermont)—From Twig Farm, pressed, raw goat's milk, similar to Elk Mountain

STANSER CHUA FLADÄ—*see* Fladä

STANSER RÖTELI—*see* Innerschweizer Weicher

STANSER SCHAFCHÄS (Switzerland)—Firm, moist, pressed, washed rind, raw sheep's milk, similar to Fium' Orbu

STANSER SCHAF REBLOCHON—*see* Innerschweizer Schafchäs

STILTON (England)—Firm, pressed, pasteurized cow's milk, blue, similar to Fourme d'Ambert

SUMMER TOMME (Vermont)—Semisoft, herb encrusted, sheep's milk, similar to Fleur du Maquis

T

TALEGGIO (Italy)—Semisoft, lightly pressed, washed rind, cow's milk, similar to Grayson

TARENTAISE (Vermont)—Hard, cooked, pressed, raw cow's milk, similar to Abondance

(LA) TAUPINIÈRE (France)—Semisoft, goat's milk, similar to Valençay

(QUEIJO) TERRINCHO (Portugal)—Firm, pressed, raw sheep's milk, similar to Evora

TESSINER GEISSKÄSE (Switzerland)—Firm, moist, pressed, washed rind, raw goat's milk, similar to Mont St. Francis

TÊTE DE MOINE (Switzerland)—Hard, cooked, pressed, washed rind cow's milk, similar to Gruyère

TÉTOUN DE SANTA AGATA (France)—Semisoft, peppercorn studded (at base and tip) goat's milk, similar to Valensole

THYM TAMARRE (France)—Semisoft, herb crusted (thyme), goat's milk, similar to Mothais à la Feuille

THOMASVILLE TOMME (Georgia)—Pressed, washed rind, raw cow's milk, similar to Orb Weaver

TICKLEMORE (England)—Firm, pasteurized goat's milk, similar to Garrotxa

TOMA, AKA TOMINO (Italy)—A family of firm, pressed, mostly raw goat's, sheep's, or cow's milk, similar to Tomme de Savoie (Toma Piemontese is the DOP version; Toma del Maccagno and Toma Val Casotto are other versions)

TOMME, AKA TOME, AKA TOMETTE (France)—A family of firm, pressed, mostly raw cow's and/or goat's and sheep's milk, similar to Toma or Tomino (includes Tome des Bauges and Tomme de Savoie)

TOME DES BAUGES (France)—Firm, pressed, raw cow's milk, similar to Tomme de Savoie

TOMME FERMIÈRE D'ALSACE (France)—Semifirm, pressed, washed rind, raw cow's milk, similar to Morbier

TOMMETTE DE LARUNS (French Pyrénées)—Pressed, firm, raw sheep's milk, similar to Ossau-Iraty

TOMME VAUDOISE (Switzerland)—Soft, bloomy rind, cow's milk, similar to Riesling x Sylvaner

TORTA DEL CASAR (Spain)—Usually soft, thistle renneted, raw sheep's milk, similar to (Queso de la) Serena

TORTITA DE BARROS—Identical to Torta del Casar, in smaller format, without DOP

TOURMALET (French Pyrénées)—Pressed, firm, raw sheep's milk, similar to Ossau-Iraty

TRADE LAKE CEDAR (Wisconsin)—Firm, pressed, raw sheep's milk, similar to Ossau Iraty

TRIPLE CRÈMES (France)—A family of bloomy-rind cheeses, made from cow's milk with added cream, similar to Coulommiers; includes Pierre-Robert, Brillat-Savarin, Explorateur, St. André, Gratte-Paille, etc.

TRUFFE DE VALENSOLE (France)—Semisoft, goat's milk, similar to Taupinière or Wabash Cannonball

TUMALO TOMME (Oregon)—Pressed, raw goat's milk, similar to Tomme de Chèvre

U

UBRIACO (Italy)—A family of pressed, cow's milk cheeses, bathed in wine musts of various varietals to varying degrees, similar to Weinkäse; example: Ubriaco Prosecco

UP IN SMOKE (Oregon)—Semisoft, gently smoked, pasteurized goat's milk, unique

UPLANDS PLEASANT RIDGE RESERVE—*See* Pleasant Ridge Reserve

URNER ALPKÄSE (Switzerland)—Hard, cooked, pressed, raw cow's milk, similar to Höbelkäse

V

VACHERIN DU HAUT-DOUBS/MONT D'OR (France)—Soft, bark encircled (spruce), raw cow's milk, similar to Bergfichte

VACHERIN FRIBOURGEOIS (Switzerland)—Firm, pressed, cow's milk, similar to Fontina Val d'Aosta

VAL BAGNER (Switzerland)—Firm, cooked, pressed, raw cow's milk, a raclette cheese similar to Fontina Val d'Aosta

VALDEÓN (Spain)—Firm, moist, pasteurized, leaf-wrapped, cow's and/or goat's milk, blue, similar to Echo Mountain

VALENÇAY (France)—Firm, moist, goat's milk (raw if AOC), similar to Pouligny-Sainte-Pierre

VERMONT SHEPHERD (Vermont)—Hard, pressed, raw sheep's milk, similar to Ossau-Iraty

W

WABASH CANNONBALL (Indiana)—Semisoft, mold ripened, pasteurized goat's milk, similar to Bonne Bouche

WENSLEYDALE (England)—Firm, pasteurized cow's milk, similar to Cornish Yarg

WIMER WINTER (Oregon)—Semisoft, washed rind, raw goat's milk, similar to Mont St. Francis

WINNIMERE (Vermont)—Semisoft, bark encircled (spruce), lightly washed, raw cow's milk, similar to Bergfichte

WINCHESTER AGED GOUDA (California)—Cooked, pressed,

waxed, cow's milk, similar to Goudse Boerenkäse (aged farmhouse Gouda)

Z

(QUESO) ZAMORANO (Spain)—Hard, pressed, sheep's milk, similar to Manchego

ACKNOWLEDGMENTS

First we want to thank the team that helped us put this book together, including our agent, Angela Miller, who has become a serious and successful cheese farmer in her own right; our photographers Nicolas Beckman and John Uher; our editors, Rica Allannic and Ashley Phillips; creative director Marysarah Quinn; Jane Treuhaft; Jennifer Davis; Terry Deal; and all their colleagues behind the scenes at Clarkson Potter who made it happen.

We've consulted with many Important Cheese People, interviewing some of them in depth, to fill this book with the most complete and accurate information we could find on real cheese. They have given generously of their time and knowledge, and for this we thank them gratefully. Here they are, with apologies to any we've inadvertently left out and with a hearty salute to every single artisan cheesemaker mentioned in chapters 14 through 22, a list too lengthy to print in full: Rolf Beeler; Cary Bryant and David Gremmels of Rogue Creamery; Ricki Carroll of New England Cheesemaking Supply Co.,

with special thanks for allowing us to print one of her recipes under "A Simple Cheese You Can Make at Home," chapter 3; Sue Conley, Peggy Smith, and Maureen Cunnie of Cowgirl Creamery/Tomales Bay Foods; Peter Dixon, consulting cheesemaker, with special thanks for allowing us to print one of his recipes under "A Real Cheese Recipe," chapter 3; Catherine Donnelly, Ph.D., professor, Department of Nutrition and Food Sciences, University of Vermont, and co-director, the Vermont Institute for Artisan Cheese; Mary Anne Drake, Ph.D., associate professor, microbiology and sensory analysis, Department of Food Science, North Carolina State University; Marc Druart, Vermont Institute for Artisan Cheese; Sharon Gerdes and Erin Coffield of Dairy Marketing Inc.; Dick Groves, publisher of *The Cheese Reporter;* Rob Kaufelt, Liz Thorpe, and Jason Donnelly of Murray's Cheese Shop; Cheryl Sullivan of Atalanta Corporation; Pete Kent, executive director, Dairy Farmers of Oregon; Peter Kindel; Paul Kinstedt, Ph.D.,

professor, Department of Nutrition and Food Sciences, University of Vermont, and co-director, the Vermont Institute for Artisan Cheese; Caroline and Daniel Hostettler of Quality Cheese and 55 Degrees Cool Wine and Cheese, Fort Myers, Fla.; Thomas Morell, M.D., neurologist and pain management expert; Shelli Morton, Crystal Food Importers; David Nicholson, Great Ciao; Tami Parr, Pacific Northwest Cheese Project; Cindy Tabacchi, nutritionist and nutrition consultant; Thalassa Skinner and Kate Arding, editors of *Culture;* Ig Vella.

I'd like to single out the following for their special support in helping make this book happen for me: David Gibbons; Terry Deal; Max Lau; Daniel Perretti, and, of course, my daughter Scarlett McCalman.

Thanks to my colleagues on the staff at the Artisanal Premium Cheese Center: Mourad Abouettahir; Waldemar Albrecht; Toni Amira; Ondine Appel; Craig Brady; Michelle Caruso; Colby Chambers; Diana Chiodi; Brian Cooper; Denis Cottin; Dan Dowe and the entire Dowe family; Gabriel Edelman; Chris Farris; Heather Figgins; Holly Garçia; Keith Geter; Hannah Goldberg; Freddy Gomez; Fernando Gonzalez; Irem Greenfield; Erin Hedley; Charles Henderson; Gerald Hylla; Sulayman Jasseh; Melanie Kahn; Valentino Lee; Jon Lundbom; May Matta-Aliah; Ana V. Mateo; Howard Mears; Paolo Michel; Joseph Mikolay; Lensley Morgan; Alicia Mullenix; Nadezhda Muntyanu; Dolly Ou; Candela Prol; Hanitra Rasandiharisoa; Andre Rivera; Sebastian Robert; Jeffrey Roberts; Shirley Rosas; Matt Russo; Matt Shale; Josh Shaub; Miguel Suarez; Verna Valencia; Jessica Wurwarg; Ivan Yermolayev; Josh Zizmor.

Thank you to my co-workers at Picholine: Mishu Abdul; Edwin Aguilar; Jose A. Alvarado; Charley Beronio; Romeric Blanvillan; Efrain Cajisaca; Alex Carvajal; Sarah Chalfy; Jeffrey Churchill; Eric Collins; Heather Cook; Matthew Dahlberg; Carmine DiGiovanni; Tony Di li Coli; Danny Ettinger; Alex Garcia; Jose Herrera; Eric Hipp; Phil Johnson; Jorge Landi; Luis Landi; Rodna Lee; Mark Lockard; Jason Mabile; Ramiro Molina; Delfino Moran; Fortunato Moran; Marin Nadalin; Manuel Panameno; Phil Pastou; Guy Rabarijaona; Mesias Riera; Luis Rios; Eric Smades; John Tarleton; Daniel Tenen; Luis Tito.

And also to Xavier Villasuso, Chantal Giverd, and Charles Mahal at Artisanal Brasserie and Wine Bar in Seattle.

I want to extend a big thank-you to all the hundreds of people I've worked with in the cheese industry and its affiliates, including the educators and their sponsors, the market vendors, the restaurants, hotels, transportation industry, charitable events, and the press, among them: Paul Bonneau; Sandra Bowern; Neal Brown; Frank Buatti; Sebbie Buehler; Michelle Buster; Gianaclis Caldwell; Enric Canut; Nora Carey; Jonathan Cohen; Mike Collins; Giorgio Cravero; Charles Curtis; Mike Darby; Gerry Dawes; Francine Diamond; Debra Dickerson; Linda Dutch; Lyn Farmer; Balázs Zalán-Szabolcs Fekete; Aaron Foster; Nadia Gil; Jill Glomb; Mike Gorner; Chris Gray; John Grogan; Richard Groves; Mila Guerra; Sam Gugino; Suzanne Hassenstein; Tyler Hawes; Jason Hinds; Randolph Hodgson; Allison Hooper; Craig Hopson; Hannah Howard; Fred Hull; Mari-anne and Scott Hunnel; Jim Hutchin-son; Christine Hyatt; Mary Janssen; Sarah Jennings; Mark Johnson; Leah Juhl; George Kao; Jordan Kaplan; Constantine Karvonides; Akiko Katayama; Tia Keenan; Mateo and Andy Kehler; Irina Kim; Peter Kindel; Juliana King; Bernhard Klotz; Carole Kotkin; Paula Lambert; Alexandra Leaf; Giuseppe Licitra; David Lockwood; Jim MacPhee; Cynthia Major; Olivier Masmondet; Joel and Susan Mendel; Jessica Miller; Matt Mirapaul; David Moran; William Oglethorpe; Cesar Olivares; Greg O'Neill; Haleigh and Jena Paxton;

Daphne Payan; Francis Plowman; John and Janine Putnam; Nancy Radke; Scott Rankin; Rachel Riggs; Cornel Ruhland; Philip Ruskin; Matt Russo; Monika Samuels; Diane Sauvage; Anne Saxelby; Judy Schad; Walter Schmuckenschlag; Michael John Simkin; Pam Smith; Olaug Srand; Cathy Strange; Daniel Strongin; Miguel Suarez; Oriol Urgell; Stephane Vivier; Min Wang; Wendy Whitehurst; Liz Wight; Marci Wilson; Mark Windt; Suzanne Wolcott; Ellen Yin.

And to my colleagues on the ACS Fromager Certification Committee: Matt Benson, Sasha Davies; Steve Ehlers; Laurie Greenberg; Kathy Guidi; Sara Hill; Jeff Katcher; Dave Leonardi; Emilio Mignucci; Sue Sturman; Sara Vivenzio; Daphne Zepos.

And finally, to Cecilia M. Brancato for her encouragement and love, right through to the book's final stages of production.

—MAX McCALMAN

Thanks to all the people who kept me going personally during the researching and writing of this book, especially my mother Mary W. Gibbons, my children Marley and Will, and to Serena R. Castelli, for her love and support.

—DAVID GIBBONS

Photographs on pages 7, 12, 13, 15, 17, 22, 23, 24, 29, 30, 31, 32, 35, 36, 40, 42, 48, 53, 56, 58, 60, 66, 67, 68, 71, 72, 73, 75, 81, 83, 84, 86, 87, 95, 97, 99, 101, 102, 104, 113, 114, 115, 116, 129, 131, 136, 137, 138, 148, 155, 162, 163, 165, 170, 171, 175, 177, 179, 180, 182, 183, 184, 187, 192, 195, 201, 207, 209, 215, 217, 223, 226, 244, 261, 266, 267, 274, 276, 277, 278, 279, 281, 291, 308, 309, 310, 311, 314, 318, 319, 320, 321, 322, 338, 344, 345, 350, 351, 353, 358, 359, 360, and 361: copyright © 2009 by Nicolas Beckman

Photographs on pages 2, 4, 8, 10, 18, 21, 39, 49, 79, 93, 132, 135, 146, 156, 159, 169, 188, 191, 205, 219, 220, 225, 228, 230, 232, 236, 247, 256, 257, 258, 262, 265, 288, 293, 303, 304, 307, 313, 317, 325, 328, 330, 332, 337, 343, 349, 354, 357, 362, and 378: copyright © 2009 by John Uher

p. 17, top: © Patricia Morford
p. 34: © Vermont Cheese Council
p. 43: © F. V. Kosikowski LLC
p. 44: © Michael Ward
p. 45, top: © Tim Calabro/First Light Studios
p. 45, middle: © Sharon Bice
p. 45 bottom © 2009 Randolph Hodgson
p. 46: © Rosemary Wessel/Three Salamanders Design Studio
p. 50: © David Gibbons
p. 55: © Tami Parr
p. 60: © Tami Parr
p. 67: © David Gibbons
p. 68, top: © Kathleen Bauer, GoodStuffNW
p. 68, middle: © Kathleen Bauer, GoodStuffNW

p. 75: © Tami Parr
p. 86: © David Gibbons
p. 94: © CoRFiLaC
p. 120: © Mike Gingrich
p. 122: © Greg Redfern
p. 127: © Curran Photography
p. 130: © Sharon Bice
p. 160-164, all photos: © David Gibbons
p. 166, top and bottom: © David Gibbons
p. 269, top: © Curran Photography
p. 269, middle © Tim Calabro/First Light Studios
p. 269, bottom: © David Gibbons
p. 271: © Jasper Hill Farm
p. 273, top and bottom: © Tomales Bay Foods
p. 277: © Vern Caldwell
p. 278: © Patricia Morford
p. 280: © Lewis Harrington
p. 283: © Tami Parr
p. 285: © Emily T. Johnson
p. 286: © John Ater
p. 287: © Joel McNair, Graze Magazine.
p. 297, top and bottom: © Quality Cheese
p. 298: © Alberto Venzago
p. 299: © Rolf Beeler Selections
p. 345, bottom: © David Gibbons

Piper's Pyramid with saké: Japan's so-called rice wine finds pairings with cheeses friendly to light, aromatic white wines.

A

B